MY HEART
I OFFER

MY HEART
I OFFER

Daily Reflections
on the Journey of Faith

By Calvin College Alumni and Friends

Calvin Alumni Association
Grand Rapids, Michigan

Published 2000 by the Calvin Alumni Association
Calvin College, 3201 Burton Street S.E., Grand Rapids, Michigan 49546

Library of Congress Cataloging-in-Publication Data

A catalog record for this book is available
from the Library of Congress

ISBN 0-9703693-3-6

The Calvin Alumni Association gratefully acknowledges those authors
and publishers listed in the Notes and Acknowledgments section
who have given permission to reprint copyrighted materials.

Contents

Foreword

To write is to risk. To put pen to paper or fingers to keyboard and to express oneself to the world is not easy. Once the words are written, anyone may read them. Once the words are down on paper, the writer no longer controls how they are received. To write is to risk.

To speak about one's own journey of faith is also a risk. To tell how God has worked in your life — the things he has taught you, the things he has done — is not always easy. God speaks and acts in the lives of all of us, to be sure, but his methods vary. To speak specifically about how God has worked in your life, how a certain Scripture passage brings insight, how an event in your life viewed years later bears God's fingerprints — to talk about such things is a risk. It is a risk because you put yourself in the place of naming God, of declaring that he is alive and well. "Look," you say, "here he is!" The risk is that someone else might look where you are pointing and not see — or might not even be willing to look.

A year ago we asked over three hundred friends of Calvin College (alumni, faculty, staff, parents, students) to accept both of these risks: to write and to write about faith. What you are holding in your hands is a collection of devotionals written by risk takers. Most of the authors published here would never call themselves authors. But when asked for a devotional to place in this collection, they took the risk: They wrote, and they wrote well.

As a committee we were heartened by the responses that came flowing in — so many fine pieces, such diversity in topic and text and life situation, such rich insights into the relationship with God which we all seek to foster. Although the work involved in this project was significant, those of us who served on the editorial committee are unanimous in our delight in being a part of it. This project affirmed what we already suspected about Calvin alumni and friends: that they are intelligent and insightful and compassionate. It also inspired and affirmed each of us in our individual journeys of faith. Even as we read, evaluated, and edited the words penned and typed and e-mailed, God used these words to shape our souls. We are confident that this collection of the writings of risk takers will do the same for you.

Our committee gives its thanks to Susan Buist of the Calvin Alumni and Public Relations Office and to Amanda Van Til of the Calvin Development Office, who received all the devotions, formatted them, and sent them on to us. We are particularly thankful for Susan's constant vigilance and attention to detail, which kept this project on course and made our work as committee members much easier. We also thank our editor, Jan Walhout, who used her skills of precision and clarity to make the content of this book consistent while at the same time being mindful of each writer's style. Book designer Klaas Wolterstorff matched the written efforts with creative visuals. Wallace Bratt served as our patient and affable committee chair, leading us with wisdom and sensitivity. We are grateful that even in retirement he continues his service to Calvin College. Each committee member deserves thanks for reading and often rereading these devotionals, for offering good ideas and insights, and for taking on editing, proofreading, and biblical and theological evaluations as well. To Tracey Gebbia, Scott Hoezee, Sunmee Jo, Lois Konyndyk, and Michael Van Denend, thank you.

To write is to risk, and to write about issues of faith is an even bigger risk. Our highest thanks go to all who took the risk and made this book what it is. You offered your hearts, promptly and sincerely, and we thank you.

To God alone be the glory!

For the committee,
Mary S. Hulst Antonides

God with Us

Psalm 139:1

Cornelius Plantinga, Jr. '67
Calvin dean of the chapel;
Grand Rapids, Michigan

O LORD, you have searched me and you know me. (Ps. 139:1)

The psalmist prays to the inescapable God. We can shield our thoughts from each other, but not from God. We can hide our shame, but not from God. We can outsmart our competitors, but nobody outsmarts God. Even death brings no escape. People who hope to end it all discover God on the other side and have to face him again.

It can make a person crazy. Everywhere we go, there is God. Even inside our own brain, there is God. We always have company. We never have privacy. God is always before us, and, as Paul Tillich wrote, this is why people always try to kill him. Our Savior ended up on a Roman cross because he brought God much too close.

But even "the death of God" brings no end to God. Human wickedness does its worst, and God absorbs it. Then God transcends it. According to the Easter gospel, God rises above our evil and fills the world as never before.

The stubborn fact is that we can't get away from God. Where would we go? There's no exit. There's no place that's out-of-bounds. We are metaphysically outflanked by God, and our only choice is to surrender. Inside the cradle of grace, our only choice is to take our heart in our hands and offer it to God. The result is a miracle. To give ourselves up to God is to find our destiny with the one "whom to serve is perfect freedom." In that perfect freedom we can confidently and joyfully say, "O Lord, you have searched me, and you know me. You know me in the light and in the shadows. You know me in my pride and in my despair. You know what I said and what I almost said. You know my secrets, and you love me still. Nothing I do will make you love me more. None of my doubts will make you love me less. And when my end comes, I shall awake and discover that you are with me after all."

1

A New Beginning

Dirk Jasperse '76   Psalm 118:24
Teacher; Escondido, California

One of the great things about life as God has ordered it is the repetition of units of time. In one sense, time is one undivided continuum. But in our experience, that continuum of time is divided into distinct units — days, months, years — that help us structure our lives and classify our past and our future. Having the whole span of our earthly existence is a wonderful blessing, but having units of time is also a blessing from the wise Creator.

The instant one unit of time expires, another follows right behind. Because units of time continuously repeat, we are always making new beginnings. Our lives and our work in God's kingdom are full of them — new calendar years, new school years, new months, new weeks, new days. Each of these gives us a chance to start over, to clear the slate, to put our mistakes and failures behind us, and to begin afresh. This multitude of new beginnings is a gift from God. It is part of his forgiveness, a way of putting closure to one period of life with its sins and shortcomings and of opening a new one. Having fresh, new days, weeks, and years is a way by which God encourages us along the road of sanctification. It is God's way of allowing us to put a period at the end of the old year, week, or day with its disappointments and discouragements and to start over again.

"This is the day the LORD has made; let us rejoice and be glad in it" (Ps. 118:24). A new day, a new week, or a new year stands before us. What a blessing to have time divided up into distinct units that give us so many new beginnings. We are God's, time is God's, our work, our families, and all our efforts are God's. What an encouragement for us as we go forward into each day knowing that God is intimately with us as we make another new beginning with him.

Romans 14:7-8   Wilbert M. Van Dyk '52
Calvin Seminary professor emeritus;
Grand Rapids, Michigan

> Q. *What is your only comfort in life and in death?*
> A. *That I am not my own, but belong — body and soul, in life and in death — to my faithful Savior Jesus Christ.*
>
> (Heidelberg Catechism, Q. and A. 1*)

There is so much misery in the world that it seems both desperately needful and yet despairingly futile to speak of comfort. It is desperately needful because the world that bleeds out of a million wounds cries for comfort. It seems despairingly futile to speak of comfort because there is no end to trouble. In the book of Job, Eliphaz was on target when he said, "Human beings are born to trouble" (Job 5:7, NIVI).

Comfort. The word suggests quiet composure and inner strength. It is a gift of God's grace in Jesus Christ. In his sacrificial death and victorious resurrection he delivered the ultimate blow to evil, to injustice, and to all misery. Knowing that we belong to him enables us to face life's vicissitudes with the confidence that we are not on our own. Secure as his possessions, we have strength to endure trouble, courage to face challenges, and eagerness to anticipate the joys that he has designed for us.

Of course, belonging to Jesus entails more than the promise of his protection; it also expects our commitment, and commitment is sometimes very expensive, as the pig in the following anecdote realized. A pig and a chicken were looking for a restaurant. They finally found one with this sign: "Ham and eggs are our specialty." The chicken wanted to go in, but the pig refused, explaining, "All they expect from you, my dear hen, is a contribution. From me they expect total commitment." For us, too, commitment means *even unto death*.

But in life and in death, body and soul, we belong to him who purchased us with his blood and who now makes us willing and ready to live for him. Paul says it this way in Romans 14:8: "If we live, we live to the Lord; and if we die, we die to the Lord. So, whether we live or die, we belong to the Lord." That's comfort!

Where Is God in All This?

James R. Kok '56
Pastor; Bellflower, California

Psalm 30:2, 5

> *O LORD my God, I called to you for help and you healed me. . . . Weeping may remain for a night, but rejoicing comes in the morning.* (Ps. 30:2, 5)

I once promised a mother mourning the death of her child that "the Lord is weeping with you." She lifted her head for the first time in months. I then reworded a blessing of Jesus: "In as much as it happens to the least of these my little ones, it happens to me." She nodded assent, finding deep comfort that Jesus totally identified with her. I had this comfort straight from Scripture, but it had taken me a while to grasp the message.

Years ago I had stumbled across Genesis 6:6. The words had thrilled me. I was looking through a window into the heart of God: "The Lord was grieved . . . and his heart was filled with pain." Never had I seen the Creator like that — heartbroken, hurt. What emerged for me is a very personal, vulnerable, passionately involved God, a God touched, affected, disturbed over the hurts, messes, and tragedies in our lives. This God is always present when things go wrong — not only present, but concerned, brokenhearted, at work to restore and heal.

The Bible tells story after story like this. "The Israelites groaned in their slavery and cried out, and their cry for help . . . went up to God. God heard their groaning and he remembered. . . . God looked on the Israelites and was concerned" (Exod. 2:23-25). Their cries triggered the exodus. Remember the king who was told he would die? Devastated, he turned to God, praying and weeping. God's prompt response: "I have heard your prayer and seen your tears; I will heal you" (2 Kings 20:4).

My favorite Bible verse is from the sad eviction of Hagar and Ishmael by Sarah and Abraham. Mother and child lay doomed in the hot desert. Both were weeping. Then "God heard the boy crying" (Gen. 21:17), and he rescued them. God touched by a baby's tears? Incredible! God wants us to know this: "I hear your cries. I am touched. I will lift you and carry you to a new place."

God is always with us, caring, touched, hurting for us, and lifting us to our feet again. God's presence can be counted on to heal and to blow on us a fresh breeze of hope. "Weeping may remain for a night, but rejoicing comes in the morning" (Ps. 30:5).

Have I Practiced Yes Today?

Mark 10:13-16   Michael Kelly Blanchard

Calvin parent/songwriter; Unionville, Connecticut

Have I practiced "Yes" today
Peeked some blue sky through the gray,
Stuck a smile to what I say to face a frown of fear?
Or nervous have I practiced "No"
Shut a door, closed down a show
Told an aching heart to go find another ear?
Have I practiced "Yes" today
Looked for goodness on the way
Interwoven my work with play to keep the child alive?
Or darkened have I practiced "No"
Let the seeds of sadness sow
Helped the hopeless habits grow dynasties inside?
For in the final frame of things
When standing at the door,
The only keys upon my ring
Will be the ones I've used before.
Have I practiced "Yes" tonight
In the darkness laughed its light
Taken time to make things right, before I turn the page?
Or angry have I practiced "No"
Let icy winds of bitter blow
Hid my heart deep in the snow of unforgiven rage?
Have I practiced "Yes" tonight
Spoke it with a hug so tight
Wrapped it in a kiss goodnight, then washed it down with prayer?
Or busy have I practiced "No"
Forgot that love is tell and show
Overlooked how fast they grow and that soon they won't be there?
"Let the children come to me,"
The Son of God said once so tenderly.
"For in these little ones I see my Father's loving will.
Yes, in our country all you need
Is simply the will to believe
That 'Yes' is why you were conceived and, yes,
I love you still."
For in the final win or lose,
The truth no more, no less,
The only way I'll be refused
Is if I say "No" to "Yes."

In God's Name, Bless

Elaine Rosendall De Stigter '70   Numbers 6:22-27
Teacher; Grand Rapids, Michigan

January 6, 1993 (Epiphany): Today a friend of mine was called by a Hospice nurse. "Come quickly," she said. My friend's father, a strong man whose body had been weakened too soon by leukemia, was dying. As she and her husband left their home, my friend pocketed a copy of the words from Numbers 6:24-26. So often she had heard this Old Testament blessing at the end of worship. Now these were the words she knew would be appropriate as the sweet chariot would swing low to carry her father home: "The LORD bless you and keep you; the LORD make his face shine upon you and be gracious to you; the LORD turn his face toward you and give you peace." She could not know that these were the very words her husband would tenderly speak to his father-in-law as her own fingers closed around the paper folded in her pocket.

A coincidence? I think not.

When I heard this story, the practice of blessing took on new meaning for me. I had thought that only God and ministers bless. Generations have prayed for God's blessing. As a child I sang "Make me a blessing . . ." God indeed blesses. We *are* blessed. We can *be* a blessing. But we are also told *to* bless in the name of God (Num. 6:22-23). And when we bless, we are blessed. It happens in children's worship centers every Sunday with an intimate touch on the head or shoulder of a child and the simple words "God be with you." It happens each day in my kindergarten classroom as we sing a blessing to one another. Sometimes we are unaware when we bless, but blessing is always powerful.

January 20, 1999 (epiphany): Early this evening I received a phone call from my brother. I heard him say, "Dad's breathing has become more shallow. I'll meet you at the nursing home." In recent years our father had been fighting a fear-filled battle with declining health. His mind was ravaged by dementia, his body racked with pain. He had no peace. For the past several days this once strong servant of God, schooled in a devout but never confident version of the faith, had been weakening. Now, exactly fifty years to the day after his own father's death, my father lay dying — and disturbed. At first I sang from the *Psalter.* Then, remembering my friends on that day of Epiphany six years before, I read, "The LORD bless you and keep you; the LORD make his face shine upon you and be gracious to you; the LORD turn his face toward you and give you peace." Not long after, my father died — quietly. Grace. Peace. At last.

A coincidence? I know it was not. I believe it was the blessing.

Job, Isaiah, and South Africa

Job 24:1-24; Isaiah 61:1-9

Nancy Jacobs '84
Professor; Providence, Rhode Island

To say someone has suffered or is suffering the trials of Job says a lot, but I would hazard to say it about the black people of South Africa. The way Job 24 resonates with events in the history of rural South Africa is uncanny.

Under colonial rule black South Africans lost much of their farmland and pastures (Job 24:2), so they began working on farms and in cities and mines owned by others (Job 24:6). Under apartheid many black people lost their homes and were removed to barren areas where they suffered great poverty (Job 24:5, 10). In 1983 the government of the homeland of Bophuthatswana killed nearly twenty thousand donkeys, without compensation to their owners (Job 24:3). These animals had been very useful to the poor South Africans, but they competed on communal land with the cattle owned by the well-connected elite. In Job 24, Job is not recounting tribulations he himself suffered but instead is amassing a catalogue of iniquities that God needs to come around to avenge. He is asking, "Where is justice?" The same question cries out in South Africa.

Justice is a much more pervasive theme in Isaiah 61, and here, too, the conditions in South Africa come to mind — the faith of oppressed Christians, their steadfast vision of comfort, liberation, and renewal, their eventual reward. The transition to majority rule did not solve all problems of the country, but 1994, when the back of apartheid was broken, probably was the closest to the year of the Lord's favor that most of us will ever see in the history of modern nations. Many South Africans thank God for this blessing and continue to be wonderful examples of faith and discipleship in the cause of justice.

I see two lessons in this juxtaposition of Job, Isaiah, and twentieth-century South Africa. First, injustices in the modern world are sadly reminiscent of those decried in the Old Testament. Christians must expose them with narratives of inequity and redemption. Second, this world is still rife with injustice. Christians must never grow complacent about oppression. May God give us vision to see and courage to act.

The Sound of Beauty

Judi De Jager '95   Psalm 19
Oceanography instructor; Lyons, Illinois

> Wind and snow outside.
> Clear skies
> reveal starry eyes.
> Silhouetted, bare trees.
> pillared bushes
> the sound of beauty.

I grew up in upstate New York, where I lived in a house that had many windows but only one on its northwest side. Fortunately, the bedroom with the one northwest window was mine. I spent an inordinate amount of time gazing out that window. I practically memorized the view of the Big Dipper above the neighboring rooftops, the pine trees guarding the shimmering driveways, and the forested backdrop of the entire neighborhood. As a meditational routine I would kneel below the windowsill, fold my hands, and reiterate the psalmist's words: "The heavens declare the glory of God" (Ps. 19:1). Spring, summer, fall, and winter I would look out that window.

Now I am older and live in an urban area of the Midwest, in Chicago, Illinois. I don't see as many pine trees and forested backdrops, and I am rarely able to find the Big Dipper. It is possible, however, every day, to hear the sound of beauty. Listen.

Cardinals

Luke 12:6-7

Daniel J. De Witt '77
Psychologist; Grand Rapids, Michigan

Are not five sparrows sold for two pennies? Yet not one of them is forgotten by God. Indeed, the very hairs of your head are all numbered. Don't be afraid; you are worth more than many sparrows. (Luke 12:6-7)

Outside my office window I stock a bird feeder. It attracts a variety of feathered friends throughout the year. Goldfinches, chickadees, nuthatches, titmice, cardinals, and sparrows entertain my clients and me with their visits. I like to think that my seed offerings provide some sustenance to the birds which inhabit the woods behind our building. I find myself at times feeling sorry for the birds, especially on the coldest days of our Michigan winters. How do their bare feet feel as they cling to the metal perches? How do they keep warm and find the energy to fly when all they have for fuel are cold, hard seeds? I imagine them freezing solid and falling off their branches as they quietly await dawn in subzero temperatures. My empathy for them motivates me to buy an occasional bag of seed and trudge out to fill the feeding tubes once or twice a week. I don't really have a personal relationship with these birds. I haven't named them as one might name a pet parakeet kept indoors. We don't communicate with each other. I don't even hear their songs, because my windows are nearly always shut.

What impact, I wonder, would it have on me if one of these birds would suddenly fail to show up for its meager meal? I might notice if one of the cardinals chose to frequent another feeding station. They are large and showy. My clients usually comment to me when the cardinals come to feed. Yes, they would be conspicuous by their absence. But the truth is that most of the individual birds could leave and not return without my noticing.

It is not uncommon for my clients to comment to me about their own relative unimportance in the bigger scheme of things. They feel very much alone with their pain. They feel like a common sparrow at the big bird feeder of life — unloved, unappreciated, and unnoticed. Is that an accurate perception of their human condition and position? The feelings certainly may reflect painful and inadequate relationships with family, friends, and church here on earth. Even with good intentions we often fail to recognize and attend to one another's needs and difficulties.

Luke reminds us, however, that we are never really alone and overlooked. God is always watching, and he considers each of us to be special and distinct. We are all cardinals at our Lord's feeder.

Duty

Gaylen Byker '73 Romans 12:1-3
Calvin president; Grand Rapids, Michigan

Duty has become a four-letter word. In fact, it's become one of the few unfashionable four-letter words. People hear *duty*, and they think of KP. They think of homework. They think of being thirteen and having to pull weeds. *Duty* reminds people of work they don't necessarily like. It may also remind them of God, the sovereignty of God, and the commands of God. And people have trouble here, too. They don't like the idea that somebody else might presume to legislate for them, impose obligations on them.

Of course, human beings since Adam and Eve have had a tendency to reject this or that particular duty. But since the Enlightenment, people have tended to reject every external moral claim. They reject the whole idea that somebody else, even God, has the right to tell them how to think and what to do.

What a relief it is to have our minds renewed by the gospel, as commanded by Paul: "Do not conform any longer to the pattern of this world, but be transformed by the renewing of your mind. Then you will be able to test and approve what God's will is — his good, pleasing and perfect will" (Rom. 12:2). How wonderful to hear the gospel of grace that speaks a transforming word. How wonderful to let the fresh winds of the gospel blow away some of our complaints and excuses. The gospel says that to work in God's garden is our destiny. To work by God's side is our delight. In his *Letters to Olga* and in each of his plays, Vaclav Havel asserts or implies that human responsibility is not merely an arbitrary set of rules and relationships but rather is essential to the very nature of human existence. He says, "Responsibility is the root, the center of gravity, the constructional principle or axis of identity ... the mortar binding it together.... We are not responsible because of our identity; instead, we have an identity because we are responsible."

Of course there is work to do, but work in the kingdom of God is work we offer out of grateful hearts. Grateful hearts are light hearts. We may offer our work in company with others who are like-minded, who are also offering their work to God, trying to do the duty that God has given all of us and to do it *coram Deo*, as Calvin said, "before God," "before the face of God."

The place to start is right where we are — in our homes, our own classrooms, our own offices and workstations. "Do the duty which lies nearest thee," said Thomas Carlyle, and "thy second duty will already have become clearer."

In His Hands

Psalm 31:15

John Suk '79
Editor; Grand Rapids, Michigan

My times are in your hands. (Ps. 31:15)

Once at a Christmas party for the staff of *The Banner,* the late Dr. John Kromminga, former president of Calvin Theological Seminary, was sitting in my living room, where he had a view of the street outside. He asked if the intersection he was looking at was that "odd one" where five streets come together onto Seminole Road. I said it was.

That launched Kromminga into some reminiscing. He told us that when he first moved to Grand Rapids, he was the designated driver for the family because his father, Rev. Dietrich Kromminga, didn't like driving. With a gleam in his eyes, Kromminga confessed that he remembered the big intersection because he used to "do doughnuts" there in the snow with the family's Model T when he was alone. It had been fun — more than sixty years ago.

Later, Kromminga's recollections led me to wonder about all the other stories that my house has been in on but that I am unaware of. Which now long-dead residents might have seen John Kromminga doing doughnuts more than sixty years ago? Had they chuckled, seeing Kromminga's delight, or had they clucked disapprovingly about how preachers' kids are a bad lot?

Sometimes I catch myself looking around my living room, wishing I could get a glimpse of it seventy years ago, when the house was new. I can guess from the layers of paint what the colors were. I've detected plaster repairs that give away the locations of light fixtures long gone. But what was the furniture like? Who were the people who lived here before? What kinds of hopes and dreams, beliefs and doubts filled their lives? What would this living room look like fifty years from now?

I don't know, but this line of thought is great for dreamers like me. And never threatening either. After all, "from the womb of the dawn" (Ps. 110:3) until Jesus comes again "like a thief in the night" (1 Thess. 5:2), all my times are most securely in his hands (Ps. 31:15).

No matter who is tearing around the house!

Holding Hands

Mary S. Hulst Antonides '91   Isaiah 42:6
Pastor; Grand Rapids, Michigan

> *I, the LORD, have called you in righteousness;*
> *I will take hold of your hand.* (Isa. 42:6)

In this little verse tucked away in the forty-second chapter of Isaiah, the prophet gives us a comforting picture of God. Like a mom taking her son's hand as they go across a street or like Dad reaching out for the hand of his daughter in the middle of a crowd, Isaiah tells us, God reaches out to take our hands — to protect us, guide us, lead us, comfort us.

The taking of a hand is an intimate gesture; it means different things at different times. Lovers hold hands walking in the park, signifying affection and the willingness to display that affection to the world. Parents hold the hands of children, sometimes to signal affection, often to provide a deterrent to the child's innate desire to wander. Sometimes parents grab their children's hands to pull them away from harm. Nurses take the hands of patients to help them out of bed or assist them on a walk down the hall.

The taking of our hands by God can mean all of these things. We can imagine God, like one who loves us, holding our hands to show his affection. We can picture God, as our parent, swallowing up our small hands in the protective, guiding grip of his large hands. We can picture God, as our caregiver, coming to our aid with his strong, supportive hand.

The prophet has given us a picture of our loving, hand-holding God. May we have hands that are able to be held — not fists of anger that are hard to grip nor hands so full of the stuff of life that they have no openness to God's care or direction. May we come to God with empty hands, open hands, hands like those of a child: ready to be held, willing to be directed, open to receive love, glad to accept protection. In the words of the spiritual, may each of us ask the precious Lord to take our hands and lead us home.

Used by God

2 Kings 13:20-21

Tim Becksvoort '97
Teacher; Bellflower, California

Elisha died and was buried. Now Moabite raiders used to enter the country every spring. Once while some Israelites were burying a man, suddenly they saw a band of raiders, so they threw the man's body into Elisha's tomb. When the body touched Elisha's bones, the man came to life and stood up on his feet (2 Kings 13:20-21).

God is gracious, merciful, and faithful to his people — often using his chosen ones as vehicles of his goodness. This is perhaps an obvious conclusion, but one that we need to be constantly reminded of nevertheless. Elisha was a chosen one of God. God used him many times during his life and even after his death. Elisha never saw the particular manifestation of God's grace mentioned in today's passage. Why? Because he was dead when it happened. In fact, the Bible tells us that he died of an unspecified illness (2 Kings 13:14). A person of less faith might have wondered why the God that cured an enemy commander of leprosy, produced a nearly bottomless jar of oil to sustain a widow and her sons, and brought back to life a Shunammite's son chose not to make well the man through whom he had performed these miracles. It just doesn't seem fair.

But God had better plans. He chose to show how he could work miracles through one of his chosen ones even after he had died. The man who was the recipient of this miracle received one of the best gifts from God — new life.

The Old Testament story of Elisha ends there, but its implications for us are ongoing. Remain faithful to God and be active in passing on his grace and mercy to others. God has a plan, and it involves each one of us. Like Elisha, we don't know how or when God will use us — it might even be after we die. But have faith that God will be faithful even in the darkest times. And pray that God will use us to pass on the best gift of all time — eternal life.

Heroes of the Faith

Randall Heeres '74   Hebrews 11:8-28
Teacher; Cadillac, Michigan

The seventeenth-century poet John Donne often wrote of the seeming contradictions, the paradoxes, of Christian faith. Like the apostle Paul, Donne grasped that true freedom means being a prisoner of Christ, that God's grace is not cosmetic but heart-deep and thorough.

Donne and Paul also recognized doubt in the Christian life, the times of reluctance or skepticism. Hebrews 11, recalling the heroes of the faith, presents exemplary lives for us, yet these same heroes also demonstrated sin and human frailty, doubt tempered by God's faith-giving grace. We can learn from their doubt as well as from their faith.

Abraham and Moses rate many verses in Hebrews 11, which highlights their obedience to God's blessed vision. However, we know that Moses' initial reluctance to be a leader (Exod. 4) cost him entrance to the Promised Land. Abraham, too, was sometimes uncertain of his destiny (Gen. 17). Doubt gnawed at heroic faith.

After these powerhouses, Hebrews 11 lists others in less detail, heroes like Gideon and Samson. Gideon questioned where God was as the Midianites oppressed Israel. His doubt was overcome by three gracious signs: the amazing fire and the wet and dry fleeces. After the heroics of trumpets and swords, Gideon created a golden ephod, which plagued him and all Israel who worshiped it. Yet here in Hebrews 11 stands Gideon as well as the lusty and arrogant Samson and the hesitant Barak.

As aliens traveling toward our true country, we experience doubts, yet by God's grace we may be heroes of the faith. Witness the neighbor ravaged by deadly disease but still growing in faith. Witness the testimonies of those whose lives were nearly destroyed by addictions. Witness the restored harmony in a church once splintered by controversy. Witness the aged friend whose story is of God's faithfulness in the desert and beside still waters.

Like Donne, Paul, Moses, Gideon, and the whole "cloud of witnesses," we know, too, that by God's grace our faith remains despite doubts. We are sanctified sinners, made holy — heroes of faith.

Faithful in Seattle

2 John 4

Jane Plantinga Pauw '81
Pastor; Seattle, Washington

It has given me great joy to find some of your children walking in the truth, just as the Father commanded us. (2 John 4)

When I was ordained a Presbyterian minister in 1990, I knew my work would sometimes feel like an uphill battle. I had been told Seattle was the country's most unchurched area. Many northwesterners say the place they go to worship God is the mountains, not the churches. That is why stories like those of Abby and Roger have meant so much to me.

About two years ago I noticed an unfamiliar young woman in church one Sunday. I introduced myself to her and noticed she had paint on her watchband and in her hair. She said she was a painter, an artist. A few weeks later she brought Roger to church, and before we knew it, they had taken the church by storm. Even though they knew none of the hymns, they joined the choir. Roger made birdhouses on poles for an auction. Abby painted one of the Sunday-school rooms to look like a temple so the children can be transported to ancient Israel when they hear Bible stories. They began to volunteer in our women's shelter. They attended every available adult-education class, asking probing questions about faith.

Before long they began to speak about getting married. I was struck with their single-minded intent to integrate their new-found faith into their wedding. Their friends, true Seattleites, were puzzled by this new and alien turn in Roger's and Abby's lives. The wedding became an occasion for the couple to publicly profess their faith and to share it with family and friends.

This is probably the first time ever that an enthusiastic bride has asked whether ten hymns would be acceptable for the wedding service! After some discussion, we decided to stick with three. Instead of wedding gifts, the couple requested donations to Habitat for Humanity and food for the local food bank. By the beginning of the service, the church entrance was filled to overflowing with bags of gourmet packaged foods, and thousands of dollars had been collected. As Abby walked down the aisle, the choir was waiting for her at the chancel, singing through tears of joy, "Glory to God in the highest, peace to God's people on earth!"

Roger and Abby are striking testaments to the bountiful grace of God. They, and others like them, remind me and reassure us that God is faithful, even in Seattle.

Deep Water

David Van Houten '81   Luke 5:1-32
Professor; Merion Station, Pennsylvania

In the opening scene of Luke 5, we find Jesus standing on the lakeshore, surrounded by people "crowding around him and listening to the word of God" (Luke 5:1). After teaching from a boat, Jesus turns to a few fishermen and instructs them to "put out into deep water" (Luke 5:4). After some initial hesitation, they obey, and they catch more fish than they can handle.

"Putting out into deep water" is a metaphor that describes the dark side of Jesus' ministry in the Gospel of Luke. Jesus refuses to stay where it's safe or do what is expected of him. He repeatedly pushes off the shore of social respectability into the deep waters of uncertainty and risk, often confusing and alienating would-be followers. He touches a leper, forgives a man's sins, and eats with social and religious outcasts. And it is no coincidence that Jesus' command to "put out into deep water" precedes the calling of the disciples. They are asked to follow, and they often do so at great risk.

Where is our "deep water"? I suspect we feel surrounded by it. We do not have to look too far to find people whom we would rather not touch, rather not forgive, and with whom we would rather not eat. Or the deep water may be within, as we are called to honest self-examination and repentance. Following Jesus, we need to leave the security of our busyness behind and journey deep within our own souls. We put out into deep water with the assurance that Jesus is there, waiting.

May God make us people of courage and lead us deep within and far outside ourselves.

Why We Should Praise

Psalm 95:1-7

Jonathan Tamminga
Calvin student; Grand Rapids, Michigan

Come, let us sing for joy to the LORD; let us shout aloud to the Rock of our salvation. Let us come before him with thanksgiving and extol him with music and song. (Ps. 95:1-2)

Chris Rice, a Christian rock musician, has a song entitled "Cartoons." In it he sings songs of praise as though they came from the mouths of favorite cartoon characters. Fred and Wilma Flintstone sing "YabbaDabba-Lujah," Scooby-Doo and Shaggy belt out a chorus of "ScoobyDooby-Lujah," and so on. Aside from the obvious humor in this song, Rice reminds us that God must be praised and that cartoon characters are not up to the job. We must do the praising.

Why should we praise? The answers can be found outdoors, in God's creation. Everywhere we look we should be reminded of him, because everywhere we look we can see him. We can find God in the color that paints the sky just before the sun bottoms out. We can see him along a path in the woods as a fawn sips from a stream. We can see him sitting in that old oak tree at the end of the block and playing among the stars of the night sky. We must praise God for this marvelous creation.

This is, however, not the only reason for our praise. We must praise him for everything. We have life because of him, we have all our many blessings because of him, but most importantly we have salvation because of him. He sent his Son to die for us on the cross on Golgotha. His perfect Child died so that we may live. What more reason can there be for giving him praise?

So join with me, brothers and sisters, each Sunday as we gather together to sing and worship and send our thanks to God on high. But also give praise every time your husband belts out a Christmas hymn, every time your son practices his tuba, every time birds sing out in the fresh spring air. For all of these moments are gifts from God.

Praise the Lord now and forever. Amen.

Sunmee Jo '93   Psalm 139; Matthew 6:24-34
Attorney; Grand Rapids, Michigan

I did not realize I was an anxious person until my student-loan payments came due. After a grace period which was much too short, I was repaying various creditors, and I began to worry, "How am I going to make it?" I found it ironic, and was greatly ashamed, that I, a poverty lawyer representing poor people, was worrying about how not to become one of them. On top of this worry, my job was stressful. It was and still is difficult not to be overwhelmed by the tragedy, injustice, and inequities I encounter in addition to the unexpected emergencies and court dates.

When we are overwhelmed by the anxieties of daily life — financial, professional, academic, personal — Christ's peace seems terribly elusive. Yet Christ says to us, "Do not worry about tomorrow, for tomorrow will worry about itself. Each day has enough trouble of its own" (Matt. 6:34). A sermon by Rev. Marchienne Rienstra helped me rediscover Psalm 139, in which the psalmist cries, "Search me, O God, and know my heart; test me and know my anxious thoughts" (Ps. 139:23). In Matthew, Christ promises that though we will experience trouble and anxiety, God's grace is generous, abundant, and sufficient for us. The psalms tell us that God, who is omniscient and omnipotent, knows our inmost thoughts and our every need.

Reminded of this all-encompassing grace, I realize how blessed I am indeed. I am humbled every day as I serve families who have less than I do materially yet exhibit more dignity and more fruit of the Spirit (Gal. 5:22-23) than I would in similar circumstances. There are many days when I sigh, "There but for the grace of God go I." What Christ offers may not be what I want (a miraculous payoff of my loans), but I am assured that he will provide me with what I need. This peace he leaves with me in the midst of anxious times.

And so day by day I strive to "seek first his kingdom and his righteousness" (Matt. 6:33), and I pray that the Lord may search me and find the "offensive way in me, and lead me in the way everlasting" (Ps. 139:24).

Five Smooth Stones

1 Samuel 17

Anthony J. Diekema '56
Calvin president emeritus; Grand Haven, Michigan

"The LORD who delivered me from the paw of the lion and the paw of the bear will deliver me from the hand of this Philistine.". . . Then he took his staff in his hand, chose five smooth stones from the stream, put them in the pouch of his shepherd's bag and, with his sling in his hand, approached the Philistine.

(1 Sam. 17:37, 40)

This classic saga of Old Testament warfare has something in it for everyone. It's a great giant-killer story, and the warfare metaphor is ripe for fruitful application to our own lives each day.

David faced an incredible challenge. We're told that this challenge — Goliath — stood nine feet tall, wore 125 pounds of armor, and wielded a spear with an iron point that weighed almost 15 pounds. Hardly a fair fight by any measure, and David could take no encouragement from the Israelite army, which was terrified and on the run.

David obviously could not meet this challenge on Goliath's terms. But David faced Goliath on his own terms: a proven simple trust in God and a shepherd's common armament — a slingshot and "five smooth stones." David trusted God, who had been with him before and would deliver him again through the use of a simple weapon. Goliath was powerless on David's terms.

Like David, we all face extraordinary challenges from time to time. Perhaps you are confronting one today — a complicated family problem, a serious illness, a cherished relationship now in jeopardy. Perhaps you just feel overwhelmed by the general and ever-present specter of sin and evil.

What are the five smooth stones with which you can face today's challenges? Certainly, trust in God is foundational. It is nonnegotiable; it knows that God is in charge of everything. Note that David had such trust in confronting Goliath but also in tending his sheep each day. And confidence flows naturally from trust. Courage is another smooth stone; it is a gift of God engendered by trust and confidence. Like David, you may need to take actions from which those around you are refraining because they are without courage.

There are many other smooth stones — love, humility, prayer, loyalty, commitment, obedience — which may be uniquely suited to help you overcome your present challenge. Think carefully about each one. Then pick the five smooth stones that will be most likely to deliver you from your present giant, knowing that they are gifts of God for your deliverance and for your shalom.

Gratefulness

John R. Houskamp '86   Philippians 4:4-7
Physician; Byron Center, Michigan

Rejoice in the Lord always. I will say it again: Rejoice! . . . Do not be anxious about anything, but in everything, by prayer and petition, with thanksgiving, present your requests to God. And the peace of God . . . will guard your hearts and your minds in Christ Jesus. (Phil. 4:4-7)

We all know of those experiences in life when we promise God something as long as he gets us through a certain mess. Most of us have made such promises ourselves. Maybe after a hard time, such as a struggle with cancer, we promise God and ourselves that things will change and that we will keep in better contact with him. We will do things differently. We will do better, and we will become better people.

And then, of course, we don't change. In a little while things go back to the way they were, and we forget to follow through with those changes that seemed so important just a brief time before. It is not easy to keep those promises.

Maybe we shouldn't even make them. Paul says that we are to rejoice in the Lord always and that in return God will give us his peace and keep our hearts and minds in him. That is, if we are just grateful for what he has given, God will grant us his peace. We don't have to sacrifice our children or become missionaries in a foreign land or open a rescue mission in the inner city. God makes it simpler than any bargain we might make with him about what we will or won't do from now on if he grants our requests. And the beauty of it is that we don't have to face the fact over and over that we have failed again.

God says "Rejoice in what I have given you. Look around and be thankful. Appreciate my gifts. Look at the sunshine and say thanks for a new day. Listen to the sound of rain on your car window and realize what a gift it is that you can even be sitting there to hear it. Feel the love that is present in your child's embrace or the wet lick of your dog." In the play *Our Town*, Thornton Wilder encourages us to treasure each moment when he asks, "Do any human beings ever realize life while they live it? — every, every minute?"*

Thomas Merton states it differently in his *Thoughts in Solitude:* "To be grateful is to recognize the love of God in everything He has given us — and he has given us everything. Every breath we draw is a gift of His love, every moment of existence is a grace, for it brings with it immense graces from Him. Gratitude therefore takes nothing for granted. . . . "** See God in all things, make no bargains, give thanks, and rejoice.

A Broken Heart

Psalm 34:18

Barbara Carvill
Calvin professor; Grand Rapids, Michigan

A man once asked a rabbi, "Why does it say, 'You shall carry the Word of God on your heart'?" The rabbi answered, "You should carry God's Word on your heart so that God can come into your heart when your heart breaks." Only a person cured of a broken heart can know the wisdom of that rabbi's answer.

Our lives are journeys with and toward God. Sometimes we walk in the right direction; often we take false turns and get lost. There are easy, cheerful stretches on this journey but also painful, agonizing stretches, where our hearts break. At one time or another we all will experience agony and will walk in the dark valley Psalm 23 talks about. This is simply part of being human. Even Jesus cried out in agony, "My God, my God, why have you forsaken me?" (Mark 15:34). My own heart was broken when I lost my husband to cancer. He was thirty-four years old, and our daughter was not even two.

When our hearts break, something deep and profound is shattered within us, something that can never again be fully undone. We have encountered the dreadful, hideous meaninglessness of our sinful, broken world.

How can we console people who are shattered so deeply? What can we say to our brokenhearted friend in despair who feels cut off from everyone, even from God? Our human words of comfort sound trite. All we can do as friends is to be present, to pray, and to practice patient silence so that God's voice can be heard through his Word. It says, "You have a God who does not leave you alone, a God who 'is close to the brokenhearted'" (Ps. 34:18). When God comes into a shattered heart through Jesus the brokenhearted, the crucified and resurrected one, the core of our being is mended, and our broken center is held together again by the glue of God's infinite grace and love. And so, it *is* good to carry God's Word close to our heart.

The Calvin College logo is an open hand offering a pristine, perfect heart to God. Maybe that heart should be broken and battered.

Head and Heart

Ron Polinder '68   Proverbs 4:23
Principal; Lynden, Washington

Those of us who have been raised in the Reformed tradition or have adopted it somewhere along the way are wired to be rather rational about our Christian faith. We take seriously "the Christian mind," "the life of the mind," and "loving God with our mind." We are fond of verses like "Be transformed by the renewing of your mind" (Rom. 12:2), and we delight in books like Mark Noll's *The Scandal of the Evangelical Mind,* especially when he cites our tradition as one that has been something of a model of Christian thinking.

Make no mistake about it: Reformed thinkers have made huge contributions to the evangelical community and to the kingdom at large. We desperately need to pass on the Reformed vision and worldview to our children and far beyond. It is a great gift that at once flows from Scripture and helps us read Scripture. We are stewards of this worldview and take seriously the mandate to "make disciples" (Matt. 28:19).

But just as urgently we should also want to attend to Proverbs 4:23, which reminds us that our heart "is the wellspring of life." The heart is the symbolic center of our emotions, feelings, and motivations. The desires of the heart, good or evil, are powerful, often more so than our rationality. Rooted in the heart is the relational side of life. We would do well to nurture that relational part of us, to educate our emotions.

Novelist Walker Percy describes one of his characters as "one who gets all A's in school, but flunks life." In some ways this describes all of us Reformed types, wounded and broken souls that we are. It is only a transforming relationship and friendship with Jesus that offers hope, this mysterious new life "which is Christ in [us], the hope of glory" (Col. 1:27).

Part of the Story

1 Samuel 20:39

Robert Kuilema '81
Calvin administrator; Grand Rapids, Michigan

(The boy knew nothing of all this; only Jonathan and David knew.)

(1 Sam. 20:39)

Sometimes major episodes of biblical high drama seem too familiar to evoke any emotional response. All of us are familiar with Samuel's story of David and Jonathan's separation. We know how David skips Saul's royal banquet and how Saul in his rage throws a spear at his son. We know how Jonathan, now aware that his father intends to kill David, gathers his bow and arrows and a young boy and proceeds to David's hiding place. We know all aspects of this familiar story. Or do we?

Consider for a moment that young boy, the arrow chaser. He knows nothing of the court's political intrigues, nothing of David and Jonathan's secrets. Nameless, he comes onto the biblical stage for a brief moment. He has no awareness of his part in this important drama. The story cannot unfold without him, but he has no awareness of being in the story.

This young boy's story is a great antidote for those who feel that their lives lack meaning and purpose. "What's the point of my life? Why does this have to happen to me?" Such laments trouble many Christians. Since childhood we have been told that God has a plan for our lives. Yet it seems to many of us that, if God has planned our lives, we surely cannot discern the plan. If God is planning, shouldn't it be obvious and, perhaps, spectacular? Most of our lives seem quite too humdrum for God to have planned them.

Again, consider the young boy. He is, in the vernacular of today's adolescents, clueless. Like the boy, we, too, simply do not have any idea when the episodes of our lives have meaningful import. At any casual moment we, too, may be engaged in a turning point of history. It bothers our sense of autonomy that we don't choose or plan for importance or meaning in our lives. It is humbling to say to God, "Use me according to your plans, at your discretion, for your purposes." And it is sobering to realize that our lives will have moments when God's purposes are worked through us without our cognizance. Yet realizing this is a great gift because it can change forever how we live.

When we know that our lives belong to God, then we have his peace.

23

Long-term Care

Thomas Kennedy '75   Psalm 41:4
Professor; Valparaiso, Indiana

> *This life is a hospital; the sin has really been forgiven, but it has not yet been healed.* (Martin Luther*)

Some years ago Princeton theological ethicist Paul Ramsey wrote, "We are all fellow fetuses," incisively describing the likeness of all persons to the baby developing within a mother's womb. We are born not of our own wills but dependent upon the generosity and kindness of another. That dependency continues throughout our lives. We are cared for in our earliest days, and, ever dependent upon others for nurture and knowledge, we grow. Relying daily upon the goodwill of others, we flourish. Dependent upon spouses, physicians, health-care workers, and family to care for us, we decline in older age. To be human is to be dependent upon others, a hard truth to remember in a culture that valorizes adolescent independence, that is happy to make personal choice, independent will, the final arbiter of everything.

Of course, to be human is to be dependent, above all, upon the God who created and sustains the universe. As Luther reminds us, we are dependent not only upon the Creator and Sustainer of our being but also upon God the Physician, the Healer of our broken natures. Apart from God's grace there is no health in us. In Christ our healing has begun, to be sure, but we are not yet healthy. This life is a hospital. We await the full health promised to us.

It is no easy thing to live as a sick person dependent upon the advice and oversight of a physician. We may look healthy, we may feel healthy, but the temptations to overextend and overexpose ourselves are great — I feel good; never mind the physician's warning. Or perhaps we second-guess the physician, falling back upon our own private assessment of our health — I am not as healthy as the physician says; I cannot run; I cannot walk.

To learn to live as one dependent upon others, as one dependent upon the healing grace of God — that is a lesson to be learned daily.

Isaiah 1:16-17   Rachel Boehm Van Harmelen '89
Writer; Ottawa, Ontario

In the barnyard saga *Babe*, an unusual pig discovers an uncommon destiny. He becomes a "sheep pig" instead of the main course for Christmas dinner. In doing so, he upsets the balance of power on the Hoggett farm. You see, on the farm, each animal has its place and its purpose. Young Babe, befriended by sheepdogs, first views himself as equal to these useful animals. Later he discovers he's headed not for the sheep pen but the slaughterhouse.

One of my daughter's favorite parts of this movie is an exchange between a cow and Ferdinand the duck, Babe's rebellious counterpart. "The way things are is the way things are," drawls the cow lazily, arguing for the farmyard status quo, where each animal, including the pig, fulfills its destiny and never oversteps its predetermined boundaries. Ferdinand, ever the nonconformist, argues back adamantly, "Well, the way things are *stinks!*"

I guess it always pleased me that my daughter, three years old at the time, could appreciate the humorous heroism in this duck's righteous anger. When things don't seem right to her in life, I hope she'll work for change. After all, isn't that what "doing justice" is all about?

When we walk in downtown Ottawa, our home and Canada's national capital, my daughter asks a lot of questions about the people panhandling on the city streets. She also asks for money to drop in their hats. I see in her the seeds of a righteous anger against the injustice of homelessness. In this city alone, 300 to 400 men and women sleep in shelters every night. So do 150 children.

"Stop doing wrong, learn to do right! Seek justice, encourage the oppressed," wrote Isaiah (Isa. 1:16-17). I thank God Scripture has taught us to respond to questions of injustice not only with Ferdinand's recognition of brokenness and sin — "the way things are *stinks*" — but also with the certainty of renewal and redemption — hope for change, hope for the future.

In God's Hands

William Haverkamp '68   Isaiah 49:13-18
School superintendent; Kentwood, Michigan

> *See, I have engraved you on the palms of my hands.* (Isa. 49:16)

S everal years ago, while working for the Christian Reformed World Relief Committee, I visited a leper colony in Liberia. The program director there took me to a small store on the property that displayed handicrafts made and sold by the lepers to help cover the cost of their care. A small ebony woodcarving caught my eye. I knew it was the one thing I wanted to take home from this trip. I purchased it immediately. "Would you like to see the carver?" the program director asked.

When I saw the carver at work, the piece I had purchased took on new meaning. The man had no fingers on his left hand and only a thumb and part of the first finger on his right hand. He did his work by wedging a block of wood between his biceps and forearm and his chisel between his thumb and partial finger.

My purchase was the figure of a man held tightly in a hand. On the bottom of the carving was Isaiah 49:16: "See, I have engraved you on the palms of my hands." The carving has become one of my most treasured possessions — not just because of the story behind it but because of the beautiful concept it depicts.

Throughout Scripture the imagery of God's hands points to his love and care for his people. His hands heal (Job 5:17). He holds out his hands to an obstinate people (Isa. 65:2). Jesus places his hands on little children and blesses them (Matt. 19:15). And nails in Jesus' hands hold him to the cross as he dies for us. What precious hands!

God not only holds us in the palms of his hands; he has even engraved us into the palms of his hands. Engravings are permanent. We are permanently fixed in God's hands. He holds us tight and will never let go. Praise God!

Previous Arrangements

Esther 2 Ken Koeman '64
Pastor; Lynden, Washington

Nothing ever simply happens. There is no such thing as a mere event. And coincidences? They've been defined as "minor miracles in which God chooses to remain anonymous."

Esther 2 is a clear example of two events which at first reading seem to be nothing more than pure happenstance. Esther ends up in the position of queen in the palace, and her uncle, Mordecai, ends up in the annals of the heroes. So?

The name of God is never mentioned in the book of Esther. And yet he is right there in the forefront of the story. It's just that we don't see his hand until later on when we learn exactly how crucial the positions of Esther and Mordecai prove to be. The reason for Esther's position? To put her in precisely the right circumstances to lobby a capricious king on behalf of the entire Jewish people in order to save them from extermination, and, with them, the promised messiah. The reason for Mordecai's position? Not only to save him, with only minutes to spare, from what would have been certain death at the hands of Haman, his archenemy, but also to launch his promotion to prime minister in order to effect the deliverance of the Jews. Esther and Mordecai become the twin lynchpins in preventing a holocaust as serious as any God's people have known.

But notice something else. We don't even know that there is going to be such genocide against the Jews until Esther 3, where Haman's deadly plot is hatched, sanctioned, and announced. Yet, before we even learn about the problem, we are told these delightful stories of a beauty contest and a foiled assassination attempt. Why? To show us that God sovereignly places his solutions into position before the problem even appears.

Immense problems or small roadblocks may come our way today. Let us remember that the Lord, our shepherd, is always ten steps ahead of us. Arrangements have already been made.

Tapping into the System

Eleanor Danhof Den Hartigh '65 John 15:45
School superintendent; Chino, California

I love the computer, and I use one regularly at work and at home, but frequently I am frustrated by it. Over the past summer I had Word 97 installed on my work computer, and I even took a class to become more proficient in using it. I've expanded my capabilities and bravely try out new things, but I still find myself in situations that I can't figure out. Then I grow impatient and end up asking someone to get me out of the mess as quickly as possible without bothering me with the technical details. I realize that the computer's capabilities are almost limitless, but I do not really work at expanding my use of it, and so I haven't begun to tap into what is available to me with just the touch of a key or two.

While dealing with my computer, I suddenly realized one day that this is also true of my own relationship with Jesus Christ. Since childhood I have known and loved the Lord, and I am aware that he truly is the source of all things. But often in my life I become frustrated with a situation and wonder why something isn't working out the way I think it should. I believe I have a good solution to the problem, but my attempts to correct a particular situation have little effect. I grow impatient, and I want quick answers. "Lord, do something! Get me out of this mess," I pray. And then God gently reminds me, "Remain in me, and I will remain in you. No branch can bear fruit by itself; it must remain in the vine. Neither can you bear fruit unless you remain in me" (John 15:4-5).

Remaining in the vine takes work and spiritual discipline, at least as much work as it takes to become completely computer literate. May we all discover the limitless possibilities of grace, love, mercy, and peace available to us in that living vine of which we are the living branches fit for bearing fruit.

Escape from Futility

Psalm 127:1-2   Bert Witvoet '59
Editor; St. Catharines, Ontario

In vain you rise early and stay up late. (Ps. 127:2)

If you should venture out on the Queen Elizabeth Way outside our town at six o'clock in the morning, you would see people already driving to work. The traffic gets heavier around seven and eight. At home, parents are getting their children ready for school and are preparing themselves for a day's work. Radios blare out the most recent news: Students in Asia were beaten by police while we were deep in REM sleep, and the stock market took a dive hours before our alarms went off. Yes, we are a busy, busy human race. But how much of our busyness is for healing and growth, for love and for peace in this world?

In the language of Psalm 127, the opposite of doing something worthwhile is doing something in vain. That means that what you are busy with may be useless — a waste of time. And maybe not only a waste of time. It may even destroy something instead of building it up. There is no in-between kind of work in this world. Everything we do is either part of the problem or part of the solution. It is only the presence of the Lord in what we do that rescues our work from futility.

Take, for example, a good crew of builders: carpenters, electricians, plumbers, roofers, dry wallers, bricklayers. They are all busy working on a nice housing development on the good side of town. According to Psalm 127, unless the Lord is in the work being done on that housing development, those workmen labor in vain (Ps. 127:1).

Or take the example of your city's public-health and public-safety workers: police officers, firefighters, night watchmen, soldiers, ambulance personnel, nurses. Your city is in good hands, right? Maybe. Listen to the psalmist: Unless the Lord watches over your city, you are not secure (Ps. 127:1).

In vain you rise up early and stay up late to attend important meetings and do important things if the Lord is not there sustaining your families, protecting and blessing your church, and building your community and nation. Pray today that the Lord will deliver you from futility. Surrender whatever you do to him every day, and you will sleep well each night.

Created in His Image

James Vanden Bosch '70   Genesis 1:27
Calvin professor; Grand Rapids, Michigan

> *So God created human beings in his own image,*
> *in the image of God he created them;*
> *male and female he created them.* (Gen. 1:27, NIVI)

This verse from Genesis 1 should regularly catch us by surprise, for it holds in it one of the most amazing facts that we can learn about ourselves anywhere — that we humans are created in the image of God. Of course, just exactly what it means to be made in God's image continues to be disputed. It has been described variously as pointing to our free will, to our intellect, to our creativity, or to the fact that we are moral beings. But we can reasonably assume that being created in God's image means at least this: that we were created to be in a special relationship with God, to commune with God and with others created in his image.

However, we are so far from what God intended us to be, sin has so distorted us, that we sometimes assume that nothing of God's image survives in us or in others. But C. S. Lewis, in a sermon he preached in 1942, insists that even in our brokenness we display "the weight of glory" that he associates with being made in God's image:

> It is a serious thing to live in a society of possible gods and goddesses, to remember that the dullest and most uninteresting person you talk to may one day be a creature which, if you saw it now, you would be strongly tempted to worship, or else a horror and a corruption such as you now meet, if at all, only in a nightmare. All day long we are, in some degree, helping each other to one or other of these destinations. It is in the light of these overwhelming possibilities, it is with the awe and circumspection proper to them, that we should conduct all our dealings with one another, all friendships, all loves, all play, all politics. There are no ordinary people. You have never talked to a mere mortal.

This is not the end of the matter, but it is a very good place to start.

Missing the Messages

Psalm 119:97-104

Jane Bos Luimes '86
Writer/editor; Hudsonville, Michigan

Little slips of paper litter my house and my car. These scraps, most with ragged edges, come in fluorescent green, yellowed white, or sticky pink. On them I've scribbled little bits of wisdom. They're snippets of sermons I've heard, something else I've read, or maybe a Bible verse. I hang them on the refrigerator, stuff them in drawers, lay them near the kitchen sink, or stick them on my nightstand. Some are quick reads; others take a moment to scan.

"Pray often," one of them states in fading blue ink. Another one, a quick summary from an awesome sermon, reads, "What is a disciple? Someone who wants to be like Jesus. Now get the passion and the courage to do it." One stuck on my dashboard reads, "Let the peace of Christ rule in your hearts" (Col. 3:15). Neatly, on a perfectly square piece of green paper, I wrote, "How to make your faith complete," then listed eleven ways to do just that. They include such things as "Be quick to listen and slow to anger. . . . Heal your tongue of gossip and profanity. . . . Help those in need. . . . Don't discriminate or stereotype. . . . Don't be negative. . . . Forgive others." Crammed in my sock drawer, another well-worn piece of paper says, "Consult the Lord's will." Still another asks, "What would you give in exchange for your soul? Deny yourself and take up the cross and follow him."

Powerful messages indeed.

Yet in our busy lives it's so easy to ignore them. I do. Here they are, in plain sight. But I've seen them so often that they hardly register anymore. They've become part of the background of my daily life.

Let's pray for new passion, asking for new eyes to see the many signs that our God reigns and Jesus lives.

February

Sherry Smith Levy
Calvin parent/writer; Grand Rapids, Michigan

Matthew 10:41

Anyone who receives a prophet because he is a prophet will receive a prophet's reward, and anyone who receives a righteous man because he is a righteous man will receive a righteous man's reward. (Matt. 10:41)

I hear a bird singing today.
Yesterday too his song
broke nature's silence.
In yesterday's brilliant sunshine
the melting ice was cheered on
by his song.
Today in the blowing snowstorm
he is a prophet
proclaiming promises.

A Command Performance

1 Timothy 1:1   Richard J. Mouw
Former Calvin professor/seminary president;
La Canada, California

Paul, an apostle of Christ Jesus by the command of God our Savior and of Christ Jesus our hope. (1 Tim. 1:1)

The apostle Paul, at the beginning of his first letter to Timothy, adds an interesting phrase to his usual mode of greeting: He tells us that his apostolic status comes "by the command of God."

A. W. Tozer has a nice way of characterizing what Paul is saying here. Paul sees his service to the kingdom, Tozer explains, as "a command performance." When you are summoned to perform in the presence of royalty, it isn't the kind of invitation you can politely turn down. You had better show up — and be at your best. And that is how Paul sees his apostolic work.

But it isn't just New Testament apostles who get invitations to give command performances. It's what the Christian life is all about. We live our lives — to use a favorite Reformed phrase from the past — *coram deo*, "before the face of God." And this applies to all of life. God cares deeply about how we eat and play and work and study. There is no distinction between our private and public lives in God's eyes: "'Who can hide in secret places so that I cannot see them?' says the LORD. 'Do I not fill heaven and earth?'" (Jer. 23:24).

God's omnipresence can be a frightening thought at times. My own temptation is to want some secret places in which I can simply be on my own. But that does not work. All of life is a command performance.

But the realization of God's constant presence can also be a wonderful comfort. It is a good thing to know that we are never alone. God is not only always with us to offer guidance in the difficult places; he also knows what it is like for us to be there as vulnerable creatures. God sent Jesus into the world to find that out. And Jesus in turn sends the Holy Spirit into our lives to provide us with the strength that is necessary each day for our command performances.

Love Casts Out Fear

Harvey Brink '66   1 John 4:18
Pastor; Pella, Iowa

I continue to be amazed at how much anxiety remains in my life. My particular brand of anxiety is fear. I fear a lot. One would think that years of experience, maturity, or faith would remove all fear, but I still have more anxiety than I want or am comfortable with. I am anxious about fitting in: Will people like me, respect me, or allow me to be a part of their lives in a meaningful way? Will we mutually understand the meaning? Do I matter to them as they matter to me? I am also anxious about being fit: Am I up to snuff physically, professionally, and personally? I am anxious about being alone and being lonely. And I fear making wrong decisions.

I take comfort that I am not the only person who feels this way. Scripture records messengers from God needing to reassure people not to fear. We can expect fear in a divine-human encounter, but why do we have fears in so many other areas of life? John tells us that such fear arises out of expectation of punishment. Our humanness prepares us for the expectation that we will suffer the consequences of certain actions. We expect to bear the consequences because we think we are in charge.

I am grateful that along the way God has shown me his love and that his love is sufficiently complete to drive out fear. I respect John's use of a word here that contains an element of force in its meaning. Fear needs to be cast out, thrust away, thrown down — by complete love. But I am attached to my fear because it is connected to my desire to be in charge of my life. God's acceptance of us — in love — casts out our fear. And he does that also in community. He provides and uses the love of people to diminish and remove the lingering shreds of fear that bind us up. We are being set free to set others free from fear.

The World's True Hope

Lamentations 3:1-26

Randy Vander Weit '91
Youth director; Troy, Michigan

When I was in Madagascar on a mission trip, God took me on a spiritual journey which reminded me of the core of the gospel — God's love for us and his promise that because of our faith in Jesus he will forgive us our sins and prepare a place in heaven for us.

Even though I had ministered for eight years in a low-income neighborhood in the United States, I was not prepared for what I saw in Madagascar, one of the poorest countries in the world — children digging through rat-infested garbage heaps, looking for something to eat or sell, families living in cardboard boxes under bridges. When I saw these things, I questioned whether God is truly enough for the Malagasy people. I made the common mistake of viewing the possession of material goods as a sign of God's love.

But then I was convicted by Paul's words in 1 Timothy 6:17: "Command those who are rich in this present world not to be arrogant nor to put their hope in wealth, which is so uncertain, but to put their hope in God." That message was very powerfully communicated to me as I watched an ill-clothed, hunchbacked mother and her mentally challenged daughter go forward at an evangelistic meeting to accept Jesus Christ as their Lord and Savior. This woman knew what I had forgotten: The Lord's "compassions never fail. . . . The LORD is good to those whose hope is in him . . ." (Lam. 3:22, 25). Seeing two people who in my mind had every right to feel hopeless accept the world's true hope brought me from questioning whether God is truly enough for the Malagasy people to knowing he is more than enough for them.

The same is true for all of us. When we lose our jobs, when our marriages fall apart, or when a loved one dies, we realize that our hope does not lie in tangible things or in circumstances but in the unshakable, immovable love of God. His love is new every morning, and his faithfulness is great (Lam. 3:23). Let us hope in him.

Give Him Your Heart

Kathleen Hofman Smith '80   Proverbs 23:26
Ministry coordinator; Ada, Michigan

My son, give me your heart
and let your eyes keep to my ways. (Prov. 23:26)

"In order to give really good pastoral care, you have to be willing to give away your heart." That's what Professor Nydam teaches us at Calvin Seminary. If you want to give care to other people, you have to be willing to really care yourself. And you can't care without giving your heart.

It isn't easy to give away your heart. But if you do, you are not only obeying God's Word in Proverbs 23:26; you also are acting out God's image in you. That is what it means to be a person after God's own heart. After all, he cared enough to give away his heart to us, so we should be willing to do likewise.

Calvin's motto is "My heart I offer to you, Lord, promptly and sincerely." And offering their hearts is what many at Calvin do. From my college days at Calvin in the late seventies I remember professors who befriended me, listened to my concerns, and counseled me. They gave me their hearts. I remember dorm staffers who took time to help me through tough times — they gave their hearts. I think of teachers who were passionate about literature, art, science, and languages and put their hearts into their teaching. I see the same attitudes now at Calvin Seminary.

I remember seeing a report a few years ago that noted the unusually high percentage of Calvin graduates who go into service-related careers. I think that is evidence that Calvin's motto sticks to its students. They go on to lives of giving their hearts — first to God, then to others. The many Calvin College grads at the seminary are also evidence of this. They give their hearts to others as they offer them good news through preaching, teaching, and pastoral care.

In offering our hearts to others, we not only emulate our God but also bring honor and glory to him. As you think about honoring God in your life, think of the children's song "What Can I Give Him?" and answer as it does, "Give him my heart."

Talents

Matthew 25:14-30

Amy Cloud
Calvin student; Edwardsburg, Michigan

> *But the man who had received the one talent went off, dug a hole in the ground and hid his master's money.* (Matt. 25:18)

Reading this parable always brings to my mind the image of the ostrich — its head voluntarily buried in sand, lanky legs quivering, and hind quarters exposed in a most embarrassing fashion — the fastest bird in the world racing to put its awesome talent to foolish disuse. In a similar way, the servant entrusted with only one talent raced to hide his possibilities, his life's work, his future.

The parable tells the story of a master about to begin a journey. He calls his servants to him and gives each of them talents — money — "according to his ability" (Matt. 25:15) — five talents for one servant, three for another servant, and one talent for the third servant. The first two servants take their talents and perform what is expected of trustworthy, hardworking servants: "From everyone who has been given much, much will be demanded" (Luke 12:48). They both double what they have been given. But the plot turns with the third servant. It is expected that he, like the other two servants, will double his one talent and appear before the master with two. Whether out of fear or laziness or pride or misunderstanding, the third servant instead buries his master's talent in a hole in the ground. He offers as his reason that he knew the master to be a "hard man" (Matt. 25:24), and so he was afraid.

I struggled through four years of college before I realized that I was the one-talent servant — not in money, but in gifts. Every year I would come back to college wondering where I fit in as a student, a roommate, a child of God. Why didn't I have deeper insights, look prettier, act more boldly in my witness? I could list five talents I lacked before I realized that my cup was overflowing with my one talent. I was too absorbed with the talents of others, too fearful of the power of the one talent I did possess, to pull my head out of the sand, straighten my legs, and plant myself firmly toward the one-talent task ahead.

I still struggle with comparison and envy, but now they are tempered by a better understanding of my one talent. As servants of our great Master, who gives us the talents of our lifetimes, each of us must engage the world, seeking ways to make use of all our gifts rather than seeking to bury any of them in the sand.

Laughter

Michael Van Denend '78   1 Thessalonians 5:12-24
Calvin administrator; Grand Rapids, Michigan

Be joyful always. (1 Thess. 5:16)

Everyone knows that the shortest verse in the Bible is "Jesus wept" (John 11:35). Nine letters. This is a good passage to commit to memory, not because it's easy to remember but because it shows us that Jesus cared deeply for his friends — and that means us. It is also comforting to know that Jesus understands our sorrows and loss. He experienced sadness, as we do. He even cried.

I wish there were another passage in the gospel account that included the words "Jesus laughed." That's a mental picture we rarely allow ourselves to see. But surely Jesus did laugh. The people he met certainly gave him enough reason to do so.

Although there's no "Jesus laughed" to be found in Scripture, another text coming in relatively close behind "Jesus wept" is Saint Paul's suggestion to "be joyful always" from 1 Thessalonians. Fourteen letters.

This verse has been underused in most Christian traditions. Robert Farrar Capon wrote that the real tragedy of the cross is not Christ's death but the "funeral that the Christian church has been conducting ever since." Christians seem to have as hard a time as anybody warding off a negative and cynical view of life. Perhaps it is time to be reminded that we can join the "wife of noble character" described in Proverbs and "laugh at the days to come" (Prov. 31:25).

But how can we do this? How can we *not* do this? How can we not see things positively when the end of the story of history has already been written and we know the happy ending? Our heavenly Father, who knows every little thing about us, good and bad, will say, "Welcome home! Thanks to Jesus, I can't think of a single reason why you shouldn't join me in heaven forever. Let the celebration begin!"

We all have bad days, and some people have long, difficult periods of suffering to endure. Others live their entire lives under the shadow of persecution, death, and evil. But even to these Jesus says, "Blessed are you who weep now, for you will laugh" (Luke 6:21).

Laugh today. You have at least one good reason for doing so.

The Scandal of Grace

Luke 7:36-50

Kathleen Apol Lucas '74
Nurse; Midland Park, New Jersey

I magine the scene. A Pharisee invites Jesus to his home for dinner. Other invited guests are present, but it is an uninvited guest who holds the spotlight during this meal. Luke describes her simply as "a woman who had lived a sinful life in that town" (Luke 7:37). She finds out that Jesus is dining at Simon's home and appears. Certainly the town prostitute is not a welcome presence in the home of a man who scrupulously follows every detail of the law. In fact, it must have taken considerable courage for her to enter a home where she is seen only as a woman with a past. But then, she is a stranger to proper decorum. After pouring precious perfume over Jesus' feet, she lets down her hair and wipes them with it — something no respectable woman in Jewish society would do. Jewish law prevented even touching a prostitute.

A host's traditional Mideastern welcome was to wash a guest's feet, dusty from the roads of Palestine, to offer a glass of cold water, or to anoint the guest's head with oil. But Simon offers Jesus none of the standard rituals of hospitality. Instead, Jesus is welcomed by the woman, and what he receives is far more than a welcome. Forgetting herself, the woman is overwhelmed by forgiveness and grace. Her gift is all about extravagant, unrestrained love for Jesus. Jesus chides Simon for not extending him hospitality. The Pharisee, however, an ardent law keeper, is stuck on a tally of right and wrong — of his own law keeping and of the woman's wrongdoing. Jesus looks beyond the woman's sinful past and unconventional social behavior and sees her for who she really is. In fact, he holds her up as a model for Christians of all times. According to Matthew's Gospel, Jesus states that wherever the gospel is preached, this story will be told. Jesus joyfully receives the woman's gift from the heart.

To know Jesus is to realize that the gift of uncalculated love is the best we can offer. It is at the heart of everything else we bring him.

Living in Exile

Susan Bruxvoort Lipscomb '96 Jeremiah 29
University instructor; Flora, Indiana

Two and a half years ago I moved to a town set on a flat table of fields. It is dirt-colored and dry in winter and oven hot and damp in summer. There are no coffee shops, symphonies, art galleries. It often smells of manure. Some of my friends call it exile.

Exile. The word can mean either a forced removal or a voluntary absence from one's country or home. Adam and Eve were the first exiles. By their own choice they separated themselves from God, and then God forcibly removed them from the Garden of Eden.

In a way, all Christians live in exile, separated too far from God, in forced removal from the perfection of the Garden. Sinners, we are like the Jews in Babylon, living among strangers. We are God's children, but his paradise is not yet our home.

God gave specific, concise instructions to his people exiled to Babylon. He told them to plant gardens and have children, to seek the peace and prosperity of their city of exile, and to pray for it (Jer. 29). I take these instructions quite literally — to plant gardens, to have children, to promote peace, and to pray. I think the Israelites did, too. I'm sure they worked those beautiful hanging gardens of Babylon as well as gardens of their own for food. I'm sure they prayed for Babylon, for its peace, for its prosperity, for their enemies. God did not ask his people to accept their place of exile as it was when they arrived, but instead to water the ground, increase the population, and work for peace.

I have planted a garden in my exile. Only tomatoes and beans flourish in the clayey soil. Our summers shrivel sweet peas, and last year's drought produced small, bitter green peppers. But row upon row of canned tomatoes, rust red in glass jars, mark what I have done with my captivity. They are one way I bless my temporary home.

I pray for the prosperity of my garden, that my peppers will do better this year than last, and for the prosperity of my town, that the hog farmers will get better prices, that my neighbors will find jobs. Without children of my own, I'm at least increasing the Sunday-school population occasionally by bringing the sticky-faced neighbor kids along. And I pray for the peace of the city to which I have been carried into exile.

Being an exile is really a matter of bringing blessing wherever you are.

Psalm 30:5   Marcia Voortman Van't Land '68
Writer; Chino, California

Weeping may remain for a night, but rejoicing comes in the morning.
(Ps. 30:5)

It was my forty-sixth hospitalization in nineteen years of living with a rare illness called acute intermittent porphyria (a sister disease of multiple sclerosis and lupus). During the night my IV had infiltrated, and it had taken three tries to start a new one. The lab technician needed to poke me three times to get blood, my pain medication wasn't strong enough to handle the pain, and I hadn't slept much in the last few days and nights. A pity party was in the making.

I said, "God, I'm so tired. I can't do this hospital stuff anymore."

God replied, "Go on, my child."

"I could be a better witness of your love if I didn't have to tend to my illness all the time. Think of all the energy I'd have."

This dialogue went on for half an hour, and then I turned on the television. Immediately Channel 30 began filling my room with ocean waves and sandy beaches against the background of a sunrise. The words of a song spoke to me: "O love that will not let me go, I rest my weary soul in Thee. I give Thee back the life I owe, that in thine ocean depths its flow, may richer fuller be."* God was saying, "Marcia, I love you, and I will never let you go. I will give you more patience and courage." My heart responded in turn with the words of that great hymn of affirmation "Great Is Thy Faithfulness." A calm, soothing atmosphere filled my room, and I felt bathed in God's presence, love, and concern.

Three hours later I tried to get Channel 30 again, but all I got was a fuzzy screen. Later, when I mentioned to a nurse, "I was able to get Channel 30 during the night, but I can't get it now," she looked at me with a strange expression and said, "We don't get Channel 30 here."

Again I felt bathed in God's love. I told my wheelchair, parked in the corner of my room, "Give me a few days, and I'll be needing you again."

Towers

Carol Slager '71   Psalm 48
Teacher; Ripon, California

Were you one of the millions of TV viewers who watched the year 2000 arrive time zone by time zone? If so, you saw spectacular celebrations take place in the world's major cities, each celebration staged at the base of a particular city's landmark tower.

Awed by these sights, I found myself thinking about all those towers. Almost every city builds one, even if it's only a simple water tower. Towers are the high places that give cities identity and evoke pride, so there we were, ringing in the next millennium and showing off our high-tech towers.

The Bible has something to say about towers. Psalm 48 describes Mount Zion, the city where God lives with his people, as having walls fortified with numerous towers. The city inhabitants are encouraged to boast about God's construction project: They are urged to count those towers — massive evidence of the security God provides — and to "tell of them to the next generation" (Ps. 48:13). This psalm made me wonder when the last time was that I boasted about the mighty deeds of God and the delights of living with him.

Besides the towers on the walls, ancient cities often built a tower at city center. Usually the residence of the king, this central tower was also the provision storehouse and the last stronghold during a siege. Psalm 61 calls God that "strong tower against the foe" (Ps. 61:3). What a picture that is! God — my king, my provider, my invincible protector. Proverbs 18:10 tells us, "The name of the LORD is a strong tower; the righteous run to it and are safe." Yes, I want to claim citizenship in the city where God's name can serve as a tower of refuge.

As I thought about towers, I wondered how God saw the millennium tower extravaganza. I wondered whether he spotted any Towers of Babel there (Gen. 11:1-9). I wondered whether I have built towers of arrogant self-sufficiency that I need to demolish. And I promised to keep my focus daily on God as my tower of refuge and strength — without waiting for a special occasion.

Sacred Spaces

Genesis 28:16-17

Phil Reinders '87
Pastor; Calgary, Alberta

When Jacob awoke from his sleep, he thought, "Surely the LORD is in this place, and I was not aware of it." He was afraid and said, "How awesome is this place! This is none other than the house of God; this is the gate of heaven."

(Gen. 28:16-17)

Geography is simply a visible form of theology.

(Jon Levenson, *Sinai and Zion*)

Most followers of Christ can't help seeing the grandeur of God in creation. For years I've lived in western Canada, on both sides of the Canadian Rockies, where it seems God felt the compulsion to exaggerate that grandeur. Dwarfed by a mountain peak, staring in disbelief at the electric blue of a glacial lake, hearing the growling rumble of an avalanche, a person feels it's almost belaboring the obvious to mention God. Every molecule seems to scream out the untamed and fierce grace of God. Theology takes a backseat to geography in these spaces.

But it's not only in nature that geography speaks of God; it's also in the particulars of a place itself. We often live asleep to the reality that God inhabits not only mountain vistas and sunsets but also kitchen sinks and geriatric wards. What gives our spirituality a biblical spine is the reality that God chooses to be known in the particularities of life, particularities like place.

Throughout the story of salvation, places are not merely geographic locations. They are also sacred spaces where the elements are aflame with the divine. Jacob's stony pillow, the fiery thicket calling to Moses, Elijah's broom tree, and Paul's Damascus road are prosaic places that shimmered through with holiness. We, too, can hardly begin to speak of our spiritual journeys without a reference to place. These places are not merely parcels of real estate but, as Jacob describes them, gates of heaven. They are sacred spaces, very much like the wardrobe in C. S. Lewis's Chronicles of Narnia, where the ordinary conditions of our lives break open to a world of wonder and God is mediated.

Like Jacob, we live much of our lives on the run, very often unaware of God's presence. It's frightening to consider how much of God we miss simply through dimness, through inattention. Sacred spaces awaken us to the holy center in life, giving us a fresh orientation in our world, sending us off on the journey again. The best we can hope for is the sense to spot the holiness and walk through the gates that open before us.

The Best Deal

Kent Van Til '80
Pastor; Brookfield, Wisconsin

Matthew 16:24

I spend much of my life making agreements and then keeping or breaking them. I agree to pay the baby-sitter a certain amount, I agree to do a job, I agree to serve on a board, and the people I make the agreements with expect me to fulfill them. If I don't, there will be consequences, some swift and sure, others slow and insidious. The trick, then, seems to be to make the best deals possible — ones that I can and want to keep.

The problem is that other persons are trying to make the best deals they can make, too — the baby-sitter would like a better wage; the boss and school board would like more of my time.

Into this world of bargains and deals explodes the divine gift. God says, "I will give you everything, and you can repay me nothing. There is no bargaining. The 'deal' is — take it; it's yours before you even asked. While you were working against me, I came and gave everything for you." The gift annuls deal making; it requires humble receptivity.

The world doesn't understand this kind of transaction. It writes books about succeeding through negotiation and winning through intimidation. The art of the deal is central to success. In the marketplace something free seems valueless. But, in truth, that which we least bargained for is the greatest deal.

How can a "gifted" people live in a world of deal makers? How can people who are subject to the economy of this world and the economy of God's kingdom negotiate between the two? For starters, they must recognize that winning and losing have opposite meanings in the two worlds. In God's kingdom, whoever loses life gains it, and whoever seeks honor must first serve. Christ's gifted children are not finally concerned about success as defined by Wall Street or *Fortune* magazine. They cling to the immeasurable gift of salvation. The past carries no regrets — the gift covered them. The future carries no anxiety — the gift has secured it. The present can be lived in pure devotion to the gift giver. The only string attached to the gift is the requirement to pass it on, to go and do likewise.

So give up your fruitless search for satisfaction in the next great deal; leave everything and follow the giver of the gift. Receive the gift; it satisfies into eternity.

On the Road with Jesus

Luke 24:15

Nathan Bos '91

Graduate student; Ann Arbor, Michigan

Jesus himself came up and walked along with them. (Luke 24:15)

For me, bad suspension makes for good meditation. The Number 2 bus I take every morning is loud and bumpy, and if I can, I sit in the back, where it's loudest and bumpiest. It's the feeling of movement that I like. The physical movement helps my weak mind in the difficult task of trying to apprehend, through prayer and meditation, the spiritual movement in my life.

The disciples on the road to Emmaus would have understood. Less fortunate disciples had to stay behind, motionless in locked rooms, waiting for their risen Lord to come to them. How hard it must have been to sit and do nothing. How much better to be one of the disciples on the road, walking and talking and unknowingly entertaining their Lord. The message given those on the road was the same as that given to the disciples back behind closed doors: God's plan moves forward, relentlessly. But I think it takes less effort to believe that God is still moving the world when one can see and feel the world going by.

Riding on a bus is even better than walking like those disciples, I think, because I am not the one providing the locomotion. In the backseat I can sit perfectly still, close my eyes, do nothing at all to contribute to forward progress, and the sense of motion will still be there. I need to convince myself of this same thing about prayer, over and over. God is taking me where he would have me go, whether or not my own legs would be strong enough to take me there alone. The challenge of prayer is not to make the journey happen but only to try to perceive the forward motion.

Perhaps it is a weakness of faith not to be able to feel the journey's passing without visual aids. A hero of faith might certainly feel God's mighty wind blowing by, even indoors with the windows closed. But for me, Jesus, please agree to meet and talk as we go along.

Rejoice in Each Day

Henry Ploegstra '56   Ecclesiastes 11:9
Teacher; Dallas, Texas

> *You who are young, be happy while you are young, and let your hearts give you joy in the days of your youth. Follow the ways of your heart and whatever your eyes see, but know that for all these things God will bring you to judgment.*
> (Eccles. 11:9, NIVI)

Every morning when I arrive at school, I am greeted by the smiling and cheerful, though sometimes drowsy, faces of my students. They bring to their school and work an enthusiasm and cheerfulness and aliveness sometimes lacking in older people. For them, each day is an adventure, a new opportunity to work and play and socialize and eat lunch and live fully in an unreflective way — though plenty of reflection goes on as well.

I also see some faces, both of students and adults, that do not have this sparkle, faces of people who seem to slog their way through life, for whom every day is a burden. Of course, some of them do have heavy loads to bear—problems with health or family or money—but for some of them, the burden is self-imposed. At moments like these, I think of the second part of the exhortation from Ecclesiastes: "for all these things God will bring you to judgment" (Eccles. 11:9).

What the writer means, I think, is that we will not be brought into judgment for rejoicing in our youth—no matter what our age—but for not rejoicing in it. We will be judged for how we spend our days and our assets, for the quality of the enthusiasm and elan that we bring to our lives. We are exhorted to live fully, to live cheerfully, to enjoy what we do and what we see. We will be brought into judgment for forgetting that "this is the day the LORD has made" (Ps. 118:24) and for not rejoicing and being glad in it. Jesus himself berated the Pharisees for being overly serious; he himself spent time eating and drinking and enjoying it.

The challenge, of course, is how to put these ideas into practice every day. Sometimes external circumstances make rejoicing difficult, but for most of us most days, life is beautiful. Rejoice in a fragrant cup of coffee, the crunch of toast, the bittersweet tang of marmalade; rejoice in the sunshine or even in the poignant gloom of rain and snow. Keep the senses alert and the mind clear for the greatness that surrounds us every day. If we do so, we may yet earn the final accolade: "Well done, good and faithful servant!" (Matt. 25:21).

Doing the Impossible

Luke 1:26-38
Beverly J. Luchies Stephenson '81
Homemaker; West Olive, Michigan

The Lord is with you. . . . For nothing is impossible with God.
(Luke 1:28, 37)

Recently this passage from Luke sent my thoughts spinning to twelve years ago, when my husband and I were expecting our first child. I smiled as I recalled how I had reassured myself that God would not allow our child to be born handicapped because he knew that I could not cope with it. But our daughter Nicole was born three and a half months early, has spent many months of her life in intensive-care units, and is severely mentally and physically handicapped. Five years ago my husband and I held our son Dylan as he took his last breath. Once again God was asking me to do the impossible. And again I had not asked for this responsibility.

When the angel came to Mary to announce that she would be the mother of Jesus, he framed his message between two amazing statements: First he said, "The Lord is with you" (Luke 1:28), and finally he said, "For nothing is impossible with God" (Luke 1:37). The angel gave Mary very few details beyond the beginning of the story — "you will be with child" (Luke 1:31) — and the big picture into which that Child would fit — "his kingdom will never end" (Luke 1:33). Yet Mary responded with faith: "I am the Lord's servant" (Luke 1:38).

We all know that sometimes God allows the impossible into our lives: "The tumor is malignant." "I'm having an affair." "Your child is in serious trouble." "You are expecting triplets." At those moments we need to hear and believe the angel's message to Mary: "The Lord is with you" (Luke 1:28). God can do in and with us what seems impossible to us.

After our son's death, God reminded me of the big picture. The resurrection of Jesus Christ had turned Dylan's death into victory; our son is with Christ for eternity. Whenever someone asks how we can care for Nicole year after year, we respond, "Only by the grace of God." We love Nicole and thank God for her life, but caring for her is exhausting, messy, lonely, and inconvenient. On our own it is impossible. Only by the grace of God can we go on. For learning that, I am grateful. Today I know that "nothing is impossible with God" (Luke 1:37) and that "the Lord is with [me]" (Luke 1:28). With this assurance I, as a servant of the Lord, do the impossible every day.

A Discerning Ear

Joan Vander Veen Borst '78   Psalm 103:2-5
Social worker; Grand Rapids, Michigan

I could hear my mother's labored breathing when I opened the door to my parents' home, and I knew this would be the day she would die. The spread of her cancer had been relentless despite the good and bad days. I had brought a recording of psalms and hymns for her to listen to, but as the magnitude of what the day would bring settled in, I put all thoughts of playing music aside. After hours of relentless pacing and whispered prayer, I realized that the only sound in the house was the sound of impending death. I turned to the music I had brought and turned up the volume to match the sound coming from my dying mother. The sounds came together in a surprising duet that filled the house with hope and praise — not hope and praise for the healing of my mother but for a future that included the presence of God. I felt courage to stand straight even in my tears and to face a future I knew would be without my mother but not without the security and comfort of God's loving hands. Time passed, and before long the only sound filling the room was the sound of singing: "Praise, my soul, the King of heaven; to his feet your tribute bring."*

Every day, even on the days that seem most bleak and without God, if we listen with a discerning ear, we can hear the blending of earthly and heavenly voices. They join in a duet which the Spirit uses to direct us to praise the King of heaven. In all the sounds that fill our lives there is a song that blends with the sounds of the ocean or of city traffic, a duet that unites with the screaming of a child or the noise of a raucous gathering. The song enters the silence of even the deaf and lonely. By his sacred presence God promises to blend the pain and the beauty of our days into that song. And then, at the end of our lives, there will be finally the single voice — the one remaining sound of eternal praise.

Called by Name

John 10:2-3

Joanne E. Haan De Jonge '63
Teacher/writer; Surprise, Arizona

The ancient Hebrews attached much more importance to a name than we do today. More than a label, a name ideally captured the essence of a person's character, life, or work. Witness the name changes given to Abram and Jacob after each had a close encounter with God. The inner core of each man had been changed by his experience; his old name no longer described him accurately.

With that in mind, we can understand God's answers to individuals who asked his name. To Jacob he said, "Why do you ask my name?" (Gen. 32:29). How can one presume to ask God who he is? To Manoah he added, "It is beyond understanding" (Judg. 13:18). Of course God is beyond our understanding! His name, his essence, is beyond our comprehension.

But it is not beyond our reach. Jesus said, "You may ask me for anything in my name, and I will do it" (John 14:14). Our "sins have been forgiven on account of his name" (1 John 2:12). Someday, at the name of Jesus every knee shall bow. It's a bit overwhelming to realize that we invoke all the power in the universe when we call on God's name or ask in Jesus' name.

It's truly overwhelming to know that God calls our names, too. The power of the universe has granted us use of his name, and he calls our names! God told the ancient Israelites, "I have summoned you by name; you are mine" (Isa. 43:1). He knew them clear down to their wandering hearts and minds; yet he called them back to him. Jesus said that a good shepherd calls his sheep by name. He knows each of them fully, and he cares for them individually. He added, "I am the good shepherd" (John 10:11).

The good shepherd calls us each by name; he knows each of us fully, to our inner core, our essence. He calls us and he cares for us, by name. What more can we ask? What more do we need?

Peter Kok '67
Attorney; Ada, Michigan

Philippians 4:8

All of us have some of it, but no one knows how much of it anyone has. When it is gone, no one can get any more of it. Accordingly, most would agree that having enough of it is more precious than gold.

The commodity described is, of course, time. If you have enough of it, almost anything is possible, but if you are in short supply, virtually nothing is possible. Too often we squander this valuable resource on the tedious, the foolish, or the wasteful — on TV viewing, on golfing, coffee kletzing, and shopping.

But how should we spend the time we have? In Ecclesiastes the Teacher makes work of answering that question by investing his time in alternately pursuing the goals of pleasure, wealth, and wisdom. He finds them all ultimately unsatisfying, and he says so: Pleasure? "Laughter . . . is foolish. And what does pleasure accomplish?" (Eccles. 2:2). Wealth? "Whoever loves money never has money enough" (Eccles. 5:10). Wisdom? "For with much wisdom comes much sorrow; the more knowledge, the more grief" (Eccles. 1:18).

Perhaps out of frustration, the Teacher concludes his teaching by simply advising, "Fear God and keep his commandments, for this is the duty of every human being" (Eccles. 12:13, NIVI).

Of course. But how should we spend our time? A glance at the *New York Times* bestsellers list over the years evidences a plethora of options — many eerily mirroring the goals found to be futile millennia ago by the Teacher: *Looking Out for #1; Pulling Your Own Strings; Our Bodies, Ourselves; 9 Steps to Financial Freedom*, and on and on.

There may be many answers to how best to spend our time. The apostle Paul, however, gives a clear measuring stick for separating the valuable from the valueless. In his letter to the Philippians he urges us to think on and then do whatever is noble, right, pure, lovely, admirable, excellent, and praiseworthy (Phil. 4:8). Do this, he says, and "the God of peace will be with you" (Phil. 4:9).

Strength in Weakness

2 Corinthians 12:9

Aaron Winkle
Calvin student; Lake City, Michigan

This past summer I spent three weeks serving as a counselor and basketball coach at Spring Hill Camp in Evart, Michigan. For three weeks I awoke early and went to bed late. For three weeks I played as hard as any thirteen-year-old can play. For three weeks I watched my physical, emotional, and spiritual energy gradually slip away. Each day I awoke wondering how I would make it through another day, how I would continue to serve these kids and through them my Lord. Each night I would go to bed and say the same prayer: "Lord, give me the strength to serve and love these kids another day. Amen."

As I struggled through physical exhaustion and mental fatigue, God continued to meet all my needs. He not only met them; he provided in abundance every time. At the very moment when I felt I could not take another step, he took my hand and helped me. When I was at my most vulnerable, he provided for each one of my needs and demonstrated once again his incredible faithfulness in my life.

Through this most trying time I have come to a better understanding of God's message to Paul in 2 Corinthians 12:9: "My grace is sufficient for you, for my power is made perfect in weakness." Before my experience at camp I had read this verse and knew what it meant. I had heard it in the classroom and from the pulpit, yet I had not personally experienced it in my own life. It was only after I had been thoroughly emptied of all of my strength, as I was at camp, that I truly understood what Paul already knew when he wrote this letter to the Corinthians. We serve an amazing God.

It's a Matter of Time

Todd Pheifer '94   James 4:8
College administrator; Lakewood, California

Why is prayer difficult sometimes? Why do we sometimes feel more pressure to be eloquent than to be sincere? These are legitimate questions, but as Christians we are hesitant to admit that we ask them. We conclude that we feel these things because prayer is not our gift. Unfortunately, we are missing a key point about prayer.

Rather than being measured by eloquence and length, prayer should be measured by honesty and meaning. Conversations are the basis for growth in any relationship, and prayer leads to growth in our relationship with Jesus Christ. This is not a complicated concept, but it is one that we forget nonetheless. As is true in many other areas of life, so, too, in prayer wisdom is not the comprehension of the complicated but rather the application of the simple.

Imagine a family member, a spouse, or a friend who is close to you. Now consider why this person is close to you. Was your relationship automatic? Were you assigned this person, and you instantly bonded? Not likely. You are close to this person because you have spent time together. You've laughed, cried, and shared. You've been honest and have provided a safe haven for vulnerability.

Now consider another group in your life, your acquaintances. These are people that you pass at work or wave to in your neighborhood. You may smile at them and perhaps engage in brief conversations with them, but you don't really know them. It isn't hard to figure out why. For the same reasons that loved ones are close, acquaintances are more distant. The nature of a relationship depends upon the time invested in it.

Now think about your relationship with God. Is God a close friend or a distant acquaintance? Do you seek a quiet place to have an intimate conversation with him, or do you give a quick wave as you rush through your day?

Ask yourself this: Could my relationships on earth grow on the same amount of time that I spend with God? Remember that growth won't happen overnight. It takes time.

Your close relationships started somewhere. They took honesty, patience, availability . . . and time. The time you spend with God will also determine the depth of your relationship with him.

Living Hope

1 Peter 1:3

Jack R. Van Ens '69
Pastor; Arvada, Colorado

My parents are both dead. Often as I stand at their graves in Michigan, sharp thoughts thrust themselves up inside me, like a knife cutting to the bone. Bending over their graves, I hear a voice deep within me asking, "Is it true? Is the Christian belief certain that beyond the grave there is communion with our loved ones in which we will experience God — communion featuring laughter, good times, abiding memory, and love that will not quit? Does a physical pulse of life exist beyond the grave, life such as I felt with my dad long ago in West Virginia when we arose early in the morning and went off to the woods for some target practice, when the greenery was lush, birds sang, and the air was redolent with southern honeysuckle? When I meet Dad in heaven, will there really be some of that sensation I experienced long ago with him? Will I remember again the way I felt when I sat on my mother's lap in the living room on the Victorian love seat in front of the picture window, light streaming in as she read to me? Will the security and warmth I felt in my mother's arms be replicated in the great beyond?"

Sometimes when Father Theodore H. Hesburgh, former president of Notre Dame, comes to officiate at mass in the chapel where I serve, he repeats a famous line he has used to convince the skeptic within all of us that there is life beyond the grave. Declares Hesburgh, "The one thing we really know about tomorrow is that the providence of God will be up before the dawn." I take that to mean that Christians do not base their confidence in life after death on some esoteric proofs. Nor is such confidence bred by a mystical sense that there must be more than the rattling of bones in the casket and that Easter, that mysterious festival celebrating Christ's resurrection from the tomb, involves more than some poetic snippets about his reputation outdistancing rotting flesh and the musty smells of death.

Biblical writers based their hope on God. God for them would not be God if he were not eternal. And eternity, whatever else it encompasses, means that God has neither beginning nor end, neither a birthday nor a death day. He is — always. And so he is always with those he loves, both in this life and in the next. This is why the Bible explodes with enthusiasm about life beyond the life we know. "Praise be to the God and Father of our Lord Jesus Christ! In his great mercy he has given us new birth into a living hope through the resurrection of Jesus Christ from the dead" (1 Pet. 1:3).

Singing like God

Lisa Huisman Koops '99   Zephaniah 3:17
Teacher; Holland, Michigan

> *The LORD your God is with you, he is mighty to save.*
> *He will take great delight in you, he will quiet you with his love,*
> *he will rejoice over you with singing.* (Zeph. 3:17)

Isn't it marvelous to picture God singing over us? Especially during the dark nights we all go through from time to time, it is wonderfully comforting to listen and hear God's voice guiding us through the darkness. He who lovingly formed the universe and each one of us wove music in, around, and through every inch of the creation. God, the divine musician, created us as his imagebearers. Just as we image God in our ability to love, to create, and much more, we also image him in our ability to make music.

As a musician and music teacher, I am discovering that music is much more than symbols on a printed page signaling sequences of sound and silence. It is not limited to the concert hall or the music classroom. God's music, which he planted in all of us, is evident in the shining eyes and upturned chin of a second grader who revels in the sounds of Mussorgsky's *Pictures at an Exhibition*. I hear it in the voices of my friends at Camp Sunshine for handicapped individuals as they sing praises with joyful abandon. Music, to me, is much more about people than it is about sound and silence.

As God's children, all of us are called to realize the image of God within us and let those godly characteristics shine through. Part of imaging God is to inspire others to see God's image within themselves so that they, too, will nurture the development of godly qualities. My goal as a music teacher is not to create professional musicians or the best children's choir in western Michigan; it is to nurture and inspire the gift of music, part of the image of God, in all my students.

And so I teach them to sing — even as God in his delight over us, his creatures, rejoices over us in song. Won't you sing along?

The Paradox of the Cross

John 19:28-30

Henrietta Ten Harmsel '49
Calvin professor emerita; Grand Rapids, Michigan

The cross of Christ stands at the center of the Christian faith. Here the divine Son of God gave his life to redeem his people from sin and death. What a paradox! What an apparent contradiction that is still miraculously true! In his blessed death Christ enacted the paradox which brings the miracle of life.

Christ was the Creator of all things: "Without him nothing was made that has been made" (John 1:3). This is the basic paradox: On the cross the Creator was crucified by the very creatures he had created. But the paradox deepens. As his anguish grew, Christ's thirst became unbearable; the thirst-racked Creator cried out for a drink. He who had formed the rivers, the lakes, the waterfalls, and the oceans, now paradoxically cried out, "I am thirsty" (John 19:28). What a mystery!

But there is more. In the beginning, Christ, the Word, also said, "Let there be light" (Gen. 1:3). He had created not only the world's water but also its light: the sun, the moon, and the countless stars. But in his deep pain on the cross that light forsook him. The Creator of all light now hung alone in deep darkness.

But there is still more. On the sixth day of creation Christ had gone beyond water and the light to breathe into mankind the breath of life itself: the life of Adam and Eve; of the prophets; of his mother, Mary; of every man, woman, and child that ever lived. But now, on the cross, Christ, the Creator of life, laid down his own life as he breathed his last human breath.

What painful paradoxes these seem to be! However, by God's grace, they become paradoxes of triumph and praise. When he cried out, "I am thirsty," Christ brought forth a new and endless stream of living water. By going through the darkness of Calvary, he became the eternal light of the world. And by dying on the cross, he gave his people eternal life.

This is the glorious paradox of the cross. Believe it and live forever.

The Impatience of Job

Morris Greidanus '60   James 5:10-11
Pastor; Grand Rapids, Michigan

When we are having a hard time, it's not much appreciated to hear over and over "It could be worse" while we are still trying to absorb how bad things are. To have our tear-stained noses rubbed in the patience of Job makes us feel edgy and even rather guilty.

Job is our model for proverbial patience. But Job's reputation for patience can endure only if we ignore most of what goes on in the book of Job. Usually this is what we read about Job: He accepts what comes his way, his wife is nasty, his friends should have kept quiet (so we skip their discussions with Job — why were chapters 3-38 included anyway?), and God's speech is somewhat interesting. Then we quickly go to the humble, happy ending. We bypass how Job really handled trouble.

One summer at First Christian Reformed Church, Grand Rapids, we took the time to work through most of the book of Job, trying to get the force of some of that talk. We heard Job's lament, anger, and shock. We heard the friends comforting him, getting it wrong but also keeping Job away from dangerous edges. We met a different Job this way.

The difference starts, commentator J. Gerald Janzen thinks, in chapter 2, where "a pebble is loosened within [Job] which threatens to become an avalanche." Job's steady, accepting "The LORD gave and the LORD has taken away; may the name of the LORD be praised" (Job 1:21) changes to his snarling "You are talking like a foolish woman. Shall we accept good from God, and not trouble?" (Job 2:10). Then the narrator adds, "In all this, Job did not sin in what he said" (Job 2:10). But what did Job think? One clue: When Job speaks again, he curses the day of his birth (Job 3:1).

I find this Job more real and helpful than the clichéd Job. His secret, as James says, is perseverance. He will not let go of the conviction that God is fair and full of compassion. That's what all the arguing is about. And that's what is finally confirmed for him.

May our impatient laments and the tossings and turnings of our thoughts, talk, and prayers also get us to that point so that we, too, can say with conviction, "The Lord is full of compassion and mercy" (James 5:11).

Healing Grace

2 Samuel 12:13

Robert Rozema '93
Teacher; Grand Rapids, Michigan

Canst thou not minister to a mind diseas'd,
Pluck from the memory a rooted sorrow,
Raze out the written troubles of the brain,
And with some sweet oblivious antidote
Cleanse the stuff'd bosom of that perilous stuff
Which weighs upon the heart?

(William Shakespeare, *Macbeth*, V.3.40-45)

Then David said to Nathan, "I have sinned against the LORD."

(2 Sam. 12:13)

At first glance, King David and Macbeth seem to have very little in common. One king was anointed by God to replace an unholy ruler; the other wrested the throne from his godly predecessor. The lineage of one king yielded the Messiah; the other's sole legacy was destruction. And yet, both David and Macbeth had blood on their hands. David's sin — concealing his adultery by sending Uriah the Hittite to certain death — is not far removed from Macbeth's secret murders of the king, innocent women and children, and his best friend.

One drastic difference between these two kings, however, is the way they confront their wrongdoing. Macbeth asks the doctor attending the guilt-ridden Lady Macbeth to cleanse her conscience — and, by extension, his own — with "some sweet oblivious antidote." In desperate need of forgiveness, Macbeth turns not to God but to human medicine, which he knows cannot purge his guilt. He wishes only to forget his sin, not to be forgiven for it.

In contrast, David repents before God in simple and honest language. He seeks a balm in Gilead. There are still earthly consequences for his wrongdoing: The son conceived in adultery dies, and this sorrow will never be erased from his memory. But David's relationship with God is righted, and his soul is healed. He gets up from the ground, changes his clothes, puts on lotions, and worships in the house of the Lord.

David experiences forgiveness, a renewed shalom; Macbeth seeks a poor imitation. This is the best that Macbeth or anyone can do without God's grace. With God's grace, everything changes. For David and for us, there *is* a balm in Gilead.

God's Hand in History

Robert P. Swierenga '57   Proverbs 16:9
Professor; Holland, Michigan

Absalom's rebellion against his father, David, failed because he took the bad advice of David's trusted friend Hushai rather than the good advice of his own adviser, Ahithophel. Why? It was the Lord's plan "to frustrate the good advice of Ahithophel in order to bring disaster on Absalom" (2 Sam. 17:14). This text is one of many that show God's hand in history.

Knowing that God is in control gives us comfort and strength, but we sinfully demand the details. Abraham and Sarah became impatient for their long-promised son and tried to force God's hand. The Israelites wondered when God would give them the land of promise and a king of peace to rule it. Jesus' disciples wanted the signs of the end times, and the Thessalonian Christians were overly concerned about the Day of the Lord. Today many want to know if ours is the terminal generation.

Believers look for evidences of God's hand in history precisely because they know that God is at work. He spoke creation into being, prepared for the middle cross at Calvary, and will someday ring down the curtain, even as he shut the door of Noah's ark (Gen. 7:16). History is neither cyclical, random, progressive, or spiraling ever downward. The biblical time line is forward-pointing, purposeful, and finite, because a personal God directs all things. We fulfill his sovereign purposes even in our evil ways. The Bible tells us so: "The king's heart is in the hand of the LORD" (Prov. 21:1); he hardened Pharaoh's heart (Exod. 7:3) and called Nebuchadnezzer "my servant" (Jer. 25:9).

The inspired text is very clear compared to our tentative gloss on the past. C. S. Lewis said, "I do not dispute that History is a story written by the finger of God. But have we the text?" God's plans are often inscrutable. "Who has known the mind of God?" asks the apostle Paul (Rom. 11:34). Yes, we see "through a glass darkly" and accept life's ambiguities, but we also have a unique pair of glasses, the spectacles of faith. Because "the Bible tells us so," we can know something, rather than nothing, about the meaning of human history.

Redeeming the Routine

1 Corinthians 15:58

Calvin Bratt '77
Editor; Lynden, Washington

Therefore, my dear brothers and sisters, stand firm. Let nothing move you. Always give yourselves fully to the work of the Lord, because you know that your labor in the Lord is not in vain. (1 Cor. 15:58, NIVI)

The hardest thing about life, according to a Southern spiritual, is that it's so everyday.

Probably this is a working day for you. You must head off to an office, a classroom, or a shop. Maybe your workplace is a hospital ward or a fishing boat or your own home or farm. Whatever, you must go back for another day to extract fresh meaning from familiar places and flawed people. The daily grind, we call it.

How do we redeem the routine? How is our labor not in vain in the Lord? The Bible gives us two answers. First, everything we do is service to others — and, through them, service to God. Whatever the need is, meet it, "as working for the Lord" (Col. 3:23). But there's a second motivation for our daily work. We aren't toiling away like animals only to molder to dust once our allotted time on earth is spent. No, we await a higher destiny, according to 1 Corinthians 15. These mortal bodies that "die every day" (1 Cor. 15:31) will be transformed, like Christ's, into a splendor fit for the eternal reward that God has in store for us.

Twelve years ago I stood at the casket of my mother, who in sixty-six years had poured herself out in service to others, first and foremost to her own family. All the bread she baked, we remembered through tears, the letters she wrote, the lunches she made, the bills she paid. She had stood firm through the demands and duties — the routines — of life, and she will receive her reward.

So, too, stand firm in your marriage. Stand firm in your work. Stand firm in your parenting. Stand firm in your studies. Stand firm in your community service. Stand firm in your church leadership. Stand firm in whatever tasks God has given you to do right now. They are service for others and service for God — redemption of the routine.

When you yearn for a rest in the depths of your being, remember the Bible's promise: You will receive your reward.

Divine Absurdity

Rod Jellema '51   Isaiah 40:25-26
Professor emeritus; Washington, D.C.

This is humble-pie day. For all our science, we can't measure the time we're caught in. Our hours don't add up right, so every 1,460 days we blush and announce this extra day, this leap, this little cosmic hiccup we've invented.

It's a good day to reflect on all the other upheavals and table turnings in our efforts to be orderly. Jesus' parables, for example: Think how that servant in the parable who locked the master's money in the Brinks vault was punished, while a wilder servant bet on some stock mergers and played the horses and was rewarded. Then there's the story that maybe should be titled "The Prodigal Father," because it's the father's prodigality ("reckless wastefulness") toward his son that is shocking, and the son doesn't even have to finish stammering the repentance he has urgently rehearsed. As the homecoming party rattles the skies, we're tempted to side with the elder brother — frugal, businesslike, critical. Good boy.

We want to be good in the eyes of the stern God we imagine looking down from heaven — but then are given weekly a pastor's blessing which dares to pray that he will "lift up his face upon us" and give us shalom. Lift up? Yes. The psalmist sees our Creator as sometimes hiding his face for shame. Or maybe he sees Jesus down there being a servant. Shining shoes, perhaps. Or digging up land mines.

The Christian faith is shot through with divine absurdity. The line of our reconciliation with God depends upon a hundred-year-old woman finally getting pregnant; it blesses the shocking deceits of the undeserving Jacob; the line runs on past its own lost hopes to a peasant birth in a stable. From there the revelations that are "foolishness to the Greeks" multiply rapidly.

When I was a student, I was appalled to read that Tertullian believed the faith because it is absurd. Years later, in the vision of Michelangelo's Sistine Chapel I saw Jonah — laughing — as though he had just gotten the joke: that there is no sense, but, absurdly, God's loving the world.

Shunem and Nain

2 Kings 4:1-37; Luke 7:11-17

Sidney De Waal '57
University president; Jerusalem, Israel

The young woman had just had a last look around the garden of Jerusalem University College before taking a taxi to the airport. Tears welled up in her eyes. "No, it's not what you think," she said. "I'm not sad. I'm very happy. I discovered during my studies here that my faith is not based on myths or fancy stories. It is anchored in history. I touched it."

Indeed, God's mighty acts took place in a real place, and the place itself helped to shaped the story. Take, for example, the Hill of Moreh near Mount Tabor. There on the southwest slope the well-to-do woman of Shunem built a nice apartment for Elisha. Touched by her generosity, Elisha promised this childless woman that she would become the mother of a son. A few years later the little fellow died as he was taking lunch to his dad. In effect his mother asked, "Man of God, was all this a bad joke?" And then Elisha raised the boy from the dead.

This Old Testament story reminds us that Jesus also raised a boy from the dead, the son of the widow of Nain. You may be surprised to learn that Nain was located only a few hundred yards from Shunem, on the northwest slope of the Hill of Moreh, just around the bend in the road. For generations the people in Nain had recounted the miraculous story of how Elisha had raised the son of the Shunammite woman. Unbelievable! Elisha, the prophet, had brought a boy back to life! God is great! And now see what has happened in our town. God's prophet is back among us.

No doubt Jesus' choice of Nain for his miracle of raising a child from the dead was intentional. The people make the connection: God's prophet is among us again. Up to now Jesus has been a mere rabbi, but with this miracle he becomes more than that. He's a prophet, God's special spokesperson among us. For Jesus it means that he is making progress in his self-revelation as he travels to the cross and the Easter resurrection.

Shunem and Nain — just around the bend from each other. Salvation history grows in splendor as it moves forward touching life's experiences. Our faith journey is anchored in touchable "facts on the ground."

Drafting

Darren Walhof '91   Galatians 6:2
Calvin professor; Grand Rapids, Michigan

When I go cycling with a friend, we draft off of each other, riding single file and taking turns as the lead person, who cuts through the wind. If drafting is done properly, the effect is remarkable. After you've been fighting the wind at the front, riding in the back feels like coasting, as if you are being pulled along by the front rider. Even though you are still pedaling, the absence of wind resistance allows you to rest and regain some of your strength so that you can take your turn at the front again. In this way drafting allows cyclists to maintain a higher speed over longer distances.

I find drafting to be a useful analogy for the role that a community of faith plays in my life. Though belief is necessarily personal and individual, it is, like cycling, best done in a group. We need to participate in a faith community whose members take turns at the front, doing the hardest work. For whatever reasons, there are times when we feel close to God and times when we feel removed from him, times when our faith seems unshakable and times when it seems rather fragile. At those times when we are weak and doubt ridden, we need to turn to the other members and say, "I am struggling. You need to take the lead for a while. Pray for me because I cannot pray for myself right now. Believe for me because I am not sure that I do." And when we are firm in our faith and are close to God, we need to ask others, "How can I help? How would you like me to pray? How can I pull you along?"

In Paul's words, we need to bear one another's burdens. When it comes to faith, doing so requires an extraordinary amount of openness and trust. For me, and perhaps for most of us, it is usually easier to bear the burdens of others than to allow one's burden to be borne, since this requires admitting weakness. Confessing this weakness and drafting off of others, however, is in the end a means of strengthening our faith and of strengthening the community.

Forgiveness as a Way of Life

Colossians 2:13-14   Claude-Marie Baldwin-Vos '71

Calvin professor emerita; Seabrook, Texas

He forgave us all our sins, having canceled the written code, with its regulations, that was against us and that stood opposed to us; he took it away, nailing it to the cross. (Col. 2:13-14)

Forgiveness is not really so much about the person we need to forgive as it is about us. It's about our own sense of freedom. Failure to forgive keeps us in bondage to the person who hurt us and hinders us from fully experiencing God's presence and power in our lives.

The bottom line is that God forgave us all our sins and that we are commanded to forgive all the sins of those who have offended us. Forgive an incestuous father? A business partner who brought our business to bankruptcy? A drunken driver who killed our child? "Impossible!" you say.

Yes, forgiveness is impossible without God. We can choose to forgive only because he first forgave us. But God does require us to acknowledge the sins against us and the pain they have caused and not to deny them or to excuse the perpetrators. We need to face the pain and to ask God to give us the power to forgive from our hearts as well as from our heads. We need to take the pain which poisons and embitters us and surrender it to the Lord so that it can be nailed to the cross, where it belongs. We can then walk away from the cross with the memory of the perpetrator and the event but without the pain associated with them.

How do we know that forgiveness has been accomplished? We are able to think without pain, fear, or bitterness about the person who wounded us. We are also able to bless our offenders and wish them God's blessings. We start seeing them as God sees them. Then we know that we are no longer prisoners to our own pain and anger. The door of our prison has been opened.

Set some time aside today and make a list of all those you need to forgive — family members, parents, siblings, extended family members, in-laws, teachers, clergy, friends, neighbors, bosses, or colleagues. In each case, face the hurt and choose forgiveness — nailing your hurt and their sins upon the cross.

When God Says, "Go"

Nadya Zheltuhina   Exodus 4:1-17
Calvin student; Vologda, Russia

E very now and then we come to a point in our lives when we are faced
with a decision. Our situation may be anything from whether to become a missionary or whether to be more involved in a local church. Most
of us try to turn to God for direction, but very few of us readily accept his
answer. We are aware that, when we ask for God's guidance, God can
choose to command us to do something we feel incapable of doing. He
may ask us to go to Papua New Guinea and proclaim his Word to pagan
tribes when he knows we grew up in the safe community of Holland, Michigan. He may ask us to take time from our busy schedule to talk to a
stranger or spend time with our families when he knows that we will make
less money if we do. We want God to be gentle and understanding with us;
we want to hear a command that will not take us out of our comfortable
daily routine. So we run away from God, telling him that we cannot do
what he is asking.

We are not the first hesitant people God has ever met. Moses was reluctant to go when God asked him to deliver the children of Israel from slavery. We know how Moses tried to get out of the situation: "O LORD, I have
never been eloquent, neither in the past nor since you have spoken to your
servant. I am slow of speech and tongue" (Exod. 4:10). We try to pull the
same trick on God; we find all sorts of excuses for not doing what God has
prepared for us to do.

We do not realize that, if he commands us to go, God prepares us for
an adventure in our lives. God does not leave us on our own when he commands us to come out of our comfort zone. It is through these hard experiences that we learn to trust. Every step of Moses was directed by God's
hand. God never says, "Go," without telling us, "and surely I am with you
always, to the very end of the age" (Matt. 28:20).

So next time God says, "Go," obey and enjoy the adventure, knowing
that God will never leave your side.

Beyond the Devotional

1 Corinthians 10:31; Colossians 3:17   Lisa Ponstine

Calvin student; Grandville, Michigan

Y ou are reading a devotional right now. Why? Is it because this is your devotional time? Did you just finish dinner, and are you now reading as a family? Are you just getting up and starting the day off right? Or are you going to bed, and this is what you do at this time every night or nearly every night? Any of these reasons is a fine reason to read a devotional. But what happens when you finish this devotional? What happens when you begin to clear the dishes, when you get ready for work or school, when you fall asleep? Is God still welcome then, or is God welcome only in your devotional time?

Too often I find myself reading the Bible or a devotional book with a closed heart. I spend the time in devotion because I want to, but I don't carry anything away from it. My heart doesn't change. It's as though I offer my heart to God in my devotion time but then snatch it back as I close the book, not allowing God to take my heart, to shape it, or to change it.

Colossians 3:17 says, "Whatever you do, whether in word or deed, do it all in the name of the Lord Jesus. . . . " *Whatever* you do. *All* of it. That's difficult. That means every aspect of daily life. Every activity of every day. That means there is no separate God time because all time is God's time. That means that, when you finish a devotional, you take what you have learned and apply it to your entire life. That means that God not only receives the quality time you spend with him one-on-one or around the dinner table but also gets all of your time — even while you do the dishes, get ready for work, or fall asleep.

You are almost finished reading a devotional right now. What will you do next? End this time of devotion or continue to offer God your heart, allowing him to use you in every aspect and every activity of your life?

Through Darkness into Marvelous Light

Glen Van Andel '66   Isaiah 59:9–60:3

Calvin professor; Grand Rapids, Michigan

Twenty-eight Calvin students and two faculty members were in the middle of a sixteen-day adventure in the rainforest of Costa Rica when our Outward Bound guides led us into a dark, damp cave. They urged us to follow them through the slimy, ankle-deep mud to the remote rooms where, when we turned off our flashlights and sat very still, we could hear the soft cooing of thousands of bats hanging on the ceiling all around us. The darkness was thick. We indeed could not see a hand in front of our faces.

Then the guides asked us to deposit our flashlights in their knapsacks and challenged us to find our way out of the cave. All of us were trying to deal with our deepest fears. How could we ever get out of there? It had been hard enough finding our way with flashlights, let alone without them. We joined hands and prayed, asking God for guidance and for the courage to face our fears. One person in the group offered to try to lead, and so we started out, each person hanging on to the person just ahead. After nearly an hour of blindly picking our way along the wall, we began to see a dim light shining through the entrance of the cave. Together, with God's help, we had confronted our fears and had found the way.

Life's experiences often seem to abandon us or someone we love in a dark cave without a light. Death, terminal or debilitating illness, loss of friends and family members, and broken relationships all lead us into the dark abyss. We feel lost, alone, and afraid. But be assured: No matter where we are, God is there and is ready to provide the way through the darkness into his marvelous light.

In fact, maybe he will use us to "shine like the stars in the universe" (Phil. 2:15), to hold someone's hand and encourage that person through the cave and back to the exit. Isaiah tells us that we do indeed have the light: "Arise, shine, for your light has come, and the glory of the LORD rises upon you" (Isa. 60:1). May the light go before us to show us the way, behind us to encourage us, beside us to befriend us, above us to watch over us, within us to give us peace.

The Other Prodigal

Luke 15:20; Genesis 33:4   Dick Houskamp '59
Retired social worker; Ada, Michigan

But while he was still a long way off, his father saw him and was filled with compassion for him; he ran to his son, threw his arms around him and kissed him.
(Luke 15:20)

But Esau ran to meet Jacob and embraced him; he threw his arms around his neck and kissed him. And they wept. (Gen. 33:4)

Why did it take sixty-seven years of my life for Esau's story to leap from the page? Perhaps it is because my childhood teachers painted the fair-haired Jacob, doing his mother's bidding, as good and his swarthy, selfish, impulsive brother, Esau, as evil. I was well into adulthood before I realized that the God of the covenant chose a pretty motley crew of human beings to assist him in fulfilling his covenant promises, including the great men of faith — Abraham, Isaac, and Jacob.

A second reason for my belated discovery is related to my own spiritual journey. As we get older, we become more aware of the brevity of life and our inability to achieve the sanctified state we once dreamed possible. We have not attained the success or wholeness we once envisioned. Or, if we have been successful by human standards, we have an inner, even though well-disguised, awareness that we are fragile, stumbling, very incomplete people. Regardless of our age, my pastor recently reminded us, we are in the "boot camp of our sanctification."

The parallels between the story of Jacob and Esau and the story of the prodigal son are rich. Both Jacob and the prodigal placed great value on material possessions; both expected anger and rejection from those they had hurt; both made plans to appease the aggrieved. But in both stories overflowing love overcomes evil, the past is forgiven, the false gods of material desire are exposed, and the feeble attempts to appease and manipulate are brushed aside.

The God of the Bible is a God whose love is staggering, whose grace abounds. As we get older, we know in our hearts that that is the only way it can be.

Real Treasures

Rebecca Barton   Matthew 6:19-21
Calvin student; Sterling Heights, Michigan

> *Do not store up for yourselves treasures on earth, where moth and rust destroy, and where thieves break in and steal. But store up for yourselves treasures in heaven, where moth and rust do not destroy, and where thieves do not break in and steal. For where your treasure is, there your heart will be also.*
>
> (Matt. 6:19-21)

"Treasures on earth." What do you consider your earthly treasure? Is it a prestigious occupation or academic honor? Financial security or social acclaim?

A treasure is something of great value that is cherished. It is something you would not give up for anything and would go to great lengths to protect. But in our world the idea of treasure is sometimes devalued. It often amounts to little more than wants and hopes that we mistake for needs. But a treasure should be more than just a fleeting desire. A true treasure is often unexpectedly discovered or uncovered, like the new-found love and respect a young man finds for his father, whom he once regarded as only his provider but now sees as his friend and mentor.

In the Bible, Matthew talks of treasures being stored in heaven. He provides no example for us to follow so that we may have such treasure, but he does give this one guiding principle: "Where your treasure is, there your heart will be also" (Matt. 6:21).

The Lord Jesus finds delight when we find our treasure in him. Seeking him with our whole being and finding him in our daily lives is a treasure that cannot be destroyed by "moth and rust." The treasure of an intimate relationship with Christ needs to be held close to protect it from the "thieves who break in and steal." When we find heavenly treasures, the worldly prizes we once held dear become much less important. If we reach out to Christ with open hands and open hearts, our lives will be filled with heavenly treasures.

Revelation 7:9
Marie De Vries Van Antwerpen '61
Teacher; Kentwood, Michigan

After this I looked and there before me was a great multitude that no one could count, from every nation, tribe, people and language, standing before the throne and in front of the Lamb. They were wearing white robes and were holding palm branches in their hands. (Rev. 7:9)

The music flowing from the open doors and windows of the Haitian church welcomes me into the worship service. The little building is filled to capacity with men, women, and children singing and clapping praise to the Lord. Everyone, it seems, is wearing white, and the visual image is striking. As I stand there wondering where to sit, several young boys get up and sit on the edge of the platform. I find space on the backless bench they've vacated and sit in the front row. Facing me is a young boy who is singing with enthusiasm from a small hymnal. I move over on the bench and motion for him to sit next to me. The hymns are in Creole, and my high school French allows me to follow along as we share the book together. We sit, we stand, we sing, and he points to the right verse to help me out. He stays at my side through the service, and during the preaching part I pull out paper and pencil. "Votre nom?" I write, and he writes back, "Onacis." Then he asks my name, and I pencil, "Marie." When he takes back the pencil and paper, he draws a picture and writes my name above it. This small gesture bonds us, leaping over gaps in age, culture, and language. This sketch is a keeper. Somehow I feel the same about Onacis.

He disappears during the foot washing, but when I spot him outside after church, I smile and wave. I know I will see him again when we stand together before the throne and sing to the Lamb. For now I whisper a silent prayer: "The Lord bless you and keep you, my young friend. May his face shine upon you, and may you have peace. Amen."

A Community of Faith

Erin McIlwain   Ephesians 2:19-22
Calvin student; Rensselaer, Indiana

Consequently, you are no longer foreigners and aliens, but fellow citizens with God's people and members of God's household, built on the foundation of the apostles and prophets, with Christ Jesus himself as the chief cornerstone.

(Eph. 2:19-20)

I came to Calvin College as a student breaking all the Calvin molds: I am not Dutch, I was not raised in a Christian home, I did not go to Christian schools, and I had never heard of the Christian Reformed Church. Because of my upbringing, what I knew and had experienced of Christianity and faith was very individualized. Worship, devotion, prayer, and all things religious I kept between God and me. They rarely, and only superficially, involved anyone else.

The summer before my junior year at Calvin, I began to open up a bit and discuss the possibility of being baptized. I didn't understand what baptism entails, but I knew and dreaded that I would have to stand in front of people and openly share with them my relationship with God. I truly wanted to be baptized, but I saw no reason at all that I should have to involve other people. I thought Chaplain Cooper and I could take five minutes in his office and be done with it. However, as I talked to Chaplain Cooper and others that I respected, I realized how limiting my approach was, limiting to the significance of the sacrament of baptism and, even more drastically, limiting to the importance and value of Christ's body, the church.

As I shared more and more with my close friends about this decision, I was amazed at the encouragement and support they offered me. I was even more amazed as I came to realize how each one of them had encouraged and supported me to make this big decision. No matter how I had tried to convince myself, my faith was not solely between God and me. It was, and is, between a community of believers, an eternity of members of Christ's royal household, each an individual with his or her own talents and tasks but also each a contributing part to Christ's body, the church. I never saw that church more gloriously or accurately displayed than I did the day I stood in front of my community of believers to profess my faith and be baptized in the name of the Father, the Son, and the Holy Spirit. Truly, "in him the whole building is joined together and rises to become a holy temple in the Lord. And in him [I too am] being built together to become a dwelling in which God lives by his Spirit" (Eph. 2:21-22).

A Time to Weep . . . a Time to Laugh

Ecclesiastes 3:1-4   Gail Bangma Baker '64

Environmentalist; Niceville, Florida

> *There is a time for everything,*
>   *and a season for every activity under heaven:*
>   *a time to be born and a time to die,*
>   *a time to plant and a time to uproot,*
>   *a time to kill and a time to heal,*
>   *a time to tear down and a time to build,*
>   *a time to weep and a time to laugh,*
>   *a time to mourn and a time to dance. . . .* (Eccles. 3:1-4)

It was a brilliant white day in late winter several years ago when I suddenly became a widow. Without warning and without preparation. I was forty-six years old. Afterwards I would look at my brown-haired self in the mirror and say, "You can't be a widow; widows are old ladies with white hair."

For me as for most people, the unexpected loss of a loved one brought with it a tumult of emotions: denial, despair, anger, and, perhaps most of all, the harrowing sense of being totally out of control. I felt like a fragile leaf being tossed along on a raging stream. I did not know where I would end up.

I received many expressions of sympathy. (When middle-aged people die, most of their friends and relatives are alive and able to send condolences.) One of the most meaningful was this text from Ecclesiastes and a note from one of my coworkers. It gave me peace and hope and perspective. It reminded me that I never was in control, that God is always in control.

Slowly the despair and anger turned into acceptance. I no longer felt like a wave-tossed leaf, but like a sailor in a sturdy boat. The boat was being tossed about in a storm, but I knew it would not sink, and I could see relatively calm water ahead. God provided me with the boat. God calmed the waters. I healed because God healed me.

God gives us the strength to weather all the challenges of life. Through his guidance and mercy we can accept and even embrace these challenges, realizing that though there are times to weep and mourn, there are also times to laugh and dance.

Treasuring the Word

Conrad Bult '57
Librarian emeritus;
Grand Rapids, Michigan

2 Kings 22:8-20; Jeremiah 36; Luke 4:16-21

What memories do you have about the first Bible storybook you held in your hands and read or perhaps had read to you? Many will recall the *Child's Story Bible* by Catherine Vos or a similarly treasured illustrated volume of action-filled biblical narratives. Unforgettable for me is the image of the shield-bearing Joshua leading the Israelites across the River Jordan into Canaan. This picture in the *Child's Story Bible* is as vivid in my mind today as it was sixty years ago, when I was a five-year-old.

No doubt many of you received a Bible or New Testament from your parents or grandparents. A New Testament I still have contains this inscription on the flyleaf: "To our dear little grandson Conrad John from Grandpa and Grandma, Christmas 1939." I treasure this book.

As you read the Old and New Testament passages cited for today's reading, you no doubt noted that the law of God and the words of the prophets were originally written on scrolls made from the skin of sheep or calves, as were the words of Isaiah selected by Christ for his sermon in the synagogue at Nazareth. For the listener, hearing God's words contained in these three scrolls had dynamic results. The good King Josiah tore his clothes and instituted religious reforms. His son, King Jehoiakim, not fond of Jeremiah's prophetic words, responded quite differently, cutting up the scroll as it was read to him and throwing each piece into a fire burning in a nearby brazier. Nor did Jesus' comments on Isaiah's words receive a kind reception. From Luke we learn about those in his audience who tried to kill Jesus by pushing him off a cliff outside the town.

In your home you may have the Bible your parents read or an even older Scripture volume carried across the ocean by your immigrant forebears. As you read in it, remember that you have in your hands a Bible cherished over perhaps a century or more by family members no longer alive. What you are holding is a tangible link between your faith and the faith of those in your family who preceded you in life and in death. Continue to cherish it and the words in it.

Lessons of a Broken Lent

Matthew 26:40   Anne Elizabeth Stickney Schmidt
Faculty wife/writer; Alto, Michigan

"If only Lent had been shorter," we think. Surely we could have lasted twenty days in the course we had set for ourselves. Or ten. Or maybe the short stretch from one Sunday to the next.

Instead we hear Jesus' words to the disciples in Gethsemane as if they were spoken to us: "Couldn't you keep watch with me for one hour?" (Matt. 26:40, NIVI). Could it have been so difficult to give up tobacco or wine or butter or refined sugar or meat on Fridays? Have we become so attached to the small props of our lives that we cannot relinquish them even for a short span of time? How quickly we prove ourselves to be weak vessels for the Spirit of Christ within us.

Surely Lent should be more for us than a late winter's six-week course in self-improvement. We have a sufficient number of spas and books and motivational speakers from which to choose that can start us on the course toward attaining healthier bodies and minds. And, no, Lent cannot be reduced to a simple formula for attaining spiritual growth. Keeping a Lenten fast may be commendable, but it does not win us our salvation.

Consequently, perhaps the greatest lesson of Lent is that we cannot by our own merit or will make those changes for which we are striving. When we fail to live up to our resolutions, when we fail to keep the promises we made so confidently to ourselves and to the Lord, we once against sense our need of God. And in our emptiness and need we hear his gentle invitation extended to all who trust in Christ alone for their salvation.

What shall we surrender for Lent this year? A daily cappuccino? Membership in the local health club? Aimless shopping expeditions? The danger of choosing any of these pleasures or pursuits is that our focus becomes too small. We become Pharisees who are so intent on the minutiae of the law that we miss its greater meaning.

The penitence we feel during Lent, the sacrifices we offer to the Lord, and our small attempts at change are all experienced in the knowledge that Easter morning is just ahead. Easter morning — when our tiny victories against selfishness will be overwhelmed by the triumph Christ won over death, when the faltering steps we've taken toward righteousness will be meaningless when measured against Christ's journey from death into life. Easter morning — when, to all who have been about the valiant work of remaking themselves, God calls, "Look! I am the one who makes all things new!" (Rev. 21:5, paraphrased).

The Joy of Confession

Ellen Macleod Van Tongeren '86   Psalm 32
Teacher; Grand Rapids, Michigan

If there's one thing I have regretted about being Protestant, it's that our ancestors de-emphasized the practices of individual confession and absolution after their separation from the Roman Catholic Church. Of course, they had good intentions. There had indeed been abuses of those practices during the Middle Ages. Furthermore, Protestants have tried to incorporate confession and absolution in other ways, such as prayers of confession followed by statements of pardon in the liturgy, fellowship groups, and even church-discipline practices. I think, however, it would be worthwhile for us to be more intentional in the use of confession in our devotional lives.

Here is one possibility — an exercise in confession before God through praying along with Psalm 32:

— Read Psalm 32:1-5. Ask the Holy Spirit to convict you of sin. Think back through the day or the week and see what the Spirit brings to your attention. Say aloud to God what you have done (or not done). Let yourself feel the responsibility for it. Ask God to forgive you because Jesus took your punishment. Say verse 5 out loud, saying the last phrase, "you forgave the guilt of my sin," slowly and as many times as you need to (you may also need to remind yourself of this again later, since feelings often need time to catch up with reality).

— Read Psalm 32:6-7. Picture yourself in a safe place — to represent a place where your sins can't reach you, perhaps wrapped in strong arms or inside a secure fortress.

— Read Psalm 32:8-10. Ask the Holy Spirit to teach you the way that leaves sin behind and moves toward something much better. Think about what that way will be. Ask the Spirit to soften your will and to align it with his.

— Read Psalm 32:11. Pick a song and sing it out loud to God (it's okay if you're out of tune). Know that you are counted among the righteous not because you feel really sorry, not because you'll try hard to do better, but solely because of what Jesus Christ has done on your behalf.

The Burden

Matthew 11:25-30

Lionel Basney†
Calvin professor; Lowell, Michigan

L ent is the time for repentance.

It's a hard idea and not a popular one. A theologian tells me repentance is not a popular topic even among theologians. Perhaps that is why we sometimes hear preaching meant to make us feel sorry not for our sins but for ourselves.

We live in a therapeutic culture. Among us sin is something to be cured, like a headache. The goal is not to draw closer to God but to feel free to enjoy ourselves. We may even see repentance as morbid, as pointlessly depressing.

But to believe that everything wrong with us can be fixed with an aspirin is to think too little of ourselves. For it would mean we had no really good possibilities in us to begin with — that the most anyone could expect of us was to do a little business, have a little fun.

But love has always thought better of us than this. Our parents dreamed we would become exemplary people, brave, distinguished. And God expects even more — that we will become his friends, charged with the energy and freedom of his love. Lent is the time when we renew our hope of glory.

When we do, however, we see, too, that we aren't what God hoped we would become. Something is in the way; something is deeply, not superficially, wrong.

John Bunyan opens *The Pilgrim's Progress* with a picture of it: Christian stands at the start of his journey "with a great burden upon his back." In Barry Moser's wonderful watercolor, the burden is bigger than Christian, a heap of bags and bundles. It bends Christian in half.

Christian cannot wish it away or shrug it off. It falls off when he stands at the cross, the sign that only Christ's dying and rising make repentance work at all.

Yet we need another picture, not for the fact of sin but for all the daily examples of it and how we cope with them. Maybe that picture is the canvas bag I carry my books and papers in. Shapeless, endlessly stretchable, it is always in my hand, heavier as the week goes on.

Eventually I sit down and unpack it. There is the letter I didn't answer, the favor I didn't do, the injustice I didn't repair. There are the opportunities for charity I put off.

Sometimes I find I have done well: there is a note of thanks from a student. But I had to pull out all the trash to find it.

Something's Wrong with This Picture

Sarah Potter   Galatians 2:17-21
Calvin student; Plainfield, Illinois

The cardboard trifold on the table at Arby's had a sort of mirror on it. The advertisement claimed that the blurry colors that closely resembled my grin were the face of an "Arby's Lover." Clever, I thought. In my marketing and advertising classes we had learned that advertisers try to feature people that the prospective customer can identify with. A mirror makes the person in the ad identical to the prospective customer. You can't get much close than that — except for a better-quality mirror. Arby's had that advertisement focused directly on me.

I am, our culture tells me, the most important person in my world. The nightly news boasts "news that matters to you" — like health reports, family living, and so on. Never mind news about someone who looks different and thinks completely differently from me. A popular magazine among young teens is actually entitled *All About You*.

Sadly, if my life were a magazine, it might be titled *All About Sarah*. I spend most of my time being concerned about my grades, my future, my friends, my life. Sure, God is the most important thing to me. But I don't think God enjoys having to win the priority game I play with the different parts of my life. These parts have all been revolving around me, when they should be bowing toward him.

Paul writes, "I have been crucified with Christ and I no longer live, but Christ lives in me. The life I live in the body, I live by faith in the Son of God, who loved me and gave himself for me. I do not set aside the grace of God, for if righteousness could be gained through the law, Christ died for nothing!" (Gal. 2:20-21). The people to whom Paul was writing were trying to gain salvation by keeping the law. I have a different problem: focusing on myself as the central figure in my own salvation.

When I read these verses recently, I thought, "If righteousness could be gained through me, through focusing on myself, Christ died for nothing. His sacrifice would have been unnecessary, a big waste." But it's not about me. It's really all about Christ. And the name of it is grace.

Like Children

Matthew 18:1-4   Stacey Heemstra Hollebeek '94
                                  Teacher; Rehoboth, New Mexico

In seventh-grade Bible class we were studying Acts and had just finished the story of the angel who rescued the apostles from prison. "What do angels look like?" Leanne blurted out. "Do they have hair? Eyes? They must have a mouth because they talked — and they would look really dumb with a mouth and no eyes." As a new middle-school teacher, I was learning quickly to expect questions.

"This doesn't have anything to do with the topic, but how did they decide what books go in the Bible?"

"Is God a concrete or abstract noun?"

These seventh graders expressed their endless wonder and energy not only with questions, but also with action. When I took ten girls on a service project to a downtown hotel being renovated from a crack house to a rehabilitation home, they forgot about boys and music and instead swept up huge barrels of dust, washed wooden floors, and coached old crack addicts on ways to treat women.

Although many of my students come from poor or abusive homes, they don't fret and worry about tomorrow. They focus on today and live it to the fullest. "What are we gonna do today, Mrs. H?" is their first question in the classroom.

But what is most amazing is their prayers and their trust that God will hear and answer them. They bring everything to him, whether large or small: "Please pray for my knee." "My grandpa's in a coma. Please ask God to make him better."

Almost two thousand years ago Jesus told his disciples, "Unless you change and become like little children, you will never enter the kingdom of heaven" (Matt. 18:3). Children haven't changed since then. They still ask lots of questions, still act on their beliefs, still focus on today. And they still trust in their heavenly Father with a humble faith that puts many of us educated and pious adults to shame.

The Company We Keep

Jack Roeda '67
Pastor; Grand Rapids, Michigan

Matthew 25:40

Whatever you did for one of the least . . . (Matt. 25:40)

S ue Erickson Bloland considers fame in a recent issue of *The Atlantic Monthly*. Ms. Bloland's father, Erik Erikson, became famous after his first book, *Childhood and Society*, was published. At any gathering he was "the Luminous center of attention." She recalls a party she threw for her college friends that ignited into a "charged dance" the moment her father walked into the room. Discovering that she is the daughter of the great psychoanalyst, some people would ask, "Can I touch you?"

We are drawn to the famous, even the near famous. Fascinated. Envious. Those students will not ever forget that evening with the great Erickson. Sometimes, in discussing movies and directors, someone will mention Paul Schrader. I find myself having to resist the urge to remark, "You know, I knew Paul back in college. We were quite close actually. I attended his wedding." It is as if we gain significance by association.

We do, of course, measure each other by the company we keep. Some company reflects well on us. We size up the patrons at a restaurant, the guests at a dinner party, even the saints in the pews. We prefer company that will boost our status, show the folks back home that we are successful.

Jesus turns this status seeking on its head. According to him, what gives us a place of honor in the only gathering that counts is what we have done for "the least." He says it is our care for people of no account that makes us count.

Does this mean, then, that we are to spend more of our time serving the homeless at soup kitchens and volunteering for Prison Fellowship? Perhaps, but occasional goodness is not the heart of Jesus' desire. In Matthew's Gospel, faith ignites into love, or else it is not faith. Jesus wants compassion and self-giving to shape his disciples. "I desire mercy," he said (Matt. 9:13). It is so like him.

Knowing the End of the Story

Revelation 21:1-22:21   Tom McWhertor

Calvin administrator; Grand Rapids, Michigan

Have you ever watched a squeaking-close game on videotape without stress, already knowing that your team has clinched the title in the closing seconds? Or sneaked a peak at the closing chapter before you started the book? There are advantages to knowing the end of the story ahead of time — in real life as well.

Revelation 21-22 is one of many biblical passages (Ps. 72; Isa. 49, 60-61; Zech. 14) which, in sweeping images of fulfillment and perfection, like masterful paintings on broad canvases, picture the goal to which all creation moves. The New Jerusalem is pictured as a city "coming down out of heaven" (Rev. 21:2), as a "bride beautifully dressed for her husband" (Rev. 21:2), and as a place where "there will be no more death or mourning or crying or pain" (Rev. 21:4). Those metaphors are fleshed out in these chapters to emphasize the shalom that God will surely bring in his time.

Post-resurrection believers live in the certain knowledge of how all will turn out — we have read the last chapter before living it. This should empower us to live faithfully and stand tall in everything we do. If not, we have missed the grace and strength God is providing for us between Christ's coming and his return.

Bruce Cockburn, a Christian singer-songwriter from Canada, captures the sense of this in "A Dream like Mine," from *Nothing but a Burning Light* (1991). In this lyrical call to arms set to a driving beat, Cockburn sings about a person with a dream who has "the power of a thousand generations" because he calls the listener to rise up and change the world. But Revelation 21-22 gives us more confidence than a mere dream. It portrays God's picture of the way things *will be*. Imagine that power!

Do our lives reflect the confidence they should if we really believe the story will end the way God promises? Are we walking with the power of a thousand generations empowered by the God of heaven and earth? We should be!

Gold That Never Ends

Karen Snapper Weaver '73   Revelation 21:18
Teacher; Grand Rapids, Michigan

Robert Frost's poem "Nothing Gold Can Stay" greeted my seventh graders as they entered my classroom that mild spring day in 1998. The night before, I had said a final farewell to my beloved Calvin professor and teaching mentor Kenneth Kuiper, and I was eager to share his passion for this poem with my own students.

Like all of Ken's American-literature students, I had not passed his class until I had memorized this poem, in which Frost compares the first budding leaves of spring to pure gold, a gold which soon will turn to common green. Frost saw the golds of this world, like the splendid dawn and the glorious Garden of Eden, as lasting only an hour and destined to fade, for "nothing gold can stay."

I read the poem aloud to my students, emphasizing that last line. Then I asked them to take out their journals and write a brief personal story ending with the poem's last line. Brows furrowed. Pencils scratched. Soon an eager hand waved.

Its owner read, "My dad came home from work with our new car — the first new car we had ever had. We were so excited! It was purple, shiny, and had that really new smell inside. We all climbed in to drive to my grandpa and grandma's to show it off. On the way my little brother Josh threw up all over the cloth seats. Nothing gold can stay."

Another hand. "I loved to go to my Grandma Rose's house. It was old, with a screen door that would make Grandma yell out, 'Who has come for a Grandma hug?' And then she would give me a big hug and kiss. She would always have cookies for me, and we would eat ice cream together. Last winter Grandma Rose died. Uncle Mart and Aunt Emily live there now. They put up a new metal screen door. I never want to go there again. Nothing gold can stay."

As the contributions began to wane, a hand waved from the back, followed by this epiphany: "Isn't it so cool, Mrs. Weaver? Just when one gold thing is gone, there's another one out there?"

Yes. That is cool. And as I took these seventh-grade words into my heart, I was overwhelmed by the grace of a loving God who not only fills our lives here on this imperfect earth with a stream of golden blessings but also assures us of a gold which, unlike Robert Frost's, will never end.

I thought of Ken in his final home: "Jerusalem the golden . . . the city of God's presence . . . what bliss beyond compare!"* Thank you, Lord.

'And All Shall Be Well'

Matthew 27:46

Jeremy Lloyd '94
Musician; Greensboro, North Carolina

My God, my God, why have you forsaken me? (Matt. 27:46)

Jesus knew both doubt and despair. It's a place I visit sometimes, too. But it's no vacation. One might just as well spend forty days in the desert. Or three days in a whale.

In church we don't talk freely about the country of despair. For a long time I stopped attending services because I felt like the child in "The Emperor's New Clothes" who spoke out and exposed the king. For me it was this: In spite of the way we so easily speak of the presence of God in daily life, does anyone else notice that *God is not here*?

Not long ago, in my hometown in Pennsylvania, a little African-American boy was found murdered in a nearby river. That Sunday our pastor, ignoring this horror, sermonized about how God had watched over him that week, even sending an angel to help him fix his car. "Lord, save me from your followers," I prayed, in the words of the famous bumper sticker.

In time I discovered I am not the only person who has difficulty answering the question "So what is God doing in your life today?" For people who are dogged by the need to account for or accede to the silence of God, people who often feel the groan of creation to be stronger than the pull of grace, the only possible answer to that question comes in the form of blood and tears. In Gethsemane and on Calvary Jesus was one of them.

In time I discovered one thing more. The land of doubt is on the same continent as the land of faith. In two of the four Gospels the last words of Jesus himself were words of deep despair. So I wonder whether we need to worry about those who traverse the shadowy valleys, whether we need to fear they may not make it back, when God is with them all along, even following them into hell.

There is a living answer to Jesus' question "Why have you forsaken me?" The answer is resurrection, Jesus' and ours. And in the meantime, even in our despair, the words of Julian of Norwich reflect God's promise: "All shall be well, and all shall be well, and all manner of thing shall be well."*

Carrying the Death and Life of Jesus

Dorina K. Lazo '99   2 Corinthians 4:7-12
Writer; Fresno, California

During my senior year at Calvin College, I had the opportunity to study in Central America for a semester, two weeks of which we spent in Nicaragua, a place remarkable for its contrasts. It was from one of those contrasts that I learned a hard-hitting lesson.

Perhaps the most profound contrast that I experienced was in the home where I stayed. A girl named Marcia worked there as a maid and nanny. At sixteen she was the mother of a sixteen-month-old child. The baby's father had abandoned them, and Marcia was left to care for her daughter and her aging mother. Many people would be inclined to pity someone like Marcia, but Marcia had an attitude that refused pity. She radiated love and patience as she cleaned the house and cared for her employers' children. At night she would sneak across the street to see her own little girl.

In my time in Nicaragua I took a few minutes a day to chat with Marcia. We knew each other only four short days, but our friendship felt older than that. Before I left, Marcia handed me a small scrap of paper on which she had written a poem about our friendship. With tears streaming down my face, I thanked her as well as I could in Spanish. To the family of the house, Marcia was the maid, but to me she was a symbol of hope in the midst of adversity.

One day recently, overcome by discouragement, I looked to the Bible for some comfort and strengthening. My eyes stopped on 2 Corinthians 4:7-9, which I had previously underlined:

> But we have this treasure in jars of clay to show that this all-surpassing power is from God and not from us. We are hard pressed on every side, but not crushed; perplexed, but not in despair; persecuted, but not abandoned; struck down, but not destroyed. We always carry around in our body the death of Jesus, so that the life of Jesus may also be revealed in our body.

And then I remembered my Nicaraguan *amiga*, Marcia. I was struck anew by how she carried with her both the life and death of Jesus. It was the contrast between her life and her attitude toward it that had made an indelible impression on my mind and my heart. Remembering her, I realized that even on my dark days the death and life of Jesus should carry me through. "Therefore [I] do not lose heart" (2 Cor. 4:16).

Finding Self-worth

2 Chronicles 7:14

John H. Timmerman '67
Calvin professor; Grand Rapids, Michigan

If my people, who are called by my name, will humble themselves and pray and seek my face and turn from their wicked ways, then I will hear from heaven and will forgive their sin and will heal their land. (2 Chron. 7:14)

In *The Myth of Sisyphus* Albert Camus raises a fearful and tricky question: "Should I commit suicide today?" Instead of answering yes or no straightaway, Camus first talks about how and when to ask the question. You should ask the question upon waking up each morning, says Camus. Why? For two reasons. Asking the question in the morning, when you are fresh and untarnished by the day, you are more likely to answer no. If you ask the same question at the end of the day, the day's events may well have burdened your spirit and weighted your answer toward yes. Second, because you are likely to answer no in the early morning, you thereby affirm both life and yourself. You give yourself a sense of self-worth that may even keep the demons of the day at bay.

I don't ask Camus's question. But I often do wonder how some people, myself included, can believe that they can atone for themselves, purify themselves, give themselves worth — all by themselves. Throughout history people have tried to do precisely that. It may have been by beating drums around the sweat lodge. It may have been by ascetic withdrawal to waste places. It may have been by asking Camus's tricky question, designed to affirm personal worth if asked at the right time.

The right approach to self-worth, I believe, arises from today's verse in 2 Chronicles 7, particularly in the verb to *humble* oneself. It doesn't take much to make me understand that I can't atone for myself. I can't get self-worth on my own. But I do know the alternative, though sometimes my knees are too rusty when they bend in prayer and I seek the face of God. When I take the posture of a humble suppliant, the weight of his glory and the touch of his forgiveness hold me there. I have to throw off pride like a dirty overcoat and admit my need before forgiveness happens. I have to dredge the desire for sin out of the hard, crooked corners of my heart and lay them open in repentance. Then, in my imperfect humility but still trying to hold on with baby hands of faith, I can receive God's healing restoration of my worth as a child of God.

The God Who Forgets

Duane Kelderman '73   Jeremiah 31:33-34
Pastor; Grand Rapids, Michigan

This is the covenant I will make with the house of Israel. . . . I . . . will remember their sins no more. (Jer. 31:33-34)

The promise of the Christian gospel is that God will not remember our sins. This promise reminds me of a special moment I had with my father-in-law a couple of years ago, not long before he died. My father-in-law was one of the most generous people I have ever known. Jeannette and I got married when we were only nineteen and full-time students at Calvin. Dad generously set us up in a beautiful mobile home. When Dad and Mom came to see us, they would quietly fill our freezer with the best cuts of meat and sneak plush new bath towels into our linen closet.

Jeannette and I would always say thank you, and Dad, not wanting us to feel like he was giving us anything, would always say, "Oh, Mom's got it down in the black book." This was one of my father-in-law's most famous lines: "Mom's got it down in the black book." It took me a while to figure out he was joking. But he said it every time we would thank him for something.

Eventually we finished school and were able to make it on our own. Probably twenty years passed with no mention of the black book — until a couple of years ago. Jeannette and I had done a small thing for her parents. But they were embarrassingly grateful. They kept saying, "Thank you," and, "You shouldn't have done that." (Often generous people are better at giving than receiving.) When Dad wouldn't quit thanking us, I finally said, "Hey, Dad, give it a rest. Don't you remember the black book? I think it's time you hauled it out." Without a flinch, Dad replied, "Oh, Mom lost the black book."

What a beautiful picture of forgiveness. God remembers our sins no more. He loses the book — on purpose. He destroys the record. Like Israel, we can believe God's promise: "I will remember your sins no more."

Romans 8:26; 2 Corinthians 9:15   Willis De Boer '48
Calvin professor emeritus;
Grand Rapids, Michigan

A high school student was leading the final student assembly for the school year. He had developed considerable poise during the year. He now had stage presence — the ability to keep things going with the right words and filler remarks. But at this final assembly he was caught off guard. Suddenly his parents walked on stage, followed by the principal, who proceeded to read a tribute and present him with a plaque and a five-hundred-dollar scholarship award for outstanding leadership and good citizenship. There was a long, embarrassing moment of silence. Finally the poised young leader blurted out, "All I can think of to say is thank you, and that doesn't seem to be enough!"

Words can fail us. There are situations and experiences that cause such depth of feeling and emotion that words won't work. They come off hopelessly flat and cheap. It happens when there is awful tragedy and suffering. Job's three friends, when they saw his suffering, had the good sense to hold their tongues. They sat with him in silence.

The apostle Paul has a very comfortable insight for such uncomfortable situations. When suffering so engulfs us that words fail us, "the Spirit himself intercedes for us with groans that words cannot express" (Rom. 8:26). God covers us even in the inadequacy of human language.

Words can also fail us in our moments of surprise or of satisfaction and fulfillment. Paul once exclaimed, "Thanks be to God for his indescribable gift" (2 Cor. 9:15). God's grace can so overwhelm us, his sharing his life and love so impact us, that we can't get beyond thank you — and that doesn't seem to be enough.

But here, too, we may rely on our companion the Holy Spirit. If in our suffering the Spirit groans for us, surely, in our excitement and fulfillment he revels with and sings for us. Forget the embarrassment over being tongue-tied with halting and inadequate responses. Our Friend steps in and expresses our inexpressibles perfectly.

Thanks, Lord, for covering even our moments of ecstasy and anguish.

Room for All

Sondra Dunn Sula '83
Artist; Aurora, Illinois

Hebrews 9:11-15

For months I had been reading a translation of Julian of Norwich's *Revelation of Divine Love*. Fascinated by this fourteenth-century mystic who felt deeply the love of Christ through his Passion, I was drawn to the opportunity to sign up for a silent retreat to focus on Christ's Passion and his divine love for us.

As I sat in my tiny, sparse room of retreat, an image came to me. A seemingly endless line of people stood at the entrance of what looked like the opening to a cave. The people were amazingly varied — young, old, rich, poor, and racially very diverse. One by one they were climbing into the cave. Then, as though a camera lens had pulled back, I saw the enormous form of Jesus. The opening into which the people were going was not a cave at all but the gaping wound in Jesus' side. The people were entering through it on the way to his heart, where they would find rest. It seemed impossible that everyone could fit inside that heart, but apparently the heart of my vision had an endless capacity. Then I realized that all were welcome in Jesus' heart. Within it an entire sad, broken world could fit. In the corner of my mind I could hear him saying, "Come inside me. Enter through the gates of my side. Inside is my heart. A piece of it is for you. Partake. It is all I have to give you, and it is everything."

Jesus offers his heart to each one of us — from a fourteenth-century mystic to a crying, hungry child to a successful business executive. We merely have to enter through his wounds, wounds he suffered for us so that we can be close to him. His body is the bridge, and his heart, the source of all comfort.

'Liquor Sweet and Most Divine'

Mark 14:23-24

Charlotte Fennema Otten '49
Calvin professor emerita; Grand Rapids, Michigan

Then he took the cup, gave thanks, and offered it to them, and they all drank from it. "This is my blood of the covenant, which is poured out for many," he said to them. (Mark 14:23-24)

Golgotha. A day of executions. Three stark wooden crosses, carried or dragged, added to the desolation of the Place of a Skull. On the middle cross hung a weak man. Trying to carry his cross, he had stumbled, and someone had carried it for him.

Now, blinded by blood streaming from the crown of thorns that his enemies had jokingly placed on his head, he felt blood seeping from wounds that the nails had made in his hands and feet. Since there was darkness over all the earth while he was dying, no one watching the executions could see that his blood illumined his flesh.

When his friends took him down from the cross, their loving hands wiped the blood from his eyes and wounds. They wrapped his body in a white linen cloth and buried him in a white tomb. Silence settled on the hearts of those who buried him. Darkness entered their souls.

Then something happened that not only shook the small world of his followers but also caused an upheaval in the universe. Before the sun rose on Sunday morning, the hanged one felt blood coursing through his veins. He shook off death, and for forty days he showed his friends that he was the way, the truth, and the life. Then he left again.

This time they didn't feel desolate. He had left them his blood. They remembered that, just before his death, he had blessed a cup of wine and told his disciples that they were drinking his "blood of the covenant, which [was] poured out" for them.

Centuries later, in the sunlight of his presence, his blood lights the world. Taking Communion, we drink with the seventeenth-century poet George Herbert, who reminds us,

Love is that liquor sweet and most divine,
Which my God feels as bloud; but I, as wine.*

Singin' the Blues on 92

Calvin Seerveld '52   Psalm 92
Professor emeritus/writer; Willowdale, Ontario

To hear the Lord speak through a psalm, you need to hear the ups and the downs together of the psalm. The African-American tradition of the blues has a musical scale, harmonics, and flattened notes that can catch simultaneously the ups and downs of God's Word.

God's flexible, firm voice of Psalm 92 allows us to offer up our hearts and bittersweet lives under Jesus Christ's rule as an offering to the Lord in song. Psalms are meant to be sung. So sing "Blues 92."

Blues 92

The melody lyrics, verse by verse:

Cm7 / F7:
The LORD en - joys a hot gui - tar, with
I watch the wick - ed get a - head; they
I had it bad not long a - go, double-
I'm get - ting old, bones dry - ing up, not
The LORD en - joys a hot guit - ar, with

G7 / Cm7:
drums and sax to cook it. God
know the ropes so well. "Yeah,
crossed, was on the rocks. But you
grow - ing like a tree. "Oh,
drums and sax to cook it. God

Eb / Bb7 / Ab7 / F9:
moves some - times it seems so slow, but my
those poor en - e - mies," says God,
know? the LORD was e - ven there: made me
don't you wor - ry," says the LORD, "You'll get
moves some - times it seems so slow, but my

G7 / Cm7:
LORD the Rock ain't crook - ed.
find - ing the road to hell!"
strong as a wild ox!
good fresh sap from me!"
LORD the Rock ain't crook - ed.

Making Space MARCH 29

Mark 9:36-37 James Lamse '58

Calvin professor; Grand Rapids, Michigan

It's the end of March, and I am literally ankle deep in paper again. As part of my early career pledge to make myself fully available to students, I leave my office door open during the day, and when a student enters, I push my work aside — most often onto the floor. A fair number of students have dropped in over the course of the semester, and my office shows it. It's a mess.

Recently, however, I have observed a disturbing change in my office protocol. As this semester has progressed and the workload has increased to the point that my hands are starting to shake, I seem to be hedging on my accessibility policy. The door still stands open, and I still greet each entering student with a smile and the ready "Guten Tag! Wie geht's?" but something is different. What is it? It's my book bag. The student misses the usual welcoming chair because my book bag occupies it. The hunkered-down bag communicates this message: "You are welcome as long as you can take care of your business standing up."

Catching myself in this flagrant betrayal of my career-long commitment, I feel a sense of shame, and I vow to change my behavior. But dealing with my deception by emptying the book bag and dropping it onto the floor the first thing in the morning will only partially solve my problem. Behind the failure to respond eagerly to the "least of these," I sense a more serious issue — the busyness that diminishes my welcome of God when *he* comes calling to tend to *my* needs.

And so I recognize along about this time of year again that I am running low and that the location of my book bag is a new barometer of sorts, not just of my commitment to the concerns of my students but more seriously also of my openness to the sorely needed curative visits of the great Teacher, who also had his moments but knew better than I what to do about them.

What is your book bag saying these days?

The Rest of the Story

Jack Veltkamp '66
Dentist; Lynden, Washington

John 21:25

> *Jesus did many other things as well. If every one of them were written down, I suppose that even the whole world would not have room for the books that would be written.* (John 21:25)

Wait a minute! What kind of speculation is John engaging in here? Using average-size hardcovers (assume that John was not thinking of books on disks) and laying them side to side and end to end, to cover the entire surface of the planet we would need approximately 101 quadrillion books.

This is obviously a case of literary hyperbole, perhaps a little poetic license, is it not? To encrypt on conventional pages all that is humanly observable and recordable about Jesus' thirty-three years on earth would mean at least 100 million books for every second of his life. No man's life could possibly be that full.

Or could it? What if he was the God-man, the infinite I AM, the Alpha and Omega? His description alone could well fill the aforementioned volumes to overflowing, and still we would come up short in painting a word picture of the glory "of the only Begotten."

But he did not ask us to write quadrillions of books about him. He knows our limitations, our narrow and clouded vision that prevents us from seeing him face to face. But the one book he has given is not only sufficient enough to satisfy our human curiosity but also compelling enough in its story of love and grace that we, with all the saints, can eagerly and longingly look forward to what Paul Harvey would call "the rest of the story."

The numbers John suggests are unfathomable and mind-boggling, but it is only *our* minds that are boggled. Jesus understands the numbers. Just as he counts every hair on our heads, every grain of sand on the seashore, and every star in the sky, he knows "the rest of the story." And as we give ear to what he is saying and pay heed to what he has said, he promises to fill us in.

The Many Shapes of Jesus

Galatians 2:20

Epke Vander Berg '64
Missionary; Grand Rapids, Michigan

I have been crucified with Christ and I no longer live, but Christ lives in me. The life I live in the body, I live by faith in the Son of God, who loved me and gave himself for me. (Gal. 2:20)

I've attended hundreds of Bible studies around the world, but this time it was in Dhahran, Saudi Arabia. A young man stood to speak, as is customary, and talked about his love for Jesus. One couldn't help being moved by his testimony. The poignancy and sincerity were obvious to anyone in the room. As he finished, he said that he wished all of us could meet the Jesus he had met and that all of us would have the same experience he had had. In a moment his loving testimonial had become a sermon of guidelines for anyone seeking Jesus.

I put my thoughts on hold and returned to the apartment where I was living during my summer pastorate. Perhaps the air-conditioning would help me to think through the upsetting thoughts that weltered in my mind. You see, the young man's experience of meeting Jesus wasn't like mine. Why, I wondered, do people seem to experience Jesus differently? Why is it that the Jesus that meets one person is different from the Jesus others experience? I felt like asking, "Would the real Jesus please stand up?"

My mind did not rest all night. I had cracked the door for spiritual chaos to enter, and I could feel it trying to push itself in all the way. Many hours later I was surprised by an analogy which quieted my troubled spirit.

From my meager reading in medicine, I had learned that white blood cells can take the shape of invading bacteria, match themselves with the bacteria, and destroy them. Does Jesus work something like this? Perhaps. Think about it for a moment. As bacteria invade the body and make it sick, sin comes into the human soul through some moral weakness in it. Sin has its own particular manifestation in me; it is my sin, personal and unique. When Jesus enters to heal me of my sin, he comes in the shape that fits my sin, my personal failing before God, and I experience his healing power.

That's it, I thought! That's it! Not only did Jesus become human like all of us; he also takes the shape of each of us individually to remove the personal sin with which each of us is burdened — if we call upon him for health and life. And so we all experience Jesus differently. Personalized salvation — it's a good thing, I decided.

91

Hope

Ronald M. Hofman '76
Pediatrician; Grand Rapids, Michigan

Romans 5:1-5

And we rejoice in the hope of the glory of God. Not only so, but we also rejoice in our sufferings, because we know that suffering produces perseverance; perseverance, character; and character, hope. (Rom. 5:2-4)

Ronnie was twelve years old when I met him. Born with epidermolysis bullosa dystrophica, a skin condition causing severe blistering and painful scarring, he was wheelchair bound and barely able to swallow. When he was still an infant, his fingers and toes had disintegrated from the horrific scarring of his disease. The condition was so disfiguring that his emotionally spent father disappeared when Ronnie was just a few days old. His committed mother dressed his wounds and trickled food down his constricted esophagus, sustaining him until he succumbed to the disease at age twenty. Ronnie experienced few of life's pleasures. Even his Make a Wish trip to Detroit to see the Tigers play in person was spoiled by a rainout. Ronnie personified suffering.

Every living creature comes to know suffering in some measure. Some experiences of suffering are common to many people; some, to almost all — an infant's cry over separation from mother, the finger pinched in a door, a rejection at school. Some experiences of suffering are more individualized and more devastating — a diagnosis of pancreatic cancer, entrapment in a holocaust, loss of a child, depression so deep there seems to be no hope.

When we are faced with life's burdens, it is difficult for us to believe Paul when he suggests that we rejoice in our sufferings. But the annals of history bear witness to countless examples that suffering does produce perseverance, character, and hope. In faith, individuals and communities have endured through great peril and pain: Sir Thomas More stood in defiance of Henry VIII; nineteen-year-old Joan of Arc heroically burned at the stake, committed to the hope that will not disappoint. And Ronnie, a young man of deep faith, even as he lay dying, exhorted Detroit Tiger Cecil Fielder to hit a home run.

May each of us in our suffering, great or small, be able to call upon the hope that is ours through the love outpoured by Christ, who suffered immeasurably.

The Economy of Forgiveness

Luke 23:32-38   Roberta Green Ahmanson '72
Foundation executive; Irvine, California

Father, forgive them, for they do not know what they are doing.

(Luke 23:34)

In Matthew 6:14-15 Jesus talks about forgiveness: "For if you forgive others when they sin against you, your heavenly Father will also forgive you. But if you do not forgive others their sins, your Father will not forgive your sins" (NIVI). Hard words of Jesus. Hard words for me, at least. Forgiving is one of the struggles of my life. Grudges come naturally to me. Forgiving is work. But unless we do it, we die.

My husband says that our age has forgotten what Jesus really did for us. Jesus did not accept or tolerate us; he forgave us. Forgiveness implies that a wrong must be righted; it implies a moral law. Of course, we know what that law is. It is stated in the Ten Commandments. It is written in creation. When a law is broken, it must be made right. We wrong and are wronged, so we must both repent and forgive. When we ask for forgiveness, we are set free — if the other person makes the tough decision to forgive us.

Some time ago one of the prayer counselors in my church gave me a tape on forgiveness by Episcopal Bishop David Schofield. One point Bishop Schofield makes that was new to me is that other people suffer when we don't forgive them. Not being forgiven can cause physical pain. Why? Because the weight of what they have done is still on them. They carry it around. The same is true when they don't forgive us. Then we carry the weight of the grudge on our backs. Bishop Schofield also makes another useful point: When we forgive, it isn't our forgiveness we are giving; it is God's forgiveness flowing through us.

The Christian psychologist Jay Adams has written that God's pattern is always to ask us to put off the old and put on the new. Otherwise we are houses swept clean, in danger of new demons coming in to fill the void. So, as we clean out our grudges through forgiveness, we should also fill the open space left in us by the putting on of love.

Our sin entails a great debt, a burden too great for us to bear, too heavy to be lifted by our efforts alone. But when a debt is forgiven, it doesn't have to be paid. Because our debt is forgiven, we don't have to pay, and so we can well afford to forgive others, we want to forgive others out of gratitude for our own forgiveness, and we must forgive others because Jesus told us to and showed us how. Our life depends on forgiveness — today and forever.

Marlin Van Elderen† '66   John 9
Publications editor; Grand Lancy, Switzerland

> *A second time they summoned the man who had been blind. "Give glory to God," they said. "We know this man is a sinner." He replied, "Whether he is a sinner or not, I don't know. One thing I do know. I was blind but now I see!"*
> (John 9:24-25)

If the story of Jesus healing the man born blind had stopped at verse 24 of John 9, the religious leaders would have got it right. The disability which had consigned this man to a life of begging, Jesus told his disciples, was a channel for revealing the work of God (John 9:3-4). What more fitting response to such a miracle than giving glory to God?

But the story does go on. And it shows that the religious leaders, anxious about Jesus' growing popularity, are less interested in praise and thanksgiving than in ensuring that any positive reaction to what has happened does not lead to anything they cannot control. Having failed to discredit the healing itself (John 9:18-21), they try hard to salvage their certainties about how and through whom God works (John 9:24-34). "We know this Jesus is a sinner," they insist. "We do not know where he comes from. As for us, *we* are disciples of Moses." When the former beggar dares to point out the holes in their argument, they roll out their ultimate weapon — religious authority: "You were steeped in sin at birth; how dare you lecture us!" (John 9:34). They excommunicate him.

Later, having seen Jesus and recognized the light of the world, the healed man says to him, "'Lord, I believe.' And he worshiped him" (John 9:38). If we make this simple and eloquent confession our own, let us do so in the awareness of Jesus' warning about the dangers that often accompany strong faith: the confidence that we know just how God works, the readiness to label as sinners those who disagree, the urge to prop up our own faith by cataloguing the faults of others, the habit of tailoring our theology of grace to fit the dimensions of our understanding, the impulse to exclude people who think differently. Indeed, followers of Jesus are perhaps more tempted than most to say, "What? Are *we* blind too?" Jesus' response brings us up short: "If you were blind, you would not be guilty of sin; but now that you claim you can see, your guilt remains" (John 9:40-41).

The Blessings of Pain

Job 6:10

Roger S. Greenway '55
Calvin Seminary professor; Rockford, Michigan

Then I would still have this consolation — my joy in unrelenting pain — that I had not denied the words of the Holy One. (Job 6:10)

We all want to avoid pain. Yet, by God's grace, pain can be a blessing. Pain reminds us that our bodies are gifts from God, marvelous in so many ways yet frail and susceptible to injury, disease, and eventually deterioration and death. Pain reminds us that in the last analysis our bodies are dust.

Crippling pain embarrasses us when it makes us walk slowly, limp, and climb stairs with difficulty. But these physical challenges keep us humble, and that is good. Jesus said that unless we become like little children (who stumble easily and often must be carried), we cannot enter the kingdom of God (Mark 10:15).

Pain teaches us to be compassionate toward others. It makes us sensitive to pain-causing situations like having to stand for a long time and physical barriers like stairways, long hallways, slippery sidewalks, and pushy people.

Pain reminds us that we live in a fallen world. The human race rebelled against God and now suffers the consequences (Gen. 3:16). Pain identifies us with God's whole creation, which groans along with us "as in the pains of childbirth right up to the present time" (Rom. 8:22).

Pain reminds us of the suffering of Jesus Christ, who suffered beyond measure that we might be forgiven of all our sins. Because of Christ we can bear our pain in the hope of the resurrection and of pain-free bodies someday (Rev. 21:4).

The Old Testament saint Job suffered unrelenting pain, but he clung to the promises of God and discovered joy even in pain. By God's grace we, too, can find blessings in pain.

The Broken-hearted Sacrifice

Ann Primus Berends '85 Psalm 51:16-17
Editor; Silver Spring, Maryland

If the most light we'd ever seen was the pale light of a moony night, it would seem like light enough. What was really only dimly illumined would seem to be perfectly illumined. Then, if we would wake one day to the brightness of morning sun, the world we had seen the night before by the light of the moon would, by contrast, seem smudged and blurry. *"This is light! Now we can really see!"* we would exclaim as the morning sun revealed a radiant world.

So it is when we see God. As John Calvin reminds us with his sunlight analogy, "Man is never sufficiently touched and affected by the awareness of his lowly state until he has compared himself with God's majesty" (*Institutes of the Christian Religion* I.i.2). It is this awareness of our lowly estate over against the majesty of God that kindles the sacrifice of the broken heart.

If we live with an awareness of God's glory, experiencing God's presence throughout each day, our hearts will break from sin sorrow. Our spirits will break in the effort of sin control. And we will finally turn to sacrifice our all in the fire of God's irresistible grace.

In the Old Testament, sacrifice of animals was an exercise of humility before God's glory, a daily practice of commitment to and communion with God. Whether God accepted a sacrifice or not depended upon the heart of the person bringing the sacrifice, for there beat the giver's true self. And God was looking for broken hearts. As the psalmist puts it, the only true and acceptable sacrifices to God are broken spirits and contrite hearts: "The sacrifices of God are a broken spirit; a broken and contrite heart, O God, you will not despise" (Ps. 51:17).

Since Jesus' supreme sacrifice on Calvary, the people of God need no longer bring sacrifices of sheep and goats. In the sacrifice of Jesus on Calvary the sacred blood of atonement was shed once and for all. But God still asks for sacrifices of the heart, the broken heart. Broken-hearted sacrifice is whole-hearted surrender to God. It is the humble response of the people of God to the supreme sacrifice of Jesus. When we fully grasp our darkness and our lowly estate in comparison to God's brilliance and majesty, we will humbly offer our contrite spirits up to God.

Coming to surrender isn't easy. But when we break, God is there. And when we surrender, God is there. In God's presence, brokenness sacrificed is brokenness healed, and we are transformed.

At the Cross

1 Corinthians 1:18

Bryan Dik '98

Graduate student; Minneapolis, Minnesota

My first vivid realization of God's grace packaged in the death of his Son occurred when I was an eighth grader during a Maundy Thursday Tenebrae service with dark, minor-keyed sacred songs and progressive extinguishing of candles. During this service the faith I professed became clearer, and I began to understand just who I am.

I remember staring up at the cross in front of the sanctuary, picturing the events on the day of Christ's execution. I saw the thorns embedded deep into his skull, blood cascading down his face, his back flailed open like a plowed field, flaps of skin hanging down, muscle exposed to a rough-cut cross with splinters piercing his flesh. I saw old women, young men, even children laughing at him, taunting and cursing, spitting in his face. Shaken by the thought of it, my head shamefully bowed, my mind's eye focused on Jesus' eyes, swollen with the tears of an overwhelmingly deep, lonely, anguished sadness and painfully searching for friends he knew had abandoned him, I saw Jesus as Savior for the first time. At that moment I realized he was doing this because of me, because of the daily self-centered life that I live, because of sin that I so often find myself mindlessly involved in. I was overcome by a deep sense of sorrow and remorse, as though a tremendous burden was forcing my legs to quiver, then buckle. And buckle they did, at least in a figurative sense, when my spirit stirred with a bone-shaking realization: This man had ten-inch iron spikes driven through his wrists and ankles and into that raw timber in place of me. I deserve death; he accepted death to ensure that I could have life — an unfathomable sacrifice, the perfect, sinless Son of God assuming my sin and taking on my sentence. Perhaps no one could tell as we silently filed out of that service, but I was not the same person that walked in.

It is easy to take the familiar symbol of the cross for granted. I am in the right place, however, when, with intention, I slow down to reflect on that cross, a humble reminder of the brutal, grace-filled death that led to the resurrection and saved this sinner.

Foot Washing

Lisa J. Baar Hoogeboom '89   John 13:1-17
Missionary; Grandville, Michigan

It takes only one stroll through the streets of Istanbul to see the wisdom of the Turkish custom of slipping off one's shoes at an entrance door. The dust, the coal soot, and the dung from horses that pull the gypsy wagons meld together on the pavement under the tramping of hundreds of well-polished shoes, all of which will ultimately be left at someone's door to keep from soiling the colorful carpets inside.

During one week each year the dirt underfoot gains an additional layer as preparations are made for the Islamic sacrifice holiday. Pedestrians and cars alike must then share the limited space with thousands of sheep brought in from the countryside for the sacrifices. The herds are moved from a grassy patch here to an empty lot there until all have been sold off, but not before each one has left a telltale trail behind.

During the yearly Passover celebration in Jesus' time, the streets of Jerusalem must have been like the streets of modern Istanbul. Thousands of pilgrims, sandal clad and traveling with donkeys, poured into the city from other parts of the country and the world. Undoubtedly the people, sheep, and donkeys jostled for space as they moved through crowded streets to markets or to the temple for final sacrifice preparations.

When Jesus bent down and washed his disciples' feet there in Jerusalem during his final Passover week, the putrid odor of animal dung and urine must have permeated the room. He had taken on a servant's least favorite task when he carried the basin of water and the towel around the room that evening. In a world where power and status meant everything, he became a low-level servant — and he called for his disciples to follow his example.

In this one act Jesus embodied his entire life and mission. Coming to earth as sinew, blood, and bone and then enduring the estrangement from his Father while he was being tortured on a cross was the ultimate act of servanthood. Praise God that through the flow of blood and water Jesus has washed our own dirty, dung-stained feet.

The God Who Suffers

David S. Koetje '85
Calvin professor; Grand Rapids, Michigan

Because of the LORD's great love we are not consumed. . . . great is your faithful-
ness. (Lam. 3:22-23)

Consider this quandary: If our almighty Father truly cares for us, why do we suffer? Christian friends of ours lost a mother, infant son, and father within a span of two short years. Another close friend and I lost our jobs while confronting injustices at our former institution. We now endure the pain of separation. The Calvin community also is acquainted with grief. We suffer serious medical maladies, loved ones die, children go astray, relationships strain and sometimes sever. Where is God in all this?

The prophet Jeremiah lived through the siege, slaughter, and enslavement of Jerusalem at the hand of the Babylonians. The book of Lamentations records his anguished cries as he sat alone among the desolate ruins. They are the cries of battered men left to die (Lam. 3:12), of women forced to eat the bodies of their own dead children (Lam. 2:20), of the faithful whose prayers went unanswered (Lam. 3:8). Few of us can fathom such depths of horror. Even God laments over the harsh punishment of his rebellious children (Lam. 2:11).

In this scene of utter desolation, Jeremiah's testimony is most striking: "Yet this I call to mind and therefore I have hope: Because of the LORD's great love we are not consumed, for his compassions never fail. They are new every morning; great is your faithfulness" (Lam. 3:22-23). How can Jeremiah say this? Can we, too, say it?

There is another Bible passage that portrays a man agonizing alone against the powers of darkness. He also wept over Jerusalem's sins and her refusal to repent. In Gethsemane with the sorrows of humanity weighing down until his sweat became "like drops of blood falling to the ground" (Luke 22:44), Jesus lamented for his fallen creatures. But this time *he* incurred our guilt. For our sins *he* clung to the cross and died. It wasn't the nails that held him there; it was his great love and unfailing compassion. Therein lies Jeremiah's and our hope. When we suffer, we suffer not as the hopeless; God himself assumes our grief. By Jesus' resurrection he offers victory over sin, suffering, and death. Claim his great love and faithfulness as your own.

It's Your Move

Shirley Vogelzang Hoogstra '78   John 21:1-19
Calvin administrator; Grand Rapids, Michigan

"After what he did? I can never trust him again." "I thought she was my friend. I needed her, and she never came." "I feel betrayed." "I didn't deserve that treatment." Words of pain, disappointment, and disillusionment. Chasms so wide they are unbridgeable. Years go by with only angry words spoken, words with an edge. Maybe no words at all. Love withheld for a reason.

Not so with Jesus.

In the story of the great catch of fish, Jesus appears to his disciples. He has a purpose: He is going to reinstate the wrongdoer. He is modeling reconciliation for these future leaders. Peter, by rights, should have been written off. He had abandoned Jesus at a critical moment. When the test came, he had failed in a colossal way.

But who should take the first step in the reconciliation dance? Who takes the lead? According to the human way of thinking, the wrongdoer should approach the victim. It's the wrongdoer's responsibility. What is surprising to the disciples is that Jesus makes the first move. The rejected leads the rejecter. Jesus never assumes the role of a victim waiting for an apology. After all, Peter can't really hurt him because Jesus remains at all times beloved by God, his Father. Jesus knows that Peter thinks he, Jesus, has the upper hand, that to Peter, the sinner, Jesus seems unapproachable now. So Jesus signals, by the gift of fish to a fisherman, that he wants to continue a relationship with Peter. Jesus knows Peter's needs. Jesus loves Peter in spite of all his imperfections, great as they are. He offers a perfect love that casts out Peter's fear of being rejected, even after Peter has rejected his friend.

What is Peter's response? Freedom — freedom to step out of the boat, freedom to rush toward the Master. The dam of doubt, fear, guilt, and sorrow has been broken. The assurance of feeling Jesus' love again is palpable: Jesus keeps Peter buoyant as he walks on water, and Jesus gives Peter breakfast — fish — for a fisherman from the greatest Fisherman. Having met Peter's physical needs, the Master can begin on the spiritual issues.

In this breakfast of reconciliation with Peter, Jesus points the way for us by making the first move.

Resurrection Joy

Luke 24:5-6

Margaret Venema De Boer '67
Homemaker; Calgary, Alberta

My sister once received a small plant from a friend and placed it on a shelf in her office at church. Unfortunately, because it didn't receive the attention and nurture it required, the plant soon looked like it needed emergency treatment — fast. The leaves, drooping and yellowing, cried out for help, and the soil cracked out a dusty plea for moisture and food. Feeling pangs of guilt, Mary took the measures necessary to restore abundance of life to her neglected token of friendship. After a time of intensive care, the beauty of the plant returned, and it began to flourish. Mary gave it a name to celebrate its rebirth: Phoenix, after the beautiful, lone bird in Egyptian mythology which lived in the Arabian desert for five hundred years and then consumed itself in fire, rising renewed from the ashes to start another long life. It's a symbol of rebirth, and its name is therefore fitting for Mary's little plant.

Contemplate the phoenix for a moment in the context of resurrection. Like the phoenix, Christians, too, will rise from death into immortality, eternal life. Already in this life we experience the death of self, and from the ashes of the old self we are reborn with a new nature. When we, like Mary's neglected plant, are drooping toward despair and death, God rains his grace upon us, waters our roots, and revives us again.

Remember at this season to be of good cheer, for Christ has risen, and in him we also can rise renewed from whatever conditions we are in at this moment. He is the one and only, who can raise us up in beauty from the ashes of death (Isa. 61:3) and restore the damage done by the locusts of sin (Joel 2:25). His unspeakable power has already brought about the cataclysmic change for us from mortality to immortality so that we may live in life eternal, where he is . . . forever. Alleluia! This is rich hope for our parched spirits and famished souls.

Take these thoughts with you into your spring garden as you admire the greenery erupting from the warming spring soil. Let each new shoot remind you of changes that the resurrected Christ of Easter can and will continue to bring about in you. Rise and rejoice!

101

The Tree Is Dry

Robin Tigchelaar Saylor '93

College administrator; Wenham, Massachusetts

Luke 23:28, 31

Daughters of Jerusalem, do not weep for me; weep for yourselves and for your children. . . . For if people do these things when the tree is green, what will happen when it is dry? (Luke 23:28, 31, NIVI)

When the tree was green, they put thorns into our Savior's head; they whipped him until his back was raw; they taunted and jeered at him; they nailed him to a cross; they divided his clothes; they treated him like a common criminal. How could they do all this to our Savior?

Today the tree is dry. As we scoff at those who did this to the Savior, we cannot hide from the fact that daily we join those soldiers in the nailing of Christ to the cross. As we fail to acknowledge his lordship in our lives, as we ignore injustice in the world around us, as we hold on to anger and hurt from the past, as we treat others with disdain, dislike, indifference, or disregard, as we exalt ourselves and take pride in our self-reliance, we must acknowledge that we are the "they" of the crucifixion story.

Luke records that, as our Lord hung on the cross, Jesus once again cried out to his Father, this time saying, "Father, forgive them, for they do not know what they are doing" (Luke 23:34). Maybe, amid the sounds of the nailing, the taunts, the jeers, and the laughter, nobody heard him, but his cry to the Father resounds down through the generations. As we listen closely to the Easter story, it is there: "Father, forgive them." As we listen closely throughout history, it is there: "Father, forgive them." As we listen closely today, it is there: "Father, forgive them." The message of the cross is clear: We are forgiven.

As we wait for Easter morning, let us not forget that we are the "they" of the crucifixion, but, if we listen closely, there is hope, for the cry can still be heard: "Father, forgive them, for they do not know what they are doing."

Seeing Is Believing

John 20:1-9

Rich Westmaas '54
Psychologist; Cadillac, Michigan

He saw and believed. (John 20:8)

Picture the scene. Two disillusioned, frantically excited disciples arrive out of breath. Racing to the tomb, they have come to check out the unbelievable news that the body is missing. Beating Peter to the tomb, John stops and looks inside. He sees strips of linen burial cloth, but no Jesus. Then Peter arrives and goes right inside. John follows.

Now they note the contents of the "empty" tomb in greater detail — not only the strips of linen but also the burial cloth used to wrap Jesus' head, folded and placed separately.

Processing these details is not instantaneous. John and Peter are operating without the realization that resurrection was always part of God's plan. A huge reconfiguration of meaning and reality is taking place in their heads. Perhaps it is something about the way the head cloth is folded up separately that triggers new realizations: Folded so deliberately, it would not be the work of grave robbers. Who else might have done it?

Then for John the truth hits: Jesus is alive!

John's coming to faith in the risen Lord is based on circumstantial evidence. He believes when he realizes he is seeing something that only Jesus could have done.

That is how it is with me, too. And with you? Isn't it with a catch in our breath that we, too, come to faith as we see certain things happen in our own lives or in the lives of those we care about, the kind of things that only Jesus can do?

Yes, he is here among us, too. May he keep our eyes open to his work around us and our hearts attuned to his presence.

Mary's Lament

Christina Bratt '98   John 19:25-27
Teacher; Grand Rapids, Michigan

How can a mother be where I am? I look upon the dying man — my Son — as his whole being writhes in a pain I cannot fathom. My Son. Here, at the moment of your death, my own heart collapses with grief, and my mouth becomes a source of wailing. My Son. Can my hands free you? These hands so often comforted and held you, my Son. What good are they now?

How can a woman — a virgin with a second heartbeat and a swelling belly — give birth to that which she does not understand? Young and bewildered, I bore you as God had willed. Every moment your small soul lived in me was a miracle. You are not of my flesh, and yet, my Jesus, you were half of me or more. The night I bore you was the night of our separation and the beginning of the world's race for you. When I looked on you that first night — your tiny fingers spreading, then clenched, then spreading — I wondered at the hugeness of you. My God, infinity in an Infant! How long could this earth hold you? Living with your teaching gaze, your healing hands, your guiding feet, I know that just as I have been forever changed, this earth will be new after your coming. There is no one who will be your equal again. I know this as a mother knows her child and as a creature recognizes her creator.

Now this life rejects you, my Child. I cannot help you here. Instead, I must watch you become the victim of generations of hate. My weeping is from a place deeper than my heart. How strange that you should be the one to comfort me, to give me a new son in these deepest moments of despair. My Lord and my God, what have we done to you? My dear God, you give up so much love even as your tendons snap and your blood pours out at the feet of your killers. Your arms are stretched wide — fingers limp — for all who are here. A mother's shoulders could not bear this load even for her own children.

Spread your arms wide, Lord. We know not what to do. I know not what to do. I await your return. Come quickly, my Lord Jesus.

Farewell to Innocence

Mark 4:35-41

Caspar Geisterfer '81
Missionary; Haiti

Jesus Christ extends an invitation to each of us to follow him. In the same way that Jesus invited the disciples to follow him when he said, "Let us go over to the other side" (Mark 4:35), Jesus invites us to follow into unknown places. This invitation comes to us while we are immersed in the womb-like coziness of our daily lives. Jesus invites us to go on a voyage with him into the unknown, to say farewell to the innocence of what we know.

As the disciples found out, we will see that traveling with Jesus on this voyage is more like a roller-coaster ride than like a stroll in the park. No sooner do we climb into the boat and set sail, than the storms roll in and hit us with all their fury. We fear for our lives. We wonder how wise we were to accept the invitation. We are paralyzed with fear, and this fear drives us to the depths of despair.

But something amazing is about to happen. As fear holds us in its grip, we see Jesus standing there beside us. We watch in awe as he causes the storm to subside. Our fears subside even as the sea becomes calm. We stand in awe as did the disciples when they saw Jesus alive after his crucifixion. We know that we are at the beginning of a fantastic journey with Jesus.

Seeing the Cross

Edgar Boevé '53   Matthew 27:45-46
Calvin professor emeritus; Jupiter, Florida

As an artist concerned with expressing the essential tenets of the Christian faith, I was mystified that early Christians rarely showed the crucifixion of Christ. A story so central to the biblical narrative, and in later times one of the most depicted images in the whole history of Christian art, is all but missing from the subjects represented in the early centuries of Christian iconography. It is not until the fifth century and then rarely until the seventh century that the crucifixion appears. Some art historians think that suffering by a divine Savior was too gruesome and shocking for the early church to contemplate. Perhaps the early church tended to de-emphasize Christ's suffering and death out of a denial of human suffering. However, so doing would also deny Christ's Incarnation, a dogma which early theologians asserted in strong terms. Later, the Middle Ages and Renaissance produced a wealth of works depicting the crucifixion, works which survive in great numbers even today in churches and art museums. Thus, we benefit in our time from a long and rich artistic tradition that celebrates the Passion and death of Jesus Christ.

The sacrament of the Last Supper, Communion, also reminds us of Christ's Passion and death. Through words and the elements we are reminded that Christ so loved us that he gave his body for us on the cross, that his sacrifice annulled any need for a future sacrifice and led to our redemption.

In the season of Lent we are called to remember and believe that Christ suffered on the cross, died for us, and conquered death forever in his resurrection. We who believe that Christ's sacrifice was "once and for all time" look to a cross where the body of our Lord no longer needs to hang. Christ's victory over death has banished the fear of death, and, glorying in the resurrection, we can anticipate the return of Jesus at the end of time.

May we today call to remembrance Christ in the flesh — his suffering, his death, and his resurrection — by which we are all made one with him.

God's Lilies

Luke 12:27-31

Terry Beversluis Glass '67
Librarian/teacher; Grand Rapids, Michigan

"Consider how the lilies grow" (Luke 12:27), says Jesus, speaking of the values of his kingdom. Some versions of the Sermon on the Mount use "wildflowers" instead of lilies, and we could also think of weeds growing along the road. The lilies I consider are ditch lilies, long, graceful, reddish-orange, one-day blooms, always there on the June drive home. I also love the yellow daylilies that bloom in my birthday week and the white lilies of the Annunciation paintings. The point is that all Solomon's splendor could not match God's dress for the lily. If God created lilies to be completely gorgeous though they don't toil or spin or worry, surely we as his imagebearers and his redeemed can expect to be well clothed by our Father in heaven.

I have enjoyed using "consider the lilies of the field" as a phrase reminding me to avoid fuss on clothes or hair. I believe the beauty any of us has is from God, the essence of the person seen with your eyes shut. For me, beauty is as beauty does. I think that's how God sees it. God looks on the heart. It's character, not appearances, that he sees. We, the creation of God, naked and wailing as we are born, were created in beauty, in the image of our Creator. After the sin of the fall, through Christ we are restored to his beauty. The lily bespeaks grace, an inner beauty freely bestowed.

But being clothed like the lily is about more than appearance and character. It's also about God's providence, his care, which presumes, assumes, and insists that in all our toiling and spinning, we do not have to worry. If we do, we give evidence of "little faith."

We may know ourselves to be wild and weedy rather than lily-gorgeous, but in our new clothes of Christ's atonement and resurrection, before God we are pure as the lilies of Easter. Living in the love of God, let us look for the beauty of God and the providence of God in each of his children, and our daily lives will become a joyful garden adventure of exploring the varieties of God's lilies.

Mealtime Grace

Nancy Vanderzyden Boerman '55   Luke 24:13-35
Teacher; South Holland, Illinois

For many years one of my favorite post-resurrection stories has been the one found in Luke 24. I've loved the homey details, the picture of two followers moving from dejection to exhilaration, and the special meaning it has given to me about the consecration of mealtimes.

In fact, a mentor friend of mine thinks that all churches should use this section of the Bible as the basis for their Easter-Sunday-evening sermon. She is also the one who helped me to see that the participants were probably Mr. Cleopas and Mrs. Cleopas.

If Mrs. Cleopas was the one welcoming the stranger, she was also the one who had prepared the food, including the bread, which Joel Nederhood calls "Holy Bread," in his book *This Splendid Journey*. In later years could this woman ever look at the homely shape of ordinary bread and plain food in the old way again?

But what really speaks to me is the fact that the two followers walking along the road were given a course in systematic theology, or maybe apologetics, all the way from Moses through the prophets. It was a personal, perfectly taught course. The best! And yet it all became real, clear, meaningful because of the stranger's presence. When they recognized who he is, their course work was fully integrated in what Eugene Peterson calls "the fusion of intimacy with transcendence."

Why do we have the custom of "gracing" our food and reading part of the Scripture at mealtimes? Because we believe that the risen Christ is present with us. We celebrate his resurrection every Sunday; we celebrate his presence at every meal. He enriches our food and enriches our minds as we look into his Word.

From time to time our family uses a song as a mealtime opening prayer. One of our special favorites is the one sung to the tune of the Tallis Canon. May it remind us of the real presence of the risen Christ at every gathering around the table:

Be present at this table, Lord.
Be here and everywhere adored.
These mercies bless and grant that we
May feast in paradise with thee.

Sacramental Vision

Mark 10:46-52; Psalm 135:15-18 Art Tuls, Jr. '73
Teacher; Grand Haven, Michigan

I may never see glory again the way I saw it that morning. I had decided on the lake road, a slower route that would give me more time to think about devotions for my first-hour class. A light rain had frozen on a blueberry field alongside the road, the branches now cranberry red in the mid-November sunrise. Somehow those ice-coated bushes caught just the right angle of the rising brightness, and that field lit up with the glory of God. Words are too weak to describe that icy light: maybe like sunlight shimmering on waves or a camera's flash in your eyes. Only for a couple seconds I saw it. Seconds later there was another field, just west of the road, but something had changed: no special effects there. Only dim-red bushes.

At Calvin I learned from Stan Wiersma about the "sacramental vision" of Gerard Manley Hopkins, and I remember how he used Hopkins's poem "The Windhover." Here the heroic strength of Christ flashes in the flight of a falcon. At Calvin years later I learned something else from Frederick Buechner. He spoke about "paying attention to your life," how artists and writers do that, and how Christians should, too. According to these two wise teachers, this kind of vision allows us to see God — his love, his wisdom, his majesty — in ways unexpected, even in the common or the mundane.

One blueberry field gleams with the glory of God and inspires praise. At the same time frozen bushes across the street are dull. Our own viewpoint and our own spiritual alertness make a big difference. Maybe God's presence can be seen and heard every day, anywhere, if only we have eyes to see, ears to hear.

I will never forget the glory I saw for a moment on the lake road. I also wonder how many other meaningful moments I have missed because I was not paying attention. Perhaps there are many things, many idols, that keep us from seeing or even from looking. But Christ opens the eyes of the blind. I pray he will open mine to see more flashes of glory.

Worldview

Edward A. Van Baak '45   Psalm 24:1
Retired missionary; Kentwood, Michigan

M any of us who enrolled in Calvin College in 1942 had a fairly well established world ("the earth is the Lord's") and life ("our lives are hid with Christ in God") view. But we, together with the faculty and administration, were confronted with an assault on our worldview as the chaos of World War II disrupted plans, decimated the dormitory population, and depleted classrooms. The problems of Europe and Asia challenged us on both shores and across both oceans. Suddenly our thought processes were internationalized.

The dissonance between our faith vision of a sovereign God and the savage war that raged in many countries was bridged by perceptive teachers. They taught us that the gospel had been international from the beginning, that ethnic ghettos were not in the divine order. God's people had been called from Sumerian roots, had crossed mighty rivers and daunting deserts to reach the land of the Arameans, and had settled only briefly in Canaan before spending centuries in Egypt. And when these people of God finally did lay claim to Canaan as their home, they were always interspersed with the "Canaanites, Hittites, Amorites, Perizzites, Hivites, and Jebusites." Isolationism was never an option for God's people.

The more recent heritage of the Reformed faith and its worldview was also international, multiethnic, and multilingual. Augustine of North Africa critiqued the Roman Empire and centuries later was followed in doctrine and exceeded in zeal by John Calvin, a Frenchman living in Geneva (now Switzerland). Calvin's Latin writings were popularized in a German-language catechism, refined in the Netherlands, spread into the British Isles, translated into English, and later made the foundation of courses in American literature, Reformed doctrine, Greek language, and all the sciences taught at Calvin College in the United States of America.

God is concerned about all the nations and expects that we should be concerned as well. His people of former times spent centuries under the domination of Egypt, Babylon, Assyria, Tyre, and Persia. They were threatened by the culture of Greece and the military strength of Rome. Yet none of these caused God's people to be severed from his care. In fact, the oppressors contributed to the preservation of God's people. So, too, World War II expanded the vision of a generation of Christians to encompass the entire world. Truly, the earth is the Lord's.

Recognizing Jesus with Us

Luke 24:29

Joerg Ettemeyer '79
Pastor; Dortmund, Germany

Stay with us, for it is nearly evening; the day is almost over.

(Luke 24:29)

This verse and the narrative connected with it are applicable, I think, to much more than the miracle of Easter. What happened to the two disciples on their way back home after Christ's crucifixion has always touched my heart. It is a story that comforts me in my daily life because I myself often feel like the two disciples. I often walk my pathways as though, overwhelmed by the power of death and depression, I had forgotten all about Christ's resurrection. In such sad hours of my life I need someone who accompanies me on the road back to where I belong. Then I remind myself that Christ walks the road with me and listens to what I tell him. He shares my pathway . . . and yours. He shares our feelings.

As the three arrived at the village where the two disciples were headed, the disciples asked Jesus to stay with them. Maybe they didn't want to be alone in their discouragement. Maybe they were being naturally hospitable to the stranger. Maybe they wanted more time to talk with him. Whatever the reason for the invitation, Jesus, whom they hadn't as yet recognized, stayed with them and ate with them. And the disciples recognized him as their living Lord the moment he broke the bread, gave thanks, and handed the bread to them. They remembered the Lord's Supper in the upper room just a few days before, a sacrament meant always to remind his people of his death and resurrection.

In surprising ways Jesus also comes to us, and he reminds us of what we already know: that he had to die to overcome the power of sin and death forever. He comes to me in people who tell me of the Lord's power in their lives. Such people help me remember the grace of the Lord in my own life. And he comes to me in the broken bread of Communion, which also symbolizes that Christ shares with us. He shares his love, and he wants to share his victory over death with us. He wants to share everlasting life with us. In the same way, he wants us to share with others — by confessing our faith, by helping people in need, and by questioning the social, political, and economic structures that bind them.

Christ stays with us by sharing our darkest nights, by reminding us of the everlasting life which he made possible, and by sharing the bread of Communion. He asks us to follow in his footsteps.

111

Nature Preserve

Naomi Michael Lund '99   Genesis 1

Computer service agent; Rochester, Minnesota

The ecosystem preserve is my favorite spot at Calvin. As a student I used to go there for a breath of fresh air or to take a break from studies or just for a nice walk with a friend. During my high and low points at Calvin, this was an oasis of peace and joy. Today I remember one of the highs.

It was a beautiful sunny day in early spring, warm enough to go without jackets. My dad had come from Oregon for a visit, and so together we walked through the nature preserve. Around us we saw budding trees, chirping cardinals and sparrows, and pure white trilliums. At the first turn a baby snake slithered along the side of the path, one of the few snakes I know of that I actually enjoyed seeing. From the deck overlooking the smaller pond, we noticed a bright green frog below us, enjoying the sun. We laughed at the sight of chipmunks racing each other across a nearby log. On the other side of the bridge Dad spotted a tiny turtle in the middle of a puddle. Then we noticed a crowd (five people seems like a crowd in the nature preserve) gathered around the most wonderful creature I have ever seen in the preserve. Only an arm's length away was a giant snapping turtle as big around as the circle made by my arms. I was tempted to pet it, but the snapping part of his name deterred me. We watched his slow journey back to the pond. Somehow he made two feet look like a mile. He gracefully slid beneath the surface of the water and was gone.

I felt indescribable joy that day to see just a glimpse of God's wonderful creation and to know that he cares for even the flowers of the field (Matt. 6:28-30). It was easy to understand why he considered all he had made as good.

Take time today to notice the beauty around you, and thank your Creator for his awesome creation.

Earthkeeping Day

Genesis 2:15; Romans 8:18-21

Eugene Westra '60
Teacher; Holland, Michigan

D o you have a favorite place, where you feel warm, safe, completely comfortable, and at peace? My favorite place is a high bank of the Clam River in northern Michigan with long, tapered beech boughs shading me as I read a good book.

In the Bible we are told that our Lord God also has a favorite place in the wide creation. Within that cosmos he created, God so loved the world, the planet we now call Earth, that God sent a Savior to completely rescue it and cleanse it of all evil, hurt, and death that had sullied it since the fall of the first keepers of God's garden.

Today we celebrate the good news that God will not allow Earth to be totally destroyed by people. Instead, God is already at work cleansing his favorite place. God cleanses human hearts from evil, and God is in many ways cleansing the rest of his creation, too. The creation itself is an important focus of God's saving work in Jesus, the savior and keeper of our lives.

At the very beginning of the world, God appointed Adam and Eve, the man and the woman, to be caretakers of what he had created. God, the first keeper of the Earth, asked them to become joint keepers with him. We are often reminded of God as our keeper when we speak the Aaronic Blessing: "The LORD bless you and keep you . . ." (Num. 6:24). We are called to be, like God, keepers of all that we can reach or touch in God's good creation.

On this Earthkeeping Day we again renew our vows to keep the creation clean, healthy, and productive of the food needed for all of God's creatures so that creation will continue to give God the honor and glory it was originally intended to offer by its beauty, goodness, and peace forever.

Let us love what God loves. Let us help him restore his favorite place.

Songs in the Night

Marianne Zuiderveen Schutte '77   Job 35:10; Habakkuk 3:17-18;
Homemaker; McBain, Michigan   Psalm 77

Many of us have experienced cataclysmic events of loss: the death of a child or spouse, the diagnosis of cancer, betrayal by a friend, divorce. Our lives are shattered, and God seems very far away.

The Israelites experienced cataclysmic loss when they were exiled in Babylon. Psalm 137 tells us that they sat by the rivers and wept. The Babylonians had the audacity, in the face of the pain, to ask the exiles to sing songs of Zion. In bitter response, the Israelites hung up their harps. "How can we sing the songs of the LORD while in a foreign land?" they asked (Ps. 137:4).

Paul and Silas found themselves in the "foreign land" of prison. Yet, at midnight, that darkest hour of the soul's dark night, they sang hymns to God. And the place was transformed (Acts 16:25).

In one two-week span our family experienced a spate of ills. We were victimized by crime, and two of our children were injured. I was angry at God. Just as I was crying out my "Why?" to God, I hear a song based on Acts 16 on the radio. The song emphasized praising the Lord no matter what comes our way. I wept in humility for the gift of God's assurance to hold me and all my tomorrows and to restore my voice in song to him.

Most of us will experience dark nights of the soul. We will feel exiled from God, imprisoned in hopelessness or fear or anger. The anguished cries of the psalmist give voice to the deepest of our emotions (see Psalms 13, 42, 63). What blessedness to know that our God hears and understands our every cry and that he promises to restore to us the joy of our salvation (Ps. 51:12).

When you are in the valley, tossing and turning in the blackness of the night, pray these words, as David did in the desert:

> On my bed I remember you;
> I think of you through the watches of the night.
> Because you are my help,
> I sing in the shadow of your wings. (Ps. 63:6-7)

Planning Ahead

Matthew 6:25

Jeremy Klop '94
City planner; Fort Collins, Colorado

Therefore I tell you, do not worry about your life. . . . (Matt. 6:25)

Most of us like to plan ahead. Planning ahead establishes goals to work toward, allows us to measure our progress and success, and gives us some small measure of control in a relatively unpredictable world. To control our future, the world says, we should have a financial plan for our retirement, the children's education, and that second home in the mountains. For success in the corporate world we need a business plan. We even develop plans for our cities, to enhance our communities and direct future development. With all of this emphasis on planning, it is difficult not to be anxious about tomorrow and what the future will bring.

Though society tells us our plans for the future will make us more secure, those plans often make us more anxious about successful outcomes and achievements than we would be without them. In the Sermon on the Mount, Jesus turns these worldly recommendations on their head, directing us to set aside our concern for how we are doing and focus our efforts on how God is doing: "Seek first his kingdom and his righteousness, and all these things will be given to you as well" (Matt. 6:33). This counsel to replace our plans for worldly achievement with God's plan for the kingdom is liberating: The worldly standards of success no longer apply.

God knows our needs better than we do ourselves, and he promises to provide for all of them if we seek first his kingdom and his righteousness. With these two goals in mind, we shift the focus of our plans. We begin to ask about God's plan for our lives and how we should be using our gifts to further his purposes. Our motivation to plan for the future changes from self-interest to service.

Think about your plans for the future. Are they building God's kingdom or your own? Planning ahead should not be an effort to control our future and protect our self-interest. Rather, with God's grace, it can be a faithful expression of our desire to seek the kingdom first, with the confidence that he will provide for all our needs as we work to this end.

Who Gave You This Authority?

Robert E. Vander Vennen '50   Matthew 21:23-27
Professor; Toronto, Ontario

On a certain day when he was about thirty years old, Jesus left home to start his public ministry. Jesus didn't go straight to Jerusalem to meet the high priest and suggest they draft a vision statement and plan the messianic ministry. What he did was walk to the Jordan River to be baptized by John the Baptist.

Matthew tells us in chapter 21 that late in Jesus' ministry the chief priests and the elders of the people confronted him by asking him, "By what authority are you doing these things? . . . And who gave you this authority?" (Matt. 21:23).

Jesus' response is utterly fascinating. He can't tell them what seminary he graduated from, what academic degrees he has earned. So he asks his accusers a simple question: "John's baptism — where did it come from? Was it from heaven, or from men?" (Matt. 21:25).

How could Jesus get away with seeming to avoid the question in this way? The Jewish leaders needed to answer Jesus' question because this was a standard form of Jewish argument. You could turn the accusing question back on the accusers with a question of your own, and they needed to answer your question before they could press you for your answer to theirs. The only catch was that your question needed to include elements of your own answer. The authority of Jesus was made publicly clear in his baptism by John the Baptist when the heavens opened, the Spirit descended, and the voice spoke from heaven. Jesus' response to the chief priests was a masterstroke.

As we reflect on this incident, though, we need to look beyond the high drama of it. The question of the chief priests, for all that, was very important. It is a question that is always with us. It's important in our culture, but it is also a personal question. We can't deal with authority in broad terms until we answer it in our own hearts. So the question comes to us right now, calling for our answer: By what authority did Jesus teach and act as he did, and do we accept that authority?

Finding Rest

Matthew 11:28-30

Joel Carpenter '74
Calvin provost; Grand Rapids, Michigan

Come to me, all you who are weary and burdened, and I will give you rest. Take my yoke upon you and learn from me, for I am gentle and humble in heart, and you will find rest for your souls. For my yoke is easy and my burden is light.
(Matt. 11:28-30)

I remember one tortured, sleepless night when I was a first-year graduate student. It seemed that all my obligations, worries, and failings were pressing down on me at once. I had a do-or-die examination facing me the following week. My research seemed to be headed into a dead end. My apartment mate and I were not getting along very well, I was far from home in a strange city, and I was distraught and sleepless over a recent romantic breakup. On every side, it seemed, my life was filled with anxiety, overwork, and frustration.

On every side, that is, except one. I had been attending a church in the neighborhood, and the pastor had asked me to teach a Bible class for the college-and-career group. At first I hesitated, but he insisted, so I reluctantly agreed. What better way to learn something, so the saying goes, than to teach it? So I became a Bible teacher, starting with the Gospel of Matthew, and as I read and taught, I found a remedy for my troubled heart and mind.

"Come to me, all you who are weary and burdened, and I will give you rest." The words I had been studying for Sunday's class came to me on that dark night, and they calmed my anxious spirit. In them I heard the Lord promise me that he would harness my restlessness and give me something satisfying to do for his kingdom. From then on he gave me the calm assurance of his love and care along the way. I could rest in his will, learn from his wisdom, and find the peace of soul to stay the course, wherever he was leading me. It is a promise I have not let myself forget. This passage hangs on my office wall as a constant reminder. I recommend it as a motto for your life, too.

This Is Victory

Rose Poortenga Van Reken '40   Philippians 1:21
Retired missionary; Lombard, Illinois

In his letter to the Philippians, Paul writes, "For to me, to live is Christ and to die is gain" (Phil. 1:21). But it strikes me that many of us have turned those words around: For us to live is gain and to die is Christ. There is so much living to be done and so much to gain — family and friends, position and recognition, money and possessions, health, pleasure, free time — all the things we think about and work toward and hope for. And Christ? We pray, "Please, Lord, when I die, receive me as your child into your heavenly kingdom. I really love you with my whole heart and want to spend eternity with you." Yes, it is easy to live by the motto "For me to live is gain and to die is Christ." And thus we can get our priorities mixed up.

In the light of heaven it is truly a foolish mistake, as a certain man found out. He was a man who had made an agreement with God that he could bring one full suitcase with him when he entered heaven. As he came to the gate of heaven, an angel asked him, "And what is that?"

"Oh," he replied, "the Lord is going to allow me to carry in one full suitcase when I enter heaven."

"Really?" the angel said. "And what did you bring?" The man opened the suitcase. It was packed full of gold bullion. The angel looked at the open suitcase and then back at the man. "You brought *pavement?*" he asked. Foolish indeed.

Let's pray today that we may give up our obsessions with suitcases full of gold bullion — garages full of big cars, closets full of furs and designer labels, bank vaults stuffed with stocks and bonds, tables laden with too much food, calendars burdened with good things to do — and instead sing this song:

> May the mind of Christ, my Savior, live in me from day to day,
> by his love and power controlling all I do and say.
> . . . .
> May the love of Jesus fill me as the waters fill the sea
> Him exalting, self abasing, this is victory.
>
> May we run the race before us, strong and brave to face the foe,
> Looking only unto Jesus as we onward go.*

It *Is* Enough

2 Corinthians 12:9

Harvey Kiekover '62
Pastor; Grand Rapids, Michigan

God says it, but even so, sometimes I wonder. Oh, not in those days when things are going well — when I'm up, when I feel affirmed and loved, useful and needed, when I have things in control. But those other times — when things aren't going well, when I don't feel appreciated or needed, when my prayers seem to go nowhere, when I am down in the dumps, when my life swallows me up in a welter of self-pity, well, then, yes, I do wonder. God says it, and I do want to believe it, but is God's grace really sufficient?

The words "My grace is sufficient for you" (2 Cor. 12:9) came to Paul when he was tormented by a messenger of Satan, a thorn in his flesh which he begged God to remove. But the invader didn't go away. The thorn wasn't neatly plucked out of his life as he so much wanted. It stayed, plaguing him with weakness.

"My grace is sufficient for you." The words seem vapid, empty, almost cruel when you first hear them, but they aren't. We need to hear them again: "My grace is sufficient for you, for my power is made perfect in weakness" (2 Cor. 12:9). In those moments of brokenness, of defeat, of weakness, of self-pity, grace is the answer. Grace? Yes. God's kindness, his gentleness, his favor, his love, and his presence.

Grace, God's undeserved favor, will be all that we need it to be because it is God's power, his strength, and his presence to hold us and keep us. But it has to be accepted to be that. I have to receive it in order for it to benefit me and be sufficient for me. James 4:6 says pointedly, "God opposes the proud, but gives grace to the humble." As long as we resist God and his grace, we won't experience him or his grace as enough. But when we yield to God's grace, when we embrace it and him, then it is sufficient — not only for Paul in his gigantic struggles but also for me in my struggles and for you in yours. I have seen it and experienced it.

Does grace make it easy? No, but I know this: It really *is* enough.

Praying to a Powerful, Loving God

Ron Vander Ark '66   2 Timothy 1:1-14
Technician; Phoenix, Arizona

> *For God did not give us a spirit of timidity, but a spirit of power, of love and of self-discipline.* (2 Tim. 1:7)

Did you remember to pray today? Did you hedge a little when you prayed, thinking that what you wanted was beyond God's ability to give? Did you forget that our God is a real God? Did you forget that our God is a powerful God? Our God created the heavens and the earth. Our God parted the Red Sea and the Jordan River. Our God made Daniel unappetizing and Jonah indigestible. Our God, as Jesus, healed whole communities and made demons obey him. Our God raised Jesus from the dead. That's power! So don't forget this, either: Our powerful God empowers us also to do awesome things in his name.

When you prayed, did you think that God might not answer because you did not deserve an answer? Did you think, "I'm not good enough"? Did you forget that God loves you? While you were still sinning, our God sent his own Son to die for your sins. Our God adopted you as his child. Our God placed his own Spirit inside you. Our God has prepared a wonderful place called heaven, where you can be with him forever. That's love! It is because of our God's great love for us that we are able to love even the most unlovable.

God also gave us a spirit of self-discipline so we would remember to call on him. Remember when you pray that you have a powerful God who loves you very much. Remember that our God has the power to answer your prayers and that he wants to answer them because he loves you. Pray expecting God to answer. Remember Jesus' words in John 14:14: "You may ask me for anything in my name, and I will do it." Do you believe him?

Believing Is Seeing

1 Peter 1:8   John Primus '54
Calvin professor emeritus; Grand Rapids, Michigan

Though you have not seen him, you love him; and even though you do not see him now, you believe in him and are filled with an inexpressible and glorious joy.
(1 Pet. 1:8)

The apostle Peter, along with the other disciples, had seen Jesus. They had walked with him and talked with him for three and a half wonderful years. But Peter is writing the letter of today's Scripture passage later, to Christ-followers like you and me who had not seen him in the flesh. Peter is not gloating over his personal experience with Jesus or bragging to those who had not shared in his high privilege of actually seeing Jesus. Nor is there any hint of sympathy in these words. They are simply words of blessed encouragement to those who thought they had missed out on something by not seeing Jesus.

Have you ever felt that way? When reading the Gospels, have you felt a little envious of the disciples? In fact, are we not at a serious disadvantage? We weren't there. If we could only have been there with Jesus to actually hear his words and to see him in action, how much easier faith would be.

But Peter knew that we are at no disadvantage whatsoever. In fact, the world is better off now, for since Jesus ascended into heaven, his presence is no longer limited by time and space. "And surely I am with you always, to the very end of the age," he said (Matt. 28:20). His presence today is wherever there is faith. He is with believers at prayer in a little hut in Siberia; he is with college students worshiping in a California residence hall; he is with believing Kosovars in wretched refugee camps; he is in homes and hospitals with Christians who are seriously ill. Believers everywhere, in whatever condition, have seen him after all. They have seen him with eyes of faith and have received unimaginable grace, strength, and peace.

So Peter speaks these encouraging words to us. Maybe he is thinking of his old friend Thomas as he speaks them — Thomas who insisted on the "proof" that comes with seeing. And maybe Peter is thinking of those immortal words of Jesus to Thomas: "Blessed are those who have not seen and yet have believed" (John 20:29). That blessing is for us. Claim it, and be "filled with an inexpressible and glorious joy" (1 Pet. 1:8).

Children by Adoption

Phil de Haan '84   Ephesians 1:1-8
Calvin administrator; Grand Rapids, Michigan

The word *adoption* appears only a few times in the Bible. Yet the concept of adoption, most would agree, is central to the Christian faith. Paul sets it out quite plainly in his letter to the Ephesians: "In love [God] predestined us to be adopted as his sons through Jesus Christ, in accordance with his pleasure and will — to the praise of his glorious grace, which he has freely given us in the One he loves" (Eph. 1:4-6).

These verses became more meaningful to me when my wife and I adopted our daughter, Gina Soo, in the fall of 1996. Prior to deciding to adopt, we had spent four-plus years hoping to have biological children. Slowly but surely it became plain that it was not likely to happen, and we began to consider adoption. It seemed good, but it was hard not to be just a little doubtful, hard not to think of it as the consolation prize.

Until we received Gina. The instant she was placed in our arms, she was our daughter. Every doubt and every misgiving seemed to evaporate. Her weight in our arms said simply, "This is our child." And perhaps we understood a little more deeply that day God's love for us, his adopted children.

When we presented Gina for baptism, we did so with another couple who were also presenting their Korean daughter for baptism. Together the four of us read this litany of praise and thanks that I wrote for the occasion:

> Two daughters, Lord, presented here for baptism,
> Brought from afar and claimed, made part of our families,
> Baptized once by our tears of joy, baptized today by your eternal seal,
> Even as we once were claimed and made part of your covenant.
> Your covenant, Lord: no Jew, no gentile, no east, no west,
>   no distinctions of blood nor birth.
> You simply say to all who will listen: Follow me. Believe.
>   Know that I am God.
> We praise you for that gift. And we praise you, God, for these gifts
>   of grace, these daughters.
> We pray that they may grow strong and true, servants of you.
> And even as we pray for and praise you for these two,
>   we remember the one, also sent by you,
> The one who makes this seal possible, your Child, Lord, your Son,
> Given to an undeserving world so that we might all be adopted
>   as your covenant children.

Philosophers and Faith

1 Corinthians 1:18-31   Robert Sweetman '77
Professor; Toronto, Ontario

Paul must have been quite a preacher. He could certainly turn a phrase. In today's Scripture passage he jolts his readers by mixing and matching wisdom and foolishness, Jews, gentiles, and Christ. The passage never fails to grab me when I read it. I admit that I teach ancient and medieval philosophy for a living. So maybe it's natural for me to pause before a Bible passage that alludes to the ancient philosophers. Paul at times actually cites those philosophers, but not here. Rather, I wonder whether the language of Proverbs is echoing in his head. Proverbs also pictures wisdom and foolishness in strikingly opposed images: the virgin and the whore. If Paul had Proverbs in mind in this passage, I would be tempted to understand a part of its message as follows: What looks to the philosopher as a sad and prostituted understanding (the cross) turns out to be that chaste and happy wisdom the philosopher claims to love.

Of course, the philosophers whom Paul stands on their heads could also play a mean word game. For sheer dash, it is hard to beat Plato's skewering of the teachers of rhetoric, who claimed that their art could make one wise. Socrates toys with these proud teachers until they are forced to admit that their art is not the high road to wisdom but only a humble kitchen knack, a flattery too stooped by the weight of its verbal ornament to match the lift of Socrates' plain, unadorned speech. It is probably far-fetched, but I almost see Paul in our passage out-Platoing Plato.

The passage does prove prophetic of an ancient pattern of Christian experience. Time and again in subsequent centuries, Greek and Latin students of philosophy would discover upon conversion to the Christian way of salvation that it also satisfied their philosophical yearnings. From their perspective as converts they saw that within the humble society of Christian faithful was to be found true wisdom, no longer endlessly sought but received as gift and accessible to all. I dare say that it is from something like this perspective that all authentic Christian philosophy springs, that is, thoughtful testimony to the wonder of a world viewed in the light of Christ's cross and our salvation.

Shining with Joy

Abram Van Engen
Calvin student; South Bend, Indiana

1 Peter 1:3-9

A teacher once told me that those who have the joy of Christ shine. Being a teenager, I responded, "Jesus must have been a walking light bulb then." He turned to me and coolly replied, "*Something* about him attracted twelve men who had never seen him before."

Since then I have come to realize this teacher's point: Christianity is characterized by joy. Because of Christ we can be "filled with an inexpressible and glorious joy [because we] are receiving the goal of [our] faith, the salvation of [our] souls" (1 Pet. 1:8-9). The glorious part about this joy is that it is part of both our commission and our reward.

Joy is part of our commission in that we are called to love. To love is to want what is best for another (notice: *love* does not necessarily include the concept of *like* — we can *love* our enemies, though we don't *like* them). When we begin wanting (and working) for the best of others, we empty ourselves for the sake of our neighbors. Only in this kind of selfless giving can we find joy. Sin has two important characteristics: It is the turning in on ourselves, and it is its own punishment. When we sin, we may gain temporary satisfaction, but we lose lasting joy. Only when we empty ourselves to be filled by God, can we find complete joy — joy in life itself, joy in the essence of being with God. We are like the loaves of bread which Jesus fed the crowd of five thousand; we only increase in our giving.

But joy is part of our reward as well. In our darkest moments of despair we know that at the end of the cave, at the top of the canyon, there still shines the precious light. And we know that this light has conquered all the darkness. It is because of this light that, even though we feel like our hearts have been ripped out, we still have the God-given ability to smile. We can sleep at night because we know we will be all right. We know that we have already won. Christianity is victory. To win a race can bring a grin or a big smile. To win life brings joy. And when we are filled with this joy, we do shine.

Upon reflection, I realized that there was always something about that one high school teacher that attracted me to him before I even knew him. It was his shine, his joy in Christ. Since then I have made it my own goal to shine, to be so filled with the joy of giving and the joy of Christ that I can walk down the street and people will notice a difference about me. They will notice my joy.

An Epiphany

Luke 12:4-7

Barbara Rodenhouse Van Dyken '45
Homemaker; Harpswell, Maine

It began on a bicycle tour of the Netherlands. On our second day out, as we were riding along one of those beautiful bicycle paths so common there, I unavoidably fell. I landed on my right side with great force against a concrete curb, breaking my leg. I was confined in a hospital for ten days. When the accident happened, we still had eight days of our tour left, so I prevailed upon my husband to continue the tour without me.

There I lay in a strange hospital in a strange country, alone. To myself I admitted having some fears — fears of being in the hands of unknown doctors, fears for the outcome of the mishap, fears even of the unfamiliar other patients in my room. I recall thinking of the assurance I sometimes remembered from Luke about not being afraid because one's hairs are numbered and we are worth more than sparrows (Luke 12:6-7). That helped some.

Almost immediately, marvelous things began to happen. Nurses came around often just to chat in English for a few moments. One nurse walked downtown to buy me some English-language magazines. My doctor gave me a book of short stories and also went to the trouble of having my bed wheeled to the nurses' station so that I could speak to my husband on the phone. The other three women in my room did not speak English, but, nonetheless, before long, though ill, they smiled, groped with language to communicate, and one even offered me toilet articles, since I had none.

All of these people gave me extraordinary expressions of love, love that bridged different languages, backgrounds, and situations. It was a powerful example of God's universal human family sharing the same feelings. Here was empathetic love. I warmed to them as they to me. And then I noticed my fears were gone. Serenity had come, and I remember those ten days as a precious time.

In that Dutch hospital I had a memorable, if human, experience of the assertion in 1 John 4:18: "There is no fear in love. . . . love drives out fear. . . ."

The Real World

Howard D. Vanderwell '59
Pastor; Hudsonville, Michigan

Revelation 4:1-11

> *At once I was in the Spirit, and there before me was a throne in heaven with someone sitting on it.* (Rev. 4:2)

It's a flippant little phrase that we cast around rather easily: "Welcome to the real world!" We toss it out to someone who has just encountered some jarring difficulty. We think that this difficulty has now jerked him or her out of an illusory world into the real one.

But exactly where is the real world? Is it the world students encounter when they get their first jobs? Is it the world professors stumble into when they leave their halls of academic research and deal with their own family problems? Is it the world preachers walk into when they leave their quiet studies and agonize with a young couple over their daughter's cancer or an older couple about their son's waywardness? I really began to think seriously about this subject when an acquaintance of mine asked me why I, a pastor, didn't take a job in the real world.

Where is the real world?

Are you ready for the biblical answer? It might surprise you.

The real world is the one described in John's visions in the book of Revelation. It's the world that is beyond this one. It is the world where there is a sovereign, divine King on a throne, where worship is always going on, where angels and saints are celebrating, where there is awe, obedience, and obvious divine purpose. It is the world where Jesus Christ, the Son of God, is honored as the Lamb that has been slain. True, many want to call that a fictional and fanciful world. But not so. That heavenly world shapes and influences this one, not the other way around.

Too many today assume that their grasp of reality must begin here and remain here. But the Bible teaches us a very different viewpoint. We won't understand the "here" unless we are in touch with the "there." After all, the world here is shaped and determined by the world there.

Those who keep their eyes on the real, heavenly world will find themselves more capable of understanding and living purposefully in this world. Those who try to ignore it will find they live with only half the story.

126

The Promise of Grace

Genesis 12:1-3; 21:1-7

Harriet Kuiper Eldersveld '34
Retired teacher; Crete, Illinois

Centuries ago God made a promise to a childless nomadic sheepherder. God said to Abram, "I will make you into a great nation and I will bless you . . . and all peoples on earth will be blessed through you" (Gen. 12:2-3). That promise is coming true. Two millennia ago the Savior came — the offspring of Abram who would bless millions of people on the earth.

Today, as an eighty-seven-year-old grandmother, I look forward with anticipation to my heavenly home. I look back with deep gratitude for the promise as it was kept in my family. My grandparents were transplanted to this country many years ago. One grandfather was used by God to help start Calvin College and Seminary. The other grandfather insisted on English-speaking churches to promote the promise in his new country. My dedicated parents showed our family how to live helpfully as we enjoyed telling about the promise.

I have seen children with a Dutch heritage and serious instruction in God's Word claim the promise as theirs. I have seen and heard many African-American children sing God's praise because they know the promise includes them. Among my precious friends are some who have escaped from Laos, who today also claim the promise as theirs. An immigrant student from the Ukraine knows the promise is for her. A young woman from a local bar knows the promise is for her even though she hasn't heard about it since childhood. Some prisoners in the local jail have repented of their sinful pasts and are claiming the promise for themselves. Many people all over the world are hearing about the promise on the radio, in their own languages. Some are reading about it in Bible translations that speak their native languages. The promise that all people on earth will be blessed is being fulfilled today.

The kingdom is coming. God has used even "outsiders" and disreputable people to keep that promise. He used Moses, who was trained in Pharaoh's Egyptian court. He used Jacob, who did not shrink from cheating his own brother. He used a prostitute from Jericho, a widow from Moab, a king who committed adultery and murder, a Teenager from Nazareth. He is keeping the promise made to Abram and enfleshed in Jesus just over two thousand years ago.

Believe that promise — and tell others your wonderful story of grace.

No Cowards There!

James LaGrand, Jr. '62   Revelation 21:5-8
Pastor; Gary, Indiana

> *But the cowardly, the unbelieving, the vile, the murderers, the sexually immoral, those who practice magic arts, the idolaters, and all liars — their place will be in the fiery lake of burning sulfur. This is the second death.* (Rev. 21:8)

Knowing less about hell on earth than other people, we North Americans thank God that we have escaped the Holocaust of World War II, the more recent terror in Sierra Leone, and the ethnic violence in Kosovo and East Timor. About hell itself we don't know much at all, but we do know that we don't want to go there. Christians follow the way that leads "to the city with foundations, whose architect and builder is God" (Heb. 11:10), but sometimes it is instructive to consider the alternative. It is not our business to say who goes to hell, but John's vision includes the usual suspects: vile persons, murderers, unbelievers, the sexually immoral, those who practice magic, idolaters, and all liars. But the group that heads the list is "the cowardly."

Everyone who has been instructed in the Christian faith knows that we are saved by God's grace through faith in Jesus Christ. We neither earn eternal life nor escape punishment for our sins through our own efforts, but this doctrine should not make us careless. Jesus himself warns us to "enter through the narrow gate. For wide is the gate and broad is the road that leads to destruction, and many enter through it" (Matt. 7:13). Again, Jesus warns that "anyone who does not take his cross and follow me is not worthy of me" (Matt. 10:38). When we consider the biblical meaning of faith, it is not surprising that cowardice is without eternal reward.

In the midst of temptations to avoid hardship and danger in favor of entertainment and comfort, the call to Christian discipleship is a call to courage. There are no cowards in the city of God.

Time and Eternity

1 Corinthians 2:6-10

Dennis Weidenaar '58
Professor; West Lafayette, Indiana

I recall as a youngster on a drive from Grand Rapids to Holland that my father urged me to pay close attention to what was about to appear outside the car windows as we passed through the little town of Zeeland. I sat up expectantly, only to be disappointed by the two factories across the highway from each other. My father then gleefully announced that we had just passed through time and eternity, explaining that caskets were manufactured in the factory on one side of the road and clocks in the factory on the other side. Although these words were spoken in jest, they have stuck with me and have said something to me about both the close proximity of these two concepts and the difference between them.

By the word *time* we usually mean the point or period during which a particular event occurred or didn't occur. We don't know for how long time was measured only by the alternating periods of light and darkness established by God when he created the sun and the moon. We do know that early in human history human beings felt a need to measure time more precisely, and so they used the shadows of trees and invented measuring devices like the sundial, water clock, and, in the fourteenth century, the mechanical clock, which became the precursor of the electronic and nuclear clocks available today. By these devices we were and are able to divide our days into precise, equal segments: hours, minutes, and seconds.

Defining *eternity* is much more difficult. As human beings, we can think of it only in terms of time, and even dictionaries are hard pressed to avoid words about time in order to speak of eternity: "infinite time," "duration without beginning or end," "the timeless state into which the soul is believed to pass at death," "a seemingly endless period."

But Christians have a sense of eternity not available to people without faith. Christians are practiced in talking and thinking about eternity. When God spoke of himself as I AM, he revealed his eternal nature. Eternity is the fulfillment of the promise that we will one day know and experience an abiding fellowship with God, perfect bliss such as "no eye has seen, no ear has heard, no mind has conceived" (1 Cor. 2:9). It is the glorious goal of our being and the ultimate reward prepared for us by Jesus. It's not just a measurement of time. It is a state of being.

Our pilgrimage on earth is but a journey through time that prepares us for the ultimate transcendence, abiding with God in eternity. Time is just an overture to a never-ending symphony about the presence and the grace of God.

Beyond Why

Henry J. Baron '60   Romans 8:38-39
Calvin professor emeritus; Grand Rapids, Michigan

Some words chill the bone and freeze the blood: "I'm afraid I have bad news for you . . . " All of us know someone who has heard these words and those that follow: ". . . it's inoperable"; ". . . it's a progressively debilitating disease"; ". . . we don't know the cause, and there is no cure"; ". . . we can fight it for a while, but . . . " They are words that turn dreams to dust and faith to fear.

We no longer ask why — why some should live so long that they long for death, while others, vibrant with life, should be struck down. We're tired of the whys that go nowhere, that ring their hollow echoes in our souls. Even the Lord's agonized why from the cross went unanswered.

No, we don't expect explanations on demand. God owes us none. And we realize that a tortured heart hurling its challenges at heaven's door is hardly receptive to divine reasoning even if it should be offered. We don't insist on answers. But we pray for Christ's presence.

For our Lord is acquainted with grief. He knows that hands must often ball up into fists before they can fold in prayer. He knows that voices must often rage before they whisper their faith. He knows that often the torments of despair must rack the soul before it can embrace the love of God.

We need to know that when his sheep enter the shadows of the valley, the good shepherd will hold them close. That when pain torments the body, the grace of his presence will provide balm. That when the humiliation of dependence shatters dignity, the pressure of his everlasting arms will assure us of our eternal value. That when waves of fear for self and loved ones threaten to swallow the tempest-tossed, he will walk those waves with them and turn terror into peace.

May we hear, above all the chilling words, these words of promise: Nothing "will be able to separate us from the love of God that is in Christ Jesus our Lord" (Rom. 8:39). That will be enough, for now and forever.

Healing for the Heart

2 Corinthians 3:9 Richard E. Sytsema '64

Missionary; Tokyo, Japan

In 2 Corinthians 3:9 Paul revels in the glory of the new covenant — a ministry that results in transformed hearts: "If the ministry that brings condemnation is glorious, how much more glorious is the ministry that brings righteousness!" (NIVI). God gave me a glimpse of the nature of that glory when I underwent angioplasty — the balloon treatment — after suffering a heart attack.

My team of doctors first did an angiogram. With a catheter they examined the condition of my coronary arteries. Then they wheeled a monitor over to me so I could see the angiogram. It was awesome. There on the screen was a picture of part of my right coronary artery. I could see very clearly that it was completely blocked. No blood could flow through.

Then the doctor explained that he would immediately go ahead with the angioplasty procedure to open up the artery. After this procedure was finished, they wheeled the monitor over to me again and showed me a picture of the same place in my right coronary artery that I had seen before. Again I thought, "How awesome!" I could see clearly that where there had been complete blockage, now the blood was flowing freely. The artery was open.

As I lay in the hospital, I thought about those two pictures. Both were awesome. But the awesomeness of the picture after the angiogram was nothing compared to the awesomeness of the picture after the angioplasty. The angiogram gave a very accurate picture of the condition of my coronary arteries. It defined my problem very clearly. But that is all it could do: define the problem. The balloon procedure was able to clear up the problem and give healing.

For me the difference between those two pictures became a metaphor for the difference between the old covenant and the new covenant. The law (of the old covenant) defines righteousness and shows us how unrighteous we are. But that is all it can do: define the problem. The Holy Spirit in the new covenant does so much more. He transforms our hearts and gives us the power to live righteously. Both covenants are awesome, but there is no comparison in the degree of glory.

Which Words?

Jeremiah Whittington '69   Ephesians 5:6
Physician; Novi, Michigan

Let no one deceive you with empty words, for because of such things God's wrath comes on those who are disobedient. (Eph. 5:6)

We all have experienced the power and influence of timely spoken words. And by now we're all acquainted with the computer's ability to receive, process, and store countless pieces of information. In many ways, our minds are like computers, storing words for safekeeping, for use at some future time. The question for us is this: What are we, as gatekeepers of our minds, allowing to enter the depths of our hearts? What are we rejecting?

From the resources of our minds, we speak. Rather than taking in words that harm and hurt, we should instead meditate on the Word of God — both day and night. We should take inventory of our hearts — hardware and software — to delete what is hurtful, damaging, and ugly. Then, if we move to fill the empty spaces with the Word of God, we can prevent words of wickedness from coming in to twist and deform our relationships, our understanding, our very souls. Instead, God's Word will direct our hearts to love him, to love our neighbor, and to cherish creation.

Perhaps this can be a day of perfecting and guarding our speech. We can't completely forget the words we've already processed or take back what we've said. It is too late. But we can speak *words of humility* (which is success in God's upside-down kingdom), *words of forgiveness* (healing broken hearts), *words of peace* (mending conflicts), *words of faith* (believing in miracles), and *words of hope* (dismissing discouragement and depression). And in all things, we can speak *words of love* (remembering our salvation).

Let us guard our hearts and minds from evil words. Instead, let us speak the words of our Savior, who wills above all things that we prosper and be in health — even as our souls prosper. This day I offer my heart and mind to God.

Known by Name

Psalm 8:1-4

John Timmer '54
Pastor; Grand Rapids, Michigan

David, the poet of Psalm 8, was able to see only relatively few stars — ten thousand at the most. We enlightened twenty-first-century people see infinitely more. We know that there are billions of stars in our galaxy alone and that there are billions of other galaxies, each with billions of stars, all moving at incredible speeds away from one another. David assumed that the earth was the center of the universe. We know that our world is but a tiny speck revolving around a minor star. Looking at the heavens, David humbly asked, "What are mere mortals that you are mindful of them?" (Ps. 8:4, NIVI). Measuring ourselves against the immensity of space, we feel dismayed and fearfully ask what difference it makes in the total scheme of things whether we are alive or dead, love or hate, speak the truth or lie, are faithful to our spouses or not. Does God even know we're here? Does he know my name — my first, middle, and last name? What am I that God might be mindful of me?

The first word David speaks in Psalm 8 is God's name, Yahweh. "Yahweh, our Sovereign, how majestic is your name in all the earth!" (author's translation). Yahweh — that's the Hebrew name God revealed to Moses as he stood before the bush that burned but was not consumed. Yahweh — that's the intimate name of Psalm 23: "Yahweh is my shepherd, I shall not want" (author's translation). Yahweh is the name of the God who guards his people like the apple of his eye (Ps. 17:8). Yahweh is the God who created the host of stars and numbered them, calling each of them by name (Isa. 40:26). Now, if this God is so concerned about each individual star, which today is formed by the gravitational contraction of dust and gas and which tomorrow, for want of fuel, collapses, will he not much more be concerned about us?

Yahweh, who knows each star by name, also knows our names. Therefore, when across the infinity of space we call on his name, he hears and answers us.

Qualified for Sainthood

Dave Dykgraaf '66   Colossians 1:9-14
Missionary; Niger State, Nigeria

A dear retired missionary who used to write letters of encouragement to us always used this address on the blue air forms:

> To the Saints Dykgraaf
> PO Box 261
> Jos, Nigeria

That label caused me a bit of embarrassment and brought some chuckles in the Nigerian mission office, which was also the mail distribution center for all the area missionaries. I knew I was no saint and figured that those who had to work with me on committees or projects wouldn't be so generous with their labels for me either. My wife, Jan, maybe, but not me. I never had come even close. As a student at Calvin years earlier, I would not have been singled out for recognition, certainly not for sainthood. For some years in my early missionary service I even struggled with a kind of off-putting pride. I immersed myself in African language and culture so deeply that I idealized them and alienated myself from my missionary colleagues. I got pretty good at speaking the language, but I was no fun to be with, and I certainly wasn't giving evidence of any progress on the road to sainthood.

But that retired missionary correspondent forced me to look at what Scripture says about me — and you. Paul says that God brought us out of darkness, put us into the kingdom of love, and qualified us for sainthood. Today I am grateful to be forgiven for the sin of pride that showed itself so sneakily just as I was becoming a "humble missionary." It took the blood of Christ to remove it, and that qualifies me for sainthood.

And I, along with millions of Christians everywhere, now enjoy the communion of the saints on earth — living lives worthy of the Lord, bearing fruit in every good work, growing in the knowledge of God, being strengthened with all power according to his glorious might, and joyfully giving thanks — even as we look forward to sharing "in the inheritance of the saints in the kingdom of light" (Col. 1:21).

Professor, Psalm, and Hound

Psalm 139   Vern Boerman '52
                                     Teacher; South Holland, Illinois

If your Calvin College days go back to the Franklin Campus, you maybe had one of Calvin's greatest teachers, Dr. Henry Zylstra. His arresting exterior — tall, balding, giant ears, huge hands, penetrating gaze — belied the sweet, winsome, gentle spirit within. He was a man of delightful wit, enormous erudition, and deep piety — a terrific teacher.

In December 1956, on a Sunday evening, at age forty-seven, Zylstra died at an Amsterdam bus stop. The previous Sunday he had been invited to preach at the Anglican church, and his topic had been "Our Inescapable God," based on Psalm 139.

Profound Psalm 139: a psalm about a personal God who knows me completely, unlimited by time, space, thought, or my attempted flight. A terrifying thought! Where shall I flee? To the heavens? The depths? The wings of dawn? To the far side of the sea? Into darkness? There's no escape.

A late-nineteenth-century poem that Zylstra taught with insight and conviction echoes the theme of Psalm 139. It's Francis Thompson's "The Hound of Heaven," in which the speaker of the poem is hard to separate from the poet himself. Thompson, a derelict on London's skid row who wrote poetry on paper scraps, was finally dragged away by a caring cousin — still fleeing the persistent Hound of Heaven: "I fled Him down the nights and down the days; / I fled Him, down the arches of the years; / I fled Him, down the labyrinthine ways / Of my own mind. . . ." Then he goes on to detail his avenues of escape: human friends, space, speed, children, love of nature. All eventually disappoint him.

Finally, cornered by the incarnate Hound of Heaven, he cringes, waiting for the worst: "Naked, I wait thy love's uplifted stroke!" The pursued fearfully looks up and sees Calvary "with glooming robes purpureal, cypress-crowned; / His name I know. . . ."

The majestic chase finally ends, but not in terror, because the Pursuer — amazingly — comforts the pursued, with these words: "Rise, clasp My hand and come! . . . Whom wilt thou find to love ignoble thee, / Save Me, save only Me? . . . 'Ah, fondest, blindest, weakest, / I am He Whom thou seekest!'"

In my textbook margin I wrote Zylstra's comment: "This is not only Thompson's life, but the life of every sinner who refuses to live within the generous realm of grace."

Psalm 139 ends with what ought to be every sinner's plea for grace: "Search me . . . and lead me in the way everlasting."

Patient like God

Jonathan Bradford '72
Nonprofit executive;
Grand Rapids, Michigan

Psalm 90:1-2, 4; Galatians 5:22

It's not easy to talk about God and time. One way to do it is to talk about God's timelessness, that he is eternal and lives above and apart from the human concept of time. We use time-oriented words when we talk about God because we can't think of existence without the boundaries of time. We say God existed *before* the Alps or the Rockies punched their way skyward. As we observe the passing of a year, a decade, a century, an entire millennium, we say it's just another *day* to God. But, really, the words don't do justice to God and his relationship to time.

We come a little closer when we think about the patience of God — how long he can put up with our human failings. Though we cannot experience at all what it means to be timeless like God, we can have a little idea of what it means for God to be patient. Maybe you've sat through a lecture which should have ended much sooner. Or your daughter's T-ball game, in which each inning felt like it should be the last. Only proper decorum or parental pride helps us muster the patience to get through these situations. But the patience quota here is nothing compared to the patience of God.

God's covenantal grace was planned for his children even before time began. That tells me that God was ready for us and the countless ways we would lose sight of his kingdom plan. There is no greater evidence of God's patience, his long-suffering, than his sending of Christ to die even though we were *still* sinners. In our increasingly "have it your way" and "have it now" society, we often look for immediate results from our endeavors. We want instant gratification, and if we don't get it, we are disappointed, frustrated, maybe even doubtful about our own worth or the worth of the work in which we are engaged. If so, we may be forgetting our place in God's plan and the timetable on which God works. Whether it be house painting or surgery, teaching or truck driving, all has been woven into the superstructure of a kingdom planned by a very patient God.

Remember, it was God's patience with his errant children that allowed him to give us the gift of his Son while we were still sinners. If God could do that, then surely we should be able, with the patience that comes from the Holy Spirit, to sustain our work for God in this world. God's world is not a "have it now" world. It is a divinely planned and divinely timed world, a world designed to bring eternal shalom to those who patiently trust in his covenantal love. Your patient, faithful work will hasten that shalom.

God's Rainbows

2 Corinthians 3:1-6

Douglas S. Diekema '81
Physician; Kenmore, Washington

> *You show that you are a letter from Christ, the result of our ministry, written not with ink but with the Spirit of the living God, not on tablets of stone but on tablets of human hearts.* (2 Cor. 3:3)

What a compliment Paul pays the early church at Corinth. Here was a group of believers whose lives reflected the glory of Christ. They weren't simply going through the motions, following the right rules, doing the right things. These were people who understood that being a Christian meant reflecting the person of Christ from the depths of their hearts.

Paul would have felt similarly about the people of Le Chambon, a small village in the mountains of southeastern France. Over a period of five years, its residents saved the lives of more than six thousand people who were fleeing the persecution of Nazi Germany during the Second World War. They offered hospitality and shelter to thousands despite the ever-present possibility of personal harm at the hands of their own government or German occupation forces. Yet these good people seemingly never struggled over whether to endanger themselves for the sake of others. They certainly recognized the dangers involved, but they also knew that being Christian people meant following Christ's example in meeting the needs of others. Their faith was engraved on their hearts, engraved so deeply that their lives couldn't help displaying God's goodness to others.

Philip Haillie, whose book *Lest Innocent Blood Be Shed* recounts the story of Le Chambon, tells of encountering a Jewish woman whose three children had been saved by the people of this small village. Her simple words to him reflect the profound influence Christian people can have on the world around them: "The holocaust was storm, lightning, thunder, wind, and rain. And Le Chambon was the rainbow."

What an elegant description of the Christian life. God chose the rainbow as a sign of faithfulness and hope to his servant Noah after the great flood. The "rainbows" of Le Chambon brought hope and love and faith into the lives of thousands through their simple acts of kindness. As God's people we also have the opportunity to bring faith, hope, and love to a hurting and needy world — a world badly in need of more rainbows.

Holy Rabble-rousing

Stephanie Steenbergen Disselkoen '96
Editor/writer; Barrington, Illinois

Acts 2:1-21; 4:31

The Holy Spirit's behavior at Pentecost, throughout history, and within the lives of many Christians today might aptly be termed holy rabble-rousing.

Imagine for a moment that you were present on Pentecost, when the Holy Spirit came down. What must have gone through the minds of the God-fearing Jews who experienced and witnessed the entry of the Holy Spirit into the hearts of the apostles? How would you or I have reacted to see these men literally "on fire" for God, the tongues of flame on their heads and their own human tongues flaming with the message of the gospel?

The physical evidence of the Holy Spirit — the tongues of flame and the words of the apostles — must have caused more than one knee to tremble and more than one heart to fill with terror. So confused were the Jews that they accused the apostles of having drunk too much wine.

When invited, the Holy Spirit can enter our hearts and lives with that same kind of awe-inspiring flame. Acts 2:17, quoting the prophet Joel, suggests that radical things may well happen: The Holy Spirit can make sons and daughters prophesy, young men see visions, and old men dream.

The Holy Spirit laid claim to the hearts and mouths of the apostles on Pentecost. Acts 2:41 tells the result of that day: "Those who accepted [Peter's] message were baptized, and about three thousand were added to their number that day." Not one, not ten, but three thousand people accepted the Holy Spirit into their hearts.

Invite the Holy Spirit to rabble-rouse in your heart and life today. Perhaps something as miraculous in its own way will occur as that which occurred on the first Pentecost. Perhaps what ensues will be no less bewildering, exciting, and amazing.

Being Salt and Light

Matthew 5:13-16

Nelle Vander Ark '47
Teacher; Grand Rapids, Michigan

You are the salt of the earth . . . the light of the world. (Matt. 5:13, 14)

Recently I read an article by Douglas John Hall in which he says that the postmodern world as it enters the new millennium is on four quests. One of them is "the quest for meaningful community." About the same time, I learned that some members of my own faith community are moving to places where they hope to find more neighborliness — where people will sit on the front porch with them.

These two accounts made me conclude that people are looking for something homelike, and that idea brought me to Jesus' words about salt and light. Jesus is telling us that wherever we are, we are to change the world around us. Wherever we live and work, whatever we work at, however we live, we make life more human — more homelike — when something of the love of Jesus Christ is in us and shines through us. As salt permeates the whole stew, as light illumines a space larger than its source, so, too, Christians should enhance their environment, should make it homelike.

Near the beginning of *Traveling Mercies*, her story of coming to faith, Anne Lamott relates a story told by her minister, an African-American woman named Veronica. Lamott says, "When she was about seven, her best friend got lost one day. The little girl ran up and down the streets of the big town where they lived, but she couldn't find a single landmark. She was very frightened. Finally a policeman stopped to help her. He put her in the passenger seat of his car, and they drove around until she saw her church. She pointed it out to the policeman, and then she told him firmly, 'You could let me out now. This is my church, and I can always find my way home from here.'"

Anne Lamott concluded, "And that is why I have stayed so close to mine, because no matter how bad I am feeling, how lost or lonely or frightened, when I see the face of the people at my church, and hear their voices, I can always find my way home."

Even when we succeed at making our places of worship feel like home, we need to spread the salt and the light even further, for Jesus said, "You are the salt of the *earth*. . . . You are the light of the *world*." There's a good bit of homemaking still to be done.

Reception Problems

David Hoekema '72   1 Samuel 3
Calvin professor; Grand Rapids, Michigan

One evening while I was driving home, the radio station I was listening to began fading out, and another station on the same frequency began to intrude. What I heard, to my puzzlement, was a pitched battle between the opening movement of Mahler's Second Symphony and the closing movement of Beethoven's Fifth. Beethoven's bright, brassy chords alternated every few seconds with the sinuous melodies and brooding harmonies of Mahler. These were sharply contrasting musical and emotional messages, and my radio seemed unable to embrace either one completely.

First Samuel 3 describes another sort of reception problem. Young Samuel hears his name in the night and hurries to the bedside of the priest whom he serves as an apprentice. "I did not call you," says a surprised and sleepy Eli. "Go back to sleep." Three more times Samuel hears his name and responds by going to Eli. On the third time, realizing that the boy might be tuned to a station that he, Eli, can't pick up, Eli advises Samuel to answer, "Speak, LORD, for your servant is listening."

Back in his bed, Samuel waits, wondering whether he will have a fourth chance or whether the voice will be silent forever. Then once again he hears his name, and at last God identifies himself to Samuel. And thus a great gift, long lost, is restored to Israel — the gift of hearing the voice of the Lord.

We find ourselves in an age like Samuel's. The word of the Lord is rare, and there are not many visions. Few people claim that God speaks directly to them — and most of those who do are locked up in mental institutions. Why aren't we awakened by a call in the night? Why is God so often silent, even at times of greatest need?

Perhaps the problem is not that God is silent but that we have forgotten how to listen. Are we so firmly locked on to one frequency that we cannot hear God's voice on another? Are our hearts flipping randomly from station to station, confusing God's voice with the echoes of our own pride and ambition?

By means of Scripture, worship, and the testimony of the Spirit in our hearts, God still speaks. When we learn to listen in penitence and humility, like Samuel we will finally hear God's voice.

God's Name on You

Numbers 6:22-27;
Matthew 19:13-15

Cindy Holtrop
Calvin Worship Institute administrator;
Grand Rapids, Michigan

W e all have the deep, innate longing for words that bless rather than curse. A blessing from another person is a treasured gift. Without a blessing, people young and old do not flourish in body and spirit. Children, no matter how old they are, crave a blessing from their parents. One young winner of Olympic medals once said, "I would give all of them up if I could hear words of approval from my father." Words that wound — like "you'll never amount to much" — can crush a person's spirit for a lifetime. Words that uplift — like "you are a valuable member of this family" — can nurture a person's spirit for years. Perhaps you still replay the tape of someone's one-liner that makes your heart either sting or sing.

The familiar words of Numbers 6 are a profound blessing given to God's people through the priest Aaron:

> The LORD bless you and keep you; the LORD make his face shine upon you and be gracious to you; the LORD turn his face toward you and give you peace. (Num. 6:24-26)

For centuries, God's people, hungry for words of blessing, have welcomed these words when they worshiped. With this benediction God promises to turn his face toward you, to watch over and care for you, to protect you.

Regardless of whether you have the blessing of your parents, siblings, or friends, God's blessing rests on you. God's attentive face shines on you in whatever circumstance you face. In these words God promises to be with you and to place his name on you even as he promised that Aaron and the priests would place his name in blessing on the Israelites: "So they will put my name on the Israelites, and I will bless them" (Num. 6:27). Just as Jesus placed his hands on the little children to pray for them, know that God's hand of blessing rests on you as his child.

The Evidence

Sharon R. Brinks '76   John 11:16
Attorney; Kentwood, Michigan

Let us also go, that we may die with him. (John 11:16)

As an attorney I have been trained to argue against assumptions that people make in court and to demand solid facts as evidence. Faith — which doesn't demand empirical facts and accepts some assumptions — sometimes comes very hard to my Christian life. Perhaps this is why Thomas has always been my favorite apostle.

If you ask many Christians what they know about Thomas, the phrase "doubting Thomas" will be prominent in their response. When confronted with testimony of the resurrection, Thomas demanded to see the evidence. He would not rely upon the testimony of others, which in law we call "hearsay evidence." I suspect that I, too, would have needed to see physical evidence of the living Christ in order to believe that he was alive after watching him die and be buried. I too would have wanted to see the nail marks, to feel the indentations, to put my hand into Jesus' side. Jesus accommodated Thomas. He offered his physical presence to answer the needs of this apostle, and Thomas responded by declaring, "My Lord and my God!" (John 20:28).

Thomas was a man who wanted a road map and directions. It was Thomas who asked, "Lord, we don't know where you are going, so how can we know the way?" (John 14:5). Jesus answered him by redirecting him down the road toward heaven.

But Thomas was more than a doubter. Thomas also showed great courage when the other disciples were arguing for staying where it was safe. When Jesus told his disciples that he was going near Jerusalem to raise Lazarus, it was Thomas who spoke up for dangerous and decisive action. Thomas did not try to argue with Jesus. Instead he said, "Let us also go, that we may die with him" (John 11:16).

It seems fair to assume that Thomas's personality was the same when he spoke those bold words as it was when he asked for proof of the resurrection. "Doubting" Thomas spoke boldly as a follower of Christ when it counted. His example comforts me on those days when my faith as a Christian is faint. I can follow his example to act boldly in my Christian life even if the faith part of my Christian journey says I want a road map. Jesus will meet my needs.

Don't Worry

Philippians 4:4-7

Glenn Bulthuis '77
Musician; Grand Rapids, Michigan

Rejoice in the Lord always. I will say it again: Rejoice! Let your gentleness be evident to all. The Lord is near. Do not be anxious about anything, but in everything, by prayer and petition, with thanksgiving, present your requests to God. And the peace of God, which transcends all understanding, will guard your hearts and your minds in Christ Jesus. (Phil. 4:4-7)

As I look at my life, I think it's fair to say that I've spent entirely too much time worrying. Yes, I pray, but I still worry; I still agonize; I still constantly weigh the pros and cons. Whenever I plan a major undertaking — a new job, putting on a concert — I plan and plan and plan. I lay it all out, I schedule everything, I pray, . . . and I worry. Why?

As I look back on my life, I can see God's hand clearly at work. I can point to a continuing succession of blessings, including a fine birth family, a wonderful wife, and a loving family of my own. I *know* that God is good, that he loves me, that he cares for me: I've never gone hungry; I've never slept in a cardboard box; I've never been desperately sick. Still, for some reason, when I look to the future, I don't *feel* sure. Why? Maybe it's just me, but I suspect it's part of the human condition.

The children of Israel wandered through the desert led by a column of fire and smoke. God opened up the Red Sea so they could cross, manna and quail were there for the taking every day, and yet they complained. They still couldn't see God, even though he was all around them. We're a lot like those faithless Israelites. Every morning that we wake up, our hearts have been beating silently throughout the night, and we breathe air, drink water, and fight off disease without regard for the incredible gift of life God gives each of us. We fail to see God in every moment of every day.

Clearly we need to be reminded daily to take time to pray. If we do, then we will increase our rejoicing and our thanks giving, and we will give up our obsessive worrying. We will experience the peace of God.

A Word for All Occasions

John L. Witvliet '64   Philippians 4:19
Pastor; Sioux Center, Iowa

People I know who send a lot of greeting cards often buy them by the box: birthday, get-well, or sympathy. Sometimes they buy a box of all-occasion cards, assorted cards suitable for various occasions. I find that it is sometimes difficult to find just the right card with just the right words for a particular situation and need.

But I do have just the right Bible text for any and every situation. It is the "just right" Word of the Lord when things are going well and when they are not. It is a good reminder during times of prosperity; it provides helpful encouragement in the face of economic stress. We can learn from it when we are healthy; it has a lesson for us when we are sick. It offers us a powerful truth when we are young and growing up; it provides us a very necessary truth when we are grown up and getting older. It offers a helpful anchor whatever the specifics of our lives at any given moment. I point you to the words of Philippians 4:19: "And my God will meet all your needs according to his glorious riches in Christ Jesus."

Of course, if we grasp this very precious promise, we will have to distinguish between needs and wants, but if we are able to do that, we have a most wonderful assurance. The God of the Bible will meet not some but all of our needs. And he will do it not out of but according to the riches of his grace in Christ Jesus. The God of the Bible, the God of creation and redemption, the God of the covenant and the kingdom, will not give us a token blessing, but a substantial one. The blessing will be in proportion to his lavish love and grace in Christ Jesus.

When I think about this all-occasion text, I am reminded of an old all-occasion hymn:

> If you but trust in God to guide you
>   and place your confidence in him,
> you'll find him always there beside you
>   to give you hope and strength within;
> for those who trust God's changeless love
>   build on the rock that will not move.*

I keenly hope that you are reminded, too.

Your Kingdom Come

Romans 8:31-39

Tony Van Zanten '61
Pastor; Chicago, Illinois

Lately I've been thinking about the idea of hope. I almost have to in order to make it through some days. It's my neighborhood and my friends that keep me hoping. Listen to a few of their stories.

Mack was on the streets, homeless, staying in our shelter. I taught him to say, "I am not my own but belong to Jesus." He thought it was the greatest thing he had ever heard. He was baptized. He became a church member. He got married and had three children. Today Mack is back on the street, a dope fiend again.

One day somebody came running into the Ministries Center and said, "One of your church members is in the alley. She doesn't have any clothes on." I went out there to see a two-year-old girl, not naked but close to it. I had baptized her a year earlier. Her mama had become a member of the church after coming off dope. On the day when the whole family was baptized, Mama grinned a big grin and said, "Me and my baby belong to Jesus." They laughed in joy over it. Now something had come and grabbed them. There aren't many sins bigger than leaving your baby abandoned in an alley.

A friend of mine, blind since age fifteen, told me that every morning when she wakes up she lies in her bed for a couple minutes with her eyes shut. After she is wide awake, she said, she deliberately and self-consciously opens her eyes to look around, fully expecting to be able to see again that day. "If I couldn't see yet this morning," she said, "that's okay because I know that tomorrow for sure I will see."

I want to learn to wake up every morning, look around Roseland on Chicago's south side, and fully expect to see the kingdom of God. Every day I pray, "Your kingdom come" (Matt. 6:10). Maybe today when I go back to 109th Street I'll look up and see that the kingdom of God has fully come. I'll look up and see Mack standing there with a grin on his face and his arms around his whole family. I'll see Sharon with a baby in her arms, and I'll hear them say, "Praise God. Praise God. Praise God. I still belong to Jesus. The Bible told the truth when it said that 'neither death nor life, neither angels nor demons, nor any other powers . . . will be able to separate us from the love of God that is in Christ Jesus our Lord'" (Rom. 8:38-39).

Maybe hope is not the idea I should be tossing around. Like my blind friend, I probably have to do less hoping and more believing that God will bring to pass that which he has promised.

Selfless Forgiving

Charlotte Van Oyen Witvliet '91   Colossians 3:13
Professor; Jenison, Michigan

> *Bear with each other and forgive whatever grievances you may have against one another. Forgive as the Lord forgave you.* (Col. 3:13)

When others hurt or betray us, we can choose a variety of responses. We can savor the sweetness of revenge or taste the richness of reconciliation. We can nurse grudges or grow in grace. We can dehumanize the transgressor or develop imaginative generosity, learning to see him or her as an imagebearer of God, who — like us — stands in need of grace.

When God forgives us, our sins are graciously blotted out and remembered no more (Isa. 43:25). This motivates many of us to "forgive as the Lord forgave" us. Yet in real life we can get stuck. Our misconceptions about forgiveness can leave us unable to think, feel, and maneuver through the mire of interpersonal hurts.

So what does or doesn't it mean for us to forgive? Despite the familiar cliché "forgive and forget," forgetting is nearly impossible for most of us. Forgiveness — at least for significant offenses — does not involve a literal forgetting. Instead, forgiveness involves remembering graciously: We remember the painful truth without the embellishment of choice adjectives and adverbs that stir up contempt.

Forgiveness also differs from ignoring, minimizing, tolerating, excusing, legally pardoning, liking, and reconciling. At times the church has done a disservice to survivors of neglect or abuse by suggesting that they need to reconcile with their offenders. Not so. It is wise to stay away from people who have proven themselves to be abusive or untrustworthy. Yet we still can forgive — a move that, paradoxically, frees us from the shackles of resentment and rage.

When we forgive, we relinquish grudges and vengeance against the blameworthy transgressor. We also intentionally cultivate merciful thoughts, feelings, or behaviors toward the offender. We find even small ways to genuinely wish him or her well. To forgive, we need to see the humanity of the transgressor. Though forgiveness comes more easily when the transgressor expresses contrite repentance, by the grace of God we can embody forgiveness even without it. As we look to Christ, we see the perfect model of selfless forgiving, and through him we receive the grace to "bear with each other and forgive."

Psalm 51:1 Steve J. Van Der Weele '49
Calvin professor emeritus; Grand Rapids, Michigan

S ometimes it seems that our legal system distinguishes among various offenses more justly than the Bible does. Achan is put to death for stealing, and Ananias and Sapphira die because of a lie, but the murderer on the cross receives saving grace in the last moments of his life. And the list of sins we encounter in the New Testament more or less lumps them all together. So how can we distinguish between big sins and little sins?

Biblical wisdom, of course, goes beyond legal codes. It emphasizes the state of the heart. It instructs us to examine not only the external actions but also the inner drama — intentions, motivation, attitudes. And such evaluation gives us some surprising results.

C. S. Lewis makes this case in *The Great Divorce*. Mr. Big Man, on a holiday from the infernal regions, is assigned as his mentor one of his former employees who had killed a fellow employee but who, through repentance, has come to a good end. In fact, the murderer and his victim live together in heaven. This makes no sense to Mr. Big Man. Surely our destinations should be reversed, he thinks. His mentor patiently tells him that the rules have changed. The murder? That was no big deal — an impulsive act, over before he knew it. But he does have something more serious to confess to his former employer: "I murdered you in my heart, deliberately, for years. I used to lie awake at nights thinking what I'd do to you if I ever got the chance." Then he asks Mr. Big Man's forgiveness.

In the economy of the kingdom, a seemingly inconsequential sin, practiced and unconfessed over a period of time, can place the soul in mortal danger. The secret trysts, income-tax discrepancies, the hidden lie — these are seemingly minor matters that nevertheless corrode the soul. The only remedy is a clean heart and a new spirit — the very "bleeding charity" Mr. Big Man has refused.

Creator and Reconciler of All Things

John Cooper '69   Colossians 1:9-20
Calvin Seminary professor; Grand Rapids, Michigan

If there is one passage of Scripture that clearly outlines the world and life view animating Calvin College, this it is. In just a few verses (Col. 1:15-20) Paul not only explains the person and work of Jesus Christ but also relates everything in creation and redemption to him. And he identifies the church as Christ's body, thus highlighting our place in Christ's cosmic activity.

Jesus Christ is the very image of God, the Son in whom the fullness of God himself lives. He is the creator of all things, the visible and invisible beings and dynamics of the universe as well as the tangible powers and authorities that regulate human life. Jesus Christ is the source of the good order, cooperation, and purpose of all things.

But there is a problem here. The cosmic powers and worldly authorities that move human life do not behave in an orderly, harmonious way. Dysfunctionality and conflict have attached themselves like parasites to the good creation, alienating things great and small from one another and ultimately from God. Darkness has dominion, it sometimes seems.

But the God who is fully present in Jesus Christ has been pleased to reconcile all things to himself through Jesus' death on the cross. Jesus' blood has the power to restore peace throughout the universe. He is the firstborn from the dead. He reversed the most devastating consequence of cosmic disorder and gave new life to all those who are members of his body, the church. They are the ones who have been rescued from the dominion of darkness, whose sins are forgiven, who have been brought into the light, the kingdom of his Son (Col. 1:13-14).

Paul's prayer (Col. 1:9-12) is that God will fill us who have been brought into his Son's kingdom "with the knowledge of his will through all spiritual wisdom and understanding" so that we may live lives "worthy of the Lord: . . . bearing fruit in every good work" to the glory of God. The spiritual wisdom of which Paul speaks has two parts: it is an *understanding of* God's activity in creation and redemption through Jesus Christ and faithful *participation in* it (as summarized in Col. 1:15-20).

May God continue to give his whole church spiritual wisdom, endurance, fruitful lives, joy, and peace in the coming kingdom of his Son.

It Just So Happened That . . .

Romans 8:28

Gordon Kamps '56
Retired missionary; Grand Rapids, Michigan

In Romans 8:28 we read, "And we know that in all things God works for the good of those who love him, who have been called according to his purpose." These are words of good comfort for Christians, and in a theological crunch we could probably identify these words as a proof text for the Reformed belief in God's undergirding providence. Yet in our daily lives we are sometimes careless about expressing our belief in providence. For example, we frequently and more or less offhandedly wish each other good luck — even though we don't really believe in luck — and "it just so happened that" is not at all foreign to our personal battery of cliches. Some of us often use this phrase as we recount certain events that have occurred in our lives. The use of this phrase suggests a happenstance, or chance happening, which we may not intend to convey as we tell our story. To the contrary, I am frequently struck, as many of you must be, by how the happenstances of our lives are choreographed to impress us with the fact that nothing ever "just so happens" to us.

As I write this devotional, Ruth and I have just returned from a trip to Turkey, Jordan, and Egypt, and the events of the devastating earthquakes in parts of Turkey and the crash of Egypt Air Flight 990 are fresh in our minds. These events remind us of how often on our trip we heard in response to our question "How are you?" the Arabic words for "Good, thanks be to God!"

People of the Islamic faith give expression to the direction of Allah in their lives in many ways. I can remember my parents and their friends also using similar phrases as they greeted one another personally or by letter. Sometimes these phrases, which gave recognition to God's direction and working in their lives, may have been made rather routinely, but those of us who see God's plan so marvelously and miraculously provided in our salvation and in our lives should reflect upon ways that we can give expression to the fact that nothing ever "just so happens." If we do, we may be used by God to help comfort and assure those whose recognition of God's love and direction in their lives is blurred by difficult circumstances. They need to know that "in all things God works for the good of those who love him." We need to tell them. It doesn't "just so happen."

Forgetting God

Rachael Stevenson   Isaiah 49:14-16
Calvin student; Grand Rapids, Michigan

As we grow older, we get smarter because we've taken many classes in everything from calculus and Western civilization to Spanish, biology, religion, and sociology. This feeling of intellectual maturity can lead to a loss of dependence on God, because we think we now are capable of being dependent on ourselves. As I have grown and matured in my academic studies and in my social life, I find my spiritual life dwindling away.

Sometimes I feel like the little boy who had a new baby brother named Luke. This little boy kept asking his parents if he could be alone with Luke for a little while, and this really worried the parents. What did big brother have in mind? But the little boy was persistent, and finally one evening the parents let him into Luke's room by himself. They stood outside the doorway and peeked in as their firstborn peered over the railing of Luke's crib. He looked down at the baby in the crib and said with complete sincerity, "Luke, tell me about God. I think I am forgetting him."

When we feel that we can do something completely on our own, we are in the worst kind of trouble because we are denying God's presence in our lives and in the world and our dependence upon him. We should never think we have become too smart for needing God, but sometimes the simplest things to believe are the hardest to understand.

Have faith in God every day, for every part of your life. Pray with the knowledge that the King of the universe is listening to you intently. Live knowing he holds your hand. Love everyone because he has loved you so much, and never think you can do anything without him.

Don't ever forget God. He has never forgotten you, and he never will.

Giving What We Are

Mark 12:41-44

Laura Buunk Jensen '86
Missionary; Hong Kong, China

The world's yardstick of success is very exacting. Whether it be in money or title, we can always look to another who is more or less successful than we are. The race for worldly success is one that is unfulfilling and unending.

How much more fulfilling is God's measurement of success. By the world's standards, the widow of today's text had nothing to give. In the economy of Jesus' kingdom, she gave her all in love to her God. She not only loved God through her small gift, but she also had the faith that he could be pleased with her gift and use it toward his kingdom. She had the faith to put her life completely in his hands, knowing she had given everything.

All of us have God-given gifts, and all are called to be living sacrifices to him. We cannot excuse ourselves with thoughts that, if only we had this or that talent, we could please God. God is not calling us to give what we do not have. Our attempts to please God should begin with that which he has given us. We must have the love for God to give all that we are to him and the faith that, although God needs nothing, he will be pleased with our gift and will use it for his glory. Finally, we need faith that, after we have given our all, he will provide for all our needs.

God receives our gifts in much the same way that parents receive the homemade gifts of their children — the card crudely lettered, the hand print in plaster, the macaroni flowers on a paper plate. The results may not be noteworthy or valuable by earthly standards, but these gifts are treasured because of the love in which they were created. We must learn to freely give our love gifts to God, not concentrating on the imperfection of the gift or giver but on the grace and joy of the receiver, our loving Father, who chooses to be pleased and glorified by a gift from his beloved child.

The world may view us, like the widow, as unsuccessful nobodies, but to God we are his precious children, who please him by giving him all that we are in love and in faith.

151

Tricia De Boer Koning '89   John 9:2-3
Publishing administrator; Westchester, Illinois

> *His disciples asked him, "Rabbi, who sinned, this man or his parents, that he was born blind?" "Neither this man nor his parents sinned," said Jesus, "but this happened so that the work of God might be displayed in his life."*
>
> (John 9:2-3)

For a person racked with personal pain or horrified by public violence, it takes little effort to see situations in life that call for healing or repair. In many of these cases earnest prayer and extra effort do not eliminate human suffering and struggling. Scripture gives us little reason to expect anything different if one is a believer: "for it has been granted to you on behalf of Christ not only to believe on him, but also to suffer for him" (Phil. 1:29). Suffering and even persecution for the sake of one's faith seem noble, purposeful, and almost inevitable.

But why do people suffer hardships that don't originate as a result of having faith? Take the apostle Paul, for example. In Scripture he pleads three times for the removal of his "thorn in the flesh," but it doesn't go away (2 Cor. 12:7). Look at the man born blind, in today's Scripture passage. His handicap forces him to "sit and beg" (John 9:8). He has a life of hardship for no apparent reason. He and Paul are not alone in Scripture as the only examples of people being afflicted with hardships that are not the results of their faith.

The disciples question Jesus about why the blind man is blind. What is the sense of this? Is the blind man being punished for his parents' sin? No, Jesus says, not for his parents' sin and not for his own sin. "This happened so that the work of God might be displayed in his life" (John 9:3).

Jesus restores the sight of the man born blind and so displays the work of God. Paul finds that his thorn in the flesh is a weakness through which "Christ's power may rest on me. . . . For when I am weak, then I am strong" (2 Cor. 12:9, 10). Both Paul and the man born blind lived with the constant reminder that the world is full of brokenness that needs repair. Their experiences with human struggles challenge us to believe the words of Jesus and to trust that in our troubles, diseases, and disorders "the work of God might be displayed" (John 9:3).

Jesus, in the Nick of Time

Mark 6:45-52; John 6:16-21

Lou Roossien '66
Pastor; Muskegon, Michigan

G ood ghost stories create terror and then precious relief. In the story
of Jesus stilling the storm, Jesus' friends were about to be scared silly
by an apparition skimming the waves which were threatening to swamp
their boat. Both Mark's and John's versions tell us that it was high time for
Jesus' dark-night walk on the water. Jesus saw the disciples straining at the
oars, but he had "not yet joined them" (John 6:17).

It all makes the reader wonder: How bad was the storm? Why did Jesus
decide to walk on the water? and, especially, Why did Jesus wait so long to
come?

Sometimes we find ourselves in deep water, struggling hard against
the wind, bailing for dear life. Like Jesus' friends, we've done everything we
can, been as obedient as we know how. Then the storm bursts, washing
away the naive assumption that, if we just do the right things, we'll avoid
suffering. Ask the faithful couple whose crib is empty, the parents whose
child dies before they do, the single parent who loses a son to the streets,
the family that loses everything in a disastrous "act of God." So the wind
blows, and we pray and pull harder on the oars. But where is God when we
need him? Why does he wait so long?

Maybe this little story sheds some light on why God doesn't seem to
come immediately when we call: Two maestros listen to a promising young
soprano. "What a pure, clear voice!" says the first. His friend replies, "Yes,
but she'll sing better once her heart is broken." Some lessons are learned
only through pain, and sometimes God allows us to endure the pain for
the sake of the song.

Often it's the timing that sucks us into a story as it becomes our own.
Jesus timed his walk on the water to meet his friends at their point of great-
est need. He still shows up in the nick of time in the most unlikely places:
in the kitchen, in the cell block, in the nursing home, in the boat. Yet, when
God comes, we don't always recognize him: Jesus' disciples were "terrified"
(Mark 6:50; John 6:19), for "they thought he was a ghost" (Mark 6:49).
Then fear was replaced by his presence as the I AM climbed into the boat
with them, "the wind died down," and "they were completely amazed"
(Mark 6:51).

　　　　　　　　　　　　　　　　　　　# A New Heart

Rich DeVos '47 　　　　　　　　　　　　　　　　　Philippians 4:4-7
Businessman; Manalapan, Florida

Rejoice in the Lord always. I will say it again: Rejoice! Let your gentleness be evident to all. The Lord is near. Do not be anxious about anything, but in everything, by prayer and petition, with thanksgiving, present your requests to God. And the peace of God, which transcends all understanding, will guard your hearts and your minds in Christ Jesus. (Phil. 4:4-7)

This Scripture passage is special to me. It touches my heart and truly speaks to me because it helped get me through a very anxious time in my life.

On June 2, 1997, after a stroke, a severe heart attack, two bypass surgeries, a bad staph infection, and the limitations of a badly damaged heart muscle, I had a heart transplant. Because I was seventy-one years old at the time, a heart was not available to me in the United States. However, the fact that I have the rarest blood type convinced a transplantation doctor in another country to accept me as a patient. My wife and I waited in the foreign country from January 4 to July 2, when the right heart for me became available. A thirty-nine-year-old woman was about to receive a new heart and new lungs, and her heart was a perfect fit for me in every way — even to having a strong right side, without which (the doctors told me later) I could not have survived. It was a heart that no one else in that country could use, another condition which had to be filled. Truly, God perfectly provides.

The Lord blessed me with a successful transplantation surgery, helped me through a tough recovery process, and delivered me from the danger and disappointment of rejecting the new heart. He also made it possible for one of our four children to be with us throughout the whole ordeal and for a worldwide circle of friends to lift us up continually in prayer. What a joy and encouragement it was to have so many prayer partners.

Having a new physical heart is a great blessing to me, but an even greater blessing has been the new spiritual heart I was given many years ago when I gave my life to Christ. With that heart there was never a question of rejection, for Christ has helped me to keep the heart of faith, to persevere from day to day, and for that I praise the Lord. Gifted with two "new" hearts, I try to live my life every day to fulfill the purpose for which he saved me.

Are you looking for a great Cardiologist? Than Jesus Christ there is none better. I am his witness.

Inside the Box

Romans 8:10-11

Paula Tuinstra Wigboldy '80
Speaker/agent; Chandler, Arizona

But if Christ is in you, your body is dead because of sin, yet your spirit is alive because of righteousness. And if the Spirit of him who raised Jesus from the dead is living in you, he who raised Christ from the dead will also give life to your mortal bodies through his Spirit, who lives in you. (Rom. 8:10-11)

A few weeks ago we had a visiting minister at our church. When he walked in, he went to the front and set his papers down. With them was an old box, a small box, rather tattered, brown, certainly nothing special. My daughter must have noticed the box too. She immediately tapped me on the shoulder. "Look, Mom. He's got something with him." Illustrations are a Sunday bonus for Kim. This sermon was going to be fun. We both wondered what he had in that box.

As the service proceeded, our anticipation grew. We were both rather excited about what was ahead. Would it be something the children needed to walk to the front to get? Was it something alive? Perhaps it was something very old and very special that the minister wanted to tell us about. When he walked up to begin his portion of the service, the minister grabbed his box and opened it. Inside was his Bible — something quite different from what we had imagined. But maybe this was the ultimate illustration.

When he took the Bible out of the box, it looked brand new. As I got to thinking about the protection the box provides for that Bible, I wondered whether we cherish what's inside our bodies, our box, as the minister cherishes what is inside his box. Inside our frail and decaying bodies we have very special gifts — the image of God, salvation, the power of the Holy Spirit. Do we treat these gifts inside us as though they are our prized possessions? The body is going to grow old and decay, but what's inside is everlasting. We have a heart filled with God's love. We have a soul saved by God's grace. We have a faith nurtured by God's spirit.

May we cherish what's inside us and share these gifts with a friend today.

Wonderfully Made

Christiana de Groot   Psalm 139:13-14
Calvin professor; Grand Rapids, Michigan

> *For you created my inmost being;*
> *you knit me together in my mother's womb.*
> *I praise you because I am fearfully and wonderfully made;*
> *your works are wonderful, I know that full well.* (Ps. 139:13-14)

A plumber friend had stopped by on a hot Saturday afternoon to fix a leaky toilet for me. The job finished, we sat on the steps for a while, chatting and drinking iced tea. He told me that he had come to my house from installing the plumbing in a bathroom that had been completely remodeled — new tile, new tub, and new fixtures. A peculiar thing had happened while he was working. He noticed that his cheeks were wet because his eyes were tearing. After reflecting, he concluded that there was a particular smell in that bathroom that he recognized. It came from the tile grout. He had smelled the smell before as a soldier in Korea. It was the smell of body bags. His tears, he realized, were tears of sorrow and grief, mourning those who had lost their lives in the war.

Among other things we ruminated on that afternoon was how fearfully and wonderfully we are made. We figured that his subconscious mind had recognized the smell and had triggered an emotional response of sadness, which had triggered the physical response of tears. After he became conscious of the wetness of his cheeks, he then recovered the memory that was the reason for the grief.

How interconnected the many parts of us are: sense perception, memory, emotions, the subconscious, and the conscious. We truly are integrated beings. Our minds and bodies, our pasts and presents are threads which, woven together, create the mysterious fabric of our lives. And our lives are interwoven with the lives of many others as well. We grieve when we remember those who have died — a part of us is broken. The woof and warp of our lives are intertwined with the lives of others. All together we are the wonderful work of the master weaver.

Hebrews 13:5   Grace Aukema Roossien '67
Financial planner; Vestal, New York

Keep your lives free from the love of money, and be content with what you have.
(Heb. 13:5)

During my childhood I learned that Christians should not think or talk too much about money. In fact, focusing too much on money issues was considered almost sinful. The dictum to live by was "God will provide" — and it's none of your neighbors' business.

And so, in our schools and our churches, Christians never learned much about money management. Many adult Christians (women even more so than men), therefore, are unskilled in money-management techniques and feel uncomfortable managing their God-given financial resources.

Unfortunately, although we shy away from discussions about money and from developing a careful understanding of money management, we make financial decisions almost every day of our lives. Even more unfortunately, some of our greatest relationship problems as adults stem from financial worries caused by poor communication and inadequate money-management skills.

One of the most important truths I have learned through years of working with adults in financial management is that a healthy understanding of the role money plays in our lives as Christians is fundamental to using our resources for the glory of God. For the faithful, obedient Christian, money, wealth, and financial resources of all kinds are blessings from God. With them comes responsibility, as Jesus demonstrated in his parable of the talents.

Our challenge, therefore, is to be sure that the source of our wealth is pleasing to God and not injurious to others and that we use our wealth to serve and honor God and one another.

Get Wisdom

Orin G. Gelderloos '61   Psalm 104
Professor; Dearborn, Michigan

S olomon is well-known for his wives, his wisdom, his proverbs, and the
Temple God requested him to build (1 Kings 4:29-34). He is less well-
known for his reputation as a great interpreter of all of God's creation. First
Kings 4:33-34 indicates that Solomon was knowledgeable about flora and
fauna, including the majestic cedars and the tenacious plants that grew from
the walls of the cities. Solomon was knowledgeable enough to teach about
the various species, and people from the far reaches of the then-known world
sought his opinion and knowledge. Solomon's knowledge of flora and fauna
is not described as a purely utilitarian technical skill to be used for trade or
commerce. His knowledge of the creation and its numerous species was part
of the wisdom all human beings should endeavor to acquire. He understood
the meaning of the phrase "Let every creature praise the LORD's holy name
for ever and ever" (Ps. 145:21), as expressed by his father, David, because he
recognized creation's part in praising God.

Because Solomon had great wisdom in the ways of the natural world,
he could advise on appropriate behavior for living in a way that would help
to sustain creation. He was acutely aware that God enjoys watching his
creatures play and frolic (Ps. 104:26) and that to degrade or interfere with
these activities is to dishonor the Creator. Solomon also understood that
the land needs a Sabbath so that God will be honored (Lev. 25:2) and the
land will continue to be fruitful.

Today even children can identify more than a thousand commercial
products by sight or by advertising jingle. Yet very few people know much
about the species of plants and animals that inhabit their own neighbor-
hoods. We are limited in our knowledge of the flora and fauna of creation
as well as in our knowledge of the processes by which the creation can be
maintained in all its fullness, fruitfulness, and integrity. Granted, we could
never come close to having the wisdom of Solomon with respect to the natural world, but we should really ratchet up our individual and collective attempts to make a bigger dent in it.

A wise person observes, respects, and understands God's creatures and
the natural processes upon which they depend. We may not have the
knowledge and wisdom of Solomon, but we can pray for insight and wisdom to honor God by respecting his creation in our daily lives, and we can
pray for the determination, the stamina, the financial commitment, and
the political savvy to protect our Father's world.

Who but Jesus?

John 14:1-7

Joel Edward Kok '82
Pastor; Broomall, Pennsylvania

A friend of mine goes to church, but he has abandoned the faith of his childhood. He cannot call himself a Christian, he says, because he rejects the exclusionary claims of the Christian faith. He loves non-Christians, so he refuses to accept Jesus' statement "I am the way and the truth and the life. No one comes to the Father except through me" (John 14:6).

I urge my friend and others troubled like him to consider the apostle Paul. Paul believed in Jesus Christ as the only Savior, but his faith did not turn him into an exclusionary zealot. Instead, Christ transformed Paul into a lover of all humanity. Paul's love for unbelievers came out with particular clarity and intensity in his relationship with the Jews. Paul testified, "I have great sorrow and unceasing anguish in my heart. For I could wish that I myself were accursed and cut off from Christ for the sake of my brothers, those of my own race" (Rom. 9:2-3).

Paul came to faith in Christ by means of a direct experience of Jesus' mercy to sinners. Christ's mercy led Paul through his anguish over unbelievers into an assurance that in some mysterious way God will make everything right: "For God has bound everyone over to disobedience so that he may have mercy on them all" (Rom. 11:32, NIVI), exclaimed Paul, and this led him to sing, "For from him and through him and to him are all things. To him be the glory forever! Amen" (Rom. 11:36).

Like Paul, my friend learned to love from Jesus. I hope that, like Paul, my friend also learns to express his love through a trustful hope that somehow, through Christ Jesus, "God may be all in all" (1 Cor. 15:28).

Finally, I ask my friend what I ask you: Who but Jesus perfectly reveals the heavenly Father? Whom but Jesus can we trust to judge the living and the dead? Who but Jesus is deserving of being the center of one's faith?

God-conscious

Mark Hiskes '79   **2 Corinthians 5:16-17**
Teacher; Holland, Michigan

In *Pilgrim at Tinker Creek* Annie Dillard writes, "Experiencing the present purely is being emptied and hollow; you catch grace as a man fills his cup under a waterfall."* I experienced an invigorating emptiness, and I caught some grace this summer while backpacking with friends in the Canadian Rockies. My journal tells the story:

> I haven't seen myself for days, and it's such a relief! I've got a beard growing, but I can't tell how bad it looks. I haven't combed my hair in a week (or washed it for that matter), but I can't see how greasy it is. My clothes are stained and smelly. No matter: They're warm. Come to think of it, I haven't seen one advertisement in a whole week.
>
> There are no garish billboards here in the Rockies, no sexy magazine covers, no deadening commercial breaks between mountain passes, no advertising jingles that won't go away. Back home we see 3,500 advertisements a day, they say. Here on the trail, McDonald's can't make me hungry for fries, Pontiac can't make moving slowly seem unexciting, and even L. L. Bean can't locate my address.
>
> No mirrors, no advertising. Here I can be so unself-conscious. I'm a little kid again, absorbed by everything I see and hear, shocked silent by things more worthy than myself: the ever-present Rockwall Ridge, Floe Lake at sunrise, Indian paintbrush sprinkling the meadow at breakfast, a thundering glacier at lunch time, a raging waterfall at dinner, and more grace waiting beyond each mountain pass we hike. Annie Dillard was right: "Self-consciousness is the curse of the city."* Oh, out here I feel blessed.
>
> I'd like to avoid advertisements and mirrors when I get back home, because I think God's telling me something important about being less self-conscious and more other-conscious — more God-conscious. He's showing me, I think, how to simply be that new creature Christ has seen in me all along — the one beneath the beard, the messy hair, and the dirty clothes.

Fashion Sense

Colossians 3:12-15   Connie Kuiper Van Dyke '67
Administrative assistant; Grand Rapids, Michigan

Have you ever worried about wearing the right thing? I see many beautiful and well-dressed people, and I wonder how they learned that style, where they got that fashion sense. It must be something parents teach their children, something they model for them.

My mother had very little fashion sense. She always wore a loose dress and usually an apron — one of the old-fashioned kind that covered her ample bosom and wrapped around her waist to tie in the back. She was a wonderful woman, but often, as I agonize over what to wear, I desperately wish she had taught me more about style.

My Father, however, has come to my rescue by telling me precisely what to wear: "Clothe yourselves with compassion, kindness, humility, gentleness, and patience" (Col. 3:12). I have to begin by putting away the old, dirty clothing. If I let my anger lie on the floor beside my bed, the next morning I very easily wrap myself in it again. And sarcasm fits me so easily that I rarely stop to think whether it is really becoming on a child of God.

Though I really want to be compassionate and kind and humble, I've been waiting somewhat impatiently for God to dress me that way. Instead, he asks me to act, to put on these virtues very deliberately, to wrap myself up in gentleness and wear it as a garment. Rather than an ounce of kindness, he wants enough to cover me. And then, to finish my outfit, he wants enough love to cover everything, just as my mother's aprons used to cover her other clothes.

Having a flair for clothes is a gift, but all of us are attractive when we wear the clothes God has designed for us, the clothes his Son has modeled for us, clothes available equally to all of us, regardless of our personal wealth.

Imagine the day your child comes home from school and asks for help with her clothes because she sees that John forgives others so easily, that Cindy is so kind, and that Joey is so patient that she wants to look like that, too. That's the fashion sense I want to teach my children.

Vengeance

Rozanne Meyer Bruins '72   Matthew 5:38-42
Chaplain; Grand Rapids, Michigan

All of us have an appetite for vengeance. If we know anything about ourselves, it's that we are naturally wired to retaliate. The "I don't get mad; I get even" bumper sticker plays out in our everyday lives. The car that wouldn't let us merge in the mobbed parking lot? We're not letting it in later, when its lane shuts down. It's a raw emotion, this business of vengeance, retaliation, and we think we're entitled to it.

Jesus has something to say about this, however. What he says in today's passage from his Sermon on the Mount is radical. It's controversial. But Jesus couldn't have cared less because he cares more about how his children live than about public opinion. To his followers then and now, Jesus says, "Respond in love to those who do evil to you personally." He contrasts the traditional teaching of the law with his teaching: "You have heard that it was said, 'Eye for eye, and tooth for tooth.' But I tell you, Do not resist an evil person" (Matt. 5:38-39). He then goes on to give four examples of how his children can lovingly respond to someone who has personally wronged them.

It's a tough job to put retaliation in the backseat and love behind the wheel. But we can do that by the grace of God, embodied in the cross. There the Son of God, crucified, fulfilled the traditional law. This grace of God, then, empowers us to obey Jesus' "updated law." And it gives us tremendous freedom in Christ to be agents of grace.

How is God calling you to be an agent of grace today? By breaking the chain of evil that can choke the life out of a feuding family? By practicing tough love, not for your own satisfaction but for Jesus' sake? However he calls you, return good for evil because the cross has made vengeance obsolete.

Imitation

Luke 8:26-39

Cole Ruth '95
Marketing/community relations;
Grand Rapids, Michigan

Where I work, we have sophisticated terminology for the disturbances of the mind, words like *bipolar, psychotic, schizoaffective*. You can become hard, working at a place like this. At any one time you might see a seventeen-year-old girl who never takes her hands from her eyes for fear of being seen or seeing others. Or a boy who picks at his skin and chafes himself until he bleeds. Or another girl, diagnosed as psychotic at age six, who thinks she's a Jew in World War II Germany. She calls the social worker a Nazi and believes the other patients are her enemies. Left alone in a room, she crouches along the ground or slides tiptoe along the walls, searching for hidden passages.

A psychologist explained psychosis to me in this way: a state in which a person has entered an alternative reality to escape the pain of the real one. Its onset is in early childhood. It is caused by the experience of trauma or extreme abuse. It is irreversible even with the most sophisticated drugs and therapies.

But we check them in, and we try, with a kind of madness of our own, to turn back the tide. If for a moment we forget the fine line of sanity that separates us from our patients, we find that we too begin confusing reality, that our own lives are cluttered with the same fears and anxieties, masked ever-so-thinly by the guise of the workplace or middle-class life.

Then we do what people have always done in difficult situations: We look for someone who shares our story. We look to gain strength in the solidarity of suffering, and in the community of fellow sufferers we may indirectly find a measure of healing.

Today's Scripture passage tells the story of a man named Legion because he is filled with many demons. Jesus comes to him on the hillside and talks to his demons. The demons plead with Jesus to let them remain in the man, but Jesus, seeing some pigs in a nearby field, forces the demons from Legion's body into the herd, as though by magic. And the pigs go careening over the cliff to drown in the lake below.

This, I think, is the business we Christians must be about: imitation — the business of imitating Jesus, of trying our utmost each day, one by one, to chase the demons away and force them into the abyss where they belong. Then those who are cleansed can tell "all over town how much Jesus [has] done for [them]" (Luke 8:39).

Living in God's House

Calvin B. DeWitt '57   Romans 1:20
Professor; Oregon, Wisconsin

"The heavens declare the glory of God" (Ps. 19:1). We were overwhelmed by this truth as we stood on the mountaintop singing. It was late, dark, and drizzly. We had come up by a narrow road, our headlight beams bouncing off flickering rocks and trees. Now, huddling on the top, all thirty-five of us sang. When we came to "The clouds be rolled back as a scroll," the clouds opened up, and the moon broke through wonderfully high above. Suddenly, like a huge surprise, a meteorite streamed across the clear sky. A day that had begun in fog and drizzle was ending under a cold, clear, awesome sky. It was indeed well with our souls.

At dawn the next day the whole group of evangelical relief-and-development workers from around the world gathered at the base of Mount Rainier to reflect on the testimony of creation found in Psalm 19:1 and Romans 1:20. In that marvelous temple of the outdoors, one had to believe. There was no doubt about God's divinity and everlasting power, no excuse, because the signs were all around us. The experience brought to my mind the *Psalter Hymnal* version of Psalm 29: "And through all Creation, His wonderful temple, All things He has fashioned His glory declare."*

All of creation is God's house. It is in God's great house (Gr. *oikos*) that we build our smaller houses. And it is within God's great economy of creation — God's *oikonomia* — that we build our own human economy. If ours does not mesh with God's, we build ours in vain. Respecters of God's house want everyone to live in accord with its economy. They pray, "Your kingdom come, your will be done, on earth . . ." (Matt. 6:10). When we are tuned in to God's economy, we can come out of the drizzle into silvery light and sing, "It is well, it is well with my soul."**

God in the Details

Philippians 4:6-7   Cindi Rozendal Veenstra '78
Nonprofit administrator; Kalamazoo, Michigan

On a cold, rainy September afternoon, my husband, son, and I were driving home from Chicago to Kalamazoo. About an hour and a half from home, we saw a car stuck far down in a ditch. I commented, "Wow, that seems recent." Then we noticed a man walking farther down the road. Though we generally don't pull over, this time we decided to stop to help since we had a cell phone in the car. We got off the highway and circled back to find the driver, who was still walking in the rain toward an exit. When we pulled in behind him and honked the horn, he came to the car and explained that he had hydroplaned into the ditch almost two hours earlier. He had called the police and a wrecker, but no one had come. Disregarding all we had been taught, we invited him into our car and asked him where he was heading.

"I'm a student at Calvin College," he said.

"We have a son at Calvin, Jeremy Veenstra." The young man's mouth fell, and he looked stunned.

"I'm Eric Veenstra!" Now it was time for my mouth to drop.

"Is your dad Doug, who volunteers for the Luke Society?"

"Yes."

"We're on our way back from a Luke Society meeting in Chicago. We met your dad and mom at this same meeting last year!"

In the end we waited while Eric's car was towed to Sawyer, and then we brought him home to sleep in Jeremy's bed. On the way Eric confessed that while he was walking down the road after being alone, cold, and shaken for two hours, he was praying, "God, I know you are in control, but please send some *people* here to help me." As he said the word *me,* he heard our car horn.

There was a lesson for all of us in what happened that day, and of course we've all told the story more than once. Two Veenstra males at Calvin College, the Luke Society connection, two Calvin-connected cars "recognizing" each other on a highway — you can chalk it up to Dutch bingo, the Dutch connection, or just plain luck, but to us it was plainly a lesson in God's faithfulness even in the small things of life. The clincher? God even provided a way for Eric to get back to Calvin the next morning: My husband had a meeting in Grand Rapids the next day, just a half-hour later than Eric's first class. He hadn't had a meeting in Grand Rapids for years before this.

God is surely in the big thing here — sparing Eric's life when his car left the road. But God is also in the details. Praise him for his faithfulness.

Priority Check

William D. Buursma '49 Luke 12:13-21
Retired pastor; Grand Rapids, Michigan

The reason why Jesus told the parable about the rich fool is a fascinating one. Two brothers are at odds. A bitter battle is going on between them because of a dispute over an inheritance. One has grabbed it all, much to the dismay of the other. Seething with resentment, the victim of his brother's greed comes to Jesus with the hope that the wise Rabbi from Nazareth will be able to mediate the controversy. He approaches our Lord with a request: "Teacher, tell my brother to divide the inheritance with me" (Luke 12:13).

Our Lord, who knows the hearts of all, is fully aware that the petitioner has his priorities in the wrong place. Like so many of us, he measures happiness in terms of possessions. He, like his brother, majors in minors and seeks material prosperity to the detriment of his soul. The response of the Savior is candid and curt: "Man," he says, "who appointed me a judge or an arbiter between you?" (Luke 12:14).

Today, too, many people, like the aggrieved sibling, want to enlist Jesus in their personal crusades, vendettas, and campaigns. We all want our Lord to espouse our causes, whether that is our responsibility for the needs of the Third World, a favorite political party, our side in a marital dispute, or our theological point of view.

However, the great Teacher politely but firmly declines to become captive to any ideology other than his own. He will not speak the final word in all our political, social, and ethical differences. He will not be put in a box.

In the case of the disputing brothers, Jesus looks beyond the request for arbitration to the real problem: the priorities of the petitioner. Instead of granting the man what he wants, Jesus points him to what he needs. To demonstrate this, he tells the parable of the rich fool, who is contemplating the long years of life he still expects to enjoy by cashing in his certificates of deposit, wintering in summer climates, and summering in cool northern forests. He says, "Take life easy; eat, drink and be merry" (Luke 12:19). Suddenly his reverie is interrupted when a divine voice thunders from heaven, "You fool! This very night your life will be demanded from you" (Luke 12:20).

That's the story, and this is the message: You are looking in the wrong place for happiness. When death invades the family circle and a legacy is to be divided, ask not, in the first place, how much you will get, but let the death of your dear one remind you of your own mortality. In the familiar words of our wise Rabbi and Savior, "What good will it be for you to gain the whole world, yet forfeit your soul?" (Matt. 16:26, NIVI).

Get Over It

Colossians 3:13

John J. Hoogland '55
Retired pastor; Oceanport, New Jersey

Forgive as the Lord forgave you. (Col. 3:13)

The fact that the *Titanic* sank is not exactly news. The movie — and the media coverage promoting it — served to focus our attention on this tragedy. Nearly everyone knows that the unsinkable ship hit an iceberg and sank.

Shortly after the movie came out, I saw a T-shirt that stated simply, "It Sank; Get Over It." If those words had been expressed in 1912, they would have been offensive, terribly lacking in compassion. But that was then and this is now. Today the words are somehow humorous. They have a little message for all of us: Get over it and move on with your life.

Some experiences in life are so recent and painful we simply cannot get over them easily: the loss of a job; an angry, litigious divorce; or the death of a spouse, for example. Only time and the grace of God can mend such hurts. But many of us may still be carrying much lesser wounds from home, school, work, or play. We are still angry with a relative, teacher, or classmate, a supervisor or business partner, or even a teammate or coach from earlier years. We simply cannot get over the offense and be reconciled, no matter how much time has passed.

On a surface level, all that is required is common sense — and maybe a little common grace — the common sense and the common grace that God gives to everyone. On a deeper level, however, the Christian virtues of forgiveness and reconciliation may be required. Why should we carry around a bag full of anger that weighs us down and threatens to crush our spiritual, mental, and physical health?

"Forgive as the Lord forgave you" (Col. 3:13). "Be reconciled" (2 Cor. 5:20). The past is past. Let bygones be bygones. Forgive, be reconciled, and become whole again. Get over it!

Randall Postmus '87   Philippians 2:3-5
Principal/teacher; Visalia, California

"*Whatever!*" There is nothing quite like the sound of that word echoing from the mouth of a disgruntled adolescent. What hurts even more is the growing prevalence of the "whatever" attitude in our society at large. It's part apathy, part disownment, and part denial. In other words, if something isn't going my way or the way I think it should, I'll just let it go — ouch!

Where is your attitude at this moment? Is the glass half full, half empty, or maybe never filled? What important choices or decisions have you made, are you making, or will you make? We do make important choices every moment we are alive, and they do affect every dimension of our being. More important, they affect our walk with the Lord and the witness that is seen in and through us. It's not a bad idea to ask yourself, "What would Jesus do?" (WWJD), as the popular saying goes.

Philippians 2:3-5 gives us a great help, especially in verse five: "Do nothing out of selfish ambition or vain conceit, but in humility consider others better than yourselves. Each of you should look not only to your own interests but also to the interests of others. Your attitude should be the same as that of Christ Jesus." Wow! What a powerful challenge, whatever the circumstances.

To help in the many necessary attitude adjustments or to gain an "attitude of gratitude," we need to focus on the right things. Philippians again helps out in this area with an even greater challenge, proclaiming, "Finally, brothers, whatever is true, whatever is noble, whatever is right, whatever is pure, whatever is lovely, whatever is admirable — if anything is excellent or praiseworthy — think about such things. Whatever you have learned or received or heard from me, or seen in me — put it into practice. And the God of peace will be with you" (Phil. 4:8-9).

So let the joy of the Lord be your strength, and let his attitude be your attitude. Life's not just about *Whatever!* It's about *"whatever is"* — true, noble, right, pure, lovely, and admirable. Think about these things.

Spirituality of the Road

Colossians 3:1-4, 12-17   Harry Boonstra '60
Calvin librarian emeritus; Grand Rapids, Michigan

Bookstore shelves are filled with books and other exhortations about spirituality, and I need to listen to some of what they have to say. One thing I especially need to learn from them is that spirituality requires the creation of time, of pushing for space in my calendar. We all need "to go into the hills to pray"; we have to learn withdrawal from deadlines and meetings. As my theater-trained daughter says, we need "centering" on our inner being and on God that will filter out the demands of our world.

But I also need to hear another voice, a voice which says, "Yes, we enter deeply into our union with Christ, but we are not be otherworldly." When I hear someone say that times of work or family or recreation are "moments stolen from God," my Reformed antennae start tingling. Our spirituality must maintain an earthboundness. Even though our spirits soar, in the midst of that soaring we must still say with e.e. cummings, "i thank You God for most this amazing day." And "most this amazing day" includes the laughter and tears around me as well as the blue skies and bluebooks of our everyday life. When in the midst of your quiet time you hear your daughter calling, "Dad/Mom, you said you'd go fishing with me at 9:00," you say to God, "Lord, I gotta go. Talk to you later."

All of that is summed up in a phrase I borrowed from the great missiologist David Bosch: "Being spiritual means being in Christ, whether we pray or walk or work. Spirituality is not contemplation over against action. . . . The involvement in this world should lead to deepening of our relationship with and dependence on God, and the deepening of this relationship should lead to increasing involvement in the world."

Of course, Bosch is here in the good company of Saint Paul. In Colossians Paul says, "Set your hearts on things above" — and get rid of anger right here. "Set your minds on things above" — and be compassionate to the people around you. " Your life is now hidden in Christ" — but be patient with your families. That's the kind of spirituality of the road Paul preaches.

We need to nurture spiritual discipline. But we should discipline ourselves against a world-flight spirituality. We need both — a full devotion to our calling in this life and a coming apart to be with the Lord. May we yield to the Spirit as we seek this harmony, this shalom.

Faithful Memories

George Vander Weit '64

Deuteronomy 6:7

Pastor; Troy, Michigan

Impress them on your children. . . . (Deut. 6:7)

As the water rolled down the face of the baby girl I had just baptized, I thought of Jen. Spiritual nurture had been important to her parents. They had taken their children to church each Sunday, read the Bible at home, and often gathered around the pump organ to sing the hymns of faith. In Sunday school Jen herself had taught a new generation of children the Bible stories she had been taught. And at home she continued the pattern set by her parents. She read the Bible and prayed at every meal — in Dutch, for the sake of brother Hank, whose church membership had been lapsed years ago. One day when I asked Hank what he believed, he said, "I believe the same as Jen does."

When Jen started putting sandwiches and glasses of milk in front of the pictures of her parents, she was transferred to a nursing home. As the years progressed, she increasingly lost touch with the world. Finally only one thing could get through: the psalms. I would ask, "Jen, do you remember Psalm 27?" and together we would say, "The LORD is my light and my salvation — whom shall I fear? The LORD is the stronghold of my life — of whom shall I be afraid?" (Ps. 27:1).

"And how about Psalm 23, Jen?" We would recite the entire psalm together: "The LORD is my shepherd, I shall not be in want" (Ps. 23:1). For Jen, as for so many others, the first things she learned were the last to go.

At Jen's funeral service I recited a stanza of a song Jen had sung many times: "And when these failing lips grow dumb, / And mind and memory flee, / When thou shalt in thy kingdom come, / Then, Lord, remember me."

Before she had succumbed to Alzheimer's or another senior dementia, Jen had called brother Hank back to a faith that both of them had learned in childhood. And even though Jen eventually forgot everything, I'm sure her Savior remembered her and her faith.

What a challenge it is to build the kind of memories that can call our children and brothers and sisters back. What a challenge to build the kind of memories that will remain when all else goes. What a challenge to nurture faith through which and for which we will be remembered.

A Parable for Church People

Luke 16:14, 19-31   Dirk Holkeboer '77

Nonprofit administrator; Holland, Michigan

> *Now the money-loving church members heard all this, and started booing him.*
> *He said to them, "You people make yourselves look pretty in public, but God*
> *knows your hearts. And what men praise, God abhors."*
>
> *(The Cotton Patch Version of Luke and Acts,* Luke 16:14*)

Our curiosity about what lies beyond death leads many to read the story of the rich man and Lazarus as a glimpse into heaven and hell. However, according to Dr. John Timmer, the parable is really concerned with "the way in which the kingdom [of God] breaks into the here and now."**

Jesus is heading toward Jerusalem for the last time when he speaks this parable, and he is teaching about what is important to God. To whom is he directing these teachings? The preamble to the story identifies the audience as the knowledgeable religious people of his day or, as Clarence Jordan describes them in *The Cotton Patch Version of Luke and Acts*, "money-loving church members." Jesus is speaking to us.

What insight into the kingdom is Jesus sharing? This parable is about failing to see people in need. It is about failing to see all people as God's children. The message is that care for the poor and justice for the oppressed are the appropriate responses to God's law and to the call of the prophets. The apostle John reminds us that the right response to God's law for living has been demonstrated by Jesus:

> This is how we know what love is: Jesus Christ laid down his life for us.
> And we ought to lay down our lives for one another. If anyone of you has
> material possessions and sees a brother or sister in need but has no pity
> on them, how can the love of God be in you? Dear children, let us not
> love with words or tongue but with actions and in truth.
>
> (1 John 3:16-18, NIVI)

God calls us, too, to bridge the chasms that our society has created: chasms based on economics, on race or ethnicity, on political affiliations, on religious convictions. We must remember that all people are created in God's image, not just the ones who are most like us. Let's keep our eyes open for Lazarus and others in need.

171

Living Leisurely

Nelvin Vos '54   John 10:10
Professor emeritus; Maxatawny, Pennsylvania

I have come that [you] may have life, and have it to the full. (John 10:10)

One of the first questions we expect when we meet a new person is "What do you do?" Wouldn't it be a shock if someone answered, "I live leisurely"? Instead, I frequently begin to talk of how busy I am, as if, if I didn't do so, I'm not really showing that I am doing my job.

Most of us should and could set aside more time to refresh and renew ourselves. But living leisurely is not merely to be equated with having a quantity of free time. To live leisurely is a quality of life, a way of living our Christianity.

Our word *leisure* came from roots which have the meaning of "to be permitted," "to be free." The concept of freedom is central to understanding leisure — not free time, or freedom from work, but simply freedom. Leisure is the sense of freedom in which one experiences all of living as being at rest and peace with God, self, and others.

Scripture reminds us to "be still, and know that I am God" (Ps. 46:10). To live without being ruled by the constant tempo of efficiency is to put our complete trust in the Holy Spirit, who will guide us in God's own time.

We are surrounded by God's grace. We live in it as a fish in water, without being aware of it. To be at rest at the center of our being amid the many frustrations we confront is to possess the wholeness and unity that come from the gift of God's grace.

To live leisurely in an age of anxiety is not only to be a witness to Christ's gift of grace but also to serve others. For the full life Christ speaks of is not first of all in wealth and things but in experiencing God's love and sharing that love with others. If our living is completely hectic and anxious, we are neither testifying to Christ's presence in our lives, nor are we in a position to serve others.

"This is the day the LORD has made; let us rejoice and be glad in it" (Ps. 118:24). That is living leisurely!

From the Depths

Psalm 130

Donna Kamerman-Houskamp '85
Teacher; Grand Rapids, Michigan

Psalm 130:1-2 is, with good reason, a familiar Bible passage. At one time or another we all experience the hopeless despair of being in a pit too deep, slimy, and dangerous to climb out of. We cry out to God from our pews on Sunday or from our beds at night, "O LORD, hear my voice" (Ps. 130:2).

The depths from which the psalmist is crying is neither a pit created by an enemy nor an abyss resulting simply from the fallenness of creation. This pit is one he dug himself. Although many psalms are pleas for deliverance from enemies (e.g., Ps. 30, 42, 139) or accounts of the grief God's people bear (Ps. 88), Psalm 130 acknowledges that sometimes we are the cause of our own despair.

The psalmist here is describing guilt. When we fail to repent, this guilt begins to grow. Perhaps we even admit that the unconfessed sin isn't a righteous option, but still we persist in it and do not give up the offense. Rather, we rationalize it, figuring it's not as bad as other, more atrocious evils. Perhaps we even nurse the sin along, enjoying it. Then somewhere down the line the sin casts us into the deep, slimy pit. We see the hurt we've caused others, or we reap the bitter fruit of the foolishness ourselves, or we realize we've wasted time and resources that could have served the kingdom. The guilt that has gradually become ever heavier breaks us down.

It's difficult to confess to God and ourselves that we have dug the pit ourselves, that it is an abyss of our own making. Our pride shades the truth about our sins, and meanwhile we scoop our abysses deeper and deeper. Only when we face our sin will we plead for mercy, admitting that it is our selfishness, lust, greed, pride, lack of compassion, misguided sense of justice, blindness, messed-up priorities, weakness against temptation — our turning away from God — that put us here. Only when God reaches down and pulls us up with his mighty grace will we experience joy again.

We can rejoice at our Lord's boundless love, so boundless that he was willing to leave his throne and go into the pit of pits — the grave — for us. And then he rose again, rendering all the pits of our lives ultimately harmless. Thanks be to God through our Lord and Savior, Jesus Christ, who rescues us.

Mark Vermaire '76   Psalm 148
Pastor; San Marcos, California

Praise the LORD. . . . Praise him, sun and moon. . . . Praise the LORD from the earth, you great sea creatures and all ocean depths. (Ps. 148:1, 3, 7)

Psalm 148 gets our spiritual imagination working again like that of a child. We become the conductor, tapping God's music stand and directing the cosmic orchestra in praise to God. Unfathomable heavens and angel hosts, rainbow trout and killer whales, retired school teachers and inquisitive students — these all join the cosmic symphony as we summon them to "praise the LORD" (Ps. 148:1).

The biblical vision has always been alert to such an inspired world: Trees clap their hands, the heavens judge, a star in the east leads, rocks cry out, the creation groans for all to know God's glory. If, in the words of Gerard Manley Hopkins, "The world is charged with the grandeur of God," it also responds in remarkable glory.

Exactly how does the sun or a sea monster praise God? Psalm 148 points to at least part of the answer: "Praise the LORD . . . stormy winds that do his bidding" (Ps. 148:7, 8). Summer squalls and winter blasts praise God by doing what God intended, by "doing his bidding." So, too, the lion rules and rends, just as God ordained it to do. And the whole universe, "doing his bidding," offers its Creator a world of praise.

And we join in that praise when in our daily lives we do God's bidding. We nurse the sick, plant a garden, grow a business, cuddle a child, write a paper, restore the homeless, enjoy a walk, sleep in peace. Alert to God's will and rejoicing in Jesus Christ, our Savior and Lord, we work and play and rest — all in praise to God, whose bidding we gladly do.

By doing God's bidding, we join the whole universe in praise. Look around and call the creation to worship. To the blossoming flower, "Praise the Lord!" To the swirling galaxies, "Praise the Lord!" To the majestic mountains, "Praise the Lord!" And the mountains may echo in reply, "Praise the Lord!"

Praise God, "young men and maidens, old men and children. . . . praise the name of the LORD, for his name alone is exalted. . . . Praise the LORD!" (Ps. 148:12-14).

Little Sins

James 1:22-27

Matt Poole

Calvin student; Glen Ellyn, Illinois

Recently I have felt burdened by my failure to welcome everyone I meet with love. I know I'm not responsible to be everyone's best friend, but I also know people deserve understanding that reflects their inherent worth. If each of us is truly a creation of God in his glorious image, then each time I make a snide comment or flash an excluding glance at another person, I am insulting and discounting God's creation. It is difficult to fathom this at times, and it is very easy to let that one person at work or school who is terribly cruel or persistently obnoxious bring out the worst in me. But these people — including those personalities I encounter only through the media, like professional wrestlers, corporate criminals, teen pop bands, and disagreeable politicians — are just as much deserving of our love as those who are kind and pleasant to be around. They are all God's creatures and my siblings in Christ.

Every day I let little sins leak through my nets of perception. Michael Travis, director of multicultural student affairs at Calvin College, often talks about how the obvious acts of racism are horrible but much easier to see and deal with than the hidden institutional forms of racism in organizations and people. In the same way, murder, sexual perversion, and other blatant sins need to be of great concern but are perhaps not as sinister as the perpetual, insidious sins we commit without sensing them. Imagine, if you will, that for one day everyone whom you judged, whom you looked at lustfully (including those in magazines and on TV), and whom you ignored out of spite or embarrassment quietly confronted you by saying, "I feel demeaned by you; how dare you have such disdain for God's creation?" The guilt and shame would be devastating.

God knows my heart, and even though the target of my sin might not be able to see or hear me, I am not free to demean anyone. God's creation is a precious thing in his sight, and he wants all of his daughters and sons back. Who am I to turn them away, even if only in my mind? There is a cumulative effect to all our little sins. They add up. We could better reflect Christ if we would replace our judging minds with loving hearts.

Muddy Eyes

Rebecca Warren-Van Arragon '92
Writer/editor; Bloomington, Indiana

John 9:1-11

A blind man sits by a dusty road, waiting, feeling the sun warm his face, listening to the travelers who pass by. He hears a group of men come near, talking about him as if he could not hear their accusing questions. He knows little if anything about the man Jesus, who is with them, but he can tell something of his character from the way he kindly rebuffs the other men and gently touches his diseased eyes with mud. Perhaps the blind man is hot from sitting by the road and needs a drink. Perhaps he is ready to listen to anyone who is willing to affirm his essential dignity. Perhaps he simply wants to get the mud off his face. No matter what, when Jesus speaks his next words, the blind man acts.

The miracle of this story from John 9, even more than the healing that later occurs, is this: When Jesus tells the blind man to go and wash in the pool of Siloam, he does, even though Jesus has said nothing at all about what will happen there. It would be too easy if Jesus had said it plainly: "Go and you will be healed." When he says without explanation, "Go . . . and wash," the rest is left to the blind man's imagination.

As we grow older, the mud of earth gets into our eyes, and we are no longer able to see with the imaginative insight that faith requires. We eventually stop believing that a place like Siloam could be anything more than a childish fairy tale. Yet, if we are to remain alive in faith, we must somehow be able to summon up in our mind's eye at least the slightest possibility for something miraculous, something full of grace — even as we face the inescapable harshness of life on this earth.

No one said it would be easy. Faith, like imagination, requires courage of heart. Our job is always to go on, to wipe the grit from our eyes, and to stumble, trip, and feel our way toward the pool of Siloam — with at least a hint of a chance that something miraculous just might be waiting for us when we get there.

The M & M Paradox

Luke 10:42

Paul de Vries '67
Seminary president; Ossining, New York

But only one thing is needed. Mary has chosen what is better, and it will not be taken away from her. (Luke 10:42)

Our Lord Jesus Christ was gentle with Martha — the Martha Stewart of the first century. Her efficient attention to taking care of people's needs obeyed the central teaching of the Lord. After all, he had just completed telling his famous parable about the good Samaritan (Luke 10:25-37).

What was the point of the story? We usually focus on the social responsibility we have to those in special need — those around us that are beaten up and robbed, literally and figuratively. If Martha heard this parable, she might have noted that Jesus himself was a victim, under vicious attack by Pharisees, other Jewish leaders, and even the Samaritans. She certainly would want to be a good Samaritan to Jesus. In our own time, too, Jesus is under vicious attack in many ways — verbal, spiritual, and social. His name is used in vain, people are deaf to his voice, and he is attacked when "the least" of his brothers and sisters are attacked.

If Martha was trying to obey the lessons of the good-Samaritan parable, she was wise. Still, Jesus said, there is an even greater priority. Earlier in Luke 10 he had already made this clear to his seventy disciples when they came back from fruitful ministry trips. Their work was so successful, Jesus said, that he saw Satan fall "like lightning" (Luke 10:18). Nevertheless, there was something far greater for them: "Do not rejoice that the spirits submit to you, but rejoice that your names are written in heaven" (Luke 10:20). Jesus wanted the seventy to know that even astonishing excellence in ministry will never take the place of intimacy with our Lord and Savior.

Then again, Jesus was "full of joy" at the way God reveals the truths about himself: "You . . . revealed them to little children . . . and those to whom the Son chooses to reveal him" (Luke 10:21-22). Revealing himself to us gives Jesus great joy. If only we would pay attention!

Good works and ministry service are of great value. Still, there is "only one thing . . . needed. Mary has chosen what is better, and it will not be taken away from her" (Luke 10:42) — or from us.

A Good Smell

Robert D. Bolt '80
Pastor; Grand Rapids, Michigan

2 Corinthians 2:12-17

Certain smells trigger thoughts of certain people or events in our lives. When I smell a cigar, I think of driving around in my grandpa's old white Chevy while he would puff away on an Old Dutch Masters cigar. When I smell fresh-cut grass, I am reminded of the long spring days my brother and I spent cutting yards when we ran a lawn business. When I smell wood burning, I think of pleasant times our family had around campfires on family vacations.

When my daughter was young, we would sometime leave her with a baby-sitter. She was a little apprehensive when we left, and she would almost always ask if she could have one of our bed pillows. When we would come home, my wife and I would peek in on her, and there she would be, hugging our pillow. Why did she do this? Because, she said, the pillow smelled like us. It was a smell that reminded her that we really weren't so very far away. Smells trigger memories.

Christians carry with them a certain smell, too, and God likes that fragrance. Paul tells us about it in 2 Corinthians 2:14-15: "But thanks be to God, who always leads us in triumphal procession in Christ and through us spreads everywhere the fragrance of the knowledge of him. For we are to God the aroma of Christ among those who are being saved and those who are perishing." God is using us Christians, our smell, our aroma, to tell the world that God is here. Even though we might feel insecure at times or the evil-smelling garbage of our day begins to take over, God still is with us here on this earth, and he desires to make his smell known — through us. That is some responsibility we have!

Paul is also telling us that God, like a child with her parents' pillow, likes to smell us. He likes to pick us up like a big bunch of flowers and take a good strong whiff of us. Why does he like to do this? According to Paul, when God smells us, he smells Christ. I guess the blood of Jesus, with which we have been washed, has a smell that we can never get rid of. It so deeply saturates our being that it overpowers the smell of sin.

Now that is good, comforting news. News that is worth smelling.

If You But Trust

Psalm 9:10

Willem F. Antonides '91
Health-care administrator; Grand Rapids, Michigan

Those who know your name will trust in you, for you, LORD, have never for-saken those who seek you. (Ps. 9:10)

When as a senior at Calvin I served on the Chapel Committee, one of my honors was to lead worship one last time before graduation. My time to lead worship came after I had spent the previous few months visiting and applying to seminaries. My search had ranged from California to New Jersey with Michigan in between. Finally I made a choice.

Fresh with this seemingly all-encompassing decision made, I focused chapel worship that spring day on Georg Neumark's seventeenth-century hymn "If You But Trust in God to Guide You." I took it stanza by stanza. Starting with "If you but trust in God to guide you and place your confidence in him, you'll find him always there beside you to give you hope and strength within,"* I talked about how wonderful it is to have such confidence in a sovereign God that it leads aspiring seminary students to lock up their futures even before they graduate from college.

A lot has changed since that spring day in 1991. Life did not go where I had anticipated it would go. Seminary was not where I was supposed to be. But if this hymn has taught me anything, it has taught me a powerfully simple truth, the one expressed in Psalm 9:10: God has indeed been there to guide me through difficult decisions about vocation and jobs. Job happiness and career satisfaction come and go, but God's love does give hope and strength.

I must admit having some difficulty with the second stanza in those years after college graduation: "Only be still and wait his pleasure in cheerful hope with heart content. He fills your needs to fullest measure with what discerning love has sent." Cheerful hope. Heart content. In all honesty, these are not qualities that have shaped my life or soul. Through my years of wandering and wondering, life has more often been filled with doubt and unfilled needs and unknown wants by a God whose love hasn't always appeared to be very discerning.

But the final stanza has always sustained me: "Sing, pray, and keep his ways unswerving, offer your service faithfully, and trust his word; though undeserving, you'll find his promise true to be." These words summarize what my years at Calvin taught me and prepared me for: singing, praying, service. My life may not have gone the way I planned, but through my life God has taught me that, if I but trust, he will guide.

'My Only Comfort'

Andy DeVries '70   Psalm 41:1-3
Calvin cooperative-education coordinator;
Jenison, Michigan

It was the coldest week that Rochester, Minnesota, had ever recorded. The governor had closed schools and had advised motorists to stay off the roads unless travel was absolutely necessary. I was spending that week at Mayo Clinic, hoping that the medical staff could find the reason why my misshaped liver was functioning at a reduced level. During my five-day stay I was subjected to every imaginable test and a never-ending stream of forms to be filled out. The worst part, however, was the waiting. Not knowing what to expect, not knowing what questions to ask, not getting answers to questions that I did ask — that was hard, too, but the waiting was the hardest.

After the final test had been completed on Thursday evening, I was told to go back to my room at the clinic and to expect to see the doctor in the morning. Sleep didn't come. Hundreds of questions roiled through my mind. What was wrong? Was it something that could be controlled through medication? Did I have cancer? On and on the questions continued through the night, without any answers. I tossed and turned and couldn't sleep. The room couldn't get any darker. I couldn't have felt more alone.

Then, in the middle of my despair, came one question that could be answered: "What is your only comfort in life and in death?" My catechism training immediately clicked in: "That I am not my own, but belong — body and soul, in life and in death — to my faithful Savior Jesus Christ. . . . He also watches over me in such a way that not a hair can fall from my head without the will of my Father in heaven. . . ."*

The darkness seemed to lift, my spirit soared, and I was free from the questions. Jesus had lifted me, as he had promised. I slept like a baby.

Wonder-full

Matthew 18:4

Rebecca Vander Meulen '99
Government aide; Washington, D.C.

Whoever humbles himself like this child is the greatest in the kingdom of heaven.
(Matt. 18:4)

Wonder. Children are full of it, and they don't mind saying so, much to our dismay or delight. "Look at the lights!" "Will the jelly come out of the jar if I flip it upside-down?" "That dog looks a lot like its owner — they walk the same way."

Childlike wonder — born of a naïve alertness to the everyday and to the joy of surprise in God's creation — requires humility and trust. When we are proud, we fill ourselves with ourselves and become the primary focus of our own attention. We cannot look beyond ourselves in wonder when we are absorbed in our own accomplishments, fears, and appearances. It's also hard to be wonder struck if, in our pride, we think that our understanding of the world is already complete so that we are not open to surprises. When we lack trust, we fear that taking the risk of looking beyond ourselves will land us flat on our faces. Wonder grows from a trust that our Creator will not allow that which is beyond us to consume us.

The gift of wonder, cultivated by humility and trust, in return cultivates these virtues and many others. Wonder appropriately distracts us from ourselves and displaces our boredom, ingratitude, and perception of being victimized. It's harder to be frustrated by the roots of the oak tree pushing its way through our sidewalk when we contemplate the miracle that it grew from an acorn. Or by poky driving in rare Southern snow flurries when we can wonder at how inexperience has prompted road crews to spread more salt and sand on the road than there is snow. Or by an inappropriate sneeze when we see it as the well-orchestrated response of the muscular and respiratory systems in defense against an invading allergen. When we see the wonders of our everyday existence, the everyday nuisances fall into proper perspective.

May we experience God's world with the wonder of little children, and may we — like its Creator — relish the beauty of the lily, the speech of the sparrow, the invincibility of the cockroach, the many wardrobes of the chameleon, and even the sneeze that signals an enemy pollen.

181

Perfume to Remember

Emily R. Brink '62   Psalm 141:1-2
Editor; Grand Rapids, Michigan

> O LORD, *I call to you, come quickly to me.*
> *Hear my voice when I call to you.*
> *May my prayer be set before you like incense;*
> *may the lifting up of my hands be like the evening sacrifice.*
>
> (Ps. 141:1-2)

Last year I gave a friend a very expensive bottle of perfume, something I had never done before. But I had learned something very precious from her that has helped me to pray. I hope it also has made my prayers and my life rise with a more pleasing aroma to God.

She pointed out an area of my life that needed change. Through her I saw myself in a new way, and I felt a bit broken. But then she said something I'll not forget. Remember the woman who crashed a dinner party, broke a large, expensive bottle of perfume, and poured the entire contents on Jesus' feet? All four Gospels tell the story (starting with Matt. 26:6-13). Reminding me of that story, my friend said, "Sometimes the bottle needs to be broken to let the perfume out." Though it is painful for us, God sometimes breaks something in us in order to release something more pleasing. The woman who lavished her love on Jesus had learned that.

It may be hard for us to feel such love for God because we're still hanging on to something that needs to be broken. Perhaps that's why we've not been able to revel in the aroma of Christ's love and forgiveness. We all have blind spots, and the older we get, the more blind we can become to our entrenched ways of living, praying, and worshiping. We don't really expect God to do new things in and through us. But God shows us something different: Even now we can be changed.

We all need friends like my friend, friends who know and love us enough to challenge us in encouraging ways to become more like Christ. Here is a wonderful promise that tells us we already smell sweet to God, because we are in Christ, and so it isn't every day that we need to be bitterly broken before God: "Thanks be to God, who always leads us in triumphal procession in Christ and through us spreads everywhere the fragrance of the knowledge of him" (2 Cor. 2:14).

'Standing Firm in the Faith'

1 Peter 5:6-11

Stephen P. Beals '73
Physician; Phoenix, Arizona

When the phone rang at 2:00 a.m., I caught it on the first ring. Years of conditioning had taught me to wake up fast and be alert. My mind started racing, taking inventory of who it could be. I didn't expect to hear my sister, saying, "Mom thinks Dad is having a stroke." After hanging up the phone, I began to review what this would mean in Dad's life and to ask why Dad, so soon after retirement, should have to live the rest of his life disabled.

Then I began reflecting on the truths of 1 Peter 5:6-11:

Verse 6: "Humble yourselves, therefore, under God's mighty hand, that he may lift you up in due time." When we are enduring pain and suffering, we must submit to it and its spiritual purpose in our lives. In time he will lift us up again, though maybe not in this life.

Verse 7: "Cast all your anxiety on him because he cares for you." In our state of humility our faith and dependence can only be on him.

Verses 8-9: "Be self-controlled and alert. Your enemy the devil prowls around like a roaring lion looking for someone to devour." During the time of trial in our lives, we will be tempted to blame, question, and be angry with God, giving the devil opportunity to bring bitterness and resentment into our hearts. Instead, we must "resist him, standing firm in the faith," because we know that others "throughout the world are undergoing the same kind of sufferings."

Verse 10: "And the God of all grace, who called you to his eternal glory in Christ, after you have suffered a little while, will himself restore you and make you strong, firm and steadfast." Our pain and suffering are insignificant in comparison to God's eternal plans for our lives. Our suffering is momentary in light of eternity.

Verse 11: "To him be the power for ever and ever. Amen." Hallelujah and amen!

Sharing Our Inheritance

Agatha Lubbers '59   Psalm 16:1-6
School administrator; Grand Rapids, Michigan

Twenty-five years have passed since I awoke after surgery at Rochester Methodist Hospital in Rochester, Minnesota, with the words "The boundary lines have fallen for me in pleasant places; surely I have a delightful inheritance" (Ps. 16:6) flooding my mind and giving me a great sense of peace. At the time I did not know the source of these lines, but while recovering from surgery, I had opportunity to do the necessary research to discover that these words are part of Psalm 16, the golden psalm of David. Since that time these words have often surfaced in my conscious contemplation and have become especially precious to me. I am certain that many saints have relied on this passage when they needed encouragement and comfort.

David begins the psalm with this earnest petition: "Keep me safe, O God, for in you I take refuge" (Ps. 16:1). His prayer is one of complete commitment to God — a prayer uttered not in a time of special emergency but in the course of ordinary life. Children of God share this commitment, knowing that their security in life and in death depends upon the protection and providential guidance of God. The Heidelberg Catechism summarizes it eloquently and correctly when it states that the providence of God is "the almighty and ever present power of God by which he upholds, as with his hand, heaven and earth and all creatures, and so rules them that . . . all things, in fact, come to us not by chance but from his fatherly hand."*

David affirms at the outset of the psalm that apart from God he has no good. But because of God good things abound, freeing David — and all of us — to serve God as well as others. In the presence of God our eyes are opened to take delight in others, to serve them and love them out of the bounty of God's goodness, which fills up our lives.

Those whose spiritual inheritance is as rich and deep as David's know that faith is not just about hiding oneself in God but also about looking beyond self and reaching out to others as well. With joy we can say with David, "The lot that fell to me is beautiful and fair, the heritage in which I dwell is good beyond compare." There is much in that heritage to be shared with others. May we meet the challenge and see it as an opportunity from God.

Serve with the Strength God Provides

1 Peter 4:11   Jane Bosma Vander Ploeg '78
                                           Businesswoman; Lake Oswego, Oregon

My heart I offer to you, Lord, promptly and sincerely.

(Calvin College motto)

If you serve, you should do it with the strength God provides, so that in all things God may be praised through Jesus Christ. (1 Pet. 4:11, NIVI)

Have you been here? Inspired to love a few people well or to champion a cause, you put your heart and soul into it for years. Now you feel you have aged twice as much as the time you've invested. Your heart, heavy and weary, feels pushed and pulled in many directions. You ask yourself, "Why must my heart ache over good, noble choices?"

A lesson about this kind of situation came into my life a few years ago, and it still lingers with me. I knew I had given my heart to the Lord at an early age. What I hadn't learned is that my loving God is jealous of my heart and doesn't expect me to share it with every good cause and person in my path. But, all along I had been thinking that was the assignment.

In my case, the Holy Spirit, in his counselor role, showed me that he wanted to retrieve, by his power, the portions of my heart scattered around in new and old relationships and causes. He led me specifically to sort through unresolved feelings and to sorrow over outcomes, disappointments, and farewells. Tenderly he used the prayers of loving Christians around me to do his work of reuniting my heart. His aim was that the Father could have my heart to himself.

I felt much more "together" and at peace, but I wondered, then, how to love, because I didn't want to make the same mistake again. I was led to take of the Father's love and give that out freely. His love is unending, all powerful, sufficient for every good work. His heart is big enough for the task.

When you see the Calvin logo, recall that you have given your heart to him, and, incredibly, he has given his to you.

He Means What He Says

Michelle Loyd-Paige '81   Psalm 33:8-9
Calvin professor; Muskegon Heights, Michigan

> *Let all the earth fear the LORD; let all the people of the world revere him. For he*
> *spoke, and it came to be; he commanded, and it stood firm.* (Ps. 33:8-9)

"You have until three to get in here! One, two . . ." When my three children were very young, I would sometimes issue this "three-count-to-compliance" to motivate them to action. Rarely would they allow me to get to three, because three meant that I was moving toward them with mommy wrath and judgment was about to fall. However, when my husband would try the same three-count-to-compliance, the children would often let him count to three, four, five . . . Well, you get the picture. Why? Because our children had learned from experience that Mommy meant what she said with the three-count, but Daddy didn't always follow through. I'm happy to say that those three-count days are over now, and my husband and I both enjoy the respect and prompt obedience of our children.

I wonder whether our heavenly Father can say the same thing about his children. Through his written Word, our Father has said much about his expectations for the behavior of his children. I wonder if we have gotten so comfortable with God that we take his commands as suggestions and his promises as maybes.

As Christians, we have a heavenly Father who means what he says. He always follows through on his promises. When he said, "I will never leave you nor forsake you" (Josh. 1:5), he meant it. When he said, "No weapon forged against you will prevail" (Isa. 54:17), he meant it. And when he said we could have our heart's desire, he meant it. Numbers 23:19 states, "God is not human, that he should lie, nor a human being, that he should change his mind. Does he speak and then not act? Does he promise and not fulfil?" (NIVI). God is faithful to his Word. He always has been and always will be. May he also find us faithful and quick to obey.

Lost Coins

Luke 15:8-10

Joy De Boer '65
Calvin administrator; Kentwood, Michigan

Rejoice with me; I have found my lost coin. (Luke 15:9)

In Luke 15 we have three very familiar parables — the parables of the lost sheep, the lost coin, and the lost son. The first and third parables are the most familiar to us, so familiar in fact that at times we take their messages for granted. I have heard sermons on these two parables, and I have read some wonderful books that deal with them. But what about the parable sandwiched between the other two? The parable of the lost coin is the shortest of the three, taking up only three verses of the thirty-two verses in Luke 15. I have never heard a sermon preached on this parable, and I have always supposed that in it Jesus was simply reinforcing the message of the other two, until a few years ago. At that time, in my work at Calvin College, I had the privilege of meeting with a group of women students who had one thing in common: They were all victims of sexual abuse. Gradually I realized that I was working with "lost coins." I went back to Luke 15 and took a closer look at its little story.

The woman in this story loses a coin. Why, I wondered, did Jesus use an inanimate object for this second parable? I believe it was to show his listeners and us that sometimes things and people are lost because of the carelessness or neglect of others. The coin did not make a decision to leave; it couldn't possibly even wander away unintentionally. So, too, with the young women in my group. They had no responsibility for their own lostness. Now they were all struggling with how they could understand their terrifying experiences in the light of their faith or, for some of them, their loss of faith. They were asking, "How can I believe that God, my Father, loves me when he allowed my earthly father to abuse me?" "I trusted my Sunday-school teacher, and he took advantage of me. And that was even in church! I don't want anything to do with Christianity."

To these young women and to all victims in our society who feel far from God, Jesus has this message: He understands that people, like coins, can be lost because of the cruelty or neglect of others. Our God wants those who are hurting and lost to know that he loves them, that he knows their pain, and that he wants them back in the safety of his loving arms. The Lord will not sit idly by and hope that the lost are found. He will search through all the nooks and crannies of the house. And when he finds a lost one, there will be great rejoicing among the angels in heaven. What an amazing little story to show the wonderful love of God!

Playing God's Game

Nelvin Jager '60   Genesis 3:9
Professor; Muskegon, Michigan

But the LORD God called to the man, "Where are you?" (Gen. 3:9)

This question of God to Adam has always been a very haunting one for me, even though it seems to be a rhetorical question. After all, didn't God know where Adam was? For years the question disturbed me so much that, whenever I went somewhere I shouldn't have gone or did something that I knew I shouldn't do, I heard the question — "Where are you, Adam?" — with my own name substituted in Adam's place. I had the haunting feeling that something was not right with my actions or my thinking. The result was often a sense of fear coupled with an even bigger helping of guilt. Why did this question have such a frightening effect on my young life?

When I was a boy, I often played the game of hide and seek. Who was "it" and who was hiding were questions that came straight out of the question to Adam in the Garden of Eden. And then the line "Here I come, ready or not; you shall be caught" also caught my youthful attention. What a threat, what a challenge, what a promise! Were we playing a game, or was it in the final analysis the ultimate game of life?

On the one hand, it is a frightening thing to be caught by God, as Adam was. On the other hand, it seems to be the sweetest promise possible if the game is being played by persons who have a special relationship to each other. Ah, to be caught by such a one! If God is really "it," then to be caught by him is the greatest joy one can experience or even imagine.

Adam and I both found that hiding from God is never really possible, and to sew fig leaves together in a desperate attempt to cover our spiritual nakedness is futile. How much better it is to be caught by a loving Father and clothed with the white garments of righteousness.

Though Adam feared for his life and indeed lost his close companionship with God, with God's grace we can be caught and feel the excitement of God's claim on us. It's not only pleasant and exciting to be caught by one who cares; it's the object of the whole game.

Childlike Faith

James 1:2-4

Carla Vander Weele Arensen '82
Missionary; Uganda

Nine-year-old Ruth was a student in Tanya's class at school in the capital city of Uganda. She always wore a sweater over her head. Tanya thought maybe Ruth was a Muslim, but one day she discovered that Ruth covered her head so that she wouldn't get teased. Her head was full of huge sores and scabs. Ruth had AIDS, and both of her parents were dead from the disease.

Tanya also found out that Ruth was not a Muslim. In fact, she was a Christian who loved the Lord. One day when Ruth didn't show up at school, Tanya went to the hospital to visit her in the children's ward. When Tanya arrived, she saw Ruth sitting on her bed, surrounded by about ten other children. Ruth was reading a psalm to them and explaining to them that God allows troubles into our lives for a reason. She told them that even during the hard times Jesus is in control and has a purpose for everything. Then Ruth prayed with them, and together they sang the song "Soon and very soon . . ." They sang that there would be no more crying and no more dying because "we are goin' to see the King."

After hearing this true story, I asked myself, "Is my faith as strong as Ruth's? How do I react in the face of trials much smaller than hers? Do I really believe that God allows difficulties in my life for a reason and that he is in control of all things?" Remembering the story of this faith-full child, I repeatedly pray, "Oh, Lord, let me follow the example of little Ruth."

A Matter of the Heart

Meta Brinkley Townsand '80   Psalm 108:1
Teacher/principal; Grand Rapids, Michigan

> *My heart is steadfast, O God; I will sing and make music with all my soul.*
> (Ps. 108:1)

David sings in Psalm 103:1, "Praise the LORD, O my soul; all my inmost being, praise his holy name." In Psalm 34:1 he declares, "I will extol the LORD at all times; his praise will always be on my lips."

When you look at David's life, have you ever wondered how David could be a man of praise, a man after God's own heart? After all, we can plainly see his adultery, his anger, his wrong decisions. We can see his deceit and the dysfunctional family that was produced from his loins. Our judgment on David would be easy and quick. But not God's. God turns the tables. He declares in his Word that man looks on the outward appearance, but God looks at the heart.

So God looked into the heart of David, and God saw the heart of a man who was tender and broken in repentance. God saw the heart of a man that he could trust to lead his people as king (1 Sam. 16). God saw the heart of a man who trusted in him as he fought the giant Goliath (1 Sam. 17). God saw the heart of a man obediently not killing Saul, his archenemy, even when he had the opportunity (1 Sam. 24). God saw the heart of a man go calamitously foolish in dance as he praised the mercy of God for returning the Ark of the Covenant (2 Sam.16-23). God saw the heart of a man who treasured the spirit and presence of God in his life (Ps. 51). God saw the heart of a man who continually sought after him in prayer.

Even as God saw into David's heart, he examines our hearts — when we experience the mountaintops of life, the resting places in the Promised Land, and the dry bones in the valley. God is looking for a heart that is trusting, joyful, and obedient in spite of the opposition and the burdens one must bear in order to follow Christ. To people with hearts like that he promises, "Weeping may remain for a night, but rejoicing comes in the morning" (Ps. 30:5).

Let us keep our hearts steadfast and longing for God. Let us, like David, sing and make music to him with all our being.

In the Morning of My Heart

Psalm 96

Ron Rozema '70
Nonprofit executive; Grand Rapids, Michigan

The world that I wake up to is generally a quiet place. In summer, light breaks over the city, filtering through trees to brighten our porch. In late fall, morning brings blackened skies pierced by crystalline stars and planets. Occasionally a light fog dampens the sounds of the waking city, but it's never long before car horns pierce the calm, buses rumble along the street, and city noise violates the quiet.

My internal morning world is not so different. The morning of my heart is generally a peaceful time, a time for savoring the gift of a new day, for the enchantment of twittering birds announcing first light, a time for quiet intimacy with God. Most mornings I am calm, assured that I am in a peaceful place. Rarely, though, does the quiet last. Stirrings of responsibility muster my energies — reminders to set out the trash, deadlines for the day, a computer that needs hooking up — internal postings that penetrate the calm and call me to action. Yet each day brings new awareness that I live in a sheltered corner of God's broken world. A daughter in Denver is closer to the horror of young lives tragically lost. Another in Africa knows the evil of harassment. A debilitating disease steals life from a colleague's mate. A neighbor's child is lost to the streets. My quietness is fractured; some of the breaks won't heal.

Then, stealthily, like the dawning of a new day, come reminders of God's touch. Dear saints continue to lift up their faithful prayers. The city responds to human misery. People of courage and faith share experiences even as they put God's love into action. Hearts and hands pour out the soothing, refreshing message of grace. Grace made visible offers reassurance of God's quiet places in this broken world.

In the newness of each day God calls me to be useful for restoring his peace. Each day — day after day after day — is a gift and an opportunity to give my heart and hands in service to him.

Ambassadors for Christ

Jerry Kooiman '84   2 Corinthians 5:17-21
Politician; Grand Rapids, Michigan

> *We are therefore Christ's ambassadors, as though God were making his appeal through us.* (2 Cor. 5:20)

Because I work in the world of government and politics, words like *ambassador* leap off the Bible's page at me. What an awesome responsibility to realize that the King of kings has asked us to be his ambassadors to the sinful world in which we live.

In the diplomatic world, ambassadors have a tremendous responsibility. The primary role of effective ambassadors is to be the authorized representatives or messengers of their countries. Ambassadors do not speak on their own behalf, but on the behalf of their nations' leaders. In addition, ambassadors' conduct must be above reproach, lest they bring dishonor to their countries. In order to communicate their nations' messages effectively, ambassadors must be in constant communication with their national leaders. Effective ambassadors also need to know how to articulate the message of their nations to the countries in which they serve. There are times where ambassadors must be bold and challenging; in other situations they must be diplomatic and reassuring.

I am often puzzled that God would call all of us (with all our faults and weaknesses) to be his ambassadors, but he has given us all we need to present his message. He has given us the gift of his Holy Spirit and his Word. If we are going to articulate his message in a way that is relevant, meaningful, and understandable, we need to read his Word, spend time in communication with him daily, and live our lives in such a way that we reflect our King well.

Being Christ's ambassadors is not only a responsibility. It is also an incredible honor. Webster's dictionary indicates that an ambassador "is a diplomatic official of the highest rank." The highest rank! God has not only chosen to give us the gift of salvation. He has also given us the highest possible honor by appointing us to be his ambassadors. We are the ambassadors of the King of kings. What an honor! What a responsibility!

Steps and Stops

Jeremiah 10:23

Calvin parent/retired editor; Caledonia, Michigan

I know, O Lord, that people's lives are not their own; it is not for them to direct their steps. (Jer. 10:23, NIVI)

One changed letter often changes a word's meaning. *Steps* becomes *stops.* So it is with life. We go along one step at a time — working, achieving, joyful. And suddenly — STOP.

Sometimes we stop ourselves. We fail to heed the amber caution light at the intersection. When our bones break and the car is crushed, we stop. At other times God stops us. Joseph stopped when his brothers (of all people!) sold him to desert traders (Gen. 37:28). Balaam stopped when, after three tries, his donkey simply refused to budge (Num. 22). Jonah stopped only when he found himself trapped in the stomach of a huge fish (Jon. 1:17).

I stopped when I awoke in a mental hospital. Failure. Disgrace. So I thought. God had permitted my emotional illness to force our family back to the United States from Nigeria. I spent three periods of several months over the next five years in a mental hospital, recovering from clinical depression. Here I learned painfully that "a person's steps are directed by the Lord. How then can anyone understand their own way?" (Prov. 20:24, NIVI). I learned, too, that, although his "path led through the sea" and I could not see his footprints (Ps. 77:19), he held me close.

T. S. Eliot once said that we travel to God and we travel with God; he is our destination, and he is at every point along the road. When we stop, we are in God's "direct gaze," which Richard Mouw calls "living before the face of God. When we stop, we can often see him better."* And I did.

Yes, God plans the lives of his children, and "no plan of [his] can be thwarted" (Job 42:2). The novelist Victor Hugo said, "Sorrow is a fruit. God does not make it grow on limbs too weak to bear it." If our limbs are weak, he strengthens them.

Yes, God directs our stops as well as our steps. Hallelujah!

Prodigals

Mark VandenBerge '84   Luke 15:11-32
Social worker; Grand Rapids, Michigan

I n one of my last conversations with my grandfather before his death, he made a rather startling statement. "You know, Mark," he said, "I have lived my whole life trying to please God. Yet I look back with some regrets for things I have said and done. But in my heart I cannot bring myself to call these things sin."

While I managed to find some clumsy words of counsel, I am quite sure they were inadequate. At the time, I thought what I was hearing were simply the musings of a dying man. But over time I have come to see my grandfather's words as indicative of the malaise many Christians in our community experience: ambivalence about our need for God.

We ask ourselves, "Have I done anything bad enough to warrant crying out for God's forgiveness and healing? He is busy with the prodigals out in the wild and has taken me for granted. I don't need to bother God with my uneventful life or take God's time to confess my small sins."

As a result of this attitude, we do not confess our sins, we do not receive forgiveness, and we never experience true communion with God and with others. We are like the older brother in the parable of the prodigal son, strangers in our own house, resentful and alone.

But Jesus asks us to reach out and trust him: "Whatever you ask for in prayer, believe that you have received it, and it will be yours" (Mark 11:24). Author Henri Nouwen reflects, "I can choose to dwell in the darkness . . . to wrap myself in my resentment. But I do not have to. There is the option to look into the eyes of the One who came out to search for me. . . ."

Can you trust God to break through? He searches for all of us: the prodigal and the prodigal's siblings, you and me. He wants to bring everyone to the banquet table he has set out, even on this side of heaven.

Accepting Oneself

Deuteronomy 8:2; Romans 8:15-16

Melissa Hicks '98
Campus-ministry staff member;
Pittsburgh, Pennsylvania

G od has called me to minister to college students, and I love it. But when a student asked me to accompany her on a six-week backpacking trip through the mountains of Wyoming, I questioned the calling. (I had never been camping before and had no idea what it meant to live outdoors.) Yet after much prayer I decided to journey with her and eighteen other Christians into the wilderness.

The trip quickly proved to be the greatest challenge I had ever endured. Four weeks into it I prayed, "Dear Lord, I'm grateful that you've brought me to the wilderness to test my heart. It's meant facing tough truths about myself that I'd rather not see. But now I no longer have to convince myself I'm something I'm not. I have dark, ugly sides, and that's okay. You love me immensely — no matter what. You assure me that I belong to you and am your child."

Earlier in the year God had begun teaching me how deeply and unconditionally he loves me as his child. In the wilderness he challenged me to live in that reality. It is really a challenge for all believers, because it gets at the very heart of who Jesus desires us to be. There is incredible freedom when we live in his grace, because by his death and resurrection we are adopted as God's perfect children. My identity rests solely in the fact that I belong to Christ — not in the affirmation or in the disapproval of others. As I live in this knowledge, I'm more able to receive honest feedback from others, and I'm moved to love others with the same love that God has lavished on me.

There's another by-product of accepting oneself because of Christ: the refreshment of approaching life with more playfulness and optimism. When's the next camping trip?

Finding Stillness

Darlene Kortenhoeven Meyering '69   Psalm 46:10
Calvin administrator; Grand Rapids, Michigan

Be still, and know that I am God. (Ps. 46:10)

O
ur world is far from still. Our lives are harried and noisy. Stress is at an all-time high. We are assailed by electronic images, machines, beepers, alarms, engines, stereos, and computers wherever we turn. How can we possibly find stillness?

A while ago I heard a sermon on the omnipresence of God in which the minister said, "If you want to understand the presence of God in your life, spend the next month reading, memorizing, and meditating upon Psalm 139 for twenty minutes a day." I resolved to try it.

During the same month I was meditating on the psalm, I was also reading the book *Amazing Grace* by Kathleen Norris. Norris takes words used in the Christian life and writes brief, thoughtful essays on over eighty of them to build "a vocabulary of faith." I was particularly attracted to one term that was new to me: *lectio divina,* or "holy reading." Norris defined *lectio divina* as "a daily meditation on scripture in which one reads not for knowledge or information but to enhance one's life of faith." In meditating on Psalm 139, I realized, I had been engaged in *lectio divina* and was beginning to know the familiar psalm more deeply than I had from any theological discussion, Bible study, or sermon. Why? What was different?

I had found stillness — twenty minutes of stillness each day in repetitive meditation. At first it seemed forced. But then I read aloud, using different inflections, then silently again, and then I began the conscious process of memorization. Without looking for a conclusion or for an answer to a question, I was taking the time — in stillness — to let Scripture speak. I had never read one passage over and over again for an entire month. The Scriptures are long, and it takes diligence and work to get through them even without the twenty-minute meditation method.

Spending a month on one passage was not in my game plan. But a good sermon and a good author helped me to find stillness and to know God more deeply — a God who is "familiar with all my ways" (Ps. 139:3).

From Mission Field to Mission Force

Isaiah 49:8-13   Paul J. Bergsma '65
College administrator; San Jose, Costa Rica

The Missiological Institute of the Americas, where I have served for the past sixteen years, is dedicated to the training of God's new emissaries from the Latin American countries, where the Spirit of the Lord is working mightily. It is exciting to see how God has used our former students in the coming of his kingdom in regions where his name was previously unknown. One of them recently shared with us how today's passage from Isaiah 49 took on special meaning for him in West Africa.

Jeremy is the leader of a team of Costa Rican missionaries to the Sooninke. The task of this team is to bring Jesus to this unreached people. In a recent prayer letter Jeremy explained a special relationship that exists between the Sooninke and our text from Isaiah 49.

As missionary candidates, Jeremy and others of the team studied cultural anthropology in our missions institute. In that course they learned how various societies are structured, and they learned the importance of oral history and how to learn that history by asking questions. So after arriving on the field, Jeremy applied what he had learned. He started listening to the things the Sooninke would tell him about their society, and he asked questions about their history. He learned that the Sooninke have not always lived in the area of Africa now called Mali. When Jeremy asked where they had come from, this is the answer the Sooninke gave: "A long time ago our ancestors came from the East, on the other side of the desert."

"From what part of the East?" Jeremy asked.

"From an area now covered by the great Aswan Dam," they said. When Jeremy read Isaiah 49:12 the next time, he made an important connection. According to Isaiah, people from all over the world would someday stream into God's great kingdom, and some of them would be from Sinim, which is modern-day Aswan. Sinim, thought Jeremy. Was it these people, the Sooninke, about whom the prophet Isaiah spoke when he said that people would come from the region of Sinim into the kingdom of God? Jeremy thinks so, and I agree. Today, more than 2,500 years after the prophet Isaiah spoke these words, a people originally from Sinim are receiving the good news and are being brought into the kingdom of God through the efforts of Costa Rican missionaries.

Together we can exult with Isaiah: "Shout for joy, O heavens; rejoice, O earth; burst into song, O mountains!" (Isa. 49:13). The salvation of the Lord has come to the Sooninke, the people from Sinim!

Signs and Symbols

Gary D. Vander Ark '60   Exodus 40:38
Physician; Englewood, Colorado

> *So the cloud of the LORD was over the tabernacle by day, and fire was in the cloud by night, in the sight of all the house of Israel during all their travels.*
>
> (Exod. 40:38)

The Old Testament places an important emphasis on signs and symbols. The Israelites were a visual people. Their exodus from Egypt was filled with important physical reminders of God's presence. They were always making piles of stones as reminders of God's direct intervention in their lives. New Testament Christians placed a great deal of emphasis on signs and symbols in worship, especially on the water of baptism and the bread and wine of the Lord's Supper. These are still meaningful symbols in our worship today.

Signs and symbols have a place in my own life, too. When I was a medical student, I couldn't wait to wear a white coat and drape a stethoscope around my neck. I wanted everyone to know that I was a physician. Today I have a Bible sitting in an obvious place on my desk, and I have a Physician's Prayer hanging on the wall in my examining room. In thirty years of practice, these objects have greatly enhanced my ability to minister to my patients. When someone says, "I'm glad to see a Bible on your desk," it invariably leads to talk of spiritual things. When patients comment on my wall prayer, the ensuing discussion often leads to our praying together. Sometimes my patients also display signs and symbols. When a patient is wearing a cross, for example, it is an obvious entrée to a conversation about what the cross means to him or her.

What signs and symbols do you have around your home? Our neighbor has a huge banner in front of his house that proclaims, "Denver Broncos — Champions of the World." Our house has a mezuzah at every entrance. Some people display the American flag every day. Others have a fish on the bumper of each of their cars.

But I've focused here mostly on symbols of piety and of harmless allegiance. I have not mentioned the bad signs and symbols in people's lives — the gang symbols, the hooked cross of the Nazis, the white robes of the KKK, the brand names, fur coats, and designer cars. I'm working at weeding them out of my life.

Signs and symbols can either support or undercut our witness to the gospel. Are you using the right visuals in your life?

Do It!

Hebrews 11:1-2   Rachel Schoenfuhs '99
                                                            Missionary; Taiwan

"Hey, Noah! What are you doing?"
"Uh . . . building a boat."
"Why in the world are you doing that?"
"Uh . . . I'm not really sure."

"Hey, Abraham! What are you doing?"
"I'm moving."
"Where to?"
"I don't know yet."

"Hey, Jeremiah! What are you doing?"
"I'm going to bury my belt three miles down the road."
"What for?"
"I have no idea."

If these situations seem pointless or confusing to you, imagine how Noah, Abraham, and Jeremiah felt about them. Building a boat in the middle of a field (Gen. 6)? Moving his family to no known address (Gen. 12)? Burying his belt three miles away (Jer.13)? Why would anybody do these things? Were they crazy? Bored?

No. They were obedient. If we take a look at many of the major characters in God's Word, we often find them doing the ridiculous, even the absurd. But not without reason. God told them what to do, and God thrives on challenging his people to step away from their safety nets and out of their comfort zones. What better way to teach total dependence and reliance upon him?

Are you, too, ready to go when God says, "Go"? To build a boat when God says, "Build it"? To bury a belt when God says, "Bury it"? Or would you say, "Well, yes, when I finish this," or, "Yes, when I get my finances in order," or, "Sure, when the kids finish school"? That kind of yes is really a not-so-subtle no. The problem is not that God's tasks are too impossible or even too ridiculous. The problem is that our faith is too small. It's hard to set out to do something that's not fully clear to us. But sometimes God wants us to do precisely that, trusting that "he who began a good work in you will carry it on to completion" (Phil. 1:6).

So when God says, "Build," "Move," "Bury it," say, "Yes, Lord" — and do it. Because *God* said so.

Guarding the Heritage of Faith

Corrine E. Kass '50   2 Timothy 2:14
Calvin professor emerita; Grand Rapids, Michigan

Attending Calvin College was one of many milestones in my life experiences, milestones that mark the high points of a heritage based upon a family tradition of baptizing children into the covenant and encouraging those children to claim it as their own. Early training and modeling by parents, Christian-school teachers, ministers, camp counselors, and other mentors laid the foundation for my eventual mature acceptance of the values and beliefs of my forebears.

Growing into an appreciation of Calvinistic principles was an interesting journey for me. In grade school my teacher (also my father) often talked about God's sovereignty and man's responsibility. In catechism we were drilled on sin, salvation, and service. At Calvin formal courses in Bible doctrine and Calvinism furthered my interest in the intellectual aspects of our belief system. In one of my graduate courses at the University of Illinois I wrote a paper on Calvinism and learning theory. In my teaching career at Calvin, I was often asked to spell out my faith as it relates to scholarship. How grateful I am that I could call on an entire lifetime of developing in the faith and of integrating faith and learning.

Some of us have "inherited" the faith of our parents by learning about the Christian walk from birth to maturity. With that inheritance we also inherit a tremendous responsibility to show the fruit of that faith in our daily living. None of us ever lives up to that responsibility completely, but we must try without ceasing.

As all of us struggle through our life pilgrimage — whatever our heritage, our work, our gifts, our weaknesses, and our strengths — let us ponder this verse from 2 Timothy 1:14: "Guard the good deposit that was entrusted to you — guard it with the help of the Holy Spirit who lives in us."

John 17:25-26   Mark P. Van Oyen '86
Professor; Deerfield, Illinois

Righteous Father, though the world does not know you, I know you, and they know that you have sent me. I have made you known to them, and will continue to make you known in order that the love you have for me may be in them and that I myself may be in them. (John 17:25-26)

Jesus gave them this answer: "I tell you the truth, the Son can do nothing by himself; he can do only what he sees his Father doing, because whatever the Father does the Son also does." (John 5:19)

The parent-child relationship has profound effects on our lives. Despite the things that go wrong, relationships with spouse, children, father, and mother are typically considered the most important and precious gifts of life. An example of the parent-child relationship gone wrong is an acquaintance of mine who has suffered deep wounds because his father was unable to express love verbally or even with a hug. My father, on the other hand, gave me a relationship to cherish. He died before the age of sixty, but I treasure a card he wrote to me from his hospital bed just before a serious surgery. He wrote, "What a gift it is to have a son like you! You are a real joy to Mom and me, . . . and you are a beautiful son. . . ." Even when such love is present day after day, all too often we don't really hear the message and take it in.

As much as I needed to hear that message of love and relationship from my father, the text of John 17:26 offers all of us something even more vital and more wonderful. In it Jesus prays on our behalf that we might know God the Father and his love as well as the indwelling of Jesus. In John 5:19 John also teaches us about the Father and the Son. The good lesson here is that Jesus and the Father provide a perfect model of the parent-child relationship.

In the message he preached at my mother's funeral, Rev. Jack Roeda pointed out that Jesus is a clear window to God. Not drawing attention to himself, Jesus invites us to see without any distortion at all the Father through himself. In God the Father and Jesus Christ the Son, we behold a mystery which can serve as a model for our own parent-child relationships, and we receive the indwelling grace of Jesus and the love of our heavenly Father.

Advocate, Judge, and Companion

Jim Davids '73   Micah 6:1-8
Attorney; Palos Heights, Illinois

The Bible is filled with people associated with the law. Moses gave it, David loved it, a Pharisaic lawyer summarized it, and Jesus fulfilled it. Paul's personal defense against his accusers in Acts 22 is noteworthy. But there is no better trial advocate in Scripture than the Lord in Micah 6:1-8.

In Micah 6:1 the Lord commands his recalcitrant chosen people to plead their case against him. In response to this "take your best shot" challenge, there is only silence. The speechless people have no case. The Lord then presents his case-in-chief: deliverance from slavery in Egypt, competent leadership by chosen leaders, miraculous crossing of the Jordan, and covenants with his people. This evidence is met only by silence — no rebuttal.

Having been convicted by the evidence, the people of Israel scramble to mitigate their deserved punishment. Will God the Judge accept, in lieu of punishment, material wealth in the form of yearling calves, thousands of rams, an ocean of olive oil? Apparently not. Does the Lord, like Baal, require child sacrifice? Certainly not. Then "what does the LORD require of you? To act justly and to love mercy and to walk humbly with your God" (Mic. 6:8).

Acting justly entails honesty, fair dealing, and lawfulness, that is, treating others fairly as we would want them to treat us. God also requires us to love mercy. Mercy is kindness beyond what can be claimed or expected. Mercy is, of course, best exemplified by the Lord himself. Justice requires earthly and eternal death for our sins. Yet God, through his inestimable mercy, granted us clemency from our eternal death penalty through the blood of his Son. Because of his mercy, God the Judge commands us to love mercy with our hearts.

Justice and mercy must govern our interpersonal relationships, but this is not enough. God also requires of us a personal relationship with him. This relationship must not be stagnant (we are not required merely to stand with him), but dynamic (we are to walk with him). In walking life's path, we will pass through both meadows and ravines. Yet, since we are walking in his presence, we can praise him and ask for his advice and help. When we stumble, he is there to comfort and pick us up. In the most difficult circumstances we can ride piggyback on our Advocate, our Judge, and our Companion.

God's Obelisks

Ephesians 5:15-16

Gary Schmidt
Calvin professor; Alto, Michigan

If you were to skitter around the tip of Upper Michigan's Elk Lake and head north into the orchards, you might, by chance, pick the gliding road that hosts the Obelisk — by chance, I say, because no sign marks the Obelisk's presence.

And yet, though hidden, the Obelisk is impressive in its own way. It rises twice your height with the kind of solid weight that marks a 1930s monument. Its sides display a stone for every county in Michigan, each with its name formally stamped deep into a sheer face. Though some stones are missing now, still, some grandeur remains. You approach the Obelisk tentatively, gazing up.

The Obelisk marks the 45th parallel in Michigan. You can stand there and put three-quarters of the globe at your back and know that geographers, mapmakers, navigators, all who study the world's quadrants have worked to set on the world this line that you now straddle. It is a heady straddling, even if those driving by might wonder what you are about up on that ridge.

It is worth the stopping to see this strange thing — but most of us do not. We do not stop here any more than we stop at the obelisks that the good Lord plants beside our frantic journey. We miss the obelisks because we have planned our own course, set our own timetable, and we will not be stopped, even if it is to see a strange thing. And so again and again we pass that moment, that person, that event, that sight, that breeze, that imperial sky, that poignant need, that terrible beauty that can remind us of the poles we stand between and of who, after all, set those poles in their places. God's obelisks give us the places to set our feet, the places to orient our faces, but we do not climb up the ridge to find them.

May God, our God, who is our journey and our destination both, so fill the maps of our lives with his obelisks that we can't help seeing what must ever be seen and so guide us, who are directionless without him, along a way hazardous and rough but marked by his lovely hand, until we come at last to that place where he stays, late and soon, waiting for our arrival.

Fix, Tie, Teach, Write

Milton Kuyers '56   Deuteronomy 11:18-20
Accountant; Brookfield, Wisconsin

As a very busy businessman, I have to be reminded often by God, through his Word, how I should live my life. Deuteronomy 11:18-20 has had a major impact in focusing me on those actions and activities which should be paramount in my life each day.

In this passage God starts with the most foundational issue — telling me to spend more time in his Word so that I may fix that Word in my heart and mind. The term "fix" has a very permanent quality about it. Once something is fixed, it takes some effort to dislodge it. I've learned that I can't fix something in my mind and heart without expending considerable focused effort on doing just that.

Deuteronomy 11 then goes on to tell me that I have to develop a system of reminders so that, even when I'm very busy, I don't forget what God's Word has to say ("tie them as symbols on your hands and bind them on your foreheads"). All of us have learned how to use reminders in other parts of our lives; yet we often neglect this approach to God's Word.

Then God tells me to go beyond myself in my devotion to his Word. During every bit of time I spend with my children, I need to be teaching God's words to them. I do a good job providing for my family. But that's not enough. I have to be a role model and a teacher to them whenever and wherever I spend time with them, sunup to sunset. That is an incredible responsibility. My family members sometimes listen to me. They always watch me to see whether my actions are compatible with my words. I probably teach them as much about God's words through my actions as through my speech — even as my father's actions had a greater impact on my life than his words did.

God also says "to write [these words of mine] on the doorframes of your houses and on your gates" (Deut. 11:20). What this means to me is that I have to let my neighbors, my fellow workers, and my friends know where I stand on various issues of life by making these stands visible to everyone around me. God doesn't let me get away with teaching only my children.

Yes, God has called me to an awesome task: I need to spend more time in his Word, remind myself often what he says to me in that Word, teach the Word to and be an effective role model for my family, and be willing to take a public stand for God. I believe I can do this task — but only because, through Christ, God provides me with the grace to carry it out. It must have been even harder for the people Moses addresses in the book of Deuteronomy.

The Cutting Edge

Hebrews 10:23-24   Bette DeBruyn Bosma '48
Calvin professor emerita; West Olive, Michigan

Let us hold unswervingly to the hope we profess, for he who promised is faithful. And let us consider how we may spur one another on toward love and good deeds. (Heb. 10:23-24)

When I was teaching in the Education Department at Calvin College, I would study current research in order to analyze, sift, and distill the findings that could improve classroom teaching from a Christian perspective. I called that "working at the cutting edge." I saw coworkers working at the cutting edge consistently at Calvin, in all areas. Christian scholars explore the profound array of discoveries in various natural-science fields. In many disciplines they study and evaluate new technology. Others assess current approaches in the humanities or trends in art and music.

The distinctiveness of Christ-centered work at the cutting edge lies in the purpose of the quest. A Christian works to fulfill God's command to understand and develop the immense, challenging raw materials of creation. Such work becomes determined but not rushed, persistent but not driven. Interpretations that proclaim a Christ-centered world and life view are celebrated, not envied.

In all workplaces there is a cutting edge. Is it possible to be working for a Christian world and life view in other aspects of life? I believe that in all aspects of our Christian life we can reach toward that cutting edge. We can explore ideas presented by current theologians and historians in Bible study. We can measure and evaluate environmental issues within the context of God's mandate of stewardship. We can address the needs of others with compassion.

In retirement the quest continues. Instead of resting on what has been accomplished, we explore new ideas and embrace new horizons. How do we do this? In my NIV Bible there is a subtitle in Hebrews 10, ahead of the verses quoted above. It reads, "A Call to Persevere." The call to "spur one another on to love and good deeds" (Heb. 10:24) suggests a community responsibility. To continue our work on the cutting edge for Christ, we need stimulation, encouragement, and sometimes correction. My prayer is that we may receive those necessities from one another.

Stretching

Donna Veltkamp Vander Griend '63   Isaiah 54:2
School chaplain/counselor; Bellingham, Washington

> *Enlarge the place of your tent, stretch your tent curtains wide.* (Isa. 54:2)

The years have left their stretch marks on my husband and me. During one decade of our marriage, four pregnancies birthed a daughter and three sons. God-sent joys were innumerable. Our sorrows and conflicts we tried to beat into plowshares with God's help, making fertile ground for grace and God's love lessons.

In the twenty-eight ensuing years we attempted to become holy together in our own version of the sanctification stretch, trying faithfully to "train children in the way they should go" (Prov. 22:6, NIVI). We thought this meant the perpetuation of Dutch ethnicity and loyalty to the Christian Reformed Church. After all, we had four hundred years of homogeneous ancestry as momentum.

But eventually God called us to more elasticity, to being more expansive. Our children fell in love. Their weddings stretched us; so did their spouses. The first son married a Dutch, Christian Reformed girl from our hometown; the second, a British-Canadian woman with Salvation Army background; our daughter married an Italian Catholic; and the youngest son married a Hawaiian-born young woman from the Assemblies of God denomination. We were the *Fiddler on the Roof* generation, watching our children peel off with those of "other faiths."

Now it's the seventh-inning stretch (watching from the sidelines with us are five little grandsons). From the bleachers this is what we pray for and often see: a divinely ordained diversity in our grown children, who are allowing the creativity of Christ to work in their lives. Our children — doctor, actor, therapist, teacher — and their spouses — teacher, actress, architect/lawyer, dancer — have accompanied God into public schools, theater productions, housing for the poor, and liturgical dance. We have learned much about social concerns and confession and experiencing God.

We have been stretched beyond the mindset of our youth, when movies and dancing were forbidden, when Catholics were suspect, when same-skin-color marriages were the norm, when God seemed smaller than he is now in our enlarged condition. Recently, when an after-dinner family discussion centered on the questions we are going to someday ask God, daughter-in-law Maluhia remarked, "I have a lot of questions to ask him, too, but first I'm going to ask him to dance."

The Radical Kingdom

Romans 7:4-6

Tacye Langley Clarke '93
Teacher; Vienna, Virginia

It is a strange phenomenon that some believers who attend Christian colleges come away from them cynical, rejecting the radical, triumphant nature of the gospel as a result of the examples of facile Christianity they have experienced. I came away from college dissatisfied with contemporary Christian culture, though I hadn't given up on its radical message. Struggling through shallow worship services and strained "fellowship" times, I hungered for a greater manifestation of the gritty yet glorious face of Christ I had glimpsed through literature.

For me that greater glimpse of Christ came at, of all places, an Orthodox Jewish high school where I taught. The rules were strict: I was asked never to wear pants, expose my knees, or serve my students anything baked in my kitchen. I learned that on the Jewish Sabbath a refrigerator bulb should not be permitted to go. I observed the frazzled attempts of a fellow teacher to find ten men to accompany over 150 girls on a retreat so that God would hear the girls' prayers.

In such an atmosphere I found Paul's call to be "the aroma of Christ" (2 Cor. 2:15) and "a letter from Christ" (2 Cor. 3:3) gripping. During morning prayers I would sit alone in my classroom and invoke Christ, asking him to fill me and the very building with his grace — a simple, radical prayer, given my students' scrupulous avoidance of the name Christ. I yearned to reveal to my law-bound students Christ's mercy to the unworthy, his rage at all impediments to a liberated life in the kingdom. Our study of *To Kill a Mockingbird*, *Agamemnon*, and F. Scott Fitzgerald inspired discussions about depravity, forgiveness, and redemption; *Hamlet* led me to explain the sufficiency of Christ's work.

For all its flaws, claustrophobic limitations, and extrabiblical obligations, I found Orthodox Jewish culture to be attractive and safe. All behaviors are prescribed; one's chief end is to follow the sharply delineated law — comfortingly safe, yet alien to the person and work of our Messiah, that fearful disrupter of the status quo, him who defies the notion that we get what we deserve. The experience was for me a liberating defamiliarization of my faith, and it wooed me into a richer experience of Christ's countercultural kingdom.

It's All God's Time

Marvin Kosters '60   Matthew 25
Economist; Arlington, Virginia

L ife seems much busier now than it used to be. At least that's what many people seem to think. It's not really that we have less time, of course. The question instead is how we use our time.

Some suggest that we take too little leisure. Others express concerns about shortchanging family life — we spend too little time sharing meals, nurturing children, and so on. Still others worry that we devote too little time to service, to helping others.

If we spend too little time on some things, we presumably spend too much on other things. What are those things? According to some people, we take too much leisure. According to others, work is the main culprit. One of the most obvious ways this shows up is that in many families, even families with children, both parents have jobs. Not that work is a new activity. What's new is that work increasingly involves jobs that separate people from other family members and leave less time to share with them.

But maybe we should avoid placing too much emphasis on how we divide up our time into work and leisure. It may be more important to look closely at the specific things we do with our time, whether or not we're at work. When we look at how we use our time, most of the activities in our daily lives are likely to seem ordinary and routine. Even if they are not easily described in terms of lofty goals or selfless purpose, however, we should not underestimate their importance. This is one of the lessons I draw from Matthew 25, where how the righteous receive their inheritance is described in terms of the ordinary, the commonplace. It's described in terms of small and simple things that are pleasing to God — being prepared for the Master's coming, using the talents given to us, visiting people in prison, giving food to a hungry stranger or clothes to somebody with nothing to wear.

However busy our lives and however we divide our time, we need to remind ourselves that even things that don't seem very significant in themselves, things that we do mainly out of habit, are important in God's sight. Everything we do has eternal significance.

Resting in God's Plans

Jeremiah 29:11   Sharon Van Haitsma Bytwerk '73
Professor; Grand Rapids, Michigan

"For I know the plans I have for you," declares the LORD, "plans to prosper you and not to harm you, plans to give you hope and a future." (Jer. 29:11)

When my daughter, Kate, was in sixth grade, her teacher's brother was in a serious car accident and lay in a coma for some time. The teacher shared this and the family's focus on Jeremiah 29:11. The class prayed for the young man throughout the school year and rejoiced as he returned to health. Kate knew and loved the Jeremiah verse. She wrote out a copy.

When Kate was in seventh grade, we lived in Hungary for a semester. On a weekend trip to the Tatra Mountains in Slovakia, she fell. She, too, went into a coma. But unlike her teacher's brother, she did not recover. She died. My beautiful twelve-year-old. As Kate was dying, I pleaded with God for her life. But from a deep spot in my soul, I knew I had to let God be God, and the God I wrestled with picked me up and held me close. When we returned to Michigan, I found the Jeremiah verse written in Kate's hand, taped to her mirror.

How different God's plans were from my own. Would I be able to accept God's? Was I willing? Could I trust God and his plans when he took my Kate? I could — because of his wonderful love for me in those weeks which turned into months and now have become three years. Filled with a measure of his love that I did not know was possible in this world, I found a peace that makes no earthly sense. He has carried me, set me gently down, holding my hand when the tears roll.

I miss Kate beyond words, and the plans I wanted for her. But I rest in God's plans. His plans are higher than mine. I trust them even though I do not understand them. Kate's future is eternal, and she has it with her Lord. She chose him as her Lord over a year before her death. And God has plans for me, too. He loves me, and I can trust in him whatever happens. My future has hope. The meaning of Jeremiah is indeed deep.

Mountain Majesty

Lambert '64 and Kay Youngs '61 Van Poolen   Psalm 8
Calvin professor/Homemaker; Grand Rapids, Michigan

I lift up my eyes to the hills — where does my help come from? (Ps. 121:1)

One of our most challenging excursions during a summer stay in Colorado was a hike to Emerald Lake in Rocky Mountain National Park. Though we always prepare for our summer hikes by long walks back home in Michigan, there is little we can do to acclimate ourselves to the thinner air in Colorado. To reach Emerald Lake, we had to make quite a climb in elevation, and our lung capacity was pushed to the limit. It was tempting just to put our heads down, plod on, and push ourselves to reach the lake.

But God had something else in mind for us when shortness of breath forced us to stop several times. Each time we were given the gift of a vista that was completely awe inspiring. Once it was a tiny lake nestled below in a carpet of firs and aspens as crispy white clouds floated overhead, all reminding us of God's quiet voice. Then it was a majestic snow-covered mountain range, jagged peaks reaching, reaching to the heavens above — a sign of God's power and majesty. At another stop it was a roaring waterfall spraying out just a hint of a covenant rainbow. No words were necessary as we stood in silence, hugging these images.

We need such God-given times of grandeur and beauty, but we will miss them if we don't lift our heads and look around to notice them. Not everyone can hike in the Colorado Rockies, but all can stop to examine the delicate beauty of a flower, to delight in the joy of a sun-filled day, to find pattern and picture in fleecy white clouds, to enjoy the soft drumming of rain, to wonder at the six-pointed uniqueness of a snowflake, to thrill to the happy laughter of children at play.

Yes, we did make it to the stunningly beautiful glacier-fed Emerald Lake. But we were especially thankful for the surprising gifts along the way and for a new appreciation of Psalm 121: "I lift up my eyes to the hills" — the hills of a God who never sleeps, who watches over our "coming and going both now and forevermore" (Ps. 121:8).

Most Valuable Player

Colossians 1:11   Theda Vander Meulen Williams '75
Township treasurer; Charlevoix, Michigan

Our son Tony, after taking two years off from football, decided to return to it again in his senior year. We knew that working his way onto the varsity team as a senior would be a challenge for him and for us as well. It would be his task to work hard, and it would be ours to encourage him. I spoke with him often about attitude, about not quitting, and about holding his head high. From the start of practice until the final game, I told him constantly that he was going to do something phenomenal.

Well, our team had a very disappointing season, with only one win, but we were at every game, enthusiastically cheering for the team and for Tony. I proudly carried my sign with number 82 as I rode on the parents' float for homecoming. I yelled to everyone that number 82 was awesome. When Tony had several tackles, I went berserk. When the season was over, I assured him that those tackles were the phenomenal thing he had done, and he was content with my assessment. He had persisted in spite of disappointments.

At the postseason football banquet several awards were passed out. The coaches' award was given to an athlete who was held in high regard, one who was always ready and willing to do whatever was asked of him. That award went to Tony. In our surprise and delight we agreed that this was indeed something phenomenal.

Through Tony's final high school football season, God taught me this lesson when I was at a point of spiritual weariness in life: I am on the team. Sometimes the team is doing well, and sometimes it's not. I may be part of the action, or I may be on the sidelines waiting to get back in the game. Quitting is never an option. Attitude is of utmost importance. God is in the bleachers with my number, and he is cheering for me with every move I make. He's been telling me all along that I will do something phenomenal. I believe him and trust him that I will. The award? I know that's coming when my season is over.

Helpless by the Pool

Norberto Wolf '64

John 5:1-14

Race-relations director; Bellflower, California

There is something quite intriguing in the healing of the invalid at the pool of Bethesda (John 5:1-14). There is no indication why the Lord should seek him out. He has not called for the Master. As a matter of fact, he does not even know who it is that is speaking to him. Moreover, his answer to the question "Do you want to get well?" (John 5:6) is quite oblique, certainly not revealing any expectation that something good might come from this exchange.

But then Jesus says, "Get up! Pick up your mat and walk" (John 5:8). The formidable power of God flashes through every nerve of this sad man, it softens every joint, firms every muscle, and the man is suddenly on his feet and out on the street.

This miracle is unique in the Gospels. It is not initiated by any request for help. There is no recognition of Jesus, no sense of repentance, no flickering flame of faith, and no expression of gratitude. None of the usual conditions we expect in the context of a miracle are there. There is nothing in this defeated middle-aged man to enable him to deserve what he receives.

There is a word that describes what has just happened to the helpless man by the pool. It is the word *grace.* "Grace is the sheer, self-giving love of God toward suffering and sinful humanity. It has no cause outside the love of God himself; it is not dependent on any merit or worth in the recipient" (W. Ward).

Are we able to see our faces reflected in the face of the man who left the pool? How often do we remember that, if we ourselves walk in faith, it is only because someone said to us, "Stand up and walk"? The more successful, educated, and affluent we are, the more we need to be reminded that it is all a matter of grace, yes, *all* of it. We could have been left helpless by the pool.

Hearts of Wisdom

Psalm 90:12

Janet Sjaarda Sheeres
Calvin administrative assistant; Grand Rapids, Michigan

Teach us to number our days aright, that we may gain a heart of wisdom.
(Ps. 90:12)

During a recent television interview, Billy Graham, the well-known evangelist, was asked to share the one great surprise of his life. "Its brevity," he answered. The psalmist of Psalm 90 laments life's brevity as well. The psalmist, however, goes on to admonish us to count our days so that we may at least gain a heart of wisdom — not first of all longevity or wealth or knowledge, but a heart of wisdom.

At Calvin College we are very much engaged in the quest for knowledge. We strive to instruct the students well, and the students strive to learn much. But we should also be asking these questions: Does a head full of knowledge produce a heart full of wisdom? Does knowledge translate into wisdom? And if not, how do we make it so?

The secret to developing a heart of wisdom lies in the first words of the text: "Teach us. . . . " When we say, "Teach us," we say to God, "We don't have all the answers; you teach us." We assume a stance of humility. We ask for wisdom. Those who are teachable learn best. We all have met people who are always right — at least according to their own opinion. It is difficult to teach such people because they have no receptivity to new ideas or fresh thoughts. But when we say, "Teach us," we open ourselves to God's leading and direction. His Spirit then helps us to look for ways in which we can use our head knowledge to serve him and so become wise in the process. A head full of knowledge is a wonderful thing — if it leads to a heart full of wisdom. A long life is a wonderful thing — if it leads to a heart full of wisdom.

Calvin's motto is "My heart I offer you, Lord, promptly and sincerely." May the hearts we offer God be hearts of wisdom.

Clutter Management

Steven Vryhof '77   Matthew 10:9-10
Teacher/writer; Palos Park, Illinois

The bumper sticker read, "No one should have two houses until everyone has one." I own both a beautiful home and a summer cottage. The bumper sticker and today's text pinch me. Material wealth has always been a conundrum for Christians. On the one hand, the Bible says, "Do not store up for yourselves treasures on earth" (Matt. 6:19) and "Take no bag for the journey" (Matt. 10:10). On the other hand, from Genesis to Revelation, the Bible describes the blessing of God in material terms. Nevertheless, one relentless biblical theme persists: Our stuff can easily clutter our lives and render us useless for the kingdom.

"The beginning of wisdom," says an African proverb, "is to get you a roof." Writer Annie Dillard adds, "What kind of roof? You can go too far. If you get careless, you can find yourself with a house. Then where will you be?"* The answer: maybe trapped — trapped amidst the clutter of possessions, which too often possesses us. As I once heard it said, "Wealth doesn't make you rich; it makes you busy."

How do we keep our lives light and purposeful for the kingdom when we have so much stuff to tend? Net worth is not the issue. Some people who have much hardly notice their wealth, and it takes up little space in their lives. Some people who have little obsess about possessions, and the longing consumes them. Anyone, rich or poor, can embrace the materialistic creed "Things make me happy," and anyone, even millionaires, can "take no bag for the journey."

The first step to clutter management is to look at our most deeply held values and to look at our lives to see whether we have a Christlike match between the two. Clutter management is not simply a justice issue — "No one should have two houses until everyone has one" — nor simply an ecological issue — Americans drive the distance to the planet Pluto *every day* — nor simply a personal-comfort issue — how to avoid the encumbered and dissipated feeling. Clutter management is primarily a spiritual issue: "Take no bag for the journey," and focus on Christ and his calling.

Clutter management will help us to live simply so others may simply live, to take up less space and leave a smaller ecological footprint, to keep our lives light and purposeful. Doing so enables us to offer our hearts to God, promptly and sincerely.

Remembering Not to Forget

Psalm 103:2-3

Alan Aukeman '95
Professor; Grand Rapids, Michigan

"Praise the LORD, O my soul, and forget not all his benefits," David writes in Psalm 103:2, and he then goes on to list a great many of those benefits. On the surface, David's choice of words seems strange to me: "Forget not *all* his benefits"? I like to think my memory's good; I can live life without a day planner and will jump at a game of Trivia Pursuit. I'll admit to occasionally forgetting a few things, but how could David, how could I, forget not one, not a few dozen even, but "all"? What's the psalmist so worried about? What are the chances of forgetting *all* God's benefits?

And yet I know from past experience and instructions in the book of psalms that I do sometimes forget God's commands. One of them tells me to "be still, and know that I am God" (Ps. 46:10), yet I am often not still. Maybe I forget more than I thought I did. Maybe it's a good thing David chose "all." Since he did, David must have known the feeling, too, and I would like to think he recalled the list of benefits in Psalm 103 as a tool to quicken his memory in such lapses — as I do.

Thus, it is heartening that David begins his remembering by naming a God "who forgives *all* your sins and heals *all* your diseases" (Ps. 103:3). It is true that remembering not to forget requires practice, but our diseased memories are also improved by the aid of a God who heals. The health that results goes by what John Calvin calls piety, an old-fashioned name and an old-fashioned virtue, one rarely modeled by today's cultural icons. Calvin defines piety as "that reverence joined with love of God which the knowledge of his benefits induces" (*Institutes of the Christian Religion* I.ii.1*). It exists in us, Calvin says, when we "recognize that [we] owe everything to God, that [we] are nourished by his fatherly care, [and] that he is the author of [our] every good" (*Institutes* I.ii.1). In short, we remember not to forget when we acknowledge God's providence, which, as Calvin explains, is not just God's upholding of the big picture but also "that he sustains, nourishes, and cares for, everything he has made, even to the least sparrow" (*Institutes* 1.xvi.1).

How could we possibly forget all that?

On Being Important

David Musch '76
Research scientist; Ypsilanti, Michigan

Mark 9:35

If anyone wants to be first, he must be the very last, and the servant of all.
(Mark 9:35)

A desire common to many people is to be perceived as important. I remember being interviewed almost nineteen years ago for the university faculty position I now occupy. The department chair pointed out that, should I accept the offer, I would have the potential to be a leader in my profession. That was a heady thought indeed, and at times over the years it has surfaced in both healthy and unhealthy ways. Knowing that our contributions to the family, church, and workplace are considered by others to be important leads us to have a sense of self-esteem, and surely that is healthy. But often our desire to be important dominates us to such an extent that it becomes unhealthy to relationships with others. The hyphen in *self-esteem* drops out, and we are left with *self* and *esteem*. An undue focus on either of these two concepts can lead one astray.

In a November 8, 1993, editorial in *Christianity Today*, Charles Colson refers to four great myths that define our times and challenge all faith traditions. The fourth great myth he singles out is radical individualism, which "dismisses the importance of family, church, and community, denies the value of sacrifice, and elevates individual rights and pleasures as the ultimate social values." Often the desire to be an important person is elevated to such an extent that it dominates one's life and destroys relationships.

There is a healthy middle ground, but it can be difficult to find and maintain. Placing Christ first in our lives and following his example of leading by serving are the keys to an important life. The late Dr. John Kromminga named the reward of truly important people — those who follow Christ's example — in this portion of a poem that he wrote just prior to his death:

All pomp and circumstance, all plaques and trophies
Which we have gathered and hid in their glass cases
Are outshone hundreds of times and more
By simple citizens of the life to come
Whose faces reflect the glory of their Lord,
And there is no higher compliment than "Well done."
(*The Calvin Spark*, Summer 1994)

The First Light

Genesis 1:1-3

Keith Griffioen '79
Professor; Williamsburg, Virginia

In the beginning of God's creating the heavens and the earth there was "tohu wə bohu." . . . And God said, "Let there be light," and there was light.

(Gen. 1:1-3, author's translation)

I have always loved the great creation story of Genesis, but it wasn't until a long winter's night in Utrecht thirteen years ago that a Dutch pastor opened my eyes to it as Philip opened the eyes of the Ethiopian in Acts 8:26-40. To be sure, Genesis 1 is a story about creation, but it is also a story about what the Hebrew calls *tohu wə bohu* — chaos, waste, wilderness, darkness, nothingness, emptiness, confusion — and about the dark fears that haunt us when we try to wrestle with what happened there and how. But all that fear vanishes into light when God speaks. As the story goes (in Dutch), God spends the first three days building infrastructure: *licht* ("light") on the first day, *lucht* ("air," separated from the water) on the second, and *land* ("dry land") on the third. Then God fills the world with creatures: creatures of the *licht* (sun, moon, and stars) on the fourth day, creatures of the *lucht* ("air" and water) on the fifth, and creatures of the *land* on the sixth. This story of beginnings is powerful, symmetrical, and logical, but it is not the one a modern cosmologist would tell. Somehow the mechanisms of an inflationary big bang and of supernovae explosions are beside the point here.

It was the Dutch pastor who pointed out a parallel story in the New Testament. In Mark 6:45-52 we find Jesus' disciples on the Sea of Galilee in the middle of the night as a fierce storm whips up the water. Their greatest fears torment them in the chaos. There is *tohu wə bohu* — chaos and its attendant terror, terror of a kind not apparent at the time in Genesis, where there were not yet beings who could experience terror. And then, suddenly, in the middle of it all there is light. The boatmen on the Sea of Galilee mistake Jesus for a ghost until he comes closer. Only then do they recognize the Lord, who speaks to quell their dread and calm the waters.

So, too, all our own fears — about billions of years, about sextillions of miles, about an ancient and evolving planet — vanish in the creative light of the one who still moves over the face of the deep and breathes life into the equations that govern the cosmos.

Moral Courage

Gordon Van Harn '57   Psalm 27:7-14
Calvin professor emeritus; Grand Rapids, Michigan

The book *Beating the Odds* (Hrabowski et al.) is the encouraging account of the academic success of young people from minority communities that are more often associated with statistics of poverty, crime, drugs, and violence. The authors present stories of young African-Americans selected for a university science program because of their exceptional academic gifts. As a public-school-board member in an urban district, I wanted to know more about them.

As you might expect, all of these students had at least one parent who was interested in the children's education, reading to them, helping them with homework, ensuring faithful attendance, providing enrichment opportunities, and, in general, being their advocate in school. But there is another theme throughout these stories. The effective parents taught these young people to withstand peer pressure which would destroy their academic and personal potential and to handle ridicule for their academic achievement. These parents and their churches instilled in these children the moral courage to dare to be different and do what is right.

They followed the advice of Psalm 27. First, "Teach me your way, O LORD" (Ps. 27:11) — know what is right. Second, "Do not turn me over to the desire of my foes, for false witnesses rise up against me, breathing out violence" (Ps. 27:12) — live in the presence of God rather than in the presence of evil. And, third, "Wait for the LORD; be strong and take heart" (Ps. 27:14) — have the strength to do what is right.

The young people who were part of the study are modern-day Daniels, daring to do what is right. Indeed, all young people need this courage, as do middle-agers and seniors as well. We all encounter pressures to conform to our surrounding culture. Popular entertainment, consumerist lifestyle, postmodern ideas, and increasing relativism can shape how we think and live. Living in this modern culture, we need to dare to be different; we need the moral courage to do what is right.

May God give us all — young and old and in-between — strong hearts to know what's right, to choose what's right, and valiantly to do what's right.

God in the Wilderness

Genesis 16:8   Juliana Flietstra Steensma '45
Retired rehabilitation therapist; Holland, Michigan

*And he said, "Hagar, servant of Sarai, where have you come from, and where
are you going?"* (Gen. 16:8)

When people ask me where I'm from I have difficulty giving an answer. I have lived in more than forty different houses in five states and a foreign country. Over the years I have come to see the advantages and disadvantages of this kind of life journey. I can also see that having deep roots and a hometown gives a person a sense of security. But facing new situations teaches a person to accept change and adapt to circumstances.

Hagar, the servant of Sarai, came from a difficult situation. She was a young slave girl fleeing a mistress who did not treat her kindly. Nothing but her obstinate pride and her desperation could have driven Hagar to brave a dangerous journey through the wilderness. She may have been trying to return to her own people in Egypt, but she probably would have died in the attempt if it had not been for the timely intervention of the angel of Jehovah.

The angel not only reminded Hagar of what was behind her but also gave her hope for what was ahead, and he promised her a son who would become the head of a mighty tribe. No matter how helpless and insignificant Hagar felt as a homeless slave, God knew her. She could take up her burden again because she believed God's promise concerning her future.

"Where are you going?" God asks each of us, because each one of us is of special concern to him. We may feel like strangers, we may feel abused and mistreated, we may try to run away from our troubles, but God cares for us no matter how humble our place, how sordid our situation. Even in the wildernesses of our lives, when we scarcely know where we are going, God confronts us personally with his love, his care, and his promises. And he gives us direction so that we know more certainly where we should be going.

The Virtue of Discernment

John D. Witvliet '90   Philippians 1:9-11
Calvin Worship Institute director; Jenison, Michigan

> *And this is my prayer: that your love may abound more and more in knowledge and depth of insight, so that you may be able to discern what is best and may be pure and blameless until the day of Christ, filled with the fruit of righteousness that comes through Jesus Christ — to the glory and praise of God.*
>
> (Phil. 1:9-11)

In the Scripture for today, Paul prays that the Christian community will learn and exercise the virtue of discernment. Especially in situations of conflict or confusion, we need wisdom to make good choices. Our recent disputes about how best to worship are only one example of many such situations.

What does it mean to discern? Solomon sought discernment when he asked for "a discerning heart to . . . distinguish between right and wrong" (1 Kings 3:9). Augustine defined it as "love making a right distinction between what helps us move toward God and what might hinder us." Discernment requires making choices, saying yes to some things and no to others.

Paul gives us a short recipe for discernment. Knowledge and insight are two key ingredients. They provide a measuring stick by which to judge a given innovation or practice. To make good choices, we need to ask probing questions and search for penetrating insight into truth. We need the mind of Christ.

Another ingredient of discernment is love — not a sentimental love that approves and adopts every fad, but a deep, pastoral love that nurtures long-term spiritual health. And love requires community. Psalm 19:12 asks, "Who can discern his [own] errors?" reminding us that people in isolation, by themselves, do not have the perspective to see the whole picture. That's why Paul prays for "you all" (second person plural) to determine what is best.

Finally, discernment, like every virtue, is less an accomplishment to achieve than a gift to receive. The chief ally and agent in any communal discernment process is none less than the Spirit of God. Discernment is a Pentecost virtue, a gift of the Spirit, and therefore something for which we should pray.

Ask the Spirit for help in making the choices that will produce a harvest of righteousness.

God the Builder

Ezekiel 36:24-31

Max Vreugdenhil '79
Businessman; Bradenton, Florida

I will give you a new heart and put a new spirit in you; I will remove from you your heart of stone and give you a heart of flesh. (Ezek. 36:26)

The building process begins with a survey to determine the exact boundaries and characteristics of a property. Is the site too low or wet? Is the soil unstable or polluted? Working from the survey, the contractor then determines the best location for the building. His bulldozer clears away the vegetation, then digs deep into the ground to remove muck, jagged rocks, long-forgotten fuel barrels, and other buried trash. Soon a large pile of refuse reveals the property's imperfections.

As some trucks haul off the refuse, other trucks bring in clean, sound dirt to fill the holes and level the site. A tractor compacts the dirt to remove air pockets so that the floors of the future building will not settle and crack under the building's weight. When the builder has completed these preparations, he is ready to lay the all-important foundation.

When God replaces a sinner's heart of stone with a heart of flesh, he makes it possible for the building process of salvation and regeneration to begin. As the land needs the bulldozer, the tractor, and the trucks to prepare the site and haul away the debris, so, too, the sinner needs the powerful grace of God to remove the secret and overt rebellion and disobedience from his heart. Without God's grace, assured by Christ's sacrifice on Calvary, our hearts would remain unfit sites for the spiritual temples God desires to build in our lives.

On the well-prepared ground of the heart of flesh, God lays the unfailing foundation of faith and the cornerstone, Jesus Christ. Upon that foundation and cornerstone he lays stone after stone through the work of his skilled craftsman, the Holy Spirit, until the believer is well reinforced by love, hope, patience, charity, long-suffering, and many other Christian virtues.

A Spirit-built heart is resistant to the winds of doctrine, the fires of persecution, the floods of despair. It remains a dwelling place for our Lord all the days of our lives and acts as a place of refuge and renewal to those who sense their need for rebuilding or remodeling. To them we must freely tell the name of our Builder, who made our buildings so good that, indeed, we are the temples of the living God, whose we are and whom we serve.

Evensong at Westminster Abbey

Peter A. Boelens '57   Philippians 2:6-11
Physician; Vicksburg, Mississippi

I was on my way back from my first visit to Africa, a visit which had begun with a whole succession of events that seemed to militate against
my ever getting there. The flight was supposed to have gone directly from
Atlanta to London and then on to Uganda, where I was to meet a physician
interested in starting a community health project. The plane was late leaving Atlanta. Then a woman passenger suffered a stroke that necessitated
some backtracking to Boston. My flight from London to Uganda had been
canceled, and the next one wasn't scheduled until the following week. I lost
all hope of meeting my contacts, and with Uganda in the middle of guer-
rilla warfare, my anxiety level began to rise at the thought of carrying on on
my own. Miraculously, God provided the way for me to connect with several Ugandans who were risking their lives working in the slums of Kisenyi,
and the community health project was launched.

Now I was physically a long way from Africa, in Westminster Abbey, almost breathless at the beauty of the cathedral. Still dressed in my dirty African clothes, I had arrived just in time for evensong. The music of the organ and the pure voices of the boys choir made me feel like I was sitting in
heaven. I had only recently left one of the cesspools of the world, full of suffering and heartache and killing. Why, I wondered, couldn't all of life be
perfect beauty like this?

Then, suddenly, as though I might get too enraptured by these comfortable pews and this glorious religious experience, the thought of Jesus
came to my mind: From the majesties of heaven he had come to earth for
our redemption (Phil. 2:6-8). Instinctively I knew at that moment that he
wanted me, too, to leave comfort behind and head into the dirty parts of
the world to provide the touch of his love to the hurting and hopeless. It
was fine for me to take refreshment like this from time to time, but Jesus
didn't want me to stay in this wonderful environment.

How is Jesus guiding your life? Could he be calling you to move out of
your comfortable lifestyle, to touch with love the hurting and the hopeless
in the developing world or even in your very own community?

Pigeons

1 Kings 19:1-12   Steve Baas '86
Communications director, Madison, Wisconsin

My young nieces and nephews were coming to visit me in Chicago, and it was my job to play tour guide. From the museums to the Sears Tower, from Michigan Avenue to Wrigley Field, I showed off the things that I thought were sure to dazzle them.

To my surprise, however, it wasn't any of these urban wonders that excited them. It was the pigeons. These ubiquitous dirty birds that I viewed with such contempt were, in the judgment of these children, the most wondrous thing in the city. After their visit I began to notice and appreciate more the pigeons and other commonplace wonders of the city that had always surrounded me but that I had always overlooked — flowers growing in sidewalk cracks, a homeless mother singing to her child, the sounds of birdsong and church bells.

Too often we Christians fall into the trap of looking for God in the dramatic or the overtly spiritual places of our lives. We miss the fact that God is also present in the most mundane and even earthy corners of our existence. We complain when we cannot seem to find him in the skyscraper anymore even as we fail to see him in the pigeons all around us. Like Elijah, we become bitter as we long for more of Mount Carmel's fire but forget God's presence in the still, small voice.

Some years ago a friend told me that she had resolved to look for God every day in something around her. It was always a delight to hear the amazing ways in which God surprised her with his presence. Her resolve was so well rewarded that I would recommend her approach.

If you haven't seen God today, maybe you're looking in the wrong places. If you're straining to see him in the dazzling sights and sounds of your life, maybe you've missed the gentle whisper of his still, small voice or his fluttering glory in the pigeons at your feet. Look again, and listen, for

This is my Father's world: The birds their carols raise,
The morning light, the lily white, Declare their Maker's praise.
This is my Father's world: He shines in all that's fair;
In the rustling grass I hear Him pass; He speaks to me everywhere.*

It's about Love

Louis E. Kok '53   Matthew 11:25-30
Retired chaplain; Lynden, Washington

We live in a universe God loves. Knowing and believing in God's love makes all the difference in the world. Since God loves the world, we should be able to live with a sense of safety and security. Certainly there is evil. We know evil in our own souls, and we see it around us. Still, the main premise is that God loves this old world and especially loves us as people. He loves the world in spite of the evil in it. He loves all people even though we all continue our sinful ways. In fact, it is as a result of sin that his love is most clearly demonstrated: He gave his Son for sinful people. His grace is greater than all the sin and evil that people generate. The cost of his love was the death of his Son. In the resurrection of his Son he overcame death and sin and evil. It is especially through the gift of his Son that God shows his love for the world and for us as a human race in particular.

Since we have experienced his love, that same love now lives and works in us and through us. It is that same costly and accepting love that Jesus talked about and demonstrated throughout his ministry and finally in the giving of his life on the cross. It is this Jesus kind of love that we have in our beings and that we must now show to others as we live our lives in relationship to them. Through us God has chosen to scatter his love to people around us. God's love is promiscuous, undiscriminating, and since his love is promiscuous, ours should also be. We should not require the objects of our love to be deserving, to be persons of our liking, to be good people or productive people. God did not demand that of us, or he would have passed us by. Nor may anyone or anything at all ever prevent us from spreading abroad God's love. Nothing.

This divine promiscuity seems to be difficult if not impossible, but it is the nature of God's love. God loves us; Jesus loves us; we love others. Jesus said, "My yoke is easy and my burden is light" (Matt. 11:30).

What is it all about? It's about love — God's love for the world and our love for one another.

The Patient Craftsman

Psalm 40:5

Ralph Stearley

Calvin professor; Grand Rapids, Michigan

Many, O LORD my God, are the wonders you have done. The things you planned for us no one can recount to you; were I to speak and tell of them, they would be too many to declare. (Ps. 40:5)

For the past few summers I have been repainting the exterior of my house. I have been taking my time, intensively scraping and sanding, often down to the bare wood, to prepare the surface. My neighbors walk by and ask when I will ever be done. I ask them to please be patient. I'm glad to say that they can now clearly see some progress.

Patience brings me to think of an old friend of mine. Years ago he regularly wore a button with the letters "PBPGINFWMY" on it. When asked their meaning, he would explain, "Please be patient. God is not finished with me yet." As I scrape and sand my house, I ponder the implications of PBPGINFWMY and realize that God is not yet finished with a good many things.

As a student of Earth's history, I've been privileged to examine some of the particulars of the Lord's direction of affairs on our home planet through time. This history is long by human standards, but not so by God's. The work of a master craftsman is evident in the architecture of a planet suited for abundant life and for husbandry by those beings created in his image. Yet we creatures perceive only a minimum of the foresight and planning of our covenant God. Like those who watch me working on my house year after year, we generally cannot appreciate all God's intensive work in upholding and restoring this world and our very lives.

The triune God is a God of infinite wisdom, foresight, and patience. His plans will be brought to fruition. These plans, including the redemption of his people and of the creation, will be made manifest according to his own timetable, which is not our own. Occasionally along the way we are treated to glimpses of the wonders that he is accomplishing. May God grant us greater perception of his guidance over the course of the ages and in the age to come.

Excellence

William K. Stob '52   Philippians 3:12-16
Pastor/Calvin dean emeritus; West Palm Beach, Florida

They called him Trey. The moniker stuck, and it became his trademark in his family circle. He was stimulated by strong family ties, and his competitive spirit was fueled by childhood games, sports, and the driving ambition of his parents. His childhood friends remember him as being smart — particularly good at math. His mother, Mary, was always well-organized and meticulous in her planning. These traits were passed on to her son, who wasted no time either at play or at work. Trey strove for excellence. And so the illustrious career of William Henry Gates III (Bill Gates) was begun.

Excellence is an exciting word. It triggers our imagination, and if we apply it to ourselves, it challenges us to be the very best. Tom Peters's book *In Search of Excellence* became a bestseller and influenced a whole generation of people in all walks of life to be the very best they could be.

Christians, too, are exhorted to strive for excellence, holy excellence. To be sure, we are creatures of grace, and, compared to God's blazing righteousness, our actions often resemble filthy rags. But we must press on, and, like the believers in Corinth, we should celebrate each other's gifts that make excellence possible.

The Bible gives us some guidelines for reaching holy excellence. Paul says in 1 Corinthians, "And now I will show you the most excellent way. . . . Love is patient, love is kind. It does not envy, it does not boast, it is not proud. . . . Love never fails. . . . And now these three remain: faith, hope and love. But the greatest of these is love" (1 Cor. 12:31; 13:4, 8, 13). There should be no unholy one-upmanship, no room for arrogance, in the Christian pursuit of excellence.

Furthermore, Christians in the pursuit of excellence should not be contentious persons but contributing, joyful peacemakers. Says Paul, "Rejoice in the Lord always. . . . Let your gentleness be evident to all. . . . Whatever is true, whatever is noble, whatever is right, whatever is pure, whatever is lovely, whatever is admirable — if anything is excellent or praiseworthy — think about such things" (Phil. 4:4-5, 8).

The pursuit of excellence, holy excellence — let that be *our* hallmark. Let's be driven, consumed, challenged — for Christ's sake and for his kingdom. Let's all of us make this our personal pledge: "I press on toward the goal to win the prize for which God has called me heavenward" (Phil. 3:14). That's a commitment to holy excellence!

If You Can Do Anything

Mark 9:14-32
William J. Vande Kopple '72
Calvin professor; Grand Rapids, Michigan

James Vanden Bosch and I often collaborate in teaching a course in traditional grammar. Much to the amazement of many of our friends, we enjoy this subject, including the terms associated with it, terms such as *retained object* and *zero relative pronoun.*

Once I know the name and possible forms of a linguistic element, that element tends to stand out on pages I read. Take adverbial clauses of condition, for example. Recently I was reading in Mark 9 about a man bringing his demon-possessed son to Jesus. When Jesus asks how long the boy has been tormented, the man responds that he has been possessed since childhood. Then the man begins a sentence with the conjunction *but* leading into an adverbial clause of condition: "But if you can do anything, take pity on us and help us" (Mark 9:22). One can understand the man's desperation: He has probably been trying every conceivable remedy for years, and he is speaking to Jesus immediately after some of the disciples have failed to help his son. But imagine the poignancy of the moment when Jesus, the Word through whom all things were made, responds to him with this abbreviated adverbial clause of condition: "'If you can'?"

How often do we, too, bring petitions to God without daring to believe that he has the power to respond to them? After Jesus says, "'If you can'?" he adds that not just many things are possible but that "everything is possible for one who believes" (Mark 9:23, NIVI). And throughout the Gospels he tells people that an apparently small measure of faith can lead to seemingly incredible feats.

I am not advocating working from interpretations of what we take to be God's responses to our prayers backward to judgments about how God must be measuring our faith. Some of the most devout Christians I know acknowledge that they will have to wait until eternity to understand God's responses to some of their prayers.

I am advocating that we ask God to help us overcome degrees of unbelief so that we can come before him saying, "Lord, I believe."

One Set of Footprints

Tricia Fynewever '98   1 Corinthians 1:18-31
Graduate student; Grand Terrace, California

"Didn't you promise that if I gave my heart to you, you'd be with me all the way? Then why is there just one set of footprints during my times of greatest trouble?" These haunting and somewhat accusatory questions, posed to God by the narrator of the popular footprint-shaped devotional called "Footprints," are questions like those I have asked God many times, though my questions are more likely to be something like this: "Where were you when I needed you this morning during my anatomy test?" "How am I supposed to finish all my reading, get at least four hours of sleep, and have any kind of relationship with other human beings?" "Is it imperative that I go to church today when I have eighteen hours of studying left before Monday morning?"

I've found that when the work of medical school gets harder and the hours of study lengthen, that's when everything seems to go wrong and life just doesn't feel right, doesn't even feel possible. Whenever this happens, my spirit is at its lowest point, and I feel like I've never been lonelier. What's more, I've begun to realize that it's at these hardest and most burdensome times of life that I begin to forget God and rely on my own strength. Others who experience these feelings would probably agree that it's at this point that we need God the most. What a time to forget him!

We should not rely on ourselves. If we do, we are truly foolish, for even the "weakness of God is stronger than human strength" (1 Cor. 1:25, NIVI). If we rely on God, we can be "more than conquerors through him who loved us" (Rom. 8:37). The more we rely on God, the lower life's hurdles will seem, and the more bearable life's struggles will be.

I myself have experienced the joy of conquering with God's help. As I trust more in God's strength, I enjoy even the most challenging parts of medical school. I challenge you to put a reminder of God's faithfulness where you can see it each day. My reminder is Philippians 1:6: "I always pray with joy, . . . being confident of this, that he who began a good work in you will carry it on to completion until the day of Christ Jesus."

The person in "Footprints" heard this answer from God, one that has comforted and encouraged many Christians: "My precious child, I love you and would never forsake you. During those times of trial and suffering when you see only one set of footprints, it was then that I carried you." God not only walks the hard road with us; he picks us up and carries us when the road becomes too hard for our tender human feet.

The Big Picture

Ephesians 3:14-21   Ken Bootsma '67
School administrator; Lafayette, Indiana

Where would you have to stand to get a worldview — a comprehensive view and understanding of the world around you? Would it be the Sears Tower? Half Dome? Mount McKinley? Is it possible for any of us to step back far enough to see the totality of our physical world and to develop an understanding of the beliefs of others and the interrelationships of people and nations? No, this is reserved for an omniscient and omnipotent God alone.

However, all mature, thinking individuals have a worldview, even if they are unaware of what theirs is. It's not a physical perspective on the world, but rather the philosophical perspective one takes with respect to certain facets of human thought. In his book *Faith and Reason*, Robert Nash indicates that a well-rounded worldview includes what one believes on at least five major topics: God (theology), reality (metaphysics), knowledge (epistemology), morality (ethics), and humankind (anthropology).

But it isn't enough for Christians simply to know the content of their worldview. They must move beyond the intellectual content of their faith to put that faith into action. Worldviews compete in the marketplace, and the Christian worldview *should* clash with other worldviews. Worldview battle lines are increasingly being drawn against us. As Dr. Carl Henry says, "The stakes are higher today for evangelical Christians than at any time since the Reformation. . . . Our greatest challenge is the fulfillment of our mission, position and duties . . . more so than fighting social forces or moral decay."

As Reformed Christians, we must build a sufficient worldview in order to know what the faith requires of us and to be able to defend the faith against other worldviews. But in all our intellectual approaches to faith, we need to remember that love surpasses knowledge. Listen to Paul's prayer for the Ephesians:

> I pray that out of his glorious riches he may strengthen you with power through his Spirit . . . , so that Christ may dwell in your hearts through faith. And I pray that you, being rooted and established in love, may have power, together with all the saints, to grasp how wide and long and high and deep is the love of Christ, and to know this love that surpasses knowledge — that you may be filled to the measure of all the fullness of God. (Eph. 3:16-19)

Politics and the Kingdom

Kathy Vander Ziel Vandergrift '69   Esther 7–8
Public-policy analyst; Ottawa, Ontario

The story of Esther continues to puzzle Christians. For some it is an illustration of how God preserved the Jewish people and furthered his plan of redemption. For others it is a story of self-sacrifice or a contrast between rebellious Vashti and submissive Esther. (As a woman, I sometimes feel more admiration for Vashti, who stood up to an abusive king and paid for it with her life, than I do for Esther, though I know Esther is supposed to be the heroine.)

Neither Esther nor Mordecai deserves a medal for virtue. In today's terms, Esther is a child prostitute, and Mordecai is a guardian who uses her instead of protecting her. An appreciation of how Esther turns evil into good in no way condones the sinful behavior of either Esther or Mordecai, but the story as a whole can still encourage us to be agents of justice in an alien and evil environment.

Esther is a master political strategist. Valued initially for her appearance, she becomes an effective advocate for the voiceless in the halls of power. She works hard to become a confidante of the king. At the same time, she stays in touch with her people, the victims of injustice.

To save her people, Esther identifies a specific, achievable objective that can make a crucial difference. Then she develops a careful strategy to achieve her objective. She pleads her cause in a way that appeals to the king and builds a case that the king cannot refuse. Esther knows the importance of timing and persistence. She takes life-threatening risks, but they are calculated, not reckless. Through prayer and regular consultation she involves all the people in her strategy. She is an effective agent for justice.

Today we Christians find ourselves in situations as alien as Esther's in Persia, dealing with evil spirits as powerful as King Ahasuerus. As well as celebrating Esther's role in the history of redemption, we can learn from Esther's tactics. We would do well to practice being Esthers, not passive objects in history but active and clever strategists in doing justice, moving forward step by step toward the realization of God's kingdom in society. Dare to be an Esther for the Lord.

Singing in the Kitchen

Isaiah 12

Gertrude Van Hoff Beversluis '39
Homemaker; Grand Rapids, Michigan

The Lord, is my strength and my song. (Isa. 12:2)

Of the many illuminating metaphors used for God in the Bible — shepherd, light, rock, and more — these in the book of Isaiah have been very meaningful to me through many years: He is "my strength and my song."

At first glance, those seem contradictory ideas to put together. They are like two sides of life. When you hear "strength," you think of muscle, of power, of overcoming. "Song" brings to mind light-heartedness, perhaps contentment. In the dictionary, strength is the ability to withstand or to exert great force; song is the expression of emotions. Perhaps not contradictory, but surely very different ideas.

Thoughts about both strength and song are common in the Bible, but it is unusual that they are brought together this way. God is often spoken of as "the strength of his people," the endurance and power in their lives. And the Bible persistently tells God's people to sing his praise — "the Lord's song" must be on their lips. But only in this hymn — recorded first when sung by Moses and the children of Israel (Exod.15:2) and repeated in Psalm 118 and in Isaiah — only in this hymn do we find "God *is* my song." Yes, *is* — he is music, melody, the song in our lives. And, surprisingly, in this psalm the two are put together: "The Lord Jehovah is my strength and my song."

Exactly that, I think, has been my experience of the Christian life. On some of the dreariest days, in the bumps and bruises of life, he has been my song — and so I could sing. Almost any kind of song would do: psalms we learned as children or good old *Golden Book* songs or love songs from youth. Singing made it possible to carry on. Even when problems or frustrations made me feel like not singing, somehow doing so restored my strength. Is this the experience of others who sing in the kitchen? Not the one without the other, but both together. Somehow strength generates song, and song renews strength. God is there as both. He is the strength, and he is the song.

The Food of Grace

Paul Overvoorde '90   Romans 5:20-21
Research associate; Richmond, California

Throughout history, and particularly in the story of God's people, un-expected individuals have played surprising roles. From Rahab and David in the Old Testament to Peter and Paul in the New Testament, people who might be considered the greatest of sinners have performed mighty tasks and have mobilized the kingdom of God here on earth. As the apostle Paul writes in his letter to the Romans, "Where sin increased, grace increased all the more, so that, just as sin reigned in death, so also grace might reign through righteousness to bring eternal life through Jesus Christ our Lord" (Rom. 5:20-21).

Because of the riches of divine grace, sin-filled people like us are used to fulfill God's purposes. The Communion service in my church last Sunday contained an extraordinary reminder of this grace. As individuals of all stripes — young and old, female and male, African-American and Asian, Caucasian and Indian, sharp and dull, blind and seeing — came forward to receive the elements of the sacrament, the light of God's presence burned brightly. Each person came forward to partake only after a time of self-reflection and confession of sin — sin private and personal, corporate and communal, sin of omission and commission. For some, these burdens had been carried for years; for others, they had been created during the car ride to the service that morning. Regardless, as the communicants walked past the baptismal font, a personal set of experiences drew them toward the communal act of remembering and celebrating God's unique claim on their lives.

The next time you share the cup with or pass the bread to a sister or brother in Christ, watch with new eyes, hear with new ears, and taste with a new tongue that this is the food of amazing grace.

Lessons from a Mountain Forest AUGUST 20

Psalm 104:1-6 Harlan Kredit '61

Teacher; Lynden, Washington

Today I took ten teachers hiking high into the mountains. As a biologist and naturalist, I often do this. I invite you to imagine yourself going on such a trip. Please come along.

As we climb in the rain through a majestic stand of old-growth timber, we see huge trees covered with layers of mosses and lichens. The forest floor is carpeted by a wide variety of herbs and flowers. Water drips from the trees and occasionally down our necks, too. The soil is a mixture of dark earth that looks like compost, the result of thousands of years of recycling all organic matter that has fallen to the forest floor. Gigantic fallen trees lie on the slopes in varying stages of decay. Actually they are more alive than the standing trees because they are full of thousands of different kinds of insects and fungi.

Since the sounds of the forest are absorbed by the carpet of plants, we are in a quiet place, a good place for each of us to meditate about the great questions of life. I think of Psalm 104:16, where the psalmist says, "The trees of the LORD are well watered, the cedars of Lebanon that he planted." I wonder whether the psalmist ever experienced a forest like this one. It is a powerful psalm about the Lord reveling in his creation.

What can God teach us as we quietly soak up the mood of a primeval forest shrouded in mist? Can he make it any more clear to us that he made this world for us to enjoy but not abuse? Does he expect Christians to understand stewardship of the land more deeply than most citizens on this planet do? Does he expect us to live as if we care? Could a Christian have dropped that Pepsi can along the trail?

When we leave the forest and return to our daily routine, we should look at our surroundings in a slightly different way. We should truly praise God for so clearly revealing to us every day that his world is precious to him and should be precious to us, too. Let's try.

Making Copies

Anne Zaki '99
Graduate student; Cairo, Egypt

1 Samuel 8:1-21

When I was a child, I learned to copy pictures using graph paper. Whatever picture I wanted to copy, I would divide into little squares like those on graph paper. Then I would copy each individual box separately onto the blank grid. I remember being very impressed the first time I tried this method, because as soon as I finished copying the last square, I realized that I had almost an exact copy of the original picture.

In 1 Samuel 8 all the elders of Israel gather around Samuel and ask him to appoint over them a king "such as all the other nations have." The people of Israel are so blinded by sin that they have forgotten what King they already have — a King who rules over them with justice and mercy and doesn't take their best fields, vineyards, and oil groves (1 Sam. 8:14), who does not need their sons to serve with his horses and run in front of his chariots (1 Sam. 8:11), who makes promises that only he can fulfill. They have a great King, but they are rejecting him (1 Sam. 8:7). They want to copy all the other nations.

Satan often uses the graph-paper method with us, too. Little by little we fill in the squares until we have a close copy of the original. It often begins with Satan's little questions, like "What's the big deal about lusting after this person? That doesn't make you less of a Christian!" "So what if you swear once or twice. It's all just words." "There's nothing wrong with anger, jealousy, gossip, or lying. You're only human, after all." "Do you really think it matters if you don't tithe this paycheck? You really need the money for yourself." And we keep on copying one small box after another, until before we know it, we've become carbon copies of the "people of this world" (Luke 16:8).

In contrast to the people of Israel, who wanted to copy the neighboring nations, the Bible also tells us stories of people who copied God. One copied his glory so that his face shone like God's face after being in God's presence (Exod. 34:29). Another copied God's language after living with him (Matt. 26:73). There are many more examples in the Bible of people who changed, box by box, from glory to glory, to become the image, the copy, of Christ.

Do you spend enough time in God's presence and in his Word to be transformed into a copy of him? Or do you blindly follow the ruler of this air and copy box after box his corrupting image? Do you want a face radiant with God's glory or a face deceitful with unfaithfulness? Choose for yourself today whom you will copy. Make sure the original is worth reproducing.

Praising the God of Wonders

Psalm 9:1; Psalm 40:5

Julie Feikens VanderHaagen '72
Homemaker; Williamsburg, Michigan

I will praise you, O LORD, with all my heart; I will tell of all your wonders.
(Ps. 9:1)

Many, O LORD my God, are the wonders you have done. The things you planned for us no one can recount to you. . . . (Ps. 40:5)

A ccording to weather experts, each person views the raindrops forming a rainbow from a slightly different angle. Therefore, no two people see a rainbow in exactly the same way. Twenty years ago my husband and I observed one of these weather wonders of God — from a slightly different angle. We had been married for eight years and were longing, but unable, to have children. We would be great parents, we thought. Why couldn't we be a family? What was God's plan?

Having decided to explore adoption, we were returning home from our initial meeting with social workers and numerous other prospective adoptive couples. We had been told all the depressing facts. Our eagerness to be a family had been dampened with the reality of a long wait. Now, as we drove home, our bleak mood matched the rainy weather outside. But as we came around a curve in the road, we witnessed an astonishing rainbow ahead of us. We didn't say much, but we both immediately recognized it as a sign of God's promise.

Skeptics might say that attaching significance to the rainbow is sentimental thinking. But we viewed this natural wonder of God from a different angle: God was planning an incomparable wonder for us. As the footnote to Psalm 9:1 in the *NIV Study Bible* explains, *wonders* are "God's saving acts, sometimes involving miracles . . . and sometimes not, but always involving the manifestation of God's sovereign lordship over events."

God did indeed extend his providential hand to give us two daughters, both wonderfully made, to be a part of our family through adoption. We know from experience that, in the words of the great hymn, "God moves in a mysterious way his wonders to perform."* Now we always observe rainbows from a slightly different angle, seeing God's slightly different plan for us as a family, and we praise the Lord with all our hearts as we tell of his wonders in our lives and everywhere.

Remembering God's Grace

Jeffrey DeVries '88   Joshua 24:1-15
Teacher; Lansing, Illinois

I n a recent article entitled "Poetry and American Memory," U.S. poet lau-
reate Robert Pinsky argues that many of the great issues in American
public life connect ultimately not to a political question but to a cultural
one: Who do Americans think they are? Pinsky's purpose, he tells us early
in the essay, is "to seek a vision of our future in the poetry of our past." His
argument rests on the notion that the question of our identity is largely a
matter of the past that we inherit. He finishes the essay with this bold dec-
laration: "Deciding to remember, and what to remember, is how we decide
who we are."

Joshua appears to be of a like mind. In his last official action as the
Lord's ruler over Israel, he summons all God's people together to ask them
who they are. Joshua challenges the people to renew their covenant with
God, to pledge with him to serve the Lord, but before he does this, he tells
them their history. He recounts how God liberated Abraham from false
gods, how God promised and made good on his promise to make Abraham
into a great nation, how God heard his people's cries in Egypt and delivered them, and how ultimately he led them into the promised land. Joshua
knows that the people cannot answer a question of identity, they cannot
declare themselves the people of God, without a knowledge of God's working in their past. These stories reveal who they were and are.

And so it still is today for the children of God. In deciding to remember the stories of God's grace in the sordid history of humankind and in
the daily jumble of our own lives, we discover who we are. Only when we
know our identity as adopted children of the King can we respond in gratitude by offering ourselves "as living sacrifices, holy and pleasing to God"
(Rom. 12:1).

For God's Sake, Listen

Psalm 19

Scott Hoezee '86

Pastor; Grand Rapids, Michigan

God saw all that he had made, and it was very good. (Gen. 1:31)

The heavens declare the glory of God. . . . Day after day they pour forth speech.
(Ps. 19:1-2)

Simone Weil once noted that the most striking feature of Genesis 1 is God's ability to delight in creatures other than himself. Despite the inestimable glories God possesses within himself, God is nevertheless able to "get outside himself" to celebrate others. Again and again in the creation God stops to stare at his handiwork, smiling over the sprinting of gazelles, the spouting of whales, the craning of the giraffe's improbably long neck. God keeps calling the creation "good," not as a moral assessment but as an aesthetic one. You could just as well translate all those "and God saw it was good" lines as "and God saw it was just gorgeous!"

The Bible makes clear that God enjoys noting the sights and sounds of his cosmos — to God it is nothing short of praise. As God's imagebearers, we may be the only creatures who can take similar note of creation. For instance, when we humans snorkel over a coral reef, we do so to study and appreciate the startling variety of life darting through the sea. But all those various species of fish do not make a study of one another, nor do they marvel over us human beings as we float past. It seems only we have the God-like ability to get outside ourselves so as to appreciate and study otherness. Nurturing our ability to celebrate the creation wonders around us is, therefore, a proper task for disciples — it's a way to act more like God.

Some years ago an ornithologist painstakingly counted the number of times a single red-eyed vireo sang its song one day. The final tally was 22,197. North America is estimated to be home to six billion land birds. If on just one day each of those birds were to sing its song 10,000 times, that would create a symphony of 60,000,000,000,000 (sixty trillion) songs! "Day after day they pour forth speech." And God listens. So should we, starting today.

Playing by God's Rules

Richard Bandstra '72   Psalm 119:14, 16
Judge; Grand Rapids, Michigan

> *I rejoice in following your statutes. . . . I delight in your decrees. . . .*
> (Ps. 119:14, 16)

One of Satan's biggest lies is that God's commandments are onerous constraints that prevent us from enjoying a full and satisfying life. The dark forces spread this lie throughout our culture and glorify the lifestyles of the greedy, the narcissistic, and the sex-obsessed. A second lie is that these are the paths to happiness.

Playing a well-constructed game is most fun when you follow the rules. Take chess, for example. The queen cannot be allowed to move wherever she wants. If she does, the game is destroyed or, at best, much less fun. When the queen moves the way she is supposed to, the other pieces can have their strengths and their weaknesses in proper proportion. As a result, the game can be enjoyed to its fullest.

God is like the inventors of chess, but infinitely wiser. He knows us intimately, loves us fully, and wants only the best for us. The perfect game maker, he has provided us the rules for living as joyously as possible here in a creation broken by sin.

A host of witnesses around us can tell how this works. Ask the old married couple who have lived faithfully with each other and God through all life's ups and downs. Ask the special-education teacher about her sense of satisfaction in seeing Christ in even the most challenged student. Ask the parent who models Christ with patience, humility, and wisdom in the face of a rebellious teen. Ask those struggling to meet the family budget who, nonetheless, are happiest when writing checks for kingdom causes. In our hearts we know they are right.

Maybe the rules of chess could be improved, but we can never do better than the rules God has set out for our lives. Our purest joy always comes from striving to live God's way, not going off on our own or following the suggestions of our culture.

Search for the directions of your loving Creator; play by his rules; enjoy to the fullest the life he has given you.

Earthen Vessels

2 Corinthians 4:6-5:5

Susan M. Felch
Calvin professor; Grand Rapids, Michigan

But we have this treasure in jars of clay. . . . (2 Cor. 4:7)

Imagine this scene from your favorite adventure novel: A pair of explorers tracks down a hidden cache marked by the large X on their crumpled map. They dig through the turf, pluck an undistinguished clay pot from the hole, break it open, and claim their long-sought treasure. Discarding the earthen shards in the dust, they mount their horses and ride off into the sunset.

How differently our text reads. The treasure here is indeed precious, worthy to be sought after and cherished, for it is no less than the presence of God himself, a treasure so immense the apostle Paul heaps up words to describe it: "the light of the knowledge of the glory of God in the face of Christ" (2 Cor. 4:6). But this treasure resides in earthen vessels that, unlike the clay pot in the adventure scenario, are not mere containers to be broken and discarded in the scramble to extract a valuable commodity. Though fragile, these earthen vessels are themselves precious, the means through which God chooses to display his transcendent power, "the life of Jesus . . . revealed in our body" (2 Cor. 4:11). When we are afflicted but not crushed, perplexed but not in despair, struck down but not destroyed, the treasure of God among his people shines brightly.

God loves our earthiness. He formed the dust of the ground into Adam and breathed into his creature the breath of life. He descended from heaven to assume the dusty garment of human flesh. As the master potter, he molds and shapes the clay. Now he lives in and through this motley array of clay jars; he burns his way into our flesh, reshapes us, preserves us, bears us up through life and into death. And when the fragile clay begins to crumble, as it inevitably must do, he will not discard us but will transform us from the unbearable lightness of dust into an eternal weight of glory, a heavenly tabernacle, a resurrected body. Thanks be to God.

Plugged In

Anastasia Niehof '98   John 15:5
Teacher; Cerritos, California

I love my laptop computer. It goes with me anywhere in the house — I can watch my pot of soup while using it — and anywhere in the world — I can use it on the plane or at home during my holidays. The only part I don't like about it is its battery. Its life is not nearly long enough to suit me. When I must use battery power, I keep a careful eye on how much time I have left because I know that while the computer is using battery power, my work time is limited. After a few minutes I get warning signals and flashing lights, urging me to hurry up because soon the computer will flicker and flip off, leaving me with a blank screen and no way to complete my work until the battery is recharged or I have electrical current available.

As Christians we, too, need to stay plugged in to our source of life and energy. We may get by for a few days without reliance on God's power, but the warning signs will start cropping up — a bad temper here, some lustful thoughts there, too much to drink, slacking off on church attendance, overinvolvement with self — all signs of sin slipping into our life. They mean we need to repent and draw closer to God and get recharged again.

Drawing closer to God involves coming closer to his heart in a variety of ways. First, reading his Word teaches us his way for our lives. He has left us specific instructions about how to live, and following those instructions will give us favor in his eyes. Second, prayer and meditation help us to experience God working today in us as individuals. Third, being an active member of a church keeps us in close contact with other believers working together for a common cause, which is an important part of being in God's will for our lives.

So be on the watch for flickering warning lights in your life. If you find yourself slipping away from the truths of Christianity in thought or practice, make sure to "plug yourself back in to God" — through the Bible, prayer, and the church. And rejoice in the fact that your power source never runs out. He is the very current of the universe — forever.

You've got limitless power; you've got lots of work. Do it — for the sake of the kingdom.

True Riches

Ephesians 1:3-10

Lori Bylsma Spoelhof '64
Teacher; Houston, Texas

O ur VW bus shifted into first gear to grind up the steep hill. It was dark; we were tired. The bus was taking us, the Brazilian construction team, to a Baptist church in the *flabella* ("slums") for our third long church service this weekend. The bus swerved onto a muddy, rutted road and stopped in front of the church. It was a structure similar to the one we had helped build, a twenty-by-thirty cement slab with a tin roof. This church had mud-covered brick walls, too.

Our late arrival had already caused a fifteen-minute delay in the service, but no one seemed to care. The entire congregation greeted us. We smiled to add depth to our Portuguese vocabulary of *boa noite* and *obrigada*. We were led to seats of honor. As we sat down on the sturdy wooden benches, the band began to play. The music was very loud, and the Brazilians sang lustily. The pastor spoke with passion. Brazilian faces glowed, transformed. My spirit sang without words. The warmth and love of the congregation surrounded me even though I couldn't communicate. God's presence was in this place. This was holy ground.

I lost my worshipful concentration while watching the five-year-old girl in front of me. She clapped and swayed to the music. She and her Barbie doll acted out the words to one song. Before I knew what was happening, she walked to the front, took the microphone, and sang, as the pastor translated:

> I am rich.
> I am a millionaire.
> I may not have much in this world,
> But I have a palace in heaven.
> I am rich because Jesus loves me.

I felt the Spirit speaking to me. "Who is the missionary here?"
"Not me, Lord,"
"Who has the priorities straight?"
"Help me, Lord."

I think all the *Americanos* went down the muddy hill that night changed people. I left Brazil with the knowledge that my faith is untested and my devotion is superficial. In a sense, I wanted to stay in the *flabella*. In that place, I knew, not in an intellectual way but in my deepest heart, that I am rich — because Jesus loves me.

Holy Cheerleaders

Gerry Meninga Adams '82   1 Thessalonians 5:10-11
Homemaker; Rocklin, California

God wants you and me to be holy cheerleaders. No awe-inspiring stunts or fashionable uniforms needed. The requirement for God's cheerleading squad? Accepting Jesus as the forgiver and leader of your life. Here's part of the job description: Jesus "died for us so that, whether we are awake or asleep, we may live together with him. Therefore encourage one another and build each other up, just as in fact you are doing" (1 Thess. 5:10-11).

Some time ago God used a holy cheerleader named Tim to build me up. My husband had gone to a conference, so for four days and four nights I was home alone with my three children and at the same time was experiencing the strain of a conflict at church. I felt overwhelmed. I called Tim about a music detail and ended up asking him for some godly encouragement.

He pointed out Lamentations 3:21-24: "Yet this I call to mind and therefore I have hope: Because of the LORD's great love we are not consumed, for his compassions never fail. They are new every morning; great is your faithfulness." Tim's suggestion: Why not rely on God's promise that his compassions (or his mercies) are new every morning? So in the midst of a stressful situation I could say to God, "I'm not sure I can handle all this, and I may fall apart tomorrow, but today, Lord, I'm going to depend on your mercies to get me through." Each night for the next few days, God's mercies to me were my last thoughts before sleep.

Our heavenly Father wants us to be built up and to build others up. Such encouragement can take a variety of forms — a phone call, an encouraging note, a strategic gift, a timely embrace, a prayer offered on someone else's behalf. The goal is to help lift each other's focus off self and other people and back onto Jesus. Let's be that kind of cheerleader for one another. Let us "encourage one another and build each other up, just as in fact you are doing" (1 Thess. 5:11).

In Truth, Humility, and Righteousness

Psalm 45

Gordon J. Van Wylen '42

Professor/college president emeritus; Holland, Michigan

One of the difficult challenges we face as Christians is how to live an authentically Christian life as we undertake major responsibilities in a secular society. This issue comes into particularly sharp focus in the context of our work, though we may face it in other parts of life as well. My work has been in higher education, much of it in a public university, and I frequently thought about this issue as I was involved in teaching, research, administration, and other aspects of academic life.

A fresh insight on this matter came to me some time ago as I was studying Psalm 45. This delightful psalm is a poem written to be recited at a royal wedding. The opening verses (Ps. 45:2-9) are a tribute to the king, who is described as the most excellent of men, with lips anointed with grace, and as one who loves righteousness. The poet sees the bride (Ps. 45:10-15) as a woman all glorious in her beauty, elegantly dressed, and as one called to leave her father's house to fulfill her noble role in the king's palace. Early in its history the Christian church thought of this psalm as a picture of the relationship between Christ and his bride, the church.

As I read, the phrase "ride forth victoriously in behalf of truth, humility and righteousness" (Ps. 45:4) caught my attention, for it reminded me of the issue mentioned earlier. Truth, humility, righteousness — how little these qualities and character traits are valued in contemporary society, particularly among leaders. Yet these qualities were the hallmark of Jesus' life and ministry. They were incarnate in his very being. They permeated his teaching and interactions with people. God calls us Christians, followers of Jesus, to embrace these qualities and let them permeate our lives and become the essence of our character, even as we pursue excellence in our work and community involvement. As we do so, a remarkable thing can happen. People may recognize that we have a distinctive orientation in our lives, a dimension that is authentic and even desirable. This is an important facet of the witness to which Christ calls us.

Helplessness

Arthur H. DeKruyter '47
Retired pastor; Oak Brook, Illinois

2 Corinthians 12:1-10

Helplessness is not exactly that for which we are searching. Who wants to be a sheep with its traits of defenselessness, wanderlust, and myopia? We are more willing to play the leadership role of shepherd. Isaiah says, however, that we are like sheep. And Jesus says that we *are* sheep, his sheep. But it is difficult to maintain a healthy Christian perspective without the experience of "sheeplike" helplessness. How easy it is to find security and strength in position, possessions, and health. Paul speaks to this issue in 2 Corinthians 12:1-10. He begins by revealing a secret of fourteen years: He thought for a while that he was special because of his vision of the third heaven. After all, God didn't give everyone such an ethereal experience.

But it does not work that way for Paul. A "thorn in [his] flesh" (2 Cor. 12:7) continues to plague him. He is convinced that he could be a more productive child of God if he were delivered to robust health. After three periods of wrestling with God in prayer, he finally understands that his thorn will not be going away. God has said no to his prayers.

Why would God withhold his healing touch from such a worthy servant? Paul makes the discovery himself: God is neither distant nor defeated. God does not lack wisdom or control. God is there for him, and the weak are strong when God is the source of human security. Evil cannot triumph. The cross, the symbol of the power of Caesar's Roman Empire, is no match for the grace of God.

The same grace that was sufficient for Paul is sufficient for us. It enables us to rise above every limitation, disappointment, and loss. Under this grace nothing can separate us from the love and power of our heavenly Father. Once we have experienced the grace of God in the midst of complete helplessness, we can face any enemy of soul or body with a calm spirit of confidence and peace.

Helplessness is a valuable and celebrated experience as we journey into the joy which God provides. Therefore Paul concludes by exclaiming, "When I am weak, then I am strong" (2 Cor. 12:10).

An Intellectual Christian?

2 Corinthians 10:3-5

Stan Mast '68
Pastor; Grand Rapids, Michigan

Is it possible to be both intellectual and Christian? Or is the term *intellectual Christian* an oxymoron, like jumbo shrimp, black light, icy hot?

Sigmund Freud, like many intellectuals, thought so. In a single paragraph he called religion a neurosis, an illusion, a poison, and an intoxicant. He looked forward to the day when the human race would get over its infantile fixation on God and deal with the hostility of a godless universe.

The Bible seems to give critical intellectuals some support when occasionally it seems to denigrate intellect. In his first letter to the Corinthians, for example, Paul says, "But God chose the foolish things of the world to shame the wise" (1 Cor. 1:27). Is Paul saying that Christianity is only for the unlearned?

That cannot be, given the words of 2 Corinthians 10:3-5. This passage touches on the war between the kingdom of God and the kingdom of Satan. In this battle Christians are not to use the weapons of the world, but the weapons of God. Everyone knows the famous list of divinely empowered weapons in Ephesians 6:10-20, but in 2 Corinthians 10:3-5 Paul reminds us that Christians must also use another weapon in the cosmic battle: mind, reason, intellectual sharpness, educational training. Of course, we are to use the weapon of the mind in conjunction with the other weapons, not in isolation from or opposition to them. As we struggle against Satan's kingdom, it's not faith or reason, but both. It's not evangelism or education, but both; not prayer or apologetics, but both; not the Word of God or a university degree, but both; not righteousness or intellectual rigor, but both; not the truth preached on Sunday or the truth discovered in a laboratory, but both.

An Episcopalian newspaper advertisement summed it up nicely: "He died to take away your sins, not your mind." Indeed! In the battle of the kingdoms, a strong mind shaped by a rigorous education is a crucial weapon. Make the most of school. Study hard — for the sake of the kingdom of God.

Second Sight

Arda Ringnalda Rooks '78
Teacher; Ancaster, Ontario

Ephesians 1:18-19

> *I pray also that the eyes of your heart may be enlightened in order that you may know the hope to which he has called you, the riches of his glorious inheritance in the saints, and his incomparably great power for us who believe.*
>
> (Eph. 1:18-19)

S ometimes in the middle of a routine day God gives me a moment of seeing. I might be writing, taking a walk, or cleaning the house when I am struck by something. At that moment I am filled with awe, and I see in a way I have never seen before.

Once, in late summer, while watching the sky and marveling at the green of the trees against the blue of sky, I saw an astonishing cloud drift overhead. It was long, thin, feathered, and startlingly white. As I watched, I felt a deep awe and with it an inexplicable sense of God's presence. Another time, in a wood, I was surrounded by so much silence that I felt God in the stillness.

I believe God gives such moments. They are moments when we vividly experience God in the world. These moments of awe — C. S. Lewis calls them "shafts of glory" — can be given to us at any time. If our hearts are vulnerable, they can become times of clarity, moments of seeing God's grace in the everyday.

Being human, we, like King Lear, do not always see well. Kent admonishes the old king to open his eyes, to have discernment. In Ephesians 1:18 Paul says something similar, but his words are a prayer. Paul prays that his readers will have second sight so they can "see with the eyes of their heart."

This is a prayer we all need to pray: for others, ourselves, our church, our world. Someday our hearts will be laid bare, and our eyes will be truly opened; we shall know the fullness of Christ's glory. For now, while we can't yet see through the glass sharply, we may ask to see with the eyes of our hearts. In his grace God will bless us with shafts of glory, with moments of second sight.

Meaningful Days

1 Corinthians 13

Amy B. Meyer '97
Missionary; Grand Rapids, Michigan

Another missionary once pointed out to me the emphasis implicit in the dates on gravestones — the birth date and death date, joined by a dash. The importance seems to be placed on the number of days one lives. What usually isn't emphasized is the time between the two dates — what happened from birth to death in a person's life.

Her insight set me thinking about the content of "the dash" in my life span. What will be said of the life I am living? As I look back over my life, it is becoming clearer to me how God has been working to achieve his purposes in me. My hope is that in Christ I am able to be a messenger of God's love, hope, and grace. I pray that I may see my days as opportunities to live a life of love and sincerity which thrives on seeing God's good pleasure work itself out until completion.

These thoughts inspired me to reflect on 1 Corinthians 13, the chapter of love, which reminds us of the right way to spend the days and hours and minutes of our lives:

If I speak eloquently in the language of piety and high standing but have not the love that touches the heart, I am only a babbling bystander, edifying no one.

If I have honors and degrees and can reason the perplexities of this life but have not the ability to understand love, I have nothing.

If I am able to explore and explain the events of today and tomorrow but have not the peace to trust in God's intricate and interwoven plan, I am nothing.

If I fritter my days away with appointments and activities and leave little time for my spirit to be quiet and responsive, I have not the power of his love to reach the lost.

If I spend my days conferring with my own thoughts, insights, and understanding and in so doing blame God for the difficult road I travel, I deceive myself, and his grace is far from me.

May all your days and mine be filled with receiving and giving God's love.

Faith Enough to Believe

Mary Cunningham Remein '70   Psalm 11
Human-resources specialist; Silver Spring, Maryland

G od's Word came to me with great power one day nearly three years
ago as I sat on a plane headed toward Michigan. Just a few hours earlier we had received the terrible news that our son Matthew, a senior at Calvin College, had sustained severe head injuries in a car accident. The emer-
gency-room doctor had told me that Matthew was on life support and
might not survive. I had quickly packed a suitcase but had kept my Bible
with me. When I opened it as soon as the plane was airborne, it fell open to
Psalm 11. As I read the first four verses, several phrases jumped out at me:
"In the LORD I take refuge" (Ps. 11:1); "when the foundations are being destroyed, what can the righteous do?" (Ps. 11:3); "the LORD is in his holy
temple; the LORD is on his heavenly throne" (Ps. 11:4). Immediately my desperately troubled heart was calmed. Although my world had been shaken
to its very foundation, I was reminded by God's Word that God is on his
heavenly throne; he is in control. I had nothing to fear. I thought about
Matthew and his passionate love for and commitment to Jesus Christ.
Psalm 11 says that the "LORD examines the righteous" (Ps. 11:5) and that
"upright men will see his face" (Ps. 11:7). I took great comfort in knowing
that God would not hide his face from my son.

Today Matthew lives at home. The brain trauma left him severely disabled, physically and mentally. Yet Matthew has a countenance full of love
and joy that reflects the face of God and is evidence of the presence of a
comforting Christ. God has provided loving family members, prayer war-
riors, caregivers, and therapists to come alongside Matthew. Often over the
past three years I have returned to Psalm 11 for God's assuring words —
"the LORD is in his holy temple; the LORD is on his heavenly throne.... upright men will see his face" (Ps. 11:4, 7) — and I continue to thank the Lord
for faith enough to simply believe his Word.

Putting It All Together

Job 42:1-5; Romans 1:18-20

Stu Greydanus '72
Teacher; Boynton Beach, Florida

On the first day of physics class each year, I ask my students, "What is the scientific method?" A few students try to recite three, five, or even six steps they heard in seventh or eleventh grade. Then I ask them, "What makes a good scientist?"

My questions are based on Article II of the Belgic Confession, "The Means by Which We Know God." They are designed to prompt students to think about why we should study science. Why spend time studying the details of creation? Why ask questions about Fahrenheit or centigrade?

Leading them on, I ask, "Have you read Jack London's story 'To Build a Fire'? What's the main character's name?" ("He doesn't have one.") "What happens to him?" ("He dies.") "Why?" (No response.) "Because he was a lousy scientist," I tell them. "As Jack London himself wrote, 'The trouble with him was that he was without imagination.' Here is a young kid who is good at things, but he misses the significances. And he dies because of it."

"What did Einstein think was more important than knowledge? Imagination. Imagination means the ability to see invisible things, the ability to see connections thinner than the diaphanous strands of a spider's web."

Article II of the Belgic Confession tells us how we know God. "We know him by two means: First, by the creation, preservation, and government of the universe, since that universe is before our eyes like a beautiful book in which all creatures, great and small, are as letters to make us ponder the invisible things of God: his eternal power and his divinity."* What a concept!

A student once gave me a copy of Walt Whitman's poem "The Noiseless Patient Spider." "This sounds like you," he said, "especially the part about making connections between physics and literature, science, and theology. It's our soul trying to make sense of too much information — things too awesome to comprehend in either Fahrenheit or centigrade *until* 'the gossamer thread you fling catch somewhere, O my Soul.'" Yes, until our souls find the ultimate connection — God, the Creator and Sustainer.

There it is: the Reformed perspective that brings together poet, scientist, liberal-arts thinker, and believer. That's why we study science — to see in this most elegant universe the invisible things of God.

Schools for Grace

Claudia DeVries Beversluis '74   Isaiah 66:13
Calvin professor; Grand Rapids, Michigan

Who is really prepared to be a parent? Most of us expect but are still astounded by the enormous love we feel when we first meet our children. We are less prepared for the waves of anger, guilt, envy, and vulnerability that come unbidden throughout our lives as members of families. We learn something about ourselves when we live in families, and, unfortunately, it is not all good. We fume with anger at a flawed child, only to realize that the flaw came from us in the first place. We regret something that simply cannot be undone and realize our own powerlessness in the face of pain. We are surprised by the depth of our fear. We thought we were better people than that.

Even the Bible's families, like all human pictures in the Bible, are often examples of sorrow and shortcoming. The good news of Scripture is that God works his purposes through and in spite of the weaknesses of his people — time after time after time. The good news is that forgiveness is for parents and children, for brothers and sisters, husbands and wives — real people in real families.

So why does God give us families? One reason God gives us families is that they are laboratories for loving, schools for grace. Through the daily rhythms of hurting and forgiving, loving and letting go, disappointing and accepting, playing and working, we grow into maturity as children and as parents. Life in families teaches us about God's proud delight in his creation, the stubborn relentlessness of God's love for us, the sorrowful necessity of discipline, and the grief in God's heart when we suffer.

If we think of families as schools for grace, we never have to hide our family life from God. We can accept God's forgiveness for our failings and let ourselves be bearers of grace to each other. We can bring a chastened, tender humility to our relationships.

We can join our parents and our children as the flawed but forgiven children of God, eager students in the school of grace.

Belief and Sight

Psalm 36:9 William Spoelhof '31

Calvin president emeritus; Grand Rapids, Michigan

In your light we see light. (Ps. 36:9)

On Wednesday, September 7, 1927, I entered for the first time the halls of Calvin College to register as a student. Straightway I saw above the chapel's double doors the legend which encapsulated the mission of the college as a Christian educational institution: "In Your Light We See Light."

About forty years later Calvin moved to a new campus which could accommodate the massive changes in faculty, student enrollment, and curriculum. In the transfer we took along that same legend for placement in our new chapel, inviting new generations of students once again to "See the Light."

What light of understanding, knowledge, and wisdom does this legend bring to education in this new age? Is it "seeing is believing" or "believing is seeing?" There is a difference, of course.

Ours is the "show me" age, the "prove it" culture, in which so-called objectivity can be reached only by pragmatic or demonstrable proof in a laboratory, by citing documentary evidence, by an appeal to effective experience, or by taking polls to arrive at political truth. In such an approach, seeing is believing.

The legend in our chapel, however, declares that only in the light of Christ can we see the light of truth. The opening chapters of John's Gospel plainly state, "In him was life, and that life was the light of all people. The light shines in the darkness, but the darkness has not understood it" (John 1:4-5, NIVI). We cannot see (the truth) unless we believe (Christ). Seeing, as comprehended in the legend, becomes effective only when the light is turned on, the light of him who is life — Jesus Christ.

This relationship of seeing to believing is important in all of education: in science, the liberal arts, the behavioral disciplines, and in residence life. Both "seeing is believing" and "believing is seeing" are true, but only when believing transforms seeing.

Why restrict the display of the old legend to the chapel? Wouldn't it be better placed on the signboard at our road entries, grouped with the Calvin seal, "My heart I offer to you, Lord, promptly and sincerely"? After all, it is relevant to all arenas of life, in all times and all places, not just to chapel worship.

Grace-full Days

Lynette Den Bleyker '99
Teacher; Santiago, Dominican Republic

2 Corinthians 12:9-10

Perplexing and illogical is God's grace. Why is God faithful to unfaithful and at times even faithless people? God's grace goes even beyond eternal salvation; it is sufficient, too, for our daily lives.

Truly offering our hearts to God is a risk that demands vulnerability, flexibility, perseverance, waiting. If we take the risk, our weaknesses are bound to reveal themselves. In offering our hearts to the Lord, we come face to face with our own weaknesses. What good are they anyway? In our weaknesses God reveals himself. Only when we recognize our weaknesses do we and others see who we really are: people through whom God is working and showing his power.

Several years ago, while I was attending Calvin, my father was diagnosed with cancer. A disease which always affected someone else now was taking him down. But God providentially used this experience to bless my family. When I felt overwhelmed, unable to be vulnerable or flexible, to persevere or wait, he showed me his more-than-sufficient grace. He loved me through this time — by his Word and by the fellowship of other believers.

We are very blessed to have my father healthy again. God does work miracles, and, although I don't understand all God's ways and didn't always delight in the difficult times — a sign of my weakness — God's power was made perfect in my weakness. I wanted to help my father but couldn't do so. I stood by, praying, but often felt simply helpless. God answered my prayers and those of many others who prayed with our family, and God daily showed me more of his perfect power and grace.

Learning of God's sufficient grace through my father's illness prepared me for first-year teaching in the Dominican Republic. Living away from family, friends, and the familiar schedule of a student has exposed my weaknesses. When I am unable to be vulnerable or flexible, to persevere or wait, God's love flows to and through me. I am forced daily to rely on God's perfect power and grace.

We usually try to camouflage our weaknesses, even from ourselves. But if we can look closely at them, we will realize the extent of our humanness and God's divine power so graciously given because we are weak.

Bought at a Price

1 Corinthians 6:19-20

Edward E. Ericson, Jr.
Calvin professor; Grand Rapids, Michigan

You are not your own; you were bought at a price. (1 Cor. 6:19-20)

It's easy to skip over these words from 1 Corinthians 6:19-20. They are sandwiched between the apostle Paul's rhetorical question "Do you not know that your body is a temple of the Holy Spirit, who is in you, whom you have received from God?" and the command "Therefore honor God with your body." So the verses are commonly used to remind us to take good care of our bodies. Valuable counsel, to be sure.

However, even aside from the fact that for Paul's first readers the word *body* meant the whole person, the words I have separated out for special attention give us the reason behind the counsel. And that reason is precisely where the Heidelberg Catechism starts: that we are not our own. Paul himself emphasizes this reason by repeating "bought at a price" in the next chapter, verse 23.

This passage was on my mind as I listened to President Gaylen Byker speak about duty in his Fall 1999 Opening Convocation address at Calvin College. How strange this speech would sound, I mused, to my academic peers elsewhere, where "the ethic of desire" is currently all the rage and personal pleasure is the supreme value. But there was President Byker, talking up responsibility, talking quite against the grain of today's lavishly affluent, self-absorbed consumer culture.

My mind flitted to John Stuart Mill, who already in the early 1800s pursued what he called the "ideal of self-development" by undermining "Christian self-denial" and reinvigorating "Pagan self-assertion." Maybe Mill has carried the day. But he also was working from a false dichotomy. In the Christian understanding, self-denial and self-fulfillment are not opposites. Rather, self-denial is the route to self-fulfillment. We are most fully human when we are obedient to God. That is how God made the moral universe.

Songs of Innocence and Experience

Wallace Bratt '55   Psalm 103:12
Calvin professor emeritus; Grand Rapids, Michigan

> *As far as the east is from the west, so far has he removed our transgressions from us.* (Ps. 103:12)

It is a joy and inspiration to see how so many of today's Calvin students freely and warmly speak and sing of their faith. Their songs of praise and commitment sound quite different from mine, but they carry a joy and radiant conviction all their own.

Yet many students, barely out of their adolescence, obviously have come only a limited distance in their walk of faith. For many of them, the promise of today's text about our Lord's gracious removal of our transgressions probably speaks less forcefully than it does to some of us who have lived and struggled longer.

In the winter of 1945, during the last months of Nazi terror in Germany, the imprisoned Christian martyr Dietrich Bonhoeffer wrote a moving poem entitled "Wer bin ich?" ("Who Am I?"). Am I, Bonhoeffer asks, the person the guards and most fellow prisoners think I am: cheerful, stalwart, faith filled, selfless, and at peace? Or am I at heart the person I often find myself to be: fearful, cowardly, insecure, sometimes desperate for — and even destitute of — faith? He concludes the poem by taking comfort in the assurance that, however the ledger stands, his Lord will accept him anyway.

After reading the poem with students, I once asked them which tally of their own personal characteristics would be longer — that listing their weaknesses or that listing their apparent strengths. All class members were quite confident that their strengths clearly outnumbered their weaknesses.

Many of us older Christians, I suspect, see ourselves differently. Over the years we have come to know ourselves better and have had more time to reflect on our own inconsistency, our sometimes radically unsteady walk with God.

Yet it is the gospel's clear witness that our deeper awareness shouldn't diminish our joy. Our personal spiritual ledgers may balance differently from those compiled by many younger Christians, but the knowledge of how much we have been forgiven can only increase the depth of our gratitude, till it, too, at least in our better moments, extends from east to west. We have our own songs to sing. And later our children quite surely will join in.

Strength and Help

Isaiah 43:1-2

Tom R. De Meester '59
Physician; San Marino, California

So do not fear, for I am with you; do not be dismayed, for I am your God. I will strengthen you and help you; I will uphold you with my righteous right hand.
(Isa. 41:10)

But now, this is what the LORD says — he who created you, O Jacob, he who formed you, O Israel: "Fear not, for I have redeemed you; I have summoned you by name; you are mine. When you pass through the waters, I will be with you; and when you pass through the rivers, they will not sweep over you. When you walk through the fire, you will not be burned; the flames will not set you ablaze."
(Isa. 43:1-2)

Isaiah affirms the grand truth about God: "I am with you. . . . I am your God" (Isa. 41:10). Therefore, God instructs us not to be dismayed, that is, not to look about anxiously for solutions to our difficulties. We are not to become hyperactive, discouraged, disillusioned, or terrified in our circumstances. We may be perplexed but never dismayed because, after all, "I am your God." When we might be tempted to be dismayed, we should reflect on what kind of God our God is by remembering stories about him from Scripture and by reflecting on our own past experiences in which he has seen us through difficult periods.

God tells us that he will strengthen us, that is, he will provide us with what is needed to handle our difficulties. He will empower us to cope with the circumstances. Further, he will help us, that is, he will get personally involved by upholding us with his righteous right hand. He will reach out and grip us and maintain us even though it appears that we will be submerged or swept away by the turmoil that surrounds us.

When under pressure, when perplexed, when we feel excluded, or when we suffer loss, we are to remember that our God is in control and is holding us. His concern for our well-being is reflected in these facts: He has created us; he has formed us; he has redeemed us. Consequently, he knows us, values us, calls us by name, and claims us as his own.

Shepherd and Sheep

Jan Vander Ploeg Visser '91
Teacher; Oak Forest, Illinois

Psalm 23:1-3

It wasn't until a trip to Israel that I really understood and appreciated Psalm 23. Parts of the psalm mean more to me now that I have seen the circumstances in which it was written and something of the shepherd culture of this ancient landscape.

David begins by speaking about the relationship of God to his people: "The LORD is my shepherd, I shall not be in want" (Ps. 23:1). It is like the relationship of sheep and shepherd. Shepherds go ahead of the sheep, and they provide completely for them. They are never behind the sheep, driving them; rather, they lead the flock, and the sheep must follow.

This relationship of God as shepherd and his people as sheep made me wonder: Do I follow my shepherd, or do I go my own way? Do I consciously listen for the shepherd's voice, blocking out distracting voices? If he promises that "I shall not be in want," do I rest on that promise, trusting him to provide for all my needs? I am reminded to listen to my shepherd's voice. I am comforted to know that I need not worry, because he will provide.

When David says, "He makes me lie down in green pastures" (Ps. 23:2), we often picture a huge field of green grass waiting to be grazed, as I did before I saw pastures in Israel. Because the country is hot and dry most of the year, the sheep are led among the rocks, looking for tufts of grass to eat, mouthful by mouthful. The grass quickly withers and wilts in the hot sun, but every night it is renewed by the moisture of the dew, and in the morning there is food again for the sheep. The promise that God the shepherd will provide his people with green pastures is a promise that God will give us enough for each day.

After seeing the landscape of Israel and witnessing firsthand the complete reliance of the sheep on the shepherd, I was summoned again to remember that "the LORD is *my* shepherd, I shall not be in want" (Ps. 23:1, italics added).

Others' Gifts

Luke 15:28-32

Stan Vander Klay '57
Pastor, Baldwinsville, New York

H e was a leader on the streets and a strong man in prison. But his heroin habit was stronger. No sooner had he entered the halfway house sponsored by the church I pastored than three guys came to my office to say, "Wait till you meet _____ !"

Sunday mornings his penetrating eyes stared into mine. Sometimes he smiled and nodded as I preached. It wasn't long before we were talking in my office. He seemed hungry but also hesitant to put the spoon in his mouth, counting the cost but not ready to give it up. He stayed at the house for two brief stints. Later he was sent away for homicide, a botched attempt at robbing an old slumlord.

About a decade later, before leading the funeral of another drug addict, I heard somebody call my name. When I turned around, I saw those familiar, penetrating eyes above a clerical collar. Having turned to Christ, he had been mentored and ordained by a Baptist prison chaplain. As is the custom in African-American funerals, I asked him to make a few remarks. With his first sentence he electrified the audience. I knew that my message would be anticlimactic, and it was.

That day I had to face envy straight on. "Lord, I was preaching when he was still a kid. I have never been in trouble with the law (except for a speeding ticket or two). But already he can preach me under the table!" I was nudged by the Spirit, reminded of the Scripture I needed for the moment: "Don't be an 'older brother,' Stan. Isn't this exactly what you have prayed for and longed for during most of your ministry? Join the party!" I did.

He went on to become a chaplain at the local county jail. He served there until he died of cancer, and then heaven threw another party. Though no longer in that city, I am still a pastor, preaching the best I can, blessed by those moments in the funeral home more than I can tell.

The Graceful Gift

Steven Tuit '95
Teacher; Holland, Michigan

Luke 9:23-25, 27

> *Those who would come after me must deny themselves and take up their cross daily and follow me. For those who want to save their lives will lose them, but those who lose their lives for me will save them. What good is it for you to gain the whole world, and yet lose or forfeit your very self? . . . I tell you the truth, some who are standing here will not taste death before they see the kingdom of God.*
> (Luke 9:23-25, 27, NIVI)

When I started Calvin College in the fall of 1990, I had a clear vision of what I hoped my life would be. I would double major in history and political science, go to law school, and eventually become involved in politics, moving far away from the Midwest, where I grew up. Along the way I would acquire all of the world's good things: a home on a lake, a fine car, and nice suits. I defined myself by the things I wanted and by the things that I hoped to gain. I thought of my life as empty, waiting to be filled by accomplishments and objects.

It is common for people to define themselves by what they desire to have or to be. And perhaps we do start out empty, as a blank life to be written upon. From creation's offerings we can choose things to fill that page. The true fulfillment of our selves, however, the filling up of that emptiness, occurs when we find who God created us to be, when we find the self that is rooted in Christ's choosing of us and in his image residing in us. To find ourselves, we need to listen carefully to what God has placed in us — our passions, our dreams, and the blessings we have received. And we need to be open to God's grace.

Today I am an English teacher at a Christian school in western Michigan. It is a long way from where I imagined I would be, but God has made my life fulfilling. By Christ's grace, my life is even, at times, the means of fulfillment for others. This is a biblical, paradoxical conception of the self: an otherwise empty vessel that overflows with grace because God pours his love and grace into us faster than we can lose it. That this is true is a wonder, given our natural fits and furies, but God's wide grace can flow from us into others if we deny ourselves and find our true self, that person we were created to be. When this happens, we can taste God's kingdom already.

Be Still

Psalm 46:10

Todd Huizinga '80
Vice-consul, U.S. Consulate; Hamburg, Germany

"Be still, and know that I am God" (Ps. 46:10). This admonition in Psalm 46 is an admonition and comfort to us as well. It is an admonition to us when we lose perspective and focus instead on ourselves and on our own skills, our own ability to get things done, and, if we can pray or talk the religious talk particularly well, on our own eloquence. God is too great for us to come even close to describing the wonders of his mercy, love, and power. Our attempts to approximate his greatness in our own words or actions can never be adequate. Thus, the wisest response a Christian can make to God's eternal Word of life is sometimes awed and thankful silence. The wisest reaction to God's work in the world and in our lives is sometimes a quiet acceptance of our inability to accomplish anything without him.

But this command — "Be still" — can also be a great comfort to us. It reminds us that God's attitude toward us does not depend on how eloquently we pray or on how effectively we do his will. If we come to God with a broken and contrite heart, he will make us whole again. The knowledge that God is God and that we belong to him is all the knowledge we need. It is the truth — the truth that sets us free.

A Burning Bush

Debbie Marshall '85
Legislative liaison; Alexandria, Virginia

Exodus 3:2-6

There the angel of the LORD appeared to him in flames of fire from within a bush.
(Exod. 3:2)

I have always marveled at the story of the burning bush. How wondrous and frightening it must have been for Moses to get a message straight from God. So often during my time at Calvin and in the years following, I was envious of friends who felt that God had spoken to them about their calling in life or given them the direction they needed at just the right time. I would pray, but I never felt that I got any message back about what to do. I wanted a burning bush.

When I considered moving to Washington, D.C., I was in a quandary. I could think of many reasons not to go. I prayed for guidance, but none seemed to come. I was a faithful person. Why couldn't I have a sign? Then one of my friends advised me, "Listen with your heart instead of your head, and maybe you will notice that God's signs are right in front of you." He couldn't have been more right.

I had made a list of pros and cons for the move, and they pretty much canceled each other out. My final concern was where to live. I had convinced myself that this was an insurmountable problem. I prayed again for guidance.

Yes, my burning bush was an apartment. The first place I saw was the only place I had to see. From the price to the carpet color, there couldn't have been a more perfect apartment for me at the time. And it was the only one left on my original list of apartment possibilities. As I stepped inside, I felt an inner peace come over me. My heart was open, and God was speaking to me.

I know: An apartment is no burning bush. But I got the message. Six years later I am still convinced that this is where God intends for me to be.

Working Toward Heaven

Isaiah 11:6-9

Patrick Jasperse '87
Journalist; Milwaukee, Wisconsin

I don't look forward to heaven much. It's unknown. The glimpses we get in Revelation are strange, bewildering, even terrifying. I worry I won't make it. Heaven will be preceded by the agony of death. The busyness of the present leaves little time to think about the future. I wonder whether in heaven I will be able to hold close my wife, son, mother, and father. I enjoy my life on this earth and am not eager for it to end.

Yet one of my favorite Bible passages is the picture Isaiah paints of a world where the wolf lives with the lamb, the leopard lies down with the goat, the infant plays near the hole of the cobra, and no one either harms or destroys (Isa. 11:6, 8-9). If Isaiah were writing today, he might envision a day when no child playing in her front yard is shot to death, when no parent struggles with Alzheimer's, when no one in Sierra Leone has a tongue or a hand chopped off, when planes filled with people never plunge into the ocean, when every adult can read, when the Israeli freely visits his Palestinian neighbor, when no child is ignored and no spouse is unloved, when no twenty-year-old is locked behind bars, when no man is dragged to death because of the color of his skin.

We are such creatures of this time and place, and today's problems seem so intractable that a world of peace and good is almost impossible to imagine. But what this world once was — before pollution, poverty, disease, hunger, and hate — it will be again. This is not a dream. This is God's promise. The battle already has been fought, and the victory won. Someday there "will be no more death or mourning or crying or pain, for the old order of things has passed away" (Rev. 21:4).

Knowing that should give us comfort and hope about the life to come. It should also fill us with resolve and confidence to work right now toward making this world the place that God created it to be.

Warrior Scholars

Joel Nederhood '52   1 Peter 5:8
Radio pastor emeritus; Lansing, Illinois

> *Be self-controlled and alert.* (1 Pet. 5:8)

Warrior scholars and young veterans were part of Calvin's ambience in the early fifties. Henry Zylstra brought laughter to the classroom when he described his servile experience as a lowly private browbeaten by corporals and sergeants. In Shakespeare class Falstaff would set him off, and he would tell how, on guard duty one miserable rainy night in which it was impossible for any creature to stay dry, the officer of the day had thrust his face close to Zylstra's and shouted, "Be especially watchful of fires!" Henry Stob also had war stories, but students remember most poignantly about Stob's war experiences a certain day during the Korean hostilities. In April 1951, after President Truman had relieved him of his Korean command, General Douglas MacArthur spoke to Congress, concluding with the now-famous line "Old soldiers never die; they just fade away." Stob listened to that speech and watched it on a black and white television with a full house of Calvin students in the old Franklin Street chapel. His eyes glistened, and tears rolled down his cheeks. Five years earlier, as a Navy lieutenant, he had served on the general's staff in Tokyo.

The war these men remembered and the war that took men from campus for Korean duty gave a sense of urgency to our education back then. The times seem different now; we are decidedly unwarlike. But the Bible says, "Your enemy the devil prowls around like a roaring lion looking for someone to devour" (1 Pet. 5:8). There is no reason to think that this hostility has ceased. So we must still be "self-controlled and alert." The spiritual battle goes on.

Those of us who remember Calvin's warrior scholars remember, too, that they pressed into our young minds weapons not made of nickel, lead, and steel. They showed us the power of God's truth, which is able to "demolish arguments and every pretension that sets itself up against the knowledge of God." They encouraged us to "take captive every thought to make it obedient to Christ" (2 Cor. 10:5).

Many of us will never forget our valiant mentors. What they taught us will neither die nor fade away. May the Lord Jesus, commander of heaven's hosts and of our lives, make us self-controlled and alert in his glorious service.

The Blessing of Pain

Isaiah 53:4-5

Sherri B. Ames Lantinga '89
Professor; Sioux Center, Iowa

Most of us can easily recall stories of traumatic childbirths, cancer, back problems. Pain, we think, is awful, and we try hard to avoid it. We avoid touching fire, avoid biting our tongues when chewing, and avoid injury by wearing protective gear. Pain, we think, is a result of the fall and will have no place in the new heaven and the new earth.

But pain can be a blessing in disguise. In Genesis we read, "I will greatly increase your pains in childbearing; with pain you will give birth to children" (Gen. 3:16). Consider the first part of the verse: Pain will be *greatly increased*. This suggests that pain was already present as part of God's original good creation.

But why would God create pain? Pain is a powerful warning system, a signal that something is wrong and needs immediate attention and care. People whose nerves no longer send pain messages to their brains (such as some diabetics and lepers) may not know they have been injured. A leper may step on a nail and, unknowing, continue to walk on the injured foot and cause much more injury. Pain motivates us to care for our God-given bodies. Likewise, the pain of others motivates Christians to bring grace and healing.

Why then do we hate pain so much? Like all else in the creation, the blessing of pain has been twisted so that its valuable warnings may go on too long or may create other problems in fallen creatures. It is not so much the pain that we hate as the suffering that comes with it — the emotional agony and fear and the beating that pain gives to our faith in a loving God. Prolonged pain and suffering cause us to withdraw from loved ones, to neglect our responsibilities, to feel angry, depressed, and self-absorbed. In such a situation we often don't even try to reflect the image of God. It is this awful suffering, not pain itself, that is and will be relieved with the coming of the kingdom. Come quickly, Lord Jesus.

Grace and Knowledge

Peter P. De Boer '51
Calvin professor emeritus;
Grand Rapids, Michigan

Colossians 3:21; 2 Peter 3:18

N early all my life I've been a teacher. Unfortunately, memories of my successes have tended to fade; my failures are burned in with digital clarity. Let me tell you about one of them.

A year out of Calvin and armed with a master's degree, I found myself at a Christian high school in northwest Iowa, trying to teach English literature to seniors, some of whom I thought were relatively indifferent to learning. Discouraged, I sometimes went to my colleagues for counsel. The ones I chose to listen to encouraged high intellectual standards, ruthless testing, and no apologies for low grades. "Be tough," they said. I welcomed their advice.

Meanwhile, one of my less-than-stellar students graduated from the high school and enrolled at Calvin, where, at orientation, he had to take the dreaded English screening test. Much to his surprise and pleasure, he survived the cut.

During his first Christmas vacation he visited his alma mater and looked up his "old" (was I twenty-five?) English teacher. He proudly told me of his testing experience and then scornfully added, "And you thought I didn't know nothin'." For a long time I reveled in his answer. That priceless double negative. Gotcha! I repeated the story often, always with a sense of triumph. Over the years, though, that student's reply began to gnaw at my innards. He was screaming a message that I had been too deaf to hear. So eager to be tough, I had failed to encourage him.

My shortcomings were magnified when I read some U.S. Air Force studies in leadership. Researchers had discovered that high expectations are commendable but that an effective leader combines them with compassion.

The apostle Peter has similar advice. He proposes we grow by deepening our knowledge and understanding of the gospel while at the same time deepening our ability to be gracious with others, even as God deals graciously with us.

Back in the fifties, as a novice teacher, I was only halfway there: My knowledge of God, his world, and his gospel had grown faster than my ability to be God-like in dealing graciously with struggling students. For that I am profoundly sorry. May God forgive. And may all who aspire to leadership grow in the grace and knowledge *of our Lord Jesus Christ,* for with his help they will not be in danger of embittering others to the point of discouragement.

Living without Worry

Matthew 6:25-27

Daniel Vandenbroek '98
Graduate student; Calabasas, California

What do we do when our plans for our lives don't coincide with God's plans for us? Until such a thing happens, we may not realize how difficult it is to allow God to do the decision making. In general, we want a lot of say in the outcome of our lives.

I need not look far for an example. In college I often thought that, if I would just choose the right major or get the right grades, I could somehow gain an edge and a hold on my life. I'm constantly faced with the temptation to think that with the right amount of effort I can ensure my future security.

The effort to be in control extends to nearly every facet of our lives. In our relationships we tailor our actions in an effort to influence people close to us. We think to ourselves, "If I do A, then B will fall right into place." We even go so far as to try to earn control of God's good favor. If only we do the right deeds, say the right things, and become involved in all the right places, we think, we will somehow influence God's plan for us. But we are denying God's gift of grace when we think that we have any power to make God do what we want. We can only respond to God's call, not initiate it. It is in our response that we are empowered to do what is right and to experience his love. The fact is that he comes to us regardless of our actions. God wants for us to relinquish control and open our hearts to his intentions, to admit that he knows what is best for us.

When Matthew quotes Jesus' advice of "do not worry" (Matt. 6:25), we are not to conclude that our plans will ultimately turn out okay or even that God will perfect our plans. Jesus is saying that living without worry is to actively trust God and give him control. It is to shake off any thought of influencing God; it is to allow him to influence us. Living without worry is how we acknowledge and fully accept his amazing gift of grace.

Good News to the Poor

Paul Kortenhoven '65   Luke 4:18
Missionary; Grand Rapids, Michigan

[The Lord] has anointed me to preach good news to the poor. (Luke 4:18)

Jesus said a lot of things about the poor. Once he told his disciples that the poor would always be with them (Mark 14:7), and that passage has been misinterpreted ever since. It seems that some of us want to use it as a justification for doing nothing about poverty or for the poor. After all, they will never disappear, so let's just get on with life.

The country to which I have been called is desperately poor. For years our church has tried to do something about this and, I must say, with some success. Many poor people's lives in the country of Sierra Leone were indeed improved by the generosity and perseverance of the members of the Christian Reformed Church.

But today the vast majority of citizens in this land are still poor. And that bothers me a whole lot. When Jesus spoke to his family and friends in the synagogue in Nazareth, as the physician Luke tells us, he said, "The Spirit of the Lord is on me, because he has anointed me to preach good news to the poor" (Luke 4:18).

This is one of the most amazing passages in the Bible. It is also one of the most challenging. If Jesus came to bring "good news" to the poor, as he clearly claimed, what was that good news? When I was a child growing up in a church in Chicago, I was taught that what Jesus says here really refers to people who are poor in spirit and that Jesus will bring them salvation, which will make them rich in spirit. Sounded good to me. There weren't too many poor people in Roseland in 1952, so we didn't read the Bible in terms of them.

But a career in African missions has brought me in daily overwhelming contact with physically poor people, and I no longer can spiritualize this passage. The equation is much simpler now, and maybe I understand Jesus' words in Luke 4:18 a bit more clearly: The good news to the poor is that Christians recognize that poverty is evil and that — with God's help — they are going to focus on doing something about it wherever they are and whenever they can.

God in the Emptiness

Genesis 28:10-22   James A. Holwerda '77
Pastor; Grand Rapids, Michigan

G od is invisible; God fills space unnoticeably. While this is not a particularly surprising truth, it does lead to astonishing and life-changing discoveries, of which one is that a place can be full of God, overflowing with God's saving presence, and still seem utterly empty.

Consider Jacob's situation. He is alone in the wilderness, running for his life; his brother, Esau, wants to kill him. Jacob has brought this relational disaster on himself, lying and stealing to get Esau's blessing. To make matters worse, Jacob is leaving the land that he lied and stole to get. Everything is falling apart.

"Utterly empty" describes the situation of a relapsing alcoholic whom I once visited. He talked of suicide in tones that alternated between rage and despair. Finally, in his alcohol-induced stupor, he moaned, "I'm too afraid to live and too afraid to die." Life without hope is empty — and so is death.

Sooner or later we all find ourselves in empty places. Any one of a number of things can take us there: cancer, conflict, failure, our own depravity. Any one of a number of miseries describes the emptiness: fear, regret, depression, guilt, shame. These places feel like hell: "Utter emptiness," after all, is one of the definitions of hell.

The key to leaving these awful places is to notice God's presence in them. Jacob exclaims, "Surely the LORD is in this place, and I was not aware of it" (Gen. 28:16). Nothing has changed — he is still alone, still fleeing from his brother, still leaving the promised land — but everything is different. The presence of God transforms Jacob's meager situation. Splendor pervades his misery: "How awesome is this place! This is none other than the house of God; this is the gate of heaven" (Gen. 28:17).

We do not have to fill or flee the empty places in our lives; the presence of a gracious God brings the glory of heaven into the poverty of our lives, wherever that is. It is often not easy to notice God's presence. Like Jacob we will all need our own special revelation. Thanks be to God for showing himself to anyone who asks and is willing to gaze into the emptiness.

Persistent Faith

Claire Kingma Wolterstorff '55   Matthew 15:21-28; Mark 7:24-30
Pastor; New Haven, Connecticut

J esus has come to the area of Tyre and Sidon, where Jews and an assortment of Greeks (traditional enemies) live together. One of the Greek women, a Syrophoenician, finds him and cries out, "Lord, Son of David, have mercy on me!" (Matt. 15:22). Her need emboldens her, for her daughter is possessed by a demon. She pleads for her daughter, bowing and begging before this messianic person who heals. Jesus does "not answer a word" (Matt. 15:23). Then his disciples urge Jesus, "Send her away, for she keeps crying out after us" (Matt. 15:23).

Jesus' response seems harsh. He gives the impression that he has not come to heal the likes of her daughter: "I was sent only to the lost sheep of Israel. . . . It is not right to take the children's bread and toss it to their dogs" (Matt. 15:24, 26).

The woman knows she and her daughter are "their dogs" in this scenario, with no claim to be fed. But now she is up off her knees, standing there boldly, surrounded by the hushed crowd. She is tenacious; God has loosed her courage — and her spunk, too. In desperation she whips back, "But even the dogs under the table eat the children's crumbs" (Mark 7:28).

Then Jesus, hearing God speak through her, softens. He looks at her intently, alerted by her utter trust in him. Expectant, insistent trust has made her demand the healing that is *hers by right*. Jesus marvels and says, "Woman, you have great faith! Your request is granted" (Matt. 15:28). In his mind's ear, perhaps he hears these words of Isaiah: "Foreigners who bind themselves to the LORD . . . I will . . . give them joy in my house of prayer . . . a house of prayer for all nations" (Isa. 56:6-7).

This woman, an outsider, took seriously the promises and begged, with radical faith, that they might be fulfilled in her, too. Later, no doubt, Jesus took her words and pondered them in his heart.

Getting Ready for Heaven

Revelation 5:11-14

Evert Vermeer '59
Retired social-services administrator;
Grand Rapids, Michigan

In June 1999 my wife and I were doing volunteer work with Kosovar refugees in Korca, Albania. Among the many memories of remarkable people we met there, the story of Mariana stands out.

Mariana didn't weigh eighty pounds. She no longer ate any food; when she tried to drink the water her missionary nurse, Marleen, encouraged her to take, she usually vomited it up. It would be only a few days before the cancer that had made an old woman of her nineteen-year-old body would take her life.

Growing up in the little village of Sherqeras in the Korca valley of Albania had been hard, and she had been eager at sixteen to escape the village and move to the home of her "uncle" in Italy. No one seems to know the real story of how she became a prostitute. During this time Mariana contracted venereal disease, which, untreated, had turned into untreatable cancer. In her pain and suffering she had tried to return to her village, but they didn't want her there. She and her mother moved instead to a small house on the outskirts of another village.

From the missionaries there she learned about the saving grace of Jesus. Our group of volunteers met her on our way home from a picnic when nurse Marleen had asked us to stop so she could check on a very sick patient. Mariana's mother came outside to the car and insisted we all come in to sing and pray with her daughter. Mariana cuddled like a rag doll in Marleen's arms. Mustering the little strength she had left, Mariana sang for us every Albanian gospel song she knew. We read Scripture and prayed for her while Marleen interpreted to the smiling Mariana. When we left, we took with us lifelong memories not only of Mariana's emaciated body and her euphoric smile but also of the effects of sin and exploitation, repentance and grace, rejoicing and thanksgiving, and God's love for both the one and the ninety-and-nine.

Mariana is in heaven now. Her body is renewed, and I picture her learning new songs of praise. I will remember her dying testimony as she sang — loud and clear — from the arms of her loving missionary nurse. May God bless them both.

Loving One Another

Linda Hertel Dykstra '66
Psychologist; Grand Rapids, Michigan

John 13:34-35

A new command I give you: Love one another. As I have loved you, so you must love one another. By this everyone will know that you are my disciples, if you love one another. (John 13:34-35, NIVI)

The artist Pablo Picasso painted a variety of subjects in various styles over the course of his long and prolific career. Many years ago one of his lithographs, *Dance of Youth*, done in a stark and childlike style, riveted my attention. Although it probably was not the artist's intention, for me it creatively and symbolically captured the essence of the Christian life. The print I bought of it has hung in my counseling office for nearly three decades.

In the center of the lithograph is the outline of a large dove with a palm branch in its beak. Encircling and dancing around the dove are stick figures, all in different colors, all with arms outstretched one to another, all with palm branches in their hands. In my own Christian interpretation of this lithograph, the dove represents the Holy Spirit, and the palm branches represent God's peace and love. The variety of colors of the stick people illustrates the individuality within the human race. The lithograph says to me that, as God gives his peace and love to us, we, in turn, are to give the same to others, no matter what our differences may be. We are to reach out to one another with palm branches in our hands. We are to be witnesses of God's love to us by loving our fellow human beings, no matter what their color or station in life. We understand and experience God's peace and love not only vertically, between him and us, but also horizontally, between one another, as we human beings give love and compassion to each other.

A great part of our Christian witness is in loving others as God has loved us.

Service-learning

Matthew 20:20-28

Kyle A. De Roos
Calvin student; Sheboygan, Wisconsin

Officially speaking, this past semester I tutored students at Franklin Elementary School. But that's not really the whole truth. This past semester I was allowed the opportunity and privilege to spend one hour and five minutes of each week with eight second graders from Mrs. Jipping's classroom at Franklin Elementary. From 3:35 to 4:40 p.m., my Thursdays belonged to Areceli, Fabiola, Shawnquelle, Maria, Anna, Holly, Amy, and Laura. And for that short time I was who I want to be — a teacher serving God with joy, reaching out to "the least of these."

These children needed tutoring partly because they are almost uncontrollably rambunctious. That also is part of their charm. Take Holly, for example. She never wanted to do homework and was incapable of staying in her seat. Holly was a fright in the classroom. At the end of every session she always walked to the parking lot just ahead of me and climbed into her mom's big rusted-out old van. I always wanted to go up to her mom and tell her how much of a pleasure it was to have Holly in class because she made the day full of surprises. I thought how great it would be for her mother to tell Holly on the way home how proud she was of her. But I never said anything. On the last day Holly waved to me from the van, said good-bye, and closed the passenger door. For some reason that was just as good — Holly had taken the initiative to acknowledge that we had connected.

Areceli (wonderful name!) and Fabiola weren't much easier to handle than Holly. They would get their homework finished faster than anyone else and then raise all sorts of havoc, including writing as much as possible on the outlawed but ever-so-tempting chalkboard. All the children in this class were frustrating and difficult, yet I would rather have been in that room on those Thursdays than anywhere else on this green earth just because they were so gloriously children.

My Thursday afternoons last semester were about service and about children, but they could as well have been about service and old folks or service and hospital patients. Before I went to Franklin Elementary, I thought service was a four-letter word pronounced "duty." Now I know that it is a God-given opportunity to create joy for and with other children of God. I would never say that you need to do this or that service for so much time or this often. I would urge you, though, to take advantage of the opportunities available to you for serving others in the name of God. If you're like me, that's where you will find true joy.

Working Well

Rebecca Konyndyk De Young '93   John 17:4
Calvin professor; Grandville, Michigan

> *I have brought you glory on earth by completing the work you gave me to do.*
> (John 17:4)

When I reflect on the task of raising my young children or when I attempt another revision of a writing project at the office, the thought of work which can be completed even in a full lifetime simply makes my head spin. Yet I have already had more years at this ministry of mine — at home and in my profession — than Christ himself had. Three years to preach the gospel, heal the sick, disciple the twelve, make the world whole again. Three years! Why wasn't he anxiety ridden and frantic, trying to get it all done? How did he ever make time to pray with so much to do?

Taking a moment to linger over this text helps me understand that my initial puzzlement comes from my turning everything upside-down: It is too easy to confuse kingdom fruitfulness and market-measured productivity (John 15:1-17), too easy to mistake a gift to be freely received for a burdensome obligation or task (Luke 10:38-42), too easy to substitute myself as the center of activity for the true center and central author and finisher of work (Phil. 2:13; 4:13). This work — Christ's, mine, Christ's-in-me — this is about what God is doing. He is the director and the one to whom all is directed. He gives the work; he gives the strength, the sufficient grace. His, the timing; his, the only peace.

What on earth are we working for? To "glorify God, and to enjoy Him for ever."* How will we glorify him on earth? By completing the work which he gives us to do.

Let's pray daily for strength and grace to carry on in our God-given work:

> Lord God, you call us to faithfulness, not to success or progress. We pray that, as you give us new ears to hear your Word in today's text, you will also give us new life built on trust in your power and your timing, for we want to live what we believe. Those scant three years of preaching and healing seem from the world's perspective to be hopelessly fragmentary, only a beginning, incomplete; but you judge them as having met your full redemptive purpose. Teach us to see it your way. Amen.

Anchor and Screw

Matthew 22:34-40

Ron Rienstra '87
Pastor; Grand Rapids, Michigan

Love of God and love of neighbor — on these two commandments, said Jesus, hang all the law and the prophets. They bear tremendous weight. But only if they work together.

We can think of the two commandments as twin pegs or, better, as an anchor and a screw. Sticky-tack or a simple nail in the wall works fine for hanging small objects, but hanging anything substantial requires the right hardware, usually an anchor and a screw. The plastic anchor fits snugly into a hole in the wall, and when the screw is tightened into the anchor, the anchor expands, securing them both firmly in place.

Love for God — with heart, mind, soul, and strength — is like the anchor. And love for neighbor is like the screw. We need both. Without the anchor of love for God, neighborly love is wimpy and doesn't last very long. When things get heavy, it works its way out, grinding up the wall in the process.

By the same token, what good is love for God without love for neighbor? What good is the anchor in the wall without a screw to bear weight, to do some work? We need both the anchor and the screw, love for God and love for neighbor, working together.

As our love for others goes deeper, our love for God expands. And as our love for God expands, our love for neighbors grows deeper and stronger — and we are better able to live the holy lives to which we are called by the law, the prophets, and the one to whom they point.

Restorers of the Soul

Peter Dykstra '74 Psalm 23
Data-systems executive; Glen Rock, New Jersey

He restores my soul. (Ps. 23:3)

I don't remember how old I was when I first realized that, even if I was well blessed, the business of living would involve having my soul restored over and over, sometimes almost daily. You'd think I'd have soul restoration mastered by now, but it's something I seem to need again and again. It's happening again as I write this, at age forty-seven.

I think this is why Psalm 23 has such wide appeal — the simplicity of the path it draws, from still waters and green pastures, into paths of righteousness, through the very valley of the shadow of death, to a chair and table ready and waiting in the house of the Lord. It lets us start fresh, again and again — how many times? — from a place where God restores our souls.

As I write this, I'm on a commuter train, stopped. The conductor has just said, "We will be delayed here awhile. We've had a fatality." This announcement sends a shock through the train. We've hit a person on the tracks. Who? Why? I stop writing, shaken. Strangers look at each other, joined in some unknown sorrow. What sorrow? We don't even know who has died.

What is the valley of the shadow of death? It can't be just actual death; I think it's that life itself gets old. We get worn down. The thousandth time we face the same tedious task, a demanding child, an uncooperative coworker, life gets old. We go through the motions. We need to be restored.

But some people never get restored. They seem to die gradually, barely hanging on, technically alive but withering away. Other people — the ones I want to be like — exude love and vitality, playfulness, humor. As they age, they grow in wisdom and grace. They are the saints, the cloud of witnesses, the intimations of immortality.

Christians at peace with God, regardless of their sophistication, seem rooted in a few deep and simple truths like the deep and simple truths of Psalm 23. God leads us in paths of righteousness and restores our souls.

The View from the Cistern

Jeremiah 38

Gene Rubingh '52

Retired missionary; Colorado Springs, Colorado

So they took Jeremiah and put him into the cistern. . . . (Jer. 38:6)

Standing there knee-deep in mud, Jeremiah understood rejection. This was even worse than the jail from which he had just been sprung by fickle King Zedekiah. How much abuse can a man take before he begins to wonder whether God cares?

Many of us, too, have stood in the muck of our world and have clenched an angry fist against God, screaming, "Father, where is your thunderbolt? I could use some help!" We could accept injustice more easily if we had only a puny faith. But if we believe God never fails, we need evidence in times of crisis. I wonder if Jeremiah, standing there in the cistern, voiced that cry as well.

Of course, when it comes to rejection, we aren't exactly models of faithfulness. Humanity's rejection of God is indescribable. We foul his world and gulp down its riches. We reject his gift of life and throw it away. We race down shameful alleys as he pursues us. We kill his son. We spurn his gifts.

Yet, if we should for some reason turn our faces upward, we would see a splash of sky. For Jeremiah, relief came when a black African fetched some rags for Jeremiah to put under his armpits while he was being hauled up by ropes from the cistern (Jer. 38:11). Soon Jeremiah saw more than a patch of sky. He saw green earth and a city. His life was back on track. An Ethiopian had rescued him with a couple ropes — or was it God?

We do well to turn our faces heavenward from our cisterns, too. Hope persists even in cisterns. The reason is this: Though we've slapped God in the face so often and have wrecked so much of his world, he pursues us still. Be on the lookout for an Ethiopian with rags of kindness for your pains.

If you are the Ethiopian sent by God, don't just tell people in cisterns that being there really isn't so bad. Don't talk to them of cheap grace or chide them for crying. But affirm for them that God has not let go. He proved it by sending Jesus.

The view from a cistern is terribly bleak: From the bottom we can see only a little sky. But with God's ropes for pulling and with God's rags for padding our armpits, we will stand on firm ground again with the whole beautiful sky open above our heads.

Accepting God's Plan

Jeff Elders '90
Accountant; Hudsonville, Michigan

James 1:2-3

Though He giveth or He taketh,
God His children ne'er forsaketh;
His the loving purpose solely
To preserve them pure and holy.

This stanza of "Children of the Heavenly Father" has a very special meaning to me. My wife and I and our son Jonathan had prayed for some time that God would bless us with another child. We went through all the options the fertility doctors gave us. Finally, after we had given up hope in medical science, God gave us David James. But on July 20, 1998 — 103 days later — God took him back. In September of that year my wife was again pregnant. In December she miscarried. We were on an emotional roller coaster. Often I look back and ask, "How did we get through it all? How are we still getting through it?"

God's love and never-ending mercy are the only answer. It is difficult to put into words the way I felt during the week of David's funeral. The only thing I could think about was the poem "Footprints" and how God was indeed carrying me.

It is very comforting to know that God is taking care of me, that he does have a plan, and that somehow he is using these tragedies for a purpose. Perhaps one purpose is that I am closer to God now. I am much more aware of his will in my life because I was forced to look for it. I still question why, not in defiance but in acceptance. I don't understand why this had to happen but accept that it has.

At the time of David's death, God gave his love to us in many ways. We received cards and letters of support from so many brothers and sisters in Christ that it was overwhelming. Our family, friends, and church helped with meals and shoulders to cry on. But it was time in prayer and worship with God that brought the most peace.

It is my hope that you too will find purpose in God's ways, strive to seek his will in your life, and discover his love all around you.

It Takes a Community

Ephesians 4:15

Jane Tiemersma Vogel '81
Writer/editor; Winfield, Illinois

S ince well before Hillary Rodham Clinton reminded the U.S.A. that "it takes a village," God's covenant people have known that it takes a community.

Take, for example, the Sunday I was struggling to keep our five-year-old son, Peter, from turning backward in the pew and making faces at his friend during congregational singing. I turned Peter around, but when I returned to singing, Peter thought he'd return to face-making. Meanwhile, however, a friend behind us had assessed the situation and had moved directly into Peter's line of vision so that when Peter turned around, he found himself making faces not at his friend but at the belt buckle of a retired schoolteacher who happens to stand six feet four inches tall. (I have a new picture in mind now whenever I read Ephesians 6:14: "Stand firm then, with the belt of truth buckled around your waist.")

Or take the example of my mother. My parents, former Calvin professors, felt a special concern for Calvin students long after they themselves had retired from teaching. So they were disturbed when the neighbors began complaining about the conduct of a group of Calvin students who had rented a house down the block.

One rainy night after a party had gone noisily on long after it should have, my mother, who was always practical in her theology, put a trench coat over her pajamas and knocked on the students' door. Quietly she enjoined them to show consideration for their community, consider their witness, and beware that, should the noise not stop soon, the neighbors might very well call the cops. This final warning, if nothing else, caught the attention of the young man at the door, but he wanted to know one thing more from the elderly lady standing in the rain in the middle of the night: "Who in the world are you?"

"I," answered my mother, pulling herself up to her full height of five feet five inches in bedroom slippers, "am one of the people who promised to look out for you when you were baptized."

May God grant all of us the courage to stand firm in the line of vision of those in our community who need to be confronted with the truth. And may God grant us the grace and good humor to turn our lives around when we're the ones who need to be confronted.

Telling the Story

Chris Stoffel Overvoorde   Joshua 4:2, 21-23
Calvin professor emeritus; Grand Rapids, Michigan

Joshua 3 tells the story of how God led the people of Israel through the River Jordan. Joshua 4 tells the story of the pile of stones they made to memorialize this river crossing. Having selected twelve men, one from each tribe, as God had instructed, Joshua told them to go back to the middle of the Jordan, hoist stones, one each, onto their shoulders, carry them to the place where all the people were waiting after the crossing, and set them down at the place where they were going to spend the night.

Twelve men. Twelve stones carried some two miles and arranged in some formation. Twelve stones connected with a major event. God had acted that day, and now the stones would be there to remind his people of what had happened.

The Old Testament is full of such visual reminders. The Israelites that day did something with the stones to make them unique, to make them curious to children. Joshua says,

> In the future when your descendants ask their parents, "What do these stones mean?" tell them, "Israel crossed the Jordan on dry ground." For the LORD your God dried up the Jordan before you until you had crossed over. (Josh. 4:21-23, NIVI)

In an age when everything needs to be obvious and understood immediately, it is refreshing to discover that God encourages questions, that a sense of wonder and curiosity is desirable, that not everything needs to be clear, that some things still require a connection in need of explaining by those who know. As Christians we need to recognize that when everything is clear, we are denied an opportunity to testify. We need to be challenged to tell the story. Reminders are essential for our own spiritual journeys and for our cooperative journeys as families, as congregations, as Christian agencies, as God's church, because symbolic reminders provide us with the task of spreading, the opportunity for spreading, the good news.

Visual reminders like the table for the Lord's Supper, the baptismal font, and the pulpit within our worship space are important, but they are only reminders. The real story awaits our telling. God wants us to be ambassadors who tell of, who testify to, who witness about his mighty acts and his wondrous doings in his world. We are the narrators of the stones. It is our job to tell the good news well to our descendants — and to all who will hear.

Psalm 8

Cornelia Vos
Calvin parent/psychologist;
Bowling Green, Kentucky

The blue sky above me is marked only by the white trail
Of an invisible jet,
Seemingly traveling straight upwards
Into infinity.
I pass the oak tree
Majestic and solid in its place,
And then the silver maple
Spreading its branches ever wider to receive the sunshine.
My feet move effortlessly one in front of the other
As I walk on this crisp October morning.
The birds are singing,
At first in muted choir concert,
Followed by soloist responding to soloist,
Finally giving way to a soprano melody.
Your trail is all around me, dear God,
Leading into infinity
Right here all around me,
Visible in the majestic oak,
Audible in the free song of the birds,
Sensible in my moving body,
Unmistakable in the gentle inner nudge
Of your Spirit telling me
To celebrate the gift of prayer as I walk.

After the Four-mile Mark

David A. Larsen '69   1 Peter 2:9-10
School administrator; Palos Heights, Illinois

Though it doesn't carry the prestige of the Boston Marathon, I recall a race which made a great impression on me — the annual Al's Run and Walk in downtown Milwaukee. Each fall over 25,000 people gathered to run in this thrilling and good-humored crowd event. It began with an opening pep talk from the coach — Al McGuire — patron saint of Marquette University. The talk was broadcast through a public-address system stretching for three miles along Wisconsin Avenue. Runners lined up in absolute silence for this pithy and inspiring secular call to worship.

At the starting gun, as far as I could see in front of and behind me was a thundering herd of people, all shapes, sizes, ages, costumes, and levels of endurance. All along the way I was impressed with the congeniality of the runners. We chatted with one another, joked as we ran, compared the prices of running shoes, and helped those who tripped and fell.

Until the four-mile mark. And then the silence fell.

It was every person for himself or herself after that. If you tried to joke, everyone looked at you as if you should be arrested. All I heard was the huff and puff of physical strain and the steady squish of shoes on pavement. It was a strange sort of lonely silence among thousands and thousands of people, all headed in the same direction.

I offer this story as a parable of what often happens in the Christian walk or run. Many come to the faith or grow up in the faith in the arms of the body of Christ, a caring and supportive community, one which prays for and with the young Christian, one which encourages and even admonishes. But too often and too soon matters deteriorate to good old North American individualism. Too often young babes in Christ are abandoned on the sidewalk, left at the doorstep. They get lost at church because church seems to them to be like the quiet loneliness of the four-mile mark.

If we are a "chosen people, a royal priesthood, a holy nation, a people belonging to God" (1 Pet. 2:9), Christian students shouldn't come to college enthusiastic about their faith and then have to struggle to find Christian fellowship. Nor should their peers in other situations. Those struggling with issues of culture and faith or questions of ethics and justice should be able to find others with whom they can talk. Christians struggling and in doubt should find listening ears. May conversation and community abound even after the four-mile mark.

Servants Unaware

1 Thessalonians 1:1-5

Brook Pauley
Calvin student; South Bend, Indiana

G od never ceases to amaze me. I work part-time for Young Life, a non-denominational ministry to high school students. God has consistently worked in and around me as I have been involved in Young Life, and most of the time I am not even aware of what he is doing until after the fact.

Here is just one example of God's work that has miraculously involved me. One of the girls I have been working with, I'll call her Kate, went out for coffee with me early this past fall. Kate explained to me that she had been drinking, smoking, and generally partying all summer long. She confessed that she knew she had done wrong things. Kate and I met a couple of times later, and she mentioned that she was not able to come to the weekly Young Life Bible study anymore because of her work schedule. All of a sudden a thought popped into my head: Why not get together once a week and have our own Bible study? I'm sure now that this idea was the Holy Spirit at work in me. Kate was very excited about the idea. In fact, she was so excited that she went around school asking her friends to come to this new Bible study.

It was amazing to me: God had used Kate and me, and both of us had been unaware of being used until later. I was simply available and willing to do a Bible study, and God used that. Kate was immediately excited about the idea, and I believe this was God at work in her.

Since we started the Bible study, there have been five girls coming regularly. They are learning and growing so much — all because of God's amazing and wondrous work in two people who were unaware that they were carrying out his plans. He does indeed work in mysterious ways.

I Have a Name!

Beth A. Swagman '77   Isaiah 43:1
Social worker; Grand Rapids, Michigan

> *But now, this is what the* LORD *says — he who created you, O Jacob, he who formed you, O Israel: "Fear not, for I have redeemed you; I have summoned you by name; you are mine."* (Isa. 43:1)

It seems that the world is becoming more impersonal all the time. When I call a colleague on the phone, I get a voice mailbox. When I call the doctor's office, I get a menu of options followed by a reminder to press the pound sign to hear the menu again. I can use a credit card to handle most transactions, including groceries, utility bills, tax-deductible donations, and even weekly tithing. To save time, I can purchase items online and avoid parking hassles at the neighborhood mall. Despite these many conveniences, to many companies I am just a number. If I have a problem with a bill or the product I received, the first question I'm asked is "What is your account number?" Companies don't know me, nor do they care to know about me. I'm not important to them.

In an impersonal world, I find great comfort in knowing I am important to God. I matter to him; what happens to me matters to him. He takes an interest in my life, and he knows me by name. God took an interest in you and me even before he knit us in our mothers' wombs. His interest in and love for us was so great that he chose to send his Son to redeem us. Because of God's love for you and me, nothing will ever separate us from him.

The growth of communication technology means speed and convenience, and the likely result is a world that is less and less personal. God transcends cyberspace and the information highway with a few but powerful words of comfort and acceptance. God says that we are precious to him and honored in his sight (Isa. 43:4). Forget convenience. Our God is a God of personal love, someone who knows us by name. Doesn't that feel good for a change?

Extravagant Love

Matthew 26:6-13   Kevin Jeffer '85
Copywriter; Richmond, Virginia

When the disciples saw this, they were indignant. (Matt. 26:8)

I've been thinking about receiving love lately. When my wife, Margaret, and I married, we received so many gifts that it took months just to go through them, find a place to put them, and write the thank-you notes. All the while in the back of my head I kept thinking, "I don't deserve all this." Even more troubling than the gifts was the extravagant outpouring of love that we received. It's embarrassing, and we feel the need to do something in response.

But of course we can't repay the friends and family who flew halfway around the world to be with us; or our pastor, who conducted the service in German and English; or the ladies from church who prepared and served the food, decorated the reception hall, and cleaned up afterward.

As I reflect on these extravagant offerings of love, I think of our Lord, who also received love offered extravagantly. I'm thinking, of course, of Jesus and the woman with the alabaster jar.

But Jesus knew precisely how to respond to extravagant love. The disciples were outraged, profoundly uncomfortable with the intimacy and extravagance of this gift — a natural reaction, of course, for men who often seemed consumed with questions of status and power. But our Lord knew he is worthy of all extravagance. Even more: He knew it is important to receive love — even love that goes beyond our comfort level, our sense of propriety.

So how is it with you? Can you receive Christ's love? Can you receive the love of his people? Does it make you feel rather uncomfortable, maybe even guilty? Perhaps, like me, you almost feel you need a heart transplant in order to be able to receive all the love that's coming your way.

Bring that before God, and enjoy the reservoirs of love and acceptance that are yours in Christ and in the Christian community. Indeed, you are loved — extravagantly.

The Joy of Obedience

Jan Entingh Dykgraaf '77   John 15:10-11
Missionary; Niger State, Nigeria

> *If you obey my commands, you will remain in my love. . . . I have told you this so that . . . your joy may be complete.* (John 15:10-11)

At times we become so focused on the events of our lives that we forget that our attitude should be the same as that of Christ Jesus, who "became obedient to death — even death on a cross" (Phil. 2:8). Our focus on Christ becomes blurred with cares and worries, and we forget his great example of obedience. We become too ready to say, "I don't want to." Though these words sometimes reflect a good decision — for example, when we choose not to do something morally questionable — they can, on the other hand, reflect our willful self-centeredness if they express a conflict with God's will. I know. I've been there.

In my case it happened after we had been working in missions for twenty years. At that point my husband and I decided we should return to America. Surely our families wanted this, and so did we. We would finally live together with our girls. No more boarding schools. We resigned and made our plans to reenter stateside culture. We knew that missionary positions in Africa are extremely hard to fill, and our field leader had recently asked us to consider working in northwestern Nigeria. We had experience in missions, we love Nigerian people, and we had adapted well to Nigeria's culture, climate, and food. We were well-suited. But we had other plans. We also had some pretty good reasons for not staying on the field. The main one was that I didn't want to. I really struggled with the Lord — until he reminded me that he did not want to die either. *But he did.* He was obedient . . . even unto death. Realizing that, I gave in. When I finally said, "Okay, Lord," joy flooded my heart, and the wrestling was over.

Today we still live in Nigeria. Since the day I gave in, I have realized joys that would never have been possible if I had followed my own desires and not obeyed God's call — the joy of neighbors leaving the darkness of their traditional religion for the wondrous light of our Lord, the joy of children singing praise to God, the joy of evil spirits withering at the name of Jesus.

You're looking for joy? I found it in obedience. So can you.

Psalm 146:1-2

Joan Ringerwole '65

Professor; Sioux Center, Iowa

> *Praise the* LORD. *Praise the* LORD, *O my soul. I will praise the* LORD *all my life; I will sing praise to my God as long as I live.* (Ps. 146:1-2)

There are many passages in the Bible that refer to and speak about music. Some speak about praising God and glorifying his name through music; others indicate the importance of excellence in music during our worship. From all of Scripture, the psalms are the most often quoted, for they provide us with model poetry which was usually chanted during the Old and New Testament times. Jesus himself worshiped in the synagogue and the temple, where psalms were chanted. Scripture was joined with the tune or chant in such a way that those who sang were able not only to encounter God by the close marriage of text and tune but also to commit Scripture to memory through the aid of tunes. Music, with its meter and melody, acted as servant to the text and as an aid in contributing to spirituality.

We also can enrich our lives and grow spiritually as Christians by memorizing psalms and hymns. Having memorized all the stanzas of many hymns and psalms, I now carry scriptural ideas and sometimes direct texts with me at all times. When I am doing dishes or traveling in my car, I can sing and reflect on Scripture. Because there is great variety in the texts of hymns and psalms, I can find something to fit my various moods, and often these songs I sing speak to me in ways I never would have imagined. As noted music scholar Eric Routley once said, "Each hymn has a different character, some smile at you and others frown."

The Bible shows us how music was able to soothe Saul, make the walls of Jericho come tumbling down with the sound of the trumpets, cheer prisoners in the dark of night, and be one medium of praise to God for people throughout the ages. Music is still very important in the spiritual lives of all of us. We can grow with its message, or, if the wedding of tune and text is not good, it can work as a hindrance in our worship of God. May the music with which we seek to worship God be pleasing to him and edifying to the people of his church. Let us mind both tune and text, seeking the perfect marriage for praising God.

Praise and Serve

Herb Brinks '57   Psalm 113
Calvin professor emeritus; Grand Rapids, Michigan

U sually the term *throne of God* evokes an image of distant power and glory — an outsized marble chair elevated within a formal courtyard garden. That image little resembles the throne David speaks about in Psalm 22:3: "You are enthroned as the Holy One; you are the praise of Israel." There is nothing physical about the enthronement of God here. The essence of his enthronement is his holiness and justice and care of his people, who respond to their holy King with praise. Our praise helps to build God's throne.

In the Old Testament, God's people used the psalms to praise their enthroned Lord, especially the psalms contained in the last third of the book of Psalms. These poems laud God for mighty works in nature, for guiding Israel's past, for personal comfort, for rescue — and especially for being just, merciful, gracious, and righteous.

For example, Psalm 113:5-8 declares, "Who is like the LORD our God, the One who sits enthroned on high?. . . He raises the poor from the dust and lifts the needy from the ash heap; he seats them with princes. . . . He settles the barren woman in her home as a happy mother of children." With these same words Hannah (1 Sam. 2:1-12) dedicated her son, Samuel, to the Lord's service, and centuries later Mary used them again to praise God after she understood the significance of her pregnancy: "My soul glorifies the Lord," she sang, because "he has performed mighty deeds with his arm; he has scattered those who are proud in their inmost thoughts. He . . . has lifted up the humble. He has filled the hungry with good things but has sent the rich away empty" (Luke 1:46, 51-53).

From their sons, both of them judges, Hannah and Mary expected perfect justice. Indeed, Samuel stands apart as a righteous judge, and Christ, the judge of all mankind, has established the ultimate standard of justice in Matthew 25:34-36: "Come, you who are blessed by my Father; take your inheritance, the kingdom prepared for you since the creation of the world. For I was hungry and you gave me something to eat, I was thirsty and you gave me something to drink . . . I was in prison and you came to visit me."

All this praising — by Hannah, Mary, and the psalmists — directs us, too, *to enthrone the Lord with praise* for his intervention on behalf of the poor, the needy, and the powerless and *to join him in the holy work* on their behalf that is the primary responsibility of members called to his eternal kingdom.

The Right Equipment

Hebrews 13:20-21

Stephen Chong '79
Attorney; Gotha, Florida

When I was a boy growing up playing baseball, the bat to have was a Louisville Slugger. Oh, there were other bats on the market, but all my favorite professional ballplayers seemed to use that one brand. Thus, when years later I finally got to visit the factory where these bats are made, I had to buy one for my oldest son. He was only five years old at the time and many years away from using it, but I wanted him to have the best equipment when he needed it. As his father, I wanted him to have whatever he needed to be successful.

It strikes me now that what I did for my son God has done for us Christians. He has provided us with the right equipment. To some he has given special gifts, talents, or training. To others he has given unique experiences that qualify them for certain kinds of challenging projects. For all of us God has provided two mainstays of equipment. First, he gave us his Spirit to work in us to will and to act according to his purpose (Phil. 2:13). Second, he gave us his Word in the Bible. In 2 Timothy 3:16-17 we read, "All Scripture is God-breathed and is useful for teaching, rebuking, correcting and training in righteousness, so that God's servant may be thoroughly equipped for every good work" (NIVI). This is how God intended us to be equipped for service: We are to be girded with his Word. This is the armor that God has provided in order for us to successfully do battle against the devil. These are the tools with which God accomplishes his work in and through us. Therefore, let us not fail to use the best tools on the market for spiritual success: the Holy Spirit, God's Word, special gifts, talents, training, and experiences.

Have you ever asked yourself how God would have you use the equipment he has provided for you? Whatever you have been given, know that God purposely entrusted these things to you in order that you would be properly equipped for the work that was designed for you before the foundation of the world.

Lessons from Jericho

Kevin Vande Streek   Joshua 6:1-21
Calvin professor; Grand Rapids, Michigan

The story of Joshua and the walls of Jericho is one of my favorite Bible passages. I like it because it helps me in three ways to live my life with God.

First, it teaches me to depend upon God. God knocked the walls of Jericho down. He can do anything. He created the world, sent his Son to live a perfect life, heals the sick, and raised the dead. Knowing he does all this, I can be sure he can handle anything I face in my life. Recently I had a big challenge set before me. I quickly realized it was much too big a task for me to face alone. I prayed that God would use me however it was best but acknowledged that he would have to see it through.

Second, the story of Joshua at Jericho teaches me that I need to play an active part in the challenge. The people of Israel marched — for seven days. That tells me I need to put my back into the challenge at hand. Prayer is important, financial assistance is important, but nothing replaces personal commitment to a project. I can't sit by and expect God or others to do the work for me. I have to decide which problems I think I can tackle, ask for help for those I cannot, and go to work to carry out the part of the job that is mine.

Third, the story of Joshua at Jericho teaches me about the source of all my abilities. It teaches me to whom I need to give thanks. The people of Israel, after their victory, dedicated the city to God. They realized he had given them the mental capacity to understand the directions, the courage to move forward, the physical ability to march, and the practical tools necessary to execute the plan. It is easy to accept the praise for ourselves when something goes right, easy to forget it was God's plan and his work.

God led me through my recent challenge. For that I thank him. May he lead you, too, through today's challenges as you trust in his power and use your energies for him. Glory be to God!

'Seasoned with Salt'

Colossians 4:5-6

Holly Nyenhuis
Calvin student; Jenison, Michigan

> *Be wise in the way you act toward outsiders; make the most of every opportunity.*
> *Let your conversation be always full of grace, seasoned with salt, so that you may*
> *know how to answer everyone.* (Col. 4:5-6)

It is often said that actions speak louder than words, yet as Christians we cannot ignore the importance of our words. We must be intentional about our conversations with non-Christians — it is not enough to avoid offensive speech. The *Life Application Study Bible* explains that if our conversations are "seasoned with salt," they will be "tasty" and will encourage further dialogue. People will feel free to ask questions and initiate conversations if they know we are open to and excited about how God is at work in our lives.

During this past summer I worked with missionaries in Mexico. Before I returned home, God brought today's verses from Colossians to my attention, and they made me ask myself some questions. Was I going to use my experience to glorify God? Was I going to give him all the glory for what had occurred throughout the summer? When people asked me how my summer was, would I respond by saying, "It was incredible; I learned a lot," or would I say, "It was incredible. God did amazing things, and he taught me a lot"? Both statements are true, but in the latter I would be giving the credit and praise to God. This, I think, is what it means to make the most of every opportunity and to season our conversation with salt.

We must not only intentionally season our conversation with salt by sharing how Jesus Christ is at work changing our lives, but we must also seek out such conversations. Too many of us Christians have bought into the American practice of saying that religion is a private matter. It is uncomfortable to mention Jesus with people whom we do not know well. But aren't these the very opportunities that Paul is talking about? How often do we ask God to bring us opportunities to share the gospel? If we ask him, God will give us opportunities to share with others, and he will guide us so that we can graciously draw people into "tasty" conversation about our amazing Father.

Faith, Hope, Love

Ben Beversluis '77   1 Corinthians 13:13
Journalist; Zeeland, Michigan

And now these three remain: faith, hope and love. (1 Cor. 13:13)

D reams die hard, and life's a dismal path without them.
When a short circuit in his brain stole seven-year-old Nick's speech and comprehension, he became angry, confused, agitated. Gray clouds blocked the blue-sky sparkle of his eyes. And while daily life was a struggle, perhaps worst of all was a family living on with the cold corpse of dreams. What parent hasn't hugged a newborn bundle of hope, holding tight to dreams of that infant playing Carnegie Hall, pitching a World Series shutout, captivating students, winning the Nobel Prize? The death of those dreams through illness or accident is a terrible death. It can seem the death of hope.

For some, the daily crush of a hurting life without the uplift of hope leaves decayed families, frustration, and futility. Others can accept that there is a plan, can accept that all things work together for good, however dimly they see it: a coming New Jerusalem, with "no more death or mourning or crying or pain" (Rev. 21:4). That's faith.

But beware of easy answers. A child drowns or dies in a car crash, and other children's parents so quickly say, "He's in a better place now." Temptation feeds on easy faith. When a child's pained life continues after the death of dreams, temptation whispers out of the dark on sleepless nights: Maybe now it's time for that better place, time for him to finish with this angry and disappointment-filled world. It's strong temptation in a parent's wilderness of despair.

But then comes help. God's hands on earth — the people of his church — reach out to offer comfort, to steady the unstable, to pull the desperate back from the pinnacle. And that is love.

So God's grace steadies a family on the brink. And a medical miracle brings a little boy out of his dizzy and silent world. "It's like Nick is back from the dead," says his long-loving schoolteacher — reminding us all that faith and hope were always (though at times just barely) alive. And that love, the greatest of these, still conquers death.

Praying Good-bye

Ephesians 5:20

Mary Venema Swierenga '63
Pastor; Vienna, Virginia

Our family moved recently. I knew that once the packing was done, I'd want to be alone to say farewell to 11917 Appling Valley Road, to pray my good-byes to that place. This house was unique, our children's childhood home for seventeen years. Moving from it marked the end of that era in their lives and ours. This house was also where we lived during the time I went to seminary. It is difficult to calculate the magnitude of change that decision entailed in our lives. But the transition years were over — our move signaled that. I stood on the front porch and watched the van pull out. Then, for the last time, I entered the place which had been our home for so long and significant a time.

I lingered in each room to allow the memories to ebb and flow. It took quite a while. Remembering good times and hard, I smiled and cried and was regretful and glad. In each of the kids' rooms, I recalled their pasts and entrusted their futures to God. I stood for a considerable time by the door where we'd recorded their heights over the years. I bade farewell to the familiar view outside my large kitchen window. How many times had I looked out without really seeing, as I wrote, pondered, and prayed?

I wandered outside and picked the last tomatoes from my garden, source of great satisfaction and blessing over the years. Earlier that morning I'd walked my familiar route, stopping by the pond to look for a couple strands of fragrant honeysuckle for one last wildflower bouquet. There were no more good-byes to be said. I'd prayed them all.

But there was one more thing to do. Not minding if anyone was looking, I kissed the door frame of the front door, commending the years and the memories to God. Departing with a full heart, I looked back at the house. Involuntarily my hand lifted in blessing, and I whispered a benediction on what was now the past: "Thanks be to God! Amen." It was time to leave and begin saying hello to our new home.

We Are Singers in a Choir

Louis Vos† '58   Amos 5:23-24
Calvin professor; Grand Rapids, Michigan
Richard Leach
Poet; Torrington, Connecticut

We are singers in a choir
    before the Lord our God:
in the choir are morning stars,
    with tongues of fire and light;
in the choir are countless saints,
    in a city with no night;
in the choir are seraphim,
    who soar and sing around a throne
    just past our mortal sight.
And we are singers in this choir
    with stars and saints and seraphim!

The choir in which we sing is vast,
    yet God can hear the clash and clang
    when our living and our song
    do not agree in tone and key —
singing of kindness, but not showing kindness,
singing of mercy, but not showing mercy,
singing of justice, but not doing justice —
    our dissonance is not drowned out
    by stars and saints and seraphim!

Yet when our lives come into tune
    with the song we sing —
    showing kindness, having mercy, doing justice —
we brighten the song of morning stars,
    whose tongues are fire and light;
we swell the song of the saints,
    in the city with no night;
we harmonize with seraphim,
    who soar and sing around a throne
    just past our mortal sight.
And we give glory to our God
    with stars and saints and seraphim!

The words for this hymn are based on the sermon "Living in the Wrong Key" by Louis Vos, professor of religion and theology at Calvin College; it was given on October 19, 1994, as part of a worship service by the Calvin College Alumni Choir. The sermon was based on passages from Psalms and Revelation and especially on Amos 5:23-24: "I will not listen to the music of your harps. But let justice roll on like a river, righteousness like a never-failing stream!" Music for the hymn and a subsequent anthem were written by Roy Hopp '75.

Whose Will?

Esther Timmer Koops '66   Haggai 1
Missionary linguist; Serrekunda, Gambia

Where we live in West Africa, a common response to disaster is to say, "It was the will of God." Recently I came across a setting in the Bible that made me wonder whether the people of that day might have struggled with the same mentality.

It was my rediscovery of the prophet Haggai that triggered these thoughts. Haggai was part of the small Jewish community that returned to Jerusalem from captivity in Babylon. Its goal was to rebuild the Temple and restore worship there. Surely these people had tremendous courage and a strong sense of vision. They were willing to face great hazards because of their devotion to the Lord. The book of Ezra tells us that "despite their fear of the peoples around them" (Ezra 3:3), they succeeded in rebuilding the altar and reestablishing the regular sacrifices and feasts.

About a year later they started on the Temple itself. At that point opposition became more pronounced, and eventually the project came to a halt that lasted for sixteen years. Ezra says almost nothing about that delay. So how did it happen? Why did the people lose their vision?

The book of Haggai gives us some insight into the situation. The people had turned their attention to developing their farms and building beautiful homes. Quickly they had been distracted from their original calling, and they were now telling themselves, "The time has not yet come for the LORD's house to be built" (Hag. 1:2). Perhaps in essence they were saying, "Surely God wants us to take care of ourselves, too. It must be the Lord's will that we delay his work."

Finally God sent a clear message through Haggai to wake them up. God's desire was not delay, but perseverance, in spite of obstacles. What a joyful day it must have been for the Lord and for Haggai as the people rose to the challenge.

How easy it is to make our version of God's will fit whatever it is we want. Today I'm asking myself what areas in my life are so tied up with personal concerns that I need a prophetic voice to remind me of a higher call.

Adventures

Psalm 103:11-22   David Armour '59

State-park deputy director; Lansing, Michigan

One late Friday afternoon in October, we were on our way from Michigan to West Virginia to visit our daughter and her husband. We wanted to see their new home, and we had loaded our minivan with some of their things that had been stored in our attic. Suddenly the car's lights went out, and the engine stopped. The alternator had failed, and we were stalled along a major highway, almost to Ohio. We locked the minivan and started walking. The trucks went by so fast that we felt like we were being lifted off the ground by their force. In the twilight it was a scary experience. As we walked, we prayed, asking for God's help.

After we had walked almost a mile, the driver of a two-passenger pickup truck pulled over and asked us if we had left the minivan back down the road. The young couple in the truck, on their way to Toledo on a date, had seen us get out and had decided to turn around and come back to ask what they could do to help. They were fellow Christians who even had connections with Calvin College. After driving us ten miles to the nearest exit, where we could call for help, they did not leave us until they knew a wrecker was on the way. God had indeed sent his people to help.

We were reminded of this story the other day when we were talking about traditions. One of our sons reminded us that when we have problems in our family, we call them adventures. The story recounted above was for us an adventure, not bad luck, as some would call it. Really, our whole life is an adventure here on earth. We need not worry about things because God is in control and he takes care of us every minute of the day. When troubles come, he watches from above to see how we handle the situation — whether we trust him completely or worry about our adventure. May we all pray daily that we may think of our troubles as adventures, adventures in which God is taking a hand in our lives.

Life Is an Awesome Gift

Charsie Randolph Sawyer   Psalm 69:30
Calvin professor; Grand Rapids, Michigan

I will praise God's name in song and glorify him with thanksgiving.

(Ps. 69:30)

One incident in my life that stands out vividly in my memory is that a dear college friend of mine became ill and died of cancer only a few days before graduation. The chair next to me, where she was supposed to sit, was empty, and for that reason, graduation was a bittersweet occasion. As I sat there, I recalled how she had waited for me during my final exam and had celebrated with my husband and me when I passed the test. But now she was gone, and I could not share the particular joy of graduation with her.

As we go through today, let us realize that tomorrow is not promised. Our lives are like a mist, which can evaporate at any time. Live today as if it may be your last day. Give those gifts of kindness that you have been putting off. Make those visits that you have been intending to make. Send those cards or notes that you have been meaning to write. Let go of the hurts and resentments that separate you from others. Take time to appreciate the beauty of the world around you. Cherish those who have been given into your care.

Above all, be thankful for all the precious gifts and opportunities that God continues to provide for you. Celebrate this day — and every day — with thanksgiving.

From Glory into Glory

Psalm 139:1-6

Kyliah Clarke
Calvin student; Valparaiso, Indiana

Just last week I was down in Chicago, driving toward Downers Grove. Rolling along the highway, I caught myself laughing at the city-limits signs. As a child I had viewed the Chicago-area communities as separate entities. Saying my friend Laura was from Wheaton and my friend Andy was from Itasca pointed to a significant difference in location. Now, however, it strikes me how arbitrary these lines have become. Linked by housing developments, strip malls, car washes, and hospitals, these municipalities have virtually merged into one continuous megalopolis.

Camp songs, too, are like this. "Swing Low, Sweet Chariot" can melt first into "When the Saints Go Marchin' In," then into "He's My Rock, My Sword, My Shield," and then into "I'm Gonna Sing, Sing, Sing, I'm Gonna Shout, Shout, Shout." Before the campers know it, they have sung four songs in one smoothly flowing medley. The four have been joined into one and are scarcely distinguishable from one another.

In a similar way, before I came to Calvin, my understanding of God and his presence and work in my life was divided, organized, and neatly labeled. I felt close to God sitting in a pew next to my squirming little brother. I felt close to God when I was playing outside at summer camp or competing on the Bible Quiz Team. I felt close to God out under the stars or when witnessing to a friend on the school bus.

I never gave much thought, though, to his presence at other times. I didn't see his hand when I had to do chores at home. I didn't see his purpose when I struggled with my precalculus homework or when my friend moved away. Gradually, however, I've learned that God doesn't descend once a week or only at isolated intervals. Rather, God leads me each day and in all the facets of my life, from glory into glory. I could impress you by reciting Reformed theology as a basis for this new insight. Or I could just compare it to a song that never ends. Either way it is simply beautiful.

Great and Good

Dale Cooper '64   Psalm 62:11;
Calvin chaplain; Jenison, Michigan   Heidelberg Catechism Q. and A. 26

One recent afternoon Dr. William Spoelhof, former president of Calvin College, handed me a letter he had found that morning among some of his papers. Dated October 23, 1973, it had been sent by the late Dr. Stanley Wiersma, then professor of English, to Spoelhof's wife, Ange, who had recently undergone surgery for cancer. To encourage and comfort her, Wiersma had included in the letter his translation of a Dutch hymn:

> Faith cannot do too much expecting.
> The words of Jesus all come true.
> Friends offer only weak protecting;
> Jesus the Friend will see us through.
> What limit to the love he gave us?
> All power exists for love to use.
> Since Love desires and plans to save us,
> How can Almightiness refuse?*

Said President Spoelhof to the rest of us gathered in the faculty coffee room, "How true this hymn is. In our distress God held Ange and me fast." Then, after an anointed pause, he added, "And God gave Ange to me for another twenty years."

Calvin College affirms these twin pillar truths: God is great; God is good. No less important, the Reformed Christian tradition in which Calvin College stands confesses with confidence and joy that the Lord's *power over* his children is shaped by his fatherly *love for* them. What our academic community has received from its ancestors we now long to hand on faithfully to our heirs.

Given the culture of violence and death which surrounds them daily and the atmosphere of callous injustice and of fast-paced anonymity in which they live, college-age young people today long to know for sure — deep down and beyond a trace of maybe — that they really do matter — to God and to others.

What better motto, therefore, could Calvin affirm — no, reaffirm — as it enters the third millennium than the words of the Heidelberg Catechism's Answer 26: Whatever may happen in this sometimes sad world, God "is able [to care for his children] because he is almighty God; [and] he desires to do this because he is a faithful Father."*

298

Praying like Children

Matthew 21:22

Beverly Hogberg Morrison
Calvin academic counselor; Grand Rapids, Michigan

If you believe, you will receive whatever you ask for in prayer.

(Matt. 21:22)

T hat God hears and answers our prayers is one of the greatest assur-
ances of the Christian life. Nevertheless, when I experience the fulfillment of this promise, I often respond in amazement. My apparent lack of
confidence in the certainty of this verse was initially revealed decades ago,
when our son was six years old. While looking over the school papers Hans
was sharing with me one day, I noticed that the diamond in my engage-
ment ring was missing. I did a cursory check over the floor and simultaneously estimated the replacement cost of the diamond. Consequently, I
decided to make work of finding the lost stone. Leaving my son in the care
of his older sister, I returned to my office but soon recognized the futility
of my search. I drove home dejected. Entering the house, I felt compelled to
examine the kitchen wastebasket. As a person who detests clutter, I have a
habit of reading mail or, in this situation, school papers over the wastebasket, immediately sorting out what is to be discarded. When I had removed
the last scrap from the basket, a sparkle in the bottom thrilled my heart
with relief.

The point of this narrative relates directly to Matthew 21:22. As I joyously announced my discovery to the children, Hans casually responded
with complete lack of astonishment, "While you were gone, Mom, we
prayed that you would find your diamond." His simple understanding of
this biblical promise included the assurance that his prayer would be heard
and answered; my surprise in the immediate answer suggested I was less
certain. Over the following years I have attended a seminar on prayer at Ox-
ford University and read books on the topic, yet it was this experience
shared with my son that turned my cognitive understanding of prayer into
a confident belief that God will, in his own time and according to his own
plan, graciously respond to our requests.

Mulligans of Grace

Tim Kuperus '93   Jonah 3
Pastor; Byron Center, Michigan

O ne of my favorite shots in golf is a mulligan. For those like me who have not mastered the art of hitting a round one-inch ball with a four-foot stick, a mulligan is an essential part of the game. When you sail a tee shot into the woods and quickly determine that the squirrels might as well add your ball to their collection, this shot comes in handy. Without hesitation you casually pull an emergency ball out of your pocket and declare, "I'm taking a mulligan." For some reason the term "do-over" never made its way into golf parlance.

The third chapter of Jonah records one of the great mulligans of the Bible. The city of Nineveh is in God's crosshairs on account of its violence and rebellion against God. Jonah knows it. He also knows the remedy that would spare this city. Yet Jonah decides he would far rather vacation in Tarshish than head to Nineveh and see his enemies spared. Sad but true, the prophet of God, the one whose very calling it is to tell others about God's will, abandons his calling and blatantly rejects God's will. However, God thwarts Jonah's travel plans and sends Jonah back home via a three-day ride in a deep-sea explorer. There God speaks to Jonah a second time (Jon. 3:1). Jonah needs a mulligan, and God gives him one. God profoundly yet simply demonstrates what kind of God he is, a forgiving God, a God of second chances.

Jonah eventually speaks to the people of Nineveh. The people repent, and God listens. Amazingly, God still uses Jonah, despite his initial failure, to proclaim the powerful words of hope to thousands. In the end, Nineveh is spared.

Whenever I wonder if my latest blunder is beyond the pale of forgiveness and whether God's reservoir of mercy has run dry, I remember a God who gave Jonah a mulligan. I then look to that same God and humbly say, "I need a mulligan." Praise God that through Jesus Christ God graciously keeps giving me second chances.

Hospitality

Hebrews 13:2

Carol Vandenbosch Rottman '59
Consultant; Greenville, Michigan

Do not forget to entertain strangers, for by so doing some people have entertained angels without knowing it. (Heb. 13:2)

When I was growing up, there were often new faces at our Sunday dinner table. My mom actually scouted the church each Sunday for visitors to invite for dinner. When they were reluctant, she insisted, "We can always peel another potato." With five children in the family, the potato pot was already pretty full.

I'm not sure why Mom was so hospitable, but she loved to meet new people and make them feel at home. The story goes that, when she and my dad and one small child arrived by train as total strangers to the city that was to become their home, someone heard of their coming and met them at the station. "We never had any relatives in Denver," said Mom, "but from that day on, we never lacked for friends." Some call this hospitality Western; others call it the old Dutch connection. Whatever it is, she has been paying back those original hosts for forty years by doing the same for others.

When my husband and I and two small children moved to a new city, a family like my own took us under its wing. A research pediatrician and a musician shared Sunday dinner, their own eight children, and stimulating conversation with our lonely little family. They continued to invite us frequently until we were no longer strangers in the church or in the city.

Anyone who was once a stranger because of relocation or travels or medical care in another city will recall the loneliness, the feeling of being an alien, and some know the relief of finding "family." I don't know which of the guests at my mom's table or my own were angels, but they all blessed us with their presence.

People who have plenty of family may forget the stranger. But Mom's words ring: "Anyone can peel another potato and add another chair!" We should all be seeking out the stranger in our midst.

An Eternal Perspective

Gwen Cooke De Horn '88   2 Corinthians 4:16-18
Social worker; Granger, Indiana

Getting a good perspective on time has always been a problem for me. When I was pregnant, I moaned and complained to everyone around me about having morning sickness for the rest of my life, only to wake up after several weeks feeling fine. When my children wouldn't sleep through the night for a few months, I envisioned myself sitting at college graduations in a sleep-deprived state. I often struggle along with my clients who have been battling an eating disorder for years and wonder with them whether this will ever end.

I am amazed at how our perspective on time gets skewed by trials and even the daily annoyances of life. Even though experience may tell us that life is always changing, at any given moment we often feel and act as though our current experience is here to stay. Life on this earth has a way of filling our scope and narrowing our vision so that even significant biblical truths seem far away and unimportant.

A few years ago I met a man who had been a successful businessman before deciding to devote himself and his family to church ministry. His friends and family were concerned. "You'll be poor," they said. "You'll struggle to support your family. You won't be able to have nice things and go to exotic places." His reply? "Only for fifty or sixty years." His response reflects wisdom that often evades me. We serve a God who is eternal, and our life on this earth is not even close to the sum total of our existence.

It is during times of frustration and annoyance that I so often find myself caught up in the things of this world — the immediate emotions, the temporary inconveniences, the passing discomforts. My thoughts, plans, and decisions can too quickly reflect what I am seeing now, in the present, instead of what I cannot see in eternity.

I've learned that irritating morning sickness doesn't even compare with the joy of having children. How much more will the glory of God fully revealed wipe out any memory of pains experienced on earth. It is to this truth that I hold — not just in the clearly difficult and overwhelming trials of the present age but also in the mundane activities that threaten to diminish my joy and consume my life with the temporary.

I am an eternal being. My eyes may see only this world and how it affects my life in the present, but my heart knows there's more, and that is what I am fixing on.

What Would Jesus Do?

Colossians 3:13

Paul Zigterman '79
Attorney; Lombard, Illinois

Forgive as the Lord forgave you. (Col. 3:13)

Twenty years ago at Calvin, I wrote a history paper comparing Harriet Beecher Stowe's *Uncle Tom's Cabin* and Charles Sheldon's *In His Steps*.

Sheldon asked his readers to live Christian lives by asking in everyday situations, "What would Jesus do?" Answering this seemingly simple question, however, becomes more complicated as the issues become more complex. Jesus would not lie or cheat, but what would he think about capital punishment in today's world? How would he deal with welfare issues? What would he do about distributing the world's food resources?

Stowe's Uncle Tom provides a simple answer to Sheldon's straightforward but complex question. Though Uncle Tom has become a symbol with negative connotations for many people, Stowe portrays him as a selfless Christian striving humbly to live a Christian life in the worst possible conditions. Tom was abused by wicked slave owners, but he never rebelled and never fought back. He prayed constantly, never wavered in his faith, and humbly and meekly accepted his place in life. Most important, he forgave those who abused and took advantage of him. After Simon Legree beat him almost to the point of death, Tom uttered, "I forgive ye, with all my soul." Before Tom died, he said of Legree, "Oh, if he only could repent, the Lord would forgive him now; but I'm 'feard he never will."

Maybe Uncle Tom should have rebelled, seeking relief from the injustice of slavery. Nonetheless, we can learn from his character. Harriet Beecher Stowe wrote *Uncle Tom's Cabin* to persuade a nation to end slavery, but she did so by portraying a character whose humble Christianity came from his ability to forgive those who deserved the fire of hell.

The simplest answer to "What would Jesus do?" is sometimes simply "Forgive."

Back to Basics

William J. Katt, Sr. '76 1 John 2:3-6; 5:3
Attorney; Brookfield, Wisconsin

If John is right when he says of God that "his commands are not burdensome" (1 John 5:3), why do we keep continually struggling with the same sin? If God is "able to do immeasurably more than all we ask or imagine" (Eph. 3:20), why doesn't he just handle it?

When you have that perspective on God and his commands, it is important to step back and see just why it is you are failing. Are your actions consistent with the help you are asking from God? My own life reveals that too often I look at obedience as an obligation instead of as an expression of my love for God. Likewise, disobedience is a slap in his face. When you look at obedience as an obligation, you tend to excuse yourself when you aren't completely obedient to God's command. You gossip, but not as much as you used to. You make occasional racist comments, but you are not really racist. You don't tithe, but you really give substantial amounts to the church. Isn't a *B-* in obedience good enough? John would answer with a resounding no.

Our obedience has to start with our devotional life. We will not be successful in expressing our love for God unless we are first obedient in devotions. We need to be devoted about our devotions. God gives us commands throughout Scripture to pray continually and to be prepared to answer questions about our faith. How can we possibly be obedient in daily activities if we fail to heed his admonitions to pray and study the Word? What makes us think we can take a day off from our devotional life?

The beauty of prayer and God's Scripture is that he reveals himself to us through them. He shows us that, even though we think we have been diligently praying for relief from certain sins, our lack of obedience is what continues to cause us to fail. He shows us our sin and the alternative route.

The next time you are wondering why you keep failing, check yourself. Maybe it's time to get back to basics.

Places, Promises, Praise

Philippians 1:3-6

Cheryl Poel Nielsen '71
Nonprofit administrator; Grand Rapids, Michigan

In 1964 in Jos, Nigeria, I stood with four other MKs (missionary kids) in a small chapel near Hillcrest School to profess my faith in Christ and my desire to follow him all the days of my life. Little did I know then where that commitment would take me. Not so long after, as I stood on the front porch of an unchurched family in Sun Valley, California, with my SWIM partner, knocking at the door and at the hearts of this family, I heard God's voice of encouragement: "For I know the plans I have for you . . . plans to give you hope and a future" (Jer. 29:11). More recently, as I walked along the dirt path to church in a remote village in the mountains of Yunnan Province of China, my heart overflowed with emotion when it hit me that the same God I had come to know and love in Nigeria was the God the Miao villagers were praising. In beautiful four-part harmony they were singing the familiar hymn "All Hail the Power of Jesus' Name." My ministry partners and I joined them in the song — English and Miao praising God together. A flood of God's promises and accounts of his faithfulness poured over me: "The promise is for you and your children and for all who are far off" (Acts 2:39), "go and make disciples of all nations" (Matt. 28:19), "he who began a good work in you will carry it on to completion" (Phil. 1:6), "In Christ There Is No East or West" — so many places, so many promises.

From Nigeria to California to Michigan to China, God has filled my life with his promises, his encouragement, and his good grace. Every now and then something triggers the gratitude switch in me, and I am overwhelmed by how he works in my life.

Think back to the time when you committed your life to Christ. Trace God's presence and work in you between then and today. Whether your stories take you across continents or only across town, recount his goodness and grace in your life, and you will see that he who began a good work in you is carrying it out. Let us all praise the power of Jesus' name — in every language all across the world — for bringing his work to completion in us.

Cups of Water

Rosemary Apol '87   Matthew 10:40-42
Nurse/teacher; Grand Rapids, Michigan

A few years ago my church joined our city's first chapter of the Inter-
faith Hospitality Network, a program which helps churches house
homeless families. About once every three months our church's classrooms
and fellowship hall are transformed for one week into bedrooms, a living
room, a game room — in short, a home for three or four families.

When I first heard of this program, I thought it sounded like a good
one, though I gave no thought to becoming involved personally. An unhappy chapter in our church's history had recently closed, and, if I hadn't
been married to the minister, I might have taken a leave of absence from
church. But then someone asked me not just to volunteer but to become
one of the chairpersons for the entire program. Oddly, I found myself saying yes.

Since then I have marveled at the quiet service of volunteers — a grandmother who comforts a squalling baby at two in the morning, a teenage
boy who tirelessly pulls a young child around and around in a wagon, a retired professor who curls up on the floor with a troubled three-year-old
and does the only thing that soothes the little boy — reading *Dinosaur Bob*
over and over again. It all restored what had become for me a jaded vision
of the church.

Offering a cup of cold water is not always easy. There are those who
don't want it. Others take it readily enough but without a trace of gratitude. Still others fail to note what is offered but complain about what they
perceive to be lacking.

In Matthew's Gospel, immediately after Jesus talks about cups of cold
water, he receives a message from John the Baptist, who is languishing in
prison. John wants to know whether Jesus really is the Christ after all, since
not much seems to be happening in the world. In reply Jesus sends messengers to tell John the things that are happening, including the fact that
good news is being preached to the poor.

Cups of cold water may not seem like much. They don't appear to
change the world. But we offer them anyway, and somehow we know this is
what we are called to do. Somehow we know that through small actions
like these Jesus is changing the world.

The Path to Peace

Isaiah 55:6-12

Jacki Bruxvoort Matter '78
Secretary; Lynden, Washington

"For my thoughts are not your thoughts, neither are your ways my ways," declares the LORD. (Isa. 55:8)

Decisions, decisions, decisions — we face them all the time. Some are easy — what to eat, what to wear, what brand to buy — but others are more difficult and more important, affecting us for a lifetime — whether to go to college, which career to pursue, whether to marry, whom to marry, how many children to have.

How we face these decisions in life is the key to peace. Do we flip a coin, weigh the pros and cons, take the advice of a trusted friend, or do we turn to the true source of wisdom — God and his Word?

When faced with important decisions, what we really must ask ourselves is this: What is God's will for me in this matter? What does he think is best for me? To do this we must immerse ourselves in prayer and spend time in his Word. Only by seeking God's will and following it will we know God's perfect peace, a peace which comes from knowing he loves us and has our best interests at heart.

Several years ago my husband and I faced a choice of how to build our family. We had two birth children and desired a larger family, but we wanted to seek God's will about how we should do that. Through much prayer, God led us down a path which included a miscarriage, foster children, and ultimately the adoption of three siblings, ages five, seven, and eight. As we prayed for direction, God began to close certain doors in our life and open others. He nudged us gently in a direction we had never considered in the beginning, and he prepared our hearts for this new and exciting possibility. As we followed his leading, we discovered true peace. God led us and surprised us in a marvelous way, and we look forward to more surprises as we seek his will in the decisions of our lives.

No, the paths God leads us down are not always the easy ones (we now have five teenagers!), but they are the right ones and the best ones — because they are God's.

Joy in the Journey

Eric Arnoys '92
Calvin professor; Wyoming, Michigan

Matthew 25:14-30

During my sophomore year of college I headed to the Smoky Mountains for a nontraditional spring break. I had never really hiked before, but I was ready. At least I was ready for the highs provided by mountaintop scenery and the exhilaration of achievement. And I did experience these things. But I was not prepared for what else I would face — fatigue, worry, and the pain that accompanied lugging an overweight backpack on rough terrain in unpredictable weather. By the last day of our hike I could think of nothing better than being rid of my pack and relaxing in front of a campfire.

In recent years, hiking has become much more enjoyable. My backpack is (usually) much lighter now, and my pace shows less urgency. On most hikes I focus on the journey to my destination rather than on the destination alone, and I work to enjoy the people with me and the creation surrounding me.

My old attitude of neglecting the present in deference to the future is often visible in the church as well. Jesus calls our attention to it in Matthew 25:14-30, where we find the parable of the talents. In this story the master becomes most angry with the servant who buries his money in the ground because of worry about the future. Like him, we, too, sometimes imagine that we merely need wait out the present until Christ comes and makes everything right. We too often find comfort in insulating ourselves from the difficult journey we face by looking beyond the journey to the journey's end.

But we were not put here on earth simply to sit on our hands awaiting Christ's return. We are Christ's agents on earth, joint heirs and stewards of the King. Everything that God has created is a gift, and we are to hold it and care for it as the Giver would want us to. Someday soon we will reach the destination of life's journey. In the meantime, there is much to do and plenty to see. We would do well to take our calling seriously, engaging ourselves in every moment along the way.

The Presence of God

Psalm 27:1-3

Ilga Svechs '58
Professor; Cleveland, Ohio

As an eight-year-old child in a Nazi detention camp, I learned quickly that death is a daily phenomenon. I also learned that God is and that God cares.

I have gone through the experiences of my life with the firm conviction of God's presence and with the knowledge that the greatest gift Christ left us is his ever-present Spirit in all that we do and in all that we are and are becoming. This knowledge inspires me to acknowledge life as a gift and as an opportunity given by God toward our spiritual development here and for the hereafter, where we will engage in the eternal glorification of our Creator.

God leads us in unique ways throughout this life and with a purpose which transcends our human understanding, but we do understand that he is with us in the ever-present Holy Spirit, a gift of our living Savior. As a child I opened my heart to his presence while I was witnessing the daily evil of humankind's utter inhumanity. It was then that I knew, and today I still know, that we live in God and we die in God. His living presence is with us under all circumstances because we are children of God.

In the awareness of being a child of God, one is continually blessed with the gradual development of a profound conviction about the uniqueness of the self. Although similar to others, we are all simultaneously unique in our talents and our destinies, as determined by the Creator. Thus, to love God and to fear God is to treasure the divinely determined uniqueness of one's self and of one's neighbor. The society of my childhood did not heed God's mandate to love one's neighbor as oneself because it denied this knowledge about our Creator. Instead, it divided human beings into its own self-serving categories and thus heaped up atrocity upon atrocity.

From human history we learn that the greatest testament to faith is to work toward a society that treasures the divinely ordained uniqueness of each individual, a society that will eliminate the breeding grounds for prejudice against and hatred toward the God-given qualities that make people unique.

Curtain Calls

Tim Douma '75   John 11:24-25
Pastor; Chicago, Illinois

> *Martha answered, "I know he will rise again in the resurrection at the last day."*
> *Jesus said to her, "I am the resurrection and the life. He who believes in me will*
> *live, even though he dies. . . ."* (John 11:24-25)

We came to opera later in life. A benefactor gave us tickets, and now we're subscribers. It's not that we're mavens, but we are enchanted. Maybe the magic is that opera portrays something true and wonderful about the human condition in spite of implausible plotlines that require huge leaps of faith. I know it's the simple and profound joy of being surrounded by beauty. We have no pretense about sophistication. We simply want Puccini to stir our souls. And he does. After a recent performance of *La Boheme*, we met friends in the lobby, and the gentleman said, "No matter how many times I see it and even though I know what is coming, it always gets me." If the musical *Rent*, the contemporary update of *La Boheme*, is half as mesmerizing, it's no wonder it's an award winner.

What gets us is the final act, where, after a long and bitter winter, Mimi returns in spring to her first love, Rodolfo, in order to die in his arms. Of course, I cried. And I cried again at the curtain call when Mimi came to take her bows. I cried for joy because she was alive. Silly me?

The hardest thing we face in life is dealing with loss, and the greatest loss we face is death. Our tears at the opera find their ultimate reference in the tears we shed at death. Jesus did too. "Jesus wept" (John 11:35). At death.

For losses in life and for deaths, we weep. But we grieve not as those who are without hope, because Jesus said, "I am the resurrection and the life" (John 11:25). There will be a curtain call at the end of the age, and then we'll see those we love alive again in a plot more wonderful than Puccini's: Grandma, Justine, Annie, Carla . . . alive again in everlasting life. And then we'll weep for joy.

Strength for the Weary

Isaiah 40:31

Lance Engbers
Calvin parent/school administrator;
Whitinsville, Massachusetts

But those who hope in the LORD will renew their strength. They will soar on wings like eagles; they will run and not grow weary, they will walk and not be faint. (Isa. 40:31)

Can you imagine unlimited strength and energy for the tasks you face every day? After exhausting meetings, a demanding basketball practice, and hours of struggling with your child to complete today's homework, you're sapped of all strength and perspective. What you need is a little peace and quiet and some soothing comfort. You'd like to believe the words of the prophet Isaiah, but he offers such unreasonable promises for renewed strength that you wonder. Soaring on wings like eagles? Running and not growing weary? Walking without fainting?

Without exception, runners completing a race — a marathon or even a 5K — are tired, exhausted, ready to drop (some do). Their energy, dispensed gradually, is usually calculated for depletion by the end of the race. The runner's objective is to last the longest, move the fastest, and avoid emptying all resources before the finish line. What is the secret diet, the magic formula, that unlocks the mysterious biblical promise that you "will run and not grow weary" (Isa. 40:31)?

The key to endless strength and energy is found in the first phrase of Isaiah 40:31: Those who hope in or wait on the Lord will renew their strength. Hoping in or waiting on the Lord anticipates some kind of event beyond one's own limited strength. In the face of it, before God, and in humility, we declare, "Take my heart, the core of my being, and renew me for service to you." It is an act of total trust, dedication, and devotion without reservation. It seems peculiar that the key to running without growing weary is not strong calf muscles, not an exercise program, not off-season training, not some faddish diet, and not some inspirational gimmick. In fact, the key appears to be quite unsophisticated — hoping in and waiting upon the Lord.

People may soar, run, and walk, but they also sometimes tire and fall. When we stumble while walking, trip while running, or fall after soaring, God swoops beneath us and with the strength of eagles' wings carries us with renewed energy to unanticipated heights — if we put our hope in him. So hope without weariness and soar in his service!

Providence near Disneyland

Ronald Wells   Psalm 139:1-10
Calvin professor; Grand Rapids, Michigan

The doctrine of providence usually comes to us in an abstract theological package. In practice, however, most of us understand providence to refer to the ways, beyond our knowing, that God cares for us. Let me tell a story of how I engaged providence outside Disneyland.

My business in Los Angeles was completed earlier than expected. I had never been to Disneyland, so I took a city bus out to Anaheim. I checked the time of the last return bus and then enjoyed an afternoon out in a place where even a serious historian can be a kid again. I got back to the bus stop as the winter dusk fell, only to see the bus — the last bus — pulling away. As darkness fell, I considered my options. I didn't have taxi fare back to L.A. (this was before ATMs). Already spooked by the gathering darkness and feeling unsafe, I decided to hitch a ride. But at the traffic light outside Disneyland, few people even rolled down their windows, and those who did weren't going my way.

After an hour of this, it was now fully dark, and I was fully scared. I sat on a bench and watched the next group of cars approach the light. To my astonishment the rear window of the first car had a Calvin College sticker on it. As I stumbled silently toward the car, someone inside called out, "That's Ronald Wells." Hearing my baptized name called out in the Anaheim darkness was as wonderful as it was illumining. The speaker was Lisa Cooke, a former student of mine; the driver of the car was Rev. Ed Cooke, then pastor of Rosewood CRC of Bellflower. I got in the car and was soon safely back in Los Angeles.

Some will call this luck or coincidence. Perhaps so. I think it was God's care for me in a way I can't fully explain. I don't pray for parking spaces in malls, and now I watch bus schedules carefully. But beyond my taking responsibility for my own life, there is God's undefinable care, for which I give thanks daily.

Running on Full

Philippians 2:1-11

James C. Dekker '69
Pastor; Thunder Bay, Ontario

There I was, in Thunder Bay Airport security, watching the nearly empty plane leave thirty-five minutes earlier than I had mistakenly written in my day planner. My wallet would be a hundred dollars emptier after I rebooked. Feeling as empty as my wallet was about to be, I waited for a taxi home. Because it was raining, the wait was long. A dozen people grabbed cabs ahead of me. Some looked full of their own importance, ordering baggage handlers around like slaves. Others ran out of the terminal, full of life, into the arms of lovers, friends, or family. One woman drifted back and forth, tears staining her cheeks, sometimes sobbing, waiting for someone who had not come by the time I left. A puzzling mix we were — some filled with purpose and life's good things, others running on empty for trivial or profound reasons. By tomorrow the mix would change.

But God wouldn't. The earth and all its mysterious, puzzling fullness was, is, and ever will be the Lord's. But according to the grace-filled rules God gave and personally followed, there is no eternal fullness without daily, joyful emptying. We usually don't get that point very well, but we can see astonishing hints of God's fullness if we look.

I grew up in Roseland, Chicago, blessed with a father who more than once gladly gave up promotions because he placed my mother, us children, and our church higher than company executive status. Calvin College filled my life with teachers who gave up possible national academic prestige to fill empty kids from Bellflower to Denver, from Lynden to Roseland, from Paterson to Lake Worth with goals and hopes beyond high pay and publications.

Later, Central America filled my family's life with friend Maria Rosalinda Ortega and colleague Noel Vargas. Both gave their hearts promptly and sincerely and eventually their lives. They followed their Lord Jesus' surrender to violence and oppression so others could live with physical health, with spiritual hope. I won't be full up until I see them in the fullness of God's time, when we'll all bow before the ever-emptying Christ, who fills all hearts' desires.

Harambees

Jotham Ippel '97   2 Corinthians 8:1-7, 9, 16-21
Missionary; Kenya, East Africa

Miriam Ippel '99
Campus ministry; Grand Rapids, Michigan

In this passage Paul is writing to the Corinthian church about the Jerusalem collection — an offering for the distressed Christians in Jerusalem. In Kenya this kind of effort is called *harambee*, which is a cooperative action, often including fund-raising, for a common goal. The Corinthian contribution toward the harambee for Jerusalem, however, had been put on hold because of problems and divisions within the Corinthian church.

Paul takes time in his letter to remind the Corinthians about the importance of restarting the harambee. He encourages the Corinthian Christians with the example of the Macedonians, who did not stop to calculate how much they could afford or check their tax returns to determine the amount they should give. Paul backed up these words by sending the Corinthian church a helper, Titus, a person familiar to this community.

The story of the harambee in Corinth is relevant in the life of the church today. One of its underlying principles is that even if you don't have, you can still give. In Kenya even a poor person will wish to give you chai to drink the first time you come to visit. We North Americans, however, who do have rich resources available to help others, are sometimes like the Corinthians, stalled in supporting the poor because of internal conflicts, indecisiveness, lack of focus, and, all too often, the desire to finish other projects that we have already begun. Sometimes we fail to see the urgency of a problem because it is far away from us.

The message Paul gives to us is that we need to give to and to take time for people in need. He urges us to focus not on what we don't have but on what we do have and can give. God can use us not only to provide needed finances; he also can work through us to heal the brokenness in society — if we are willing to give our time and energy and ideas.

Today is a good day to examine ourselves and learn from our mistakes. If we do so, we may be able to help heal the church and restart the harambees in our own communities.

Learning to Trust a Slow God

Psalm 40

John Van Regenmorter '70
Chaplain; Hudsonville, Michigan

I waited patiently for the Lord; he turned to me and heard my cry.

(Ps. 40:1)

Yesterday I hurriedly called a colleague to ask, "Hey, Pete, what's your e-mail address? I want to send you something right away."

Pete calmly replied, "I don't have e-mail." Mildly flustered, I called him a dinosaur and hung up.

We live in an age in which everything is supposed to happen fast. Instantly. From instant mashed potatoes to instant credit, we want service and satisfaction right now. We even carry our demands for instant action into our relationship with God. In the age of e-mail and e-commerce, we want a God who acts fast. When illness strikes, we want a God who will bring quick relief. When unexpected trouble bowls us over, we want a God who will pick us right up. If a son or daughter wanders from the faith, we want a God who will bring him or her back right now.

The Bible teaches us that God can — and sometimes does — act instantly on our behalf. But we must come to see that God's pace is not always fast. For reasons that we do not always understand, God sometimes chooses to take his time.

That's a lesson David had to learn. It is obvious from Psalm 40 that David knew what it was like to be a wanted man living away from his homeland. His enemy, King Saul, had been trying to pin him to the wall for years. David must have wondered whether he would always be a man on the run, with a price on his head. It seemed that he would never be released from the threats on his life. But by the time he wrote this psalm, Saul had died, and David was free.

It is never easy to wait patiently for the Lord. No one ever promised that it would be.

Change of Plans

Donna Praeger Walter '64
Evangelism director;
North Haledon, New Jersey

Acts 16:6-10; Jeremiah 29:10-14

If you were asked what you really wanted in life, you might say meaningful friendships, a fulfilling marriage, healthy children, or an exciting career. We all dream about what we think would make us happy, and we plan accordingly. If our dreams change over time, we adjust our plans. We go back to school or retire to another place and climate.

But life is rarely as we plan it to be. Good friends move away; loved ones die young; work can become frustrating. Perhaps our health reins us in, forcing us to face the reality that, though we wish we could do much more, God has other things in mind for us. When our dreams are thwarted, we feel our life is on hold. Then God gently teaches us this *is* our life.

The apostle Paul dreamed of going to the province of Asia. According to Acts 16:6, however, "he and his traveling companions were kept by the Holy Spirit from preaching the Word in the province of Asia." They traveled throughout Phrygia and Galatia instead. When they tried to enter Bithynia, the Spirit of Jesus would not allow them to go there either. So much for well-made plans. They journeyed instead down to Troas. Did Paul go to bed that night wondering, "Where next?" The Lord did not disappoint him. During the night Paul had a vision that they were to go over to Macedonia, and immediately following the vision, the group got ready to leave, concluding that God had called them to preach the gospel there instead.

How quickly do we respond to God's leading? As quickly as Paul, or do we wallow in our bitterness about broken dreams? Paul's plans were good, but they weren't God's plans. God's vision was better, and Paul's group knew this. Just as the Lord had plans for his Old and New Testament children, he reminds us today, "I know the plans I have for you . . . plans to prosper you and not to harm you, plans to give you hope and a future" (Jer. 29:11). He promises to be actively involved in our lives. Our response is to call upon him, pray, and seek him with all our heart. God, our plan maker, promises us in return that we will find him.

The Chief End

Colossians 3:17

Virginia Miller Lettinga '77
Professor; New Brighton, Minnesota

S ometimes I feel like a traitor. I was brought up in the Christian Reformed Church, but I like the first question and answer of the Westminster Shorter Catechism better than that of the Heidelberg. Maybe it's the Presbyterian roots on my mother's side. Maybe it's that I didn't learn it in a dimly lit church room with poor ventilation, as I did the Heidelberg.

Q: What is the chief end of man?
A: Man's chief end is to glorify God, and to enjoy Him for ever.

I now teach these two lines to my college classes each year. I help them understand "man" as the old inclusive form we now call "human," and I emphasize how inclusive the "chief end" is. I tell them, "You do not need to be intelligent to glorify and enjoy God. You do not need to be healthy. You do not need to be a responsible adult, nor do you need to be young and alert. If you were driving down the freeway tomorrow and suffered a tragic accident and were paralyzed for the rest of your life, your ability to fulfill this chief end would be unchanged. If your daughter was born with a flawed chromosome and never managed to learn to read or write, her chief end would be unchanged. This is an amazingly great — and achievable — end to which God has called us."

I think I love this question and answer because I have discovered that I really believe these words. Sixteen years ago our son was born three and a half months early. We were threatened by bankruptcy from a third of a million dollars of hospital bills; our child was predicted to have serious, lifelong limitations; my graduate-school career was in shambles; and the medication to hold off birth had left me with serious health complications.

But during that time I discovered that I really believe the words I had so blithely recited: My chief end is to glorify and enjoy God. None of these problems endangered or negated my, my husband's, or our child's ultimate calling and chief end. I sat in the midst of a North American tragedy and discovered true comfort.

Sweet Promises

Natalie Dykstra '86

Professor; Holland, Michigan

Exodus 20:1-2

> *And God spoke all these words: "I am the LORD your God, who brought you out of Egypt, out of the land of slavery."* (Exod. 20:1-2)

When God declares himself to the children of Israel, he first identifies himself by saying, "I am the LORD your God" (Exod. 20:2). What follows are the familiar Ten Commandments: We must not worship other gods; we must keep the Sabbath; we must not covet or steal or murder. These commandments enumerate what we must do and what we must not do. But these commandments also comprise a description of sorts. Indeed, the Ten Commandments address ways of acting in the world — worshiping false gods, envying your neighbor, stealing what is not yours, committing adultery — that are both born out of and result in some form of bondage. This is what bondage looks like, what it feels like, what it costs.

The good news is that God promises to deliver us from this bondage. When God declares that he is our Lord, he substantiates his claim by citing his past efforts at liberating his people. Which lord is he? He is the Lord who has brought his people "out of the land of Egypt, out of the land of slavery" (Exod. 20:2). His claim on us is that our belonging to him makes us free. So it is not the authoritative voice of God, but his abundant freedom, that commands us how to live. And the Ten Commandments seem less a list of rules to obey than a set of sweet promises to live within.

Trusting God's Plan

Jeremiah 29:11;
Genesis 37:12-18; 45:3-7

Marilyn J. Rietberg
Calvin parent/mental-health services;
Grand Rapids, Michigan

"For I know the plans I have for you," declares the LORD, *"plans to prosper you and not to harm you, plans to give you hope and a future."* (Jer. 29:11)

They happen when you least expect them, those experiences that alter your life forever. Mine began with a heart-stopping phone call: Our youngest son, Mark, age twenty-two, had been in a car accident and was in critical condition with a closed head injury.

For many days we kept a bedside vigil as Mark hovered between life and death. I often felt as though I were standing on the brink of an abyss. But hands reached across to us; countless people surrounded us with love, compassion, and prayer. The day after the accident our daughter shared with us Jeremiah 29:11. On subsequent days we often had a special verse for the day, some given to us by others and some coming softly in the still of the night. On the day Mark's condition reached a crisis, I clung to God's promise from Isaiah 43:2: "I will be with you." Yet it was the verse from Jeremiah that became our anchor. The Lord had indeed given hope that grew as our son survived and slowly began to emerge from his coma. We knew that God had given our son a future, though uncertain, and that it was in his hands.

The recovery process has been long and difficult, but it has been steady. Three years later Mark was able to return part-time to college. He has now been working with children in a preschool setting, and that has been rewarding for him. Although life took an unexpected turn, God has a plan for our son, and we take comfort that that plan will prosper him and give him hope and a future.

Sooner or later each of us faces trials, disappointments, and heartaches. Hope dims, and the future looks bleak. We wonder how this can possibly be part of God's plan for us. That is a good time to reread the story of Joseph, who surely experienced some of life's most difficult challenges. Yet God had a plan for his life, and Joseph trusted God's plan. In our darkest hour, like Joseph, we, too, can trust his plan for us. He will restore our hope and give us assurance that in him our future is secure.

God's Glory

Nicholas Wolterstorff '53   Psalm 19:1
Professor; New Haven, Connecticut

The heavens declare the glory of God. (Ps. 19:1)

The psalmist is struck with religious awe upon viewing the heavens; had he known what we now know, he would no doubt have found them even more awesome. The particular form his awe takes is that of finding the awesomeness of the heavens bespeaking the glory of God, their Maker.

References to God's glory abound in Scripture — "Glory to God in the highest" (Luke 2:14), "The glory of the Lord shone around them" (Luke 2:9). But what does it mean?

The biblical writers have in mind God's excellence. There's excellence all around us — the excellence of a fellow human being, the excellence of a sunset. But the excellence of God far transcends that of anything to be found in creation. God's excellence is glorious. The glory of God is God's supreme excellence.

The idea of God's glory is thus not a moral idea; it doesn't have to do with God's giving us a law for our lives. The psalmist also extols the law of God, the Torah, but, when he is awed by the glory of God, he has something even more fundamental about God in mind. The best analogue to contemplating the glory of God is contemplating the excellence of a painting. Glory and beauty aren't far apart.

Some people don't see it. When contemplating the heavens, they feel no religious awe, or, if they do, they do not see the awesomeness of the heavens as declaring the glory of the one who made them. Such people are blind to God's glory; they're like those who are blind to beauty. They are secular. To be secular is to fail to see the world and one's fellow human beings as displaying the supreme excellence of God.

Prominent in that version of the Reformed tradition which lies behind Calvin College is the image of God as lawgiver. More prominent in the original version of the tradition, that of John Calvin, is the near-aesthetic image of God as glorious. Calvin was echoing the awe felt by the biblical writers when face-to-face with the supreme excellence of God: Great and glorious is our God.

320

Knowledge and Love

1 Corinthians 13

Thomas K. Dykstra '57
Executive; Pittsford, New York

Now I know in part; then I shall know fully, even as I am fully known.
(1 Cor. 13:12)

It might seem a bit odd that this short commentary on knowledge pops up near the end of Saint Paul's sublime passage on love. But we must remember that one of love's attributes is its power to carry the moral burden of having knowledge. Certainly our knowledge needs such power. Without love, knowledge becomes arrogant, exploitative, and manipulative. Every day we see it happen: marital and familial abuse, political dirty tricks, international treachery, exploitation of our natural world, and the list goes on.

The old saying that a little knowledge is a dangerous thing is certainly true, but in a different sense, perfect knowledge would probably be even more deadly if it was not tempered by love. With our tendency toward sin, if we knew anything perfectly, our irresistible urge to exercise power over it would result in its destruction. The advantage we would wield over spouses, friends, and others would make them have to hide from us. So it's a good thing that for now we only "know in part" (1 Cor. 13:12).

There is, of course, one who knows everything, including each of us, completely and perfectly (Ps. 139). Fortunately, we need not hide from God as our friends would have to hide from us or as Adam and Eve mistakenly hid from God because they didn't realize that "perfect love drives out fear" (1 John 4:18). And the good news of today's text is that one day, when our capacity to love can handle it, we will have the delight of knowing fully even as we are now fully known.

Meanwhile, the message is clear: As we strive to know anything or anyone, we must strive even more to love so that our knowledge does not lead to sin. Because knowledge gives us power, what we need is the *agape* sort of love, the kind that neither needs nor expects a payback, the love Paul describes in 1 Corinthians 13.

Ask God daily for the love that sanctifies knowledge.

Melinda

Paul Diekema '88   Matthew 5:14-16
Teacher; Grand Rapids, Michigan

I remember Melinda well. She was born with spina bifida and wore two clumsy metal-and-leather braces that enabled her to walk, albeit awkwardly. Some days Melinda cried, frustrated by the stares of older students or her inability to run. Many days Melinda was absent, too sick for school. Most days she radiated happiness. What I remember most vividly about Melinda is her long, curly eyelashes, her loving smile, and her beautiful brown eyes, wide with joy.

Melinda died before we reached the second grade. The home bulletin ran a picture of her along with a brief eulogy. I don't remember crying, but I couldn't let go of Melinda, so I kept that newsletter. Coming across it over the years during my annual inventory adjustments, I would study her photo, read the eulogy, and then nestle it safely back into my paper archives. After twenty years of safekeeping, I hesitantly discarded the yellowed home bulletin, but in my mind's eye I still see the photo of Melinda, joy lighting her features.

Melinda was like a light on a hill, burning briefly but brightly for all to see. Her life beautifully illustrates for me how the seemingly insignificant can have a powerful effect. I sometimes imagine her watching from heaven, reminding me to share the love of God with others, even if only through a friendly smile or my zest for life. She shows me I don't have to be famous to qualify as a source of light for others. Life brought Melinda joy as only God's love could allow amidst her pain. And Melinda brought other people joy because her face was a reflection of Christ.

I thank God for Melinda and for many others who have blessed me with glimpses of Christ. They have given me comfort, hope, joy, and ever-strengthening faith. I pray that God will help me in the busyness of life to stay alert for little flashes of light from others and will help me to send out a few of my own. And I look forward to entering heaven one day, where I will see Melinda in the distance, run to take her hand, and dash off to the monkey bars with her to play, laugh, and talk as only healthy children can.

Mark 1:35 Ken Joling '77
Teacher, Olympia, Washington

I was once invited to work on a subcommittee for national teacher standards. My first thought was, "Where am I going to find the time? I'm a teacher, a husband, and the father of two very active young boys. There's just no way!" The subcommittee's responsibility? Professional reflection. Reluctantly I agreed to be part of the committee.

When we all got together, the committee members quickly agreed that reflection is important for growth, that we all reflect very unsystematically on what we do, and that teachers, ourselves included, need to think systematically about what they have done and are doing if they want to improve their teaching.

The consequences of unreflective teaching were obvious to us: Instead of thinking about what you are doing in relation to where you want to go, you become more focused on filling up tomorrow's class time than on preparing meaningful educational experiences that help students to grow personally and academically. We discovered, too, that when our profession became a drudgery to us, it wasn't the profession that was the problem; rather, it was the way we were applying ourselves.

As I went through this process with my colleagues, I found the parallels to my religious life compelling. When I didn't stop to think about what I was doing and why, I found myself going through the motions of worship and the Christian life, but without any purpose. The actions were there, but without meaning, and without purpose there is tedium rather than joy.

What I've come to realize is that there are always good reasons for me not to spend the time I should spend as a teacher and as a Christian reflecting on what I'm doing. However, I also know that both in my profession and in my walk with Christ, I must follow Luther's suggestion that the more I have to do, the more time I need to spend praying, reading, and reflecting.

Let Me Be a Light

Patti Navis Hathaway '82   Romans 12:1
Public speaker/writer; Westerville, Ohio

For most women who attended the spiritual retreat, it was one of those mountaintop experiences. But not for me. I spent most of the weekend in the valley, fighting for control of my soul. I had avoided going on this retreat for over two years because I knew I would be convicted of my excessive need to be in control. Prior to the retreat I had thought to myself, "You are doing such a great job managing your life. You've built a successful speaking business. You have a great husband, two adorable sons. What if you give up control? Will your whole life get messed up?" — as if I could manage my life more effectively than the Creator of the universe.

Sometimes we need to take stock of our lives and ask ourselves whether the saying "A person may know God, a person may walk with God, but yet not truly experience him" applies to us. There is a big difference between having Christ in your heart and having him on the throne of your heart. In church we sing the song "I Surrender All," yet many of us, if we were honest, would have to sing "I Surrender Some."

God calls us to be whole persons for him. This doesn't mean giving him only a part of us. It means allowing God to be an every-moment part of our lives. The result of our complete surrender is that we will be attractive to others because of our unique and life-changing relationship with God. Matthew 5:14-16 says, "You are the light of the world. . . . let your light shine before others, that they may see your good deeds and praise your Father in heaven" (NIVI).

When people are in the dark, they search for any light. We live in a dark world today. We must surrender our whole selves to God; we must be wholly consecrated to him so that we can be beacons of light in the darkness of this world.

Biking

1 Timothy 1:12-17

Gordon DeKruyter '56

Retired school administrator; Hudsonville, Michigan

Once only a dream, it was about to become a reality. Our goal was to make a cross-country biking trip from San Diego, California, to Jacksonville, Florida. The route would take us approximately 2,800 challenging miles. Little did I know this was to be an adventure which would deeply affect me personally because it put me in contact with a number of people I had never met before.

During the twenty-eight days of our trip, we saw from a unique perspective the beauty of God's nature in awesome mountains, barren deserts, and a rich variety of plant life. We also observed people from a number of cultures, nationalities, and lifestyles.

More important, however, were the unanticipated personal encounters we had with several people. There were the rich conversations with the driver of an eighteen-wheeler who had recently been to Promise Keepers and was now traveling from Michigan to San Diego. There was the missionary in San Diego who, the night before we headed east, shared with us the story of his accepting Christ's challenge for his life. We will not soon forget the "Praise the Lord" spoken by the Mexican family we could help after their car stalled along a mountain road. We still communicate by e-mail with a non-Christian young man who, after riding with us for two weeks, commented, "God has put you into my life for some purpose." And there was Nick, who rode with us for only one day in Texas but whom we could encourage as he told us about his search for faith.

Even though most Christians may never make a bike trip of this sort, their lives, too, are unpredictable adventures. And if they have a personal relationship with Christ, they will have adventures with promise. God gives purpose to each day's experiences.

May the Lord help you and me recognize and act on the opportunities that await us in the workplace or in our leisure today. May our personal relationship with him be reflected each day in all our words and deeds.

To Believe Is to Remember

Martin D. Geleynse ThM '73
Pastor; Stratford, Ontario

Psalm 78:1-17

M emory loss is a terrifying thing. Without memory you are alone in the world, floating like a dead leaf blown by the wind. Memory connects you to reality: to parents, brothers, sisters, and even to yourself. It determines who you are. Without memory you are nobody and do not belong anywhere. One terrifying form of forgetfulness is spiritual memory loss — the kind of lapse that can take away your faith and erode your relationship to God. Something like this happened once to the Israelites.

God had set the people of Israel free from their captivity in Egypt, but he did not let them wander in the desert to find their own paths. He was with them every step of the way and guided them by means of the column of cloud and fire. They followed him, and he led them to freedom. But then they forgot what he had done. They forgot God. Deliberately. The result was that they rebelled against the Lord and put him to the test.

A great comfort of the Christian faith is that God does not forget. The Lord knows our names; he remembers our place and situation. He chose us for himself before we were aware of him, and he will not forget us. Ever. Perhaps that is why near the heart of our faith is the Lord's Supper, which calls us to "remember and believe."*

Memory loss is a terrible thing, especially if we are the cause of it ourselves. If we deliberately forget, as our ancestors did in Psalm 78, then disobedience follows. Memory loss and disobedience always go together. God's Word calls us to be humble and not conceited, to go to school with the saints who walked with God and who can now teach us about the living God. God "commanded our ancestors to teach their children," the psalmist says, "so that the next generation would know [the statutes and the laws of God]. . . . Then they would put their trust in God and would not forget his deeds" (Ps. 78:5-7, NIVI).

To believe is to remember! To forget is to be lost.

The Messengers' Feet

Isaiah 52:7-10

Evelyn De Jong Diephouse '69
Pastor; Grand Rapids, Michigan

It's not hard to find people living in captivity today, whether to a corrupt regime in a poverty-stricken country or to the culture of violence in American cities. But it is hard to find people who can picture Isaiah's imagery of beautiful feet on the mountains, bringing news of rescue — since messengers don't come on foot very often anymore. "How beautiful upon the computer screen" (or over the cell phone) doesn't have quite the same poetic force.

As Isaiah sees it, though, the beauty of the messenger does not inhere in the qualities of the messenger or in the powers of the technology delivering the message; the beauty is in the message itself, in its good news, and that beauty flows over onto the messenger. The beauty of Isaiah's message is that it brings word of rescue and peace.

In war zones the question Who will reign here? means a lot more than just Who won? It's not a simple matter of who will get to lead; it's a matter of what life will be like in the future. Will the conquered people have peace and flourishing, or will they be slaves? The question Who will be in charge here? asks about the character of the conqueror. Is it someone who cares about the ordinary folk? Someone who is flattered by the wealthy? Someone who values honesty and justice?

In Isaiah 52 the answer to these questions is that the holy and righteous God of Israel is the one who rescues and reigns. It is the strength of his holy arm that sets the messengers' feet to running with the good news of salvation. God's integrity spills over onto the messengers and makes their footsteps welcome. God has plans for human flourishing that can make even the most unlikely persons serve him.

We are called to be messengers, announcing the arrival of God's realm — and so we are the messengers with beautiful feet. But the beauty of the news and the guarantee of the outcome do not depend on us. God strengthens our lame feet and makes them beautiful so that all ends of the earth will want to join us in rejoicing over the message they bring.

Work as Ministry

John Bernbaum '65   2 Corinthians 5:20
University president; Moscow, Russia

I like the word *laity*, which is derived from the Greek word *laos* and is used in the Bible to refer to "the people of God." It is an inclusive word, a word that encompasses everyone from prestigious leaders to the most powerless. However, this word has fallen into disuse today; in fact, most young people are completely unfamiliar with the term.

In Protestant circles as well as among Catholic and Orthodox believers, the old pre-Reformation distinction between "ordinary" people and professionally trained church leaders continues. Clergy, missionaries, and evangelists are often treated in the evangelical community, too, as individuals with a "higher calling." This distorted view of spirituality gives prominence to professional clergy and places everyone else in a lower, less spiritual category.

According to the Bible, all Christians are the people of God; there is no first-class or second-class status in the family of faith. All of us, as followers of Jesus Christ, have a calling, and this calling affects all facets of our lives, including our work.

This is good news, an exciting challenge. As the people of God, as laity, we are all ministers. Some of us are ministers of technology; others are ministers of homemaking; still others are ministers of education, ministers of business, or ministers of medicine. All of us have been gifted by God with our own abilities and skills. As we use these skills today in the marketplace, we are serving as ministers of God. No Christian's work is second-class work. It is all sacred service, meant to glorify God and serve our neighbors.

Viewed biblically, every Christian has ministerial rank. After all, if we are going to be ambassadors of the King, ministerial rank is required. May God grant us the strength, insight, and commitment to live as his ministers today.

In Everything Give Thanks

1 Thessalonians 5:16-18

John H. Bratt '34
Calvin professor emeritus;
Grand Rapids, Michigan

Give thanks in all circumstances, for this is God's will for you in Christ Jesus.
(1 Thess. 5:18)

Prepositions are mostly very small words, but they can be rather important parts of speech. Notice that the apostle Paul does not say to the
Thessalonian church, "*For* all circumstances give thanks." If one suffers
from terminal cancer, loses a child by death, or suffers severe losses in one's
investments, it is difficult for the Christian, if not impossible, to thank
God for those experiences. But "*in* all circumstances" is a different story.
No matter how excruciating or heart-wrenching your experience may be,
there is something in that experience for which to thank God.

In the case of terminal cancer, there are drugs which can alleviate the
pain; in the loss of a loved one, there is the comfort of friends and the so-
lace of the Spirit; in the case of bad investments, there is still bread on the
table. As the old saying has it, "Every dark cloud has a silver lining."

In the year 1943 or 1944 I met the epitome of thankfulness in adversity. He was the custodian of a church. He had lost his wife after a few years
of marriage; he had had rheumatoid arthritis for years, so his hands and
fingers were horribly misshapen; he had little of this world's goods; but he
exuded thankfulness. Once when he was reflecting on the past year, these
words came involuntarily from his lips: "What grace! What marvelous
grace God has shown to me!" That man was a living example of the kind of
thankfulness called for by the apostle Paul. He was a natural at giving
thanks.

But this attitude is not an option for the Christian, not something we
may choose to exercise or to ignore. It is laid upon us as a command. "For
this," says Paul, "is God's will for you in Christ Jesus" (1 Thess. 5:18).

Identity Crisis

James B. LaGrand '90
Professor; Shiremanstown, Pennsylvania   Exodus 6:7

> *I will take you as my own people, and I will be your God.* (Exod. 6:7)

Many voices in recent years have been telling us that true happiness and contentment will come once we cast off the old-fashioned identities given to us in the past. We will be released from these restrictions and truly find ourselves in chat rooms, online shopping centers, and hobby groups tied together only by new communications technology. Advertisements ask us, "Who do you want to be?" and promise that because of technology the answer is now finally within our control.

We are supposed to be excited about this, but I have found that even hearing about such fervent attempts to create new identities makes me anxious. I can't imagine anything more fleeting and temporary than an identity that is tied to an alias in cyberspace. Perhaps even those of us who have not fully jumped into the new technological world feel the tugs on us from different directions. What trouble me are not the restrictions from the past but the challenges of every new day, for my identity is sometimes spread too thin to be anything authentic and stabilizing. That is why God's promise that he will be our God and that we are his chosen people is so important and so comforting — especially in our times. Our identity is fixed in him. We have a place to stand and a place to rest. This is the true contentment, even in a technologically advanced world that presents a myriad of new opportunities to us.

Thinking about the identity that God gives to his chosen people, I can reaffirm that I am not my own — nor am I Microsoft's, a marketer's, or a global economic community's — but I belong to my faithful Savior, Jesus Christ.

A God Who Sings

Zephaniah 3:17

Dale Topp '59
Calvin professor; Grand Rapids, Michigan

The LORD your God is with you, he is mighty to save. He will take great delight in you, he will quiet you with his love, he will rejoice over you with singing.
(Zeph. 3:17)

Have you ever discovered a verse of Scripture that has been there all the time? That was true for me with this verse, which a student pointed out to me well past my fiftieth year. Evidently I simply had not been ready to absorb its rich meaning at an earlier time. When I was struck by it, however, its impact was powerful.

I find it incredible that God should rejoice over me with singing — that *God* should rejoice over *me* with singing! Singing is supposed to go the other way: We are supposed to rejoice over God with our singing.

Why is it such a stretch to claim the rich meaning of this verse? One reason may be our aversion to any form of pride. Some of the communities in which we grew up continue a long tradition of fighting pride in any form. Though I admire that desire, I fear that it also can tone down honest thankfulness to God for the unique and powerful gifts he has given us. A second reason we may have difficulty claiming the message of this verse for our daily lives is the weakness of our imagination. We are unable to make the mental picture of a loving father God rejoicing over his children in song. Richard Foster, in his book *Prayer*, suggests a picture helpful for me:

> One day a friend of mine was walking through a shopping mall with his two-year-old son. The child was in a particularly cantankerous mood, fussing and fuming. The frustrated father tried everything to quiet his son, but nothing seemed to help. Then, under some special inspiration, the father scooped up his son and, holding him close to his chest, began singing an impromptu love song. None of the words rhymed. He sang off-key. And yet, as best he could, this father began sharing his heart. The child relaxed and became still, listening to this strange and wonderful song. "Sing it to me again, Daddy!"

This is the kind of God Zephaniah has in mind in verse 17 of chapter 3. When we need God's help, God's comfort, God's quietness, our best prayer may simply be, "Please pick me up, God, and sing to me."

Tending God's Mysteries

Lisa De Boer '88   1 Corinthians 4:1

Professor; Santa Barbara, California

> *So then, you ought to regard us as servants of Christ and as those entrusted with the secret things of God.* (1 Cor. 4:1, NIVI)

If I was asked to pick a favorite verse, I would pick 1 Corinthians 4:1. I am a teacher. In the day-to-day rush of preparing classes, attending meetings, grading, conversing with students, keeping up with colleagues, and trying to keep my office in some semblance of order, I don't often make the time to stop and think about what it is I am really doing. Probably most of us don't make the time to stop and think about what we're really doing. Lack of time might even be a convenient excuse for our neglecting to do so.

Stopping to think can be demoralizing, even frightening. Are students learning from me what they need to learn or just what I can teach? What is the value of what I am teaching? What are students learning from me besides the content of my courses? What about those students who are not doing well? Parents, business people, pastors, students — we can all make our own list of scary questions.

Contemplating what we do, why we do it, and how others receive it can produce a sensation of spiritual vertigo. Comforting, human-sized answers are mysteriously hard to pin down. As Lionel Basney expresses it in "Dream of the School," a poem he wrote some years ago, we "work in the bewilderment of time," unable to see how our words, our deeds, our thoughts, our decisions will work in this world.

Rather than trying to deny these mysterious unknowns, though, or take flight from them, Paul exhorts us to be stewards of mysteries — of God's own mysteries. Paul couples this idea of stewarding God's mysteries with an exhortation to serve Christ. Tending mysteries is service to Christ. By serving Christ, we will become stewards of mystery. What an evocative description of the dynamic of faithful life! There are not many easy answers here, just a deep affirmation of our participation in God's own mysterious work. Where and how do you encounter God's mysteries?

Silent Light

Isaiah 60:1-3

Annelies Knoppers '67
Professor, Bergen, Netherlands

As I was growing up, I believed that, if I had faith the size of a mustard seed, there would always be light in the darkness. Now, having lived more than a half century, I have discovered that my image of God as an ever-present night-light has changed. There have been moments of complete darkness when no light was possible. My mustard-seed-size faith shrank. But now my perspective has changed.

I currently live in the Netherlands, a country well-known for its bicycles. All bicycles are required to have a working light (and bell). Every morning as I bike in the dark over the bike path, there are moments when I am all alone in the quiet dark. Then, all at once, in the distance I see a small light moving toward me. I have no idea who (and what) is on the bike, only that it is a quiet light in the dark. In the distance I see other lights silently crisscrossing through the countryside. After a while daylight gradually and silently begins to drive the dark away. As is usual for this country, there is often no sun, but there is light. Since the Netherlands is a country where it rains a great deal, every so often a rainbow appears. It hangs silently in the sky, hugging the earth in its multicolored purity, and a few minutes later it has disappeared silently without a trace.

These are the ways I now experience God as light. I can go through stretches of dark without a light coming in my direction, but eventually one will appear, not harsh or blinding but like a quiet bicycle light, a sunrise, or a rainbow. The night always ends, and the sun always rises. Always silently. This is how I perceive that God becomes visible in my life: through other people like the silent bicyclists with their lights and also through the reappearing daylight and occasional rainbow. God may not be visible or perhaps not even seem present sometimes, but he will always reappear.

Heaven's 'Great Multitude'

Douglas Bratt '80   Revelation 7:9-10
Pastor; Silver Spring, Maryland

When the apostle Paul attempts to describe heaven, he must admit it defies even the most fertile human imagination. However, the awareness of that difficulty doesn't stop the apostle John from portraying at least one aspect of heaven: its "great multitude" (Rev. 7:9).

On this side of heaven much divides Christians: factors like income level, denominational affiliation, worship style, education, and, above all, race. So we can hardly imagine what could unite us in the face of all the high barriers so frequently separating us.

John, however, can envision such unity. When he describes the prismatic myriad of people he sees crowding around Christ's heavenly throne, he talks not about many individual groups but about one multitude. The Holy Spirit showed John that in heaven God's great grace will unite his now-divided children into one exuberant worshiping community.

This dazzling vision of heaven should help give our daily lives the shape of things to come, for it challenges Christians of all nations, tribes, peoples, and languages to show that we're already united in Jesus Christ. European-Americans like me — and perhaps like you — have made it difficult for some people to feel and demonstrate that Christian unity. In the past we've even sometimes used God's Word to justify appalling enslavement and mistreatment of people of various colors, and many of us have done far too little to eradicate the noxious weed of racial prejudice within our own hearts.

So how could John's vision of heaven shape your life and mine today? Could it prompt us to respond to God's grace by confessing to God and each other our mistreatment of people, including Christians, of other races and ethnic backgrounds? Could it summon us, through the power of the Holy Spirit, to grieve over, hate, and run away from our racial prejudices?

By God's grace and healing power, such confession and repentance can help pave the way for more genuine fellowship and worship with other Christians, whatever their race or skin color. It certainly will help prepare us even today for life in God's heavenly presence with his people, our sisters and brothers in Christ from all nations, tribes, peoples, and languages.

'Oaks of Righteousness'

Isaiah 61:3   Peter Borgdorff '66
Denominational executive; Grand Rapids, Michigan

In the first stages of a new millennium, when much of society's attention is directed toward what can go wrong in the world and the momentous changes the human race will have to endure, my spirit is lifted up and my faith is increased by the message of the prophet Isaiah. He directs our attention to what God is doing in his redemptive work and how that activity is at the center of the message we believe and are called to live. The message is good news for the poor, a binding up for the brokenhearted; it promises freedom for captives and release for prisoners. The message promises hope in the place of mourning, beauty instead of decay, gladness rather than sadness, and praise instead of despair. What powerful encouragement!

The latter part of the twentieth century placed great emphasis on what individuals could achieve. Self-fulfillment and self-realization seemed to be the goal. Even spirituality and faithfulness were measured in terms of what a person had done for God. But the good news of Scripture is not about self-reliance. Rather, Isaiah points us to a greater reality, to God's purpose and goal for all who are to be counted among the redeemed: "They will be called oaks of righteousness, a planting of the LORD for the display of his splendor" (Isa. 61:3).

Can you imagine that? Majestic, enduring, and beautiful enough to be counted with the cedars of Lebanon. God does not do things halfway. If the crown of his creation is to have internal and eternal fellowship with the triune God, then externally, one day, for the whole world to see, the redeemed will display the magnificence of God's splendor. That is God's intent for us who are the sons and daughters of the living God.

There are many things that can discourage God's people. Certain events in life can be devastatingly painful. Fears about the new millennium — the environment, the stock market, AIDS, global warming, genetic mutations — can dominate our minds. At such times it is encouraging to return to the good news and from it to be reminded of God's intent and the certain outcome of his designs. Blessed be his name.

Pleroma!

Ron Nydam '70   John 10:1-10
Pastor/Calvin Seminary professor;
Grand Rapids, Michigan

The sweltering African heat had finally cooled into an evening mist that hovered all about a half-built sanctuary in the lush forest of central Ghana. With no moon shining in the heavens, it was wondrously dark. The cinder-block walls were up, but there was no roof on the building. No money for it, they said, but maybe churches are better without roofs anyway. At least this night it seemed that way. Instead, crooked branches broken from nearby trees held up torn blue tarps, which kept some of the rain out. These Christians in Ghana worship every night, so in the middle of the week the sanctuary was full. Worship is their life. They sat with flickering candles all around, praising God, bringing to God their joy for his rich blessings to them in the midst of their shoeless lives. Their joy was evident in their broad smiles, accentuated by the candlelight fighting back the darkness.

Without warning, I was asked to preach the Word. After only a few moments of reflection, I was led to speak of *pleroma* (play-roma), the word in the Bible for "fullness," for more than ample supply, when hearts and hands and stomachs have more than enough. It's the word you need to describe baskets on a hillside filled with bread and fish after five thousand people have been fed by Jesus. It's the word for the splendor of the banquet of the Christian life. It's the term that Jesus used when he said that he came to earth so that his sheep "may have life, and have it to the full" (John 10:10) — *pleroma.*

I spoke of our salvation being so much more than just forgiveness for our sins, an important corrective for unhappy Calvinists to know: There is more to the gospel than atonement. There is *pleroma* — the fullness of joy in the Spirit, who invites us to eat heartily and taste deeply the goodness of living in Christ. Yes, *pleroma* in the midst of all our suffering. Yes, *pleroma!* Candles in the open-air sanctuary, stars in the heavens, smiles on these faces. I asked the gathered congregation to say the word *pleroma.* But since Ghanians seldom use *l*'s in their native tongue, it came out *preroma* (pray-roma), the best the group could do. They grinned graciously both to themselves and to me. More smiles as this white man tried to talk about Jesus, tried to give witness in a faraway land to the truth that Jesus is Lord of richness in life, everywhere. But they already knew.

I taught them the word. They taught me its meaning.

Ephesians 1:4-14   Sheri Dunham Haan '62
                                                    Writer; Suttons Bay, Michigan

For he chose us in [Christ] before the creation of the world to be holy and blameless in his sight. (Eph. 1:4)

Already when it began, the world was bathed in hope. It was a hope of desire, its fulfillment sure because of the one who authored it.

As God stepped to the platform to begin his magnum opus, he carried hope in his heart. As he raised the baton of his voice to begin the symphony of creation, hope lived in his thoughts. And with his first breath, God almighty's immortal words brought forth not only light but also hope.

God breathed a great ball of fire and hurled it into its assigned orbit, giving it internal orders to rule the day. Then he flung the evening sentry high into the heavens, its instructions clear. With the ease of a child throwing glitter to the wind, Creator God threw countless stars into the heavens. And as he did, hope marched forward.

With stunning repetition, God's "Let there be" brought oceans of staggering size into being, each one knowing its boundaries. With the breath of his command, finned and feathered creatures appeared, each invisibly tethered to the intentions of its Designer. With mere words, the mite and the mammoth sea creature came to be, their instincts indelibly inscribed.

As each creation and creature played its melody in the Creator's grand symphony, hope was quickened.

Then God did a most amazing thing. Using his hands, he formed the crown jewels of creation, a man and a woman who would partner with him in sustaining the song of creation. They would be creatures of praise, yet far more: They would be the first of his beloved sons and daughters, the focus of hope, indeed, the reason for hope. From their creation God looked forward in time to the moment when hope would become flesh and be born in a manger.

Our Business

Lee Hardy   Matthew 4:19-20
Calvin professor; Grand Rapids, Michigan

There are two books my family reads together at Christmastime. One is *A Child's Christmas in Wales* by Dylan Thomas; the other is *A Christmas Carol* by Charles Dickens.

I imagine most of us remember how the Dickens tale begins. After grudgingly giving his employee, Bob Crachet, one day off for Christmas and pronouncing "Humbug!" on anyone who would wish him the returns of the season, Ebenezer Scrooge trudges off to his dim and austere lodgings only to be confronted by the ghost of his former business partner, Jacob Marley. Scrooge would like to dismiss this disconcerting presence as a hallucination produced, perhaps, by an ill-digested bit of beef. But the fearsome rattling of the chains wrapped about the shadowy figure convinces him otherwise. So he tries to placate the specter: "You always were good at business."

But the compliment touches a raw nerve. "Business!" cries the ghost, wringing its hands again. "Mankind was my business. The common welfare was my business; charity, mercy, forbearance, and benevolence, were all my business. The dealings of my trade were but one drop of water in the comprehensive ocean of my business!"

Evidently Jacob Marley, upon his death, acquired a broader view of his calling than he ever had in life. His repentant statement from beyond the grave should serve to remind us, too, that our vocations go far beyond the simple discharge of our occupational duties.

The Bible reminds us of this as well. If we consider the occurrences of the word *calling* in the New Testament, we will see that the primary, if not exclusive, meaning of this term refers to the calling of the gospel, pure and simple. We are called to repentance and faith (Acts 2:38); we are called into fellowship with Christ (1 Cor. 1:9); we are called out of the darkness and into the light (1 Pet. 2:9); we are called to be holy (1 Pet. 1:15; 1 Cor.1:2). Indeed, we are called to be saints (Rom. 1:7). In these passages we are not asked to choose from a variety of callings, to decide which one is right for us. Rather, one call goes out to all — the call of discipleship. It is incumbent upon all Christians to follow Christ and, in so doing, to become the kind of people God wants us to be.

What kind of people is that? A people who bear the fruit of the Spirit: love, joy, peace, patience, kindness, goodness, faithfulness, gentleness, and self-control (Gal. 5:22-23). Preparing our souls through prayer for the produce of the Spirit is what John Calvin calls the chief work of faith. As the ghost of Jacob Marley reminds us this season, it is also our most important business.

Our Greatest Joy

Revelation 21:1-4

Martin Essenburg '57
Missionary; Higashi Kurume Shi, Japan

Last night I attended a performance of Handel's *Messiah* in Tokyo. It was a very inspiring experience. Two hundred Japanese university students in the choir, a great orchestra, and outstanding soloists inspired us again through Handel's music and the words of Scripture. As I listened, I felt a little homesick, remembering how good it was to sing that oratorio each year when I was a Calvin student. I was transported in my mind back to the old college chapel on Franklin Street and to the Grand Rapids Civic Auditorium, and I gave thanks for all the good memories of choir rehearsals and performances.

But the beauty of the music and its message made me a little homesick for heaven, too. I felt a kind of holy aching for heaven, a longing for the day when we shall be "without spot among the assembly of the elect in life eternal."* If music can be this glorious here and now, imagine what it will be then and there! The idea made me remember a song we sang in my elementary school: "There's no disappointment in heaven, no weariness, sorrow or pain . . . "** And I recalled the refrain: "Sometimes I grow homesick for heaven . . . " I think it's good to experience this longing for heaven, but we need to keep our feet on the earth, too, advancing God's kingdom, sharing the good news of the gospel, and helping others through deeds of love and mercy. We do not want to be so heavenly minded that we are no earthly good, but the apostle Paul had it right when he said, "For to me, to live is Christ, and to die is gain" (Phil. 1:21).

May God enable us to serve him well through all our days on earth, and may we remember the words of Jesus to his disciples when they were rejoicing in their spectacular power and success. He told them not to rejoice in that but instead to "rejoice that your names are written in heaven" (Luke 10:20). May we find our greatest joy in that assurance of eternal life with him.

The Missing Day

Dewey Hoitenga, Jr. '52
Professor emeritus; Grand Rapids, Michigan

Mark 13:33

Be on guard! Be alert! You do not know when that time will come.

(Mark 13:33)

L ife is nothing if it is not being prepared. We saw this on a large scale at the turn of the year 2000, when the whole world prepared its computers for Y2K. We see it each day in our individual lives. We can't eat our daily breakfast unless we have prepared.

As it is with life, so it is with Jesus' coming again. We need to prepare, but when? There is no special day for it like Christmas, Good Friday, Easter, or Pentecost. On these days we look back to what Jesus has already done for us. We now have Advent, too, which was missing in my boyhood church. But during Advent, although we spend some time thinking about Jesus' second coming, we mainly prepare to celebrate his first.

As a boy, even without Advent I sometimes thought about Jesus' second coming, but I always hoped that he would wait until I grew up so I could drive a truck. Not the best way to prepare. Maybe a special day would have helped. But we still do not have one. It's a missing day in the church calendar.

Interestingly, Jesus asks us to observe only two events, his death (which we do in the Communion supper) and the day of his coming again. But when should we prepare for this? He gave us a clue: "Be alert! You do not know when that time will come" (Mark 13:33). It could be any day. So this is the day to prepare: every single day. The day isn't missing at all, but we often miss the day.

Jesus also told us how to prepare: "Trust in God; trust also in me" (John 14:1). Though simple, it's also profound advice, and sometimes difficult to affirm, especially every single day. As if to encourage us, however, Jesus went on to say, "I am going there to prepare a place for you . . . that you also may be where I am" (John 14:3). Think of it: He is preparing for us! A wonderful thought to help us prepare for his second coming — every day of the year.

He 'Who Made Himself Nothing'

Philippians 2:7

David Schelhaas '64
Professor; Sioux Center, Iowa

Your attitude should be the same as that of Christ Jesus: Who . . . made himself nothing, taking the very nature of a servant, being made in human likeness.
(Phil. 2:5-7)

Picture the Creator of the universe as a helpless babe. He who spoke creation into existence is able only to babble and cry as he waits until Mary is ready to feed him. How strange that God would use such a humiliating event — his Son becoming human — to thwart the evil one for all eternity. Yet when Christ put on human flesh and was born in a barn, Satan was dealt a deathblow. The poet Robert Southwell depicts, almost humorously, the panic in Satan's domain brought on by Christ's birth:

All hell doth at His presence quake,
Though He Him self for cold do shake.*

But what a comedown it was for the Son of God to become the Son of Man. Christ "made himself nothing," Paul tells the Philippians, so don't you go chasing after personal honors. Be like him. One of the saddest things about the church today is that it has bought into the star system of popular culture. How we fawn over big-name politicians, millionaires, athletes, and preachers. If we could only get close to them — touch the hems of their garments — how happy we would be. How excited we get when someone we know achieves star status in the eyes of the world.

Why are we so seduced by the lives of the rich and famous? Christ's birth, his life, his teachings, all argue against the star system. "Become as a little child," he says. The "first shall be last." The "greatest will be a servant." All of us know these truths. We can recite them from memory. But recitation of words is not what Christ wants.

Of course, the Christ who took on the form of a servant was also the infant King. And we who have been adopted into his family share his royalty, become "a royal priesthood." We who were nobodies are now somebodies. Still, we serve in humble anonymity until that heavenly day when "his children gather round / bright like stars, with glory crowned."** Now *there's* a star system that's worth getting excited about.

341

Perfect Comfort

Thomas Newhof '58   Isaiah 40
Engineer; Grand Rapids, Michigan

Approximately seven hundred years before Christ, the prophet Isaiah ministered to the country of Judah for sixty years. Chapter forty of the book of Isaiah presents a message of hope and comfort: The Messiah is coming as Savior. George Frideric Handel used five texts from this chapter for the libretto of his greatest of oratorios, *Messiah*.

Youth, this chapter tells us, is a time of strength. It is a time when we work hard and play hard without getting very tired. But as we mature and begin to take our place in God's world, as we get an education, find a job, marry, raise a family, and serve on church and school boards, we often feel physical, mental, and possibly even spiritual weariness. But God does not grow weary. He is "the everlasting God, the Creator of the ends of the earth. He will not grow tired or weary" (Isa. 40:28). This same God, Isaiah assures us, "gives strength to the weary" (Isa. 40:29).

This ancient prophet, inspired by God, used the mighty eagle, the king of birds, to illustrate the power of God to rejuvenate his weary people. Isaiah says, "But those who hope in the LORD will renew their strength. They will soar on wings like eagles" (Isa. 40:31). Those magnificent birds, with wingspans up to ten feet, commonly soar in thermal currents as high as ten thousand feet. What a beautiful and majestic picture of God's merciful care for his people! God assures us that, if we rely on him, our strength will be renewed; we will reach great heights.

Isaiah understands that the God-fearing people of Judah are engaged in warfare, that they must fight many battles. Therefore, already at the very beginning of this chapter, he speaks words of comfort directly from God, words borrowed by Handel to begin his *Messiah*: "Comfort ye, comfort ye my people, saith your God . . . her warfare is accomplished; . . . her iniquity is pardoned."

From his vantage point 2,700 years ago, Isaiah assures us, too, that the war is already won, the conflict is over, and the sin of God's people is pardoned. The outcome of our battles is certain. What perfect comfort.

Awaiting His Coming

Revelation 21:1-5

Cindy de Jong '81
Calvin worship coordinator; Grand Rapids, Michigan

The week before Christmas we went caroling with our neighbors. Though this may not seem to be such an unusual December activity, for me this night was packed with special significance because our next-door neighbors had invited our family and some others to join them for this night of Christmas caroling in memory of Julian and Deangelo, their two youngest sons, who had drowned the previous summer.

When we met at their house, huge flakes of snow were tumbling out of the sky onto our hats and scarves. Bundled up in boots and mittens, we trudged through the snow to any house with lights on. Though some of the youngest children hardly knew the songs, they happily cavorted in the snow. Meanwhile, the parents and older children gladly blended their voices in singing "Joy to the World," "Angels We Have Heard on High," and "O Come, All Ye Faithful," concluding at each home with "We Wish You a Merry Christmas." At nearly every home someone would come to the door beaming, often singing along. One woman simply raised her arms and proclaimed, "Praise the Lord!"

As we rounded a corner heading back toward our neighbors' home, my heart swelled with the joy of singing together on this lovely December night. And tears pricked my eyes as I remembered Julian and Deangelo, wondering how they would have liked singing in the snow and realizing how much we still missed them.

Then it struck me anew: This is what Advent is all about. Even in the midst of our joyful preparations to celebrate Christ's birth, we are often filled with sadness. So we continue to long for a Savior who will usher in a new heaven and earth where joy and peace will prevail. We long for the advent of the one who will come to make his dwelling among us and will wipe away every tear from our eyes. For then we shall join all the saints and the angels in singing a never-ending "Gloria in Excelsis Deo!" to the Prince of Peace.

Light for the World

Steven D. Jones '87
Engineer; Grand Rapids, Michigan

Isaiah 60:1-3

Come, O house of Jacob, let us walk in the light of the LORD. (Isa. 2:5)

The darkness is passing and the true light is already shining. (1 John 2:8)

I magine thousands of years ago gazing into the darkness of the night sky. When the sky was clear, the earth was illuminated with the glow of the moon and the shine of the stars. When it was overcast, the night was eerily dark, so dark that it must have been frightening. Without the light of a flame to guide the way, it must have been impossible to walk from one place to another.

Today only in the most remote parts of the world can we possibly experience the darkness that people experienced long ago. Today the glow of floodlights, porch lights, and headlights illuminates the night sky. From planes high above the earth, cities are visible from hundreds of miles away, aglow with ambient light from street lamps, car dealerships, and shopping centers. Even the countryside is now dotted with light.

Only in the last century has the earth become electrified. Now the convenience of a light switch is usually only a few steps or an arm's length away. We have only recently begun to understand the nature of light. We have learned so much about it, yet we know so little. Within the last few decades we have harnessed the power of light to transmit data, make precise measurements, perform delicate surgery, and cut metal. What a wonderful thing light is.

Without God, the path that we travel in life is shrouded in spiritual darkness, true darkness, darkness like the darkness we, living in the twenty-first century, have rarely been able to experience.

Let us pray that the light of the world will illuminate our paths so that the darkness of sin will be dispelled and we, too, reflecting his light, may show the way for others.

Waiting for His Coming

Malachi 3:1-4 — Laura Smit '83

Calvin professor; Grand Rapids, Michigan

Sometimes I think every hymn we sing in church during Advent includes the word *come*. "O come, O come, Immanuel," we sing, closely followed by "Come, thou long-expected Jesus" — then celebrate with "Joy to the world! The Lord is come." How easily we ask God to come to us.

Are we sure that his coming is something we want? The prophet Malachi promises, "Then suddenly the Lord you are seeking will come to his temple" (Mal. 3:1). Then he turns ominous: "But who can endure the day of his coming? Who can stand when he appears? For he will be like a refiner's fire" (Mal. 3:2). Each of us will have to pass through that fire. Everything in us which is not holy will be consumed.

That is not just terrifying news. It is also good news. The good news of Christ's return is this: When he comes, we will be made pure and holy so that we will be able to present ourselves to God as righteous living sacrifices. There will no longer be anything in us which separates us from God or makes us ashamed to look him in the face.

Whether you experience the second coming of Christ as terrifying or as wonderful depends on how you have experienced his first coming. If you refuse to receive him, if you try to find your identity in your own works and try to make sense of your life by your own power, then that refining fire will consume everything you are. There will be nothing left.

But if you receive him into your life, the essence of who you are will be defined by the essence of who he is. Then you will be able to say that your life is hid in Christ, who lives in you. With his help you can survive that refiner's fire and emerge as the person God always intended you to be, free from the power of sin and death, anger and hatred, fear and despair. When he comes again, you will welcome him with joy.

Come quickly, Lord Jesus.

Recognizing the Word of God

Uko Zylstra '65   John 1:1-18
Calvin professor; Kentwood, Michigan

The prologue to the Gospel of John provides marvelous insight into the mystery of God's relationship to his creation. We read that the Word was with God in the beginning and that the Word was God. Furthermore, though the Word was in the world and the world was made through the Word, the world did not recognize the Word.

How could the world fail to recognize the Word, through which the world itself was created? A major theme running through the Old Testament concerns this failure to recognize and acknowledge the Word of God. It begins in the Garden of Eden, when Adam and Eve, by their disobedience, blinded humankind to seeing the Word of God both in the creation and in the lives of the people of Israel. Later, God, in his faithfulness to the children of Abraham, sent prophet after prophet to reveal the Word of God. The prophets even performed special miracles to reveal the Word of God in all of creation. But these signs weren't sufficient. The people of Israel continued to reject God in spite of all the signs of the Word of God.

The failure of people to see and acknowledge the Word of God in all of creation finally called for the miracle of miracles: The Word became flesh and lived among humankind. The Word was no longer hidden from human eyes. The Word was right there in the flesh, and even in the flesh the Word pointed human beings to God the Father. With such a vivid display — the Word of God in the flesh — how could the people of Galilee and Judea not see God? But just as it took faith for the people of Israel to hear and see God's presence in their midst, so too it took faith for the people of Jesus' world to acknowledge and believe that God was in the flesh, dwelling among them.

In the flesh the Word no longer lives among us. May he live in spirit in our hearts.

I'll Pray for You

Ephesians 6:18

Ron Kool '85
Pastor; Grand Rapids, Michigan

As a pastor, all too often I feel the pain of what I cannot do. In the face of renegade cancer cells that are destroying the life of a friend or family member, I am reminded that I cannot heal. In the face of a family situation that seems to produce nothing but pain for everyone involved, I am reminded that I cannot bring reconciliation. In the face of a depression so heavy it feels as though it will never lift, I am reminded that I cannot make someone happy. All too often I feel that there is so little I can do.

And at those times I say the words that most of us probably say: "I'll pray for you." I have to admit: Sometimes when I say those words, they feel like a cop-out or a pious set of words that I'm supposed to say because I'm a pastor. And sometimes I get a little angry that praying is all I can do. The fact is, praying doesn't actually feel like I'm doing much at all.

And yet that is what God calls us to do. Time and time again the Bible invites us and commands us to pray. In the face of illness, when confronted with difficult challenges, in order to help spread the gospel, we are called to pray. "Pray in the Spirit on all occasions with all kinds of prayers and requests. With this in mind, be alert and always keep on praying for all the saints" (Eph. 6:18). Keep on praying, Paul says. Pray on all occasions.

I do not understand prayer. From my perspective, too often it feels like prayer is not doing anything. And yet the Bible reminds me that it is one of the most important things we can do for one another. So let today be another day of praying. As we work, as we laugh, as we share life together, as we struggle and watch others struggle, let's keep on praying for each other. It might just be the best thing we can do for each other after all.

Advent Light

Debra Huyser-Wierenga '81   Luke 1:68-79
Nurse; Edmonton, Alberta

O ur family was asked to light the candles on the second Sunday of Advent. "Why do we light this Advent candle?" Abigail asked.

Maria responded, "This second Advent candle reminds us that sometimes only one small light is all that is left to shine in the midst of darkness. But even that one small light is enough to dispel the darkness."

Earlier that year, anticipating the birth of another child, we had looked forward to the first week in December. But in mid-July, while vacationing in Michigan, we found out that our precious baby had died. Later that same day the baby was birthed. Our hearts were broken, our hopes and dreams vanished. That night, as my husband and I, our children, and my family held the tiny lifeless body of this baby, there was an outpouring of love that was life affirming. Our baby was loved and treasured in those few hours as we beheld and held, cuddled, and kissed him. Maria tenderly rearranged his little hat and blanket for over an hour. Abigail cooed, "He's so cute." We named him Alexander.

Before his little coffin was sealed, we placed articles of symbolic importance with him: a small pillow and blanket made by his sisters, a hockey puck lovingly purchased by his brother, photos, drawings, and a letter written by his grandfather. Alexander was buried on a brilliantly sunny, warm August day in Alberta. Family and friends, including many young children, stood in a circle with us. They had brought fresh flowers from their gardens. These flowers, the love of family and friends, and the beauty of playful children brought joy in a time of deep sadness. During the fall, continued support from family and friends, words from songs, the unexpectedly long season for garden flowers, and the love our family expressed for Alexander were like small lights, glimpses of God's love shining in the darkness of our grief.

There is a fine line between the opposites in our lives, between joy and sorrow, expectation and disappointment. Alexander's birth and death taught us that. Alexander was a gift, and the small lights of God's love shining in our darkness were also gifts. In this Advent season and until the day dawns when all darkness will disappear, let us thank God for these glimpses of light.

Purity of Heart

Psalm 24   C. Stephen Evans
Calvin professor/dean; Grand Rapids, Michigan

When I was a child, my parents used Ivory soap — bars of course; those were the days before soap came in little dispensers. Perhaps my parents liked its advertising slogan, one that must have enduring appeal — it is still on the bar: "99 $^{44}/100$% pure."

In the Beatitudes Jesus tells us, "Blessed are the pure in heart, for they will see God" (Matt. 5:8). Who are the pure in heart? Perhaps they are the ones with clean hands that James speaks about, metaphorically, when he says, "Wash your hands, you sinners, and purify your hearts, you double-minded" (James 4:8). James seems to make a connection between washed hands and pure hearts, and they are not characteristic of sinners, who are "double-minded." We understand the connection of the images of clean hands and pure hearts. However, it might seem initially that the opposite of purity is impurity, the characteristic of someone who does wrong, that is, of the sinner. After all, pure-hearted persons refrain from sinning, don't they? Impure people sin.

Surely yes, as James affirms. However, when James expands on the idea of impurity, he goes deeper than a mere catalogue of particular sins. Instead, he focuses on the source of all sins: a divided heart, a heart that does not seek first the kingdom of God (Matt. 6:33) and thus is beset with "desires that battle within you" (James 4:1). The problem with an idolatrous heart is not merely that God is supplanted by what is not God. It is also that, when the true God is displaced, no single rival can take his place. The substitute for God is not an idol, but idols; the evil spirit is named Legion.

Philosopher Søren Kierkegaard was so impressed with this passage from James that he wrote a whole series of devotional discourses named *Purity of Heart Is to Will One Thing*. It is only when our hearts are devoted to God that our hearts can be truly unified, for only God is truly one — not merely one good among others, but the supreme good, the source of all other goods, and the ordering principle for all other goods.

Accepting the Incarnation

Jessica Lanting '97
Teacher; Chicago, Illinois

1 Corinthians 15:13-22;
Belgic Confession, Articles 18, 19

"Take us beyond the materialism," we always pray at Christmas dinner. "Deliver us from our preoccupation with physical rather than spiritual things, Lord, especially at Christmas." Then the kids start squirming to unwrap the gifts, and we blame materialism, that rotter of society, for exaggerating the value of tangible things.

But wait. Christmas is about the value of tangibility. For this occasion spirit became eyelashes and skin, cartilage and toes. Mary wrapped that first gift in cloth strips, and shepherds ran to see organic matter lying in a manger. While we rebuke ourselves and try to detach from all the "stuff," there lies God, who had just become stuff. And Jesus did not dematerialize back to pure spirit after commending his spirit to the Father as he died. His body was wrapped again, this time for burial, and after three days, bodily, he arose. The Son of God ascended in body, and we will see him face-to-face someday.

Our faith is impotent unless Jesus is God-become-flesh. Are we properly materialistic enough to believe that salvation relies upon this? Our hope is futile unless bodies, Christ's and ours, rise from the grave. Are we materialistic enough to insist that eternal joy depends on this? It keeps us Christian to be preoccupied with these events of "substance." Without incarnation and resurrection, religion can offer only transcendence or escape from this existence, requiring that we somehow accomplish them by ourselves.

Of course, we all need reminding that our acquired possessions don't provide fulfillment. But if God's gifts and our wish lists were to exclude the material, we certainly would rot — soul and body — and all society with us.

Pray that God will forgive us for trying to disconnect from the material realm in order to be more spiritual. We can't do it, and God's gifts show us that we need not try. Thank God for joining us in our physical nature and for dying and rising to ensure that we will enjoy eternal life in perfect bodies.

Testing: 1, 2, 3 . . .

1 Corinthians 13:4-6

Ralph Honderd '62
Calvin professor; Grand Rapids, Michigan

Love is patient, love is kind. It does not envy, it does not boast, it is not proud. It is not rude, it is not self-seeking, it is not easily angered, it keeps no record of wrongs. Love does not delight in evil but rejoices with the truth.

(1 Cor. 13:4-6)

In 1 Corinthians 13 we find what is often called the love chapter of the Bible. It clearly states that love is more important than even faith and hope: "And now these three remain: faith, hope and love. But the greatest of these is love" (1 Cor. 13:13).

If we agree that God is a God of love and that he wants us to be people of love, we obviously should evaluate ourselves by the standards for love God has given us in his Word. We should ask ourselves, "How are we doing as people who love?" The following exercise might be helpful for all of us as a visual aid toward evaluating the status of our loving.

Make fists with the fingers of both hands and, with your fisted fingers on the top side, move your arms forward until they are approximately three-quarters extended, like a boxer. Say each of the ten parts of 1 Corinthians 13:4-6, one at a time. Evaluate how you are doing for each one. For example, "Love is patient." Ask yourself whether you really are patient. If you are, straighten one finger. Repeat this procedure for the remaining nine conditions of love in those three verses.

If you are truly Christlike, all your fingers will eventually be extended, and your hands will be open, extended to God in loving devotion — as your life should be. If, however, after going through verses 4 through 6, you find your fists still clenched, you should see yourself as being in a confrontational position before God.

But you ought not get discouraged if, after you did this little exercise, your hands were not completely open, because God promises that he will help us in all we do when we ask him — even in our learning to love. However, we will never realize perfection until Christ himself returns. Then, and only then, as Paul puts it, perfection comes and "the imperfect disappears" (1 Cor. 13:10).

Trusting the Father

Dan '84 and Andrea Harms '86 Van Kooten   Jeremiah 29:11
Teacher, counselor/Homemaker; Pella, Iowa

> *"For I know the plans I have for you," declares the* LORD, *"plans to prosper you and not to harm you, plans to give you hope and a future."* (Jer. 29:11)

D ay planners, appointment books, personal calendars — planning for the immediate and distant future consumes many of our hours. We plan for where to attend college — Calvin or Dordt, Iowa State or the University of Iowa. We plan for a major — geology or education, nursing or premed. We plan for where we'd like to find a job, how many children we'd like to have, and what kind of home to buy or rent.

Our goal throughout this plan making is to discern God's will for our lives. Christians with a Reformed perspective want to do God's work in his world, so we naturally want to know what God would have us do when so much needs to be done. But how can we know? Does God send us a secret message embedded in our breakfast cereal? Does his will magically appear in a chanced-upon Bible verse during personal devotions? Is the process simply an intellectual decision of weighing pros and cons?

As a married couple who have experienced vocational and geographical transition, we have found that discerning God's will is hard work that draws upon experience, prayer, and conversation, all resting firmly on the foundation of God's Word. Even then, deciding whether to stay teaching at a school we loved or to accept an overseas mission assignment was not a clear-cut decision. We agonized for weeks, seeking to know God's plan. Ultimately we found God's blessing in simply making ourselves available to do his work in either location.

As Christians, we can give up our floundering about the future because God knows the plans he has laid out for our lives. The difficulty for us is to accept his plans. Are God's plans good plans? They haven't always appeared that way to us, both in our own experience and in the experiences of those around us. Can life without a spouse or without a child lost to disease or accident be God's plan? Can life with a debilitating or handicapping condition be God's will? Paul says, "Now we see but a poor reflection as in a mirror" (1 Cor. 13:12). We simply don't see the big picture yet.

So, in the meantime, do we give in to despair and hopelessness? No. We continue to make plans, resting in the Lord's promise of his presence when lives and dreams are broken. We continue to work at trusting that the Father is in control and that he has plans for our lives.

Sowing Seeds

1 Peter 3:15; Matthew 13:1-30

Seth McCormick
Calvin student; Bay Village, Ohio

The Christmas season brings families and friends together, so when I go home from college during Christmas break, it is a time for me to catch up with what is happening in the lives of my old high school friends. At that time I am always reminded of 1 Peter 3:15, which says that we should always be prepared to talk with people about Christ and the hope he provides in our lives. God has blessed me during my breaks by opening doors to share this hope.

Because I went to a public high school, many of my friends did not know Christ. When we get together again, we swap stories about the activities of the previous semester. On numerous occasions I have shared various activities in which I participated at Calvin, many of which highlight the hope that Christ has given me. My desire is that in talking with my friends I will sow seeds that perhaps will one day sprout and grow into faith in their lives.

But this kind of witnessing is indeed a lesson in patience. Take the example of one friend of mine. In high school I never understood why, in her case, the gospel seed fell along the path and not in good soil, why her faithless friends were more successful in their seed planting than her faith-full friends. In high school this friend did accept Christ, but over time non-Christian relationships caused her to drift from faith. Later she had a trying first semester at her college, during which she searched for spiritual meaning and direction. These tough times softened her heart so that in subsequent conversations I was able to plant more seeds and to encourage her back into the way of faith.

It has only been through some personal spiritual growth and the influence of my Christian friends that I have come to see that God has his own timing and that my conversations with people can only plant seeds for him to tend and nourish.

We are all called to plant such seeds. With whom are you being led to plant seeds of salvation? Where do you see yourself planting seeds for Christ? At home? School? Work? God calls each of us to speak for him, trusting that he alone will provide the growth.

Full of Grace and Truth

Jeanette Bult DeJong '71   John 1:14
Nonprofit executive; Grand Haven, Michigan

As I was driving to church on a brisk, bright Sunday morning, a bumper sticker caught my eye: "Dear Lord, please protect me from your followers."

I was stunned. These words stung like a slap across the face of my heart. Hey, I'm a follower of the Lord. What have I done to offend this pickup driver? Hmmm. My mind turned this phrase over a few times as I drove the last miles to church.

Shock slowly turned to shame. I admitted that this prayer wasn't as outrageous as my first rush of feeling would have me argue. In fact, I had to confess that I could have uttered this prayer myself upon occasion. It's true: Other Christians, through their outrageous behavior, have embarrassed me, shocked me, and even made me angry — some of the Christians on cable TV with their tasteless sets and syrupy testimonials, Christians who work busy street corners by thrusting you're-going-to-hell tracts into the hands of any passerby too slow or nice to avoid the handoff, the Christians who are so caught up in end-times prophecies that they ignore real-time needs. Yes, there are Christians that I distance myself from.

Arriving at church, I set this internal conversation aside. Five minutes into our worship and praise opening, I was gripped by the words of a song that implored me to come to see Christ, to see his glory, to come with an honest heart to see him in his fullness. They brought to mind the words from that great first chapter of John: "The Word became flesh and made his dwelling among us. We have seen his glory, the glory of the One and Only, who came from the Father, full of grace and truth" (John 1:14).

To see all who Jesus is is to see him as full of grace and truth. This is where we followers often fail: We see only grace or truth, not both. As Neal Plantinga reminds us, we can be graceless truth tellers or graceful truth avoiders. It's probably the graceless truth tellers that were being indicted by the bumper sticker, but I realized in that worship service that Christians with both kinds of spiritual shortsightedness — those emphasizing harsh truth and those emphasizing cheap grace — need the indwelling corrective of Jesus' light.

My epiphany, my insult-turned-to-insight, fostered this prayer in my heart: "Dear Lord, protect me from my foolish self. Flood me with the light of your glory that will transform me into your likeness, full of grace and truth. Dear Lord, give me an honest heart."

'Like a Weaned Child'

Psalm 131:2

Leonard J. Vander Zee '67
Pastor; Notre Dame, Indiana

Like a weaned child with its mother, like a weaned child is my soul within me.
(Ps. 131:2)

If I was to characterize the kind of relationship I desire to have with God, it would likely be similar to that of a child at the breast, held close, sucking nourishment. Why, then, does the psalmist use a *weaned* child in his description of his relationship with God? With bottles and baby cereal, weaning is usually no big deal these days. But in earlier times a child would breast-feed three years or more. You can understand that weaning might be a traumatic moment for a child who has up to that time had as its chief joy and sole nourishment the mother's breast. Now, for some reason totally beyond the baby's ability to understand, it is refused, and some singularly unappetizing substitutes are offered. A battle ensues, the baby's hunger pitted against the mother's refusal. The process is not over in a day or two, but finally the moment comes when the baby is able to lie contentedly near its mother's breast simply enjoying the warmth and love of being near the mother.

Let's face it: Faith often begins, as life itself begins, in infancy. Our conscious need of God often starts at a point of desperation — as children asking God to save us from the monsters in the dark or as teenagers asking to be delivered from acne or failure on a test. And God does not ignore these needs. It is often the early stages of faith that are marked with supernatural intervention and spiritual exhilaration. But the weaning process soon begins. God does not want us neurotically dependent, but trusting. God's goal is not that we cling desperately to him out of fear and insecurity and need but that we come to him freely in love and faith.

In today's Scripture passage the psalmist pictures a mature faith. The child gradually breaks off the habit of regarding its mother only as a means of satisfying its own desires and learns to love her for her own sake. We also grow into loving and worshiping God for who God is rather than merely as a means of fulfilling our own desires. The center of gravity has shifted. God rather than self is at the center. It is like the child who, in the midst of playing, runs to its mother and says, "Just hold me for a minute." That is a treasured moment indeed.

Overcoming the Darkness

Sue A. Jager Rozeboom '94
John 1:5; Matthew 2:1-18
Calvin administrator; Grand Rapids, Michigan

The light shines in the darkness. . . . (John 1:5)

Sunday-school Christmas plays often lump the story of the wise men together with the story of the shepherds. The shepherds, each wearing a bath towel strapped around his head and an extra-large flannel shirt down to his knees, stroll to the manger, where Mary and Joseph gaze upon Jesus with a practiced glow. Two minutes later the wise men come, clad in silk bathrobes and tinfoil crowns. That makes for a crowd at the front of the church, and one could argue it's not a very accurate crowd, since the magi came to Bethlehem several months after Christ's birth.

But as long as we're crowding people and history in the front of church, why not add another key figure to the drama? Herod, who doesn't often make the cast. Nobody ever gets to be Herod. He's too mean and ugly. We know what he did, and we wouldn't want those atrocities to invade our Christmas joy.

But maybe Herod should be included in the cast. Maybe somebody should play Herod so we don't forget the importance of his failure. Herod is a spot of darkness in the light of the Nativity scene. But his gruesome attempt to kill the Christ Child fails, a reminder that the darkness of evil can never snuff out the light of Christ.

In our world, that promise bears repeating. Newspaper headlines and our hearts tell us so. Peace and rumors of peace are shattered by explosives on every continent. Statistics suggest that by the time you finish reading this sentence another hundred or so children will have died of malnutrition. Christians are kept from the mainstream of daily life, by oppressive regimes in some places and by repressive ideologies everywhere. Depression, disease, and disaster draw us into the shadows of doubt. Darkness seems to prevail.

But when we celebrate Christ's birth, Herod's failure to kill the Christ Child reminds us that darkness will never win, at least not ultimately. Christ is the light of the world and the light of our hearts that cannot be overcome. The Lord is our light and our salvation. What darkness shall we fear?

This Gentlest of Seasons

Luke 1:1-25, 57-80

Donald H. Postema '56
Retired pastor; Ann Arbor, Michigan

Be still before the LORD and wait patiently for him. (Ps. 37:7)

You will be silent . . . until the day this happens. (Luke 1:20)

"How silently, how silently, the wondrous Gift is given."* Each year I yearn to be more sensitive to that quiet Gift during the harried, impatient, noisy rush toward Christmas. Yet I often arrive exhausted, fragmented, empty, feeling like I've missed something of God's serene, saving presence in the Child of Bethlehem. How about you?

An angel imposed on doubting Zechariah nine months of silence as he waited for the advent of his child: "You will be silent . . . until the day this happens" (Luke 1:20). Pondering that story, I wondered whether such waiting in silence, not imposed but believingly chosen, could give a special quality to our Advent anticipation of the Child. Perhaps, along with preparing our presents and our parties, we could take this month to prepare our person for Christmas — quietly, patiently, in tranquil solitude offering our hearts to God.

Advent is not meant for agitated rushing about. This gentlest of seasons invites us to be calm instead of harried, focused instead of fragmented. It beckons us to cultivate an attitude of awed stillness before the Lord as we wait in patience for Christ to be born in our minds, hearts, and lives. During Advent maybe we could occasionally cancel church meetings so people would have a few evenings not for more frantic shopping but for more quiet contemplation. Or we could give ourselves a daily gift of ten minutes for prayer, reading, or meditation to focus on the true meaning of this sacred season.

We might have a most unspectacular Christmas, gentle as falling snow, fulfilling as an intimate moment with a Loved One, filled with wonder as at the birth of a Child. Yet we might find that we have given ourselves a lasting gift for Christmas: a spiritually precious space where we are attentive to the loving, joyous presence of God-with-us. And at the fullness of time, we might, like Zechariah, open our mouths in hushed praise to God for the wonders that affected us deeply and profoundly.

You could begin right now by savoring for a few minutes the peaceful wonder of the holy Child in the words of "O Little Town of Bethlehem."

Jane Zylstra Ophoff '70   John 1:14
Editor/teacher; Ann Arbor, Michigan

The Word became flesh and made his dwelling among us. (John 1:14)

In response to the astonishing Incarnation, I find my voice instinctively turning to the music of verse, tentatively putting one word, one rhythm, one rhyme after another while borrowing from the essential simplicity of animals to express gratitude for God's appearance in our world and his presence in our lives.

> Angel, blow thy trumpet brightly. Blow the message breathlessly.
> Blow the word, call king, call shepherd. Reach each flock,
>   each den, each herd.
> Then repeat the sounding joy, for the blessing of the boy.
> Angel, blow thy silver boldly. Blow so birds in nests can hear thee.
> Blow till fish in water, deep, answer thy fanfare and leap.
> Then repeat the sounding joy, for the naming of the boy.
> Angel, blow thy brass voice clearly. Blow more softly now,
>   more sweetly.
> Blow thy best but muted, mild, for the sleeping birthday child.
> Then repeat the sounding joy, for the being of the boy.

> *   *   *

> Bird of heaven, holy dove, avian bearer of God's love,
> come this season to the earth to bless the child's luminous birth;
> faithful fowl, peaceful dove, guard the manger from above
> and like a shepherd watching sheep protect the child in his sleep.
> Immortal bird, feathered spirit, trill good news so all can hear it.
> Unfurl your wings this Christmastide: welcome in God's joy,
>   God's pride.

Revelation 21:1-4   Laura Hoeksema Cebulski '99
After-school-program director; Jonesboro, Arkansas

S ometimes we write things that teach us something new. I'll write
something because I like the way its letters or rhythms fit together (or
maybe I just think it sounds smart!), and then it ends up showing me truth
in a way I never intended. That happened with the poem I wrote for our
wedding ceremony. Being a lover of words, I figured that such an important event was deserving of some well-thought-out sentences, so in my
naïve idealism about marriage, I wrote a poem exploring the puzzle of
God's joining two completely separate individuals into one forgiving, loving entity. A line toward the end of the wedding poem reads like this: "perhaps the joining of two into one / is not His first / nor His last / nor His
most radical invention."

Of course, I knew that marriage wasn't God's first creation, for certainly the awesome earth, the crystal waters and canyoned lands, the hot
sun and pearlescent moon preceded even the making of man and woman,
not to mention the triple union of Father, Son, and Holy Spirit, a oneness
out of three perhaps more perplexing than one from two.

And I knew that marriage wasn't God's last invention. Surely the Bible
reveals God's creative works and ideas after the Garden — Jesus defying the
Jews' social conventions and even defying gravity, inventive activities far
beyond the invention of marriage. And, of course, the most radical "invention" I had in mind when writing the poem was the sacrifice and resurrection of God's very Son.

I'm not certain, though, that I was thinking about Christ's return
when I wrote "nor His most radical invention." Now the possibilities of
that interpretation thrill me, and the depth of that imagery shocks me. The
new heaven and the new earth — an "invention" we have been promised, an
invention which in God's time has no first or last or after, an invention
which radically brings us back to the original perfect Garden, where two
were first joined into one — except that in the world to come our perfect
union will be with Perfection himself. What anticipation!

And what a mine of golden reflection marriage then becomes. There
are moments in our marriage when everything comes together, when communication is particularly clear and honest, when one is well-known and
still well loved, when tears are wiped away.

I await the new heaven and the new earth, resting upon the joy of fore-
tastes.

Echoes of Mary's Song

Douglas J. Schuurman '77   Luke 1:46-55
Professor; Northfield, Minnesota

It was my seventh year of full-time post-college study. With two small children and a third on the way, my wife and I served as resident directors in an undergraduate dorm at the University of Chicago. Prospects for employment as a faculty member were bleak. Too proud to apply for food stamps, we struggled along economically. Then the car radiator broke. The $350 to fix it might as well have been $350,000. Burdened by a load of care that had never been heavier, I phoned Starnella Johnson, deaconess of a small African-Dutch-American south-side Chicago church and begged for money. She expressed joy that I had asked for help. "Many people are too proud to ask," she said. I exhaled in relief. With a few discerning words of grace she put me at ease.

In a day or two Starnella Johnson came to our apartment to deliver the check. Our building had once been one of the more impressive ones on Chicago's south side. Al Capone had rented an entire floor in it for himself. During the time of white flight from south Chicago to the suburbs, the building had become dilapidated. Since then, the university had refurbished it as a dorm. As Starnella handed me the check, she said, "When I was a little girl, I used to play in the park across the street. I used to watch all the rich, well-dressed white people go in and out of this building. I used to wish and pray that some day I could enter this building to see what it was like inside. And today my wish came true."

It was one of those times when class, race, and gender all become sacramental realities of God's baffling presence. I heard the song of Mary echoing down the corridors of time: "The Mighty One has done great things for me — holy is his name. . . . He has brought down rulers from their thrones but has lifted up the humble. He has filled the hungry with good things but has sent the rich away empty" (Luke 1:49, 52-53). This was a *kairos* experience, a moment pregnant with new meaning, which continues to shape my view of God's ways with us. Meditating on such experiences of God's grace kindles a piety that brings a person back to the living roots of Christian calling.

Incarnation

John 1:14

Rolf Bouma '78
Pastor, Framingham, Massachusetts

. . . because there was no room for them in the inn. (Luke 2:7)

The Word became flesh. . . . (John 1:14)

If you drive south on Route 126 from Framingham, Massachusetts, where we live, you'll come upon a small shop in the Brazilian community with a delightfully descriptive name: Casa de Carne. It's a butcher shop. Casa de Carne literally means "House of Flesh" or "House of Meat."

Every time I see that sign, my mind makes the connection to the most prominent word in the Christian vocabulary from the same Latin root: Incarnation — en-flesh-ment. I'm reminded that at the heart of the Christian faith is the scandal that God actually became flesh and lived among us.

In the religious traditions of Judaism and Islam, such a notion is downright scandalous. According to those traditions, God is God, humans are humans, and never the twain shall meet. Even in Christianity the tendency is to speak as though Incarnation were nearly impossible. God is the "wholly other." Between God and humanity lies an "infinite qualitative divide." Where's the connection? How is Incarnation possible?

Perhaps we exaggerate. Already back in the second century A.D., Irenaeus suggested that God's enfleshment in Jesus Christ wasn't necessarily tied to the human fall into sin. Perhaps in creating the world God always intended to become enfleshed. Humanity's fall merely changed the agenda. While Irenaeus's suggestion is speculative, it's also provocative to think that God might always have intended to become enfleshed. It would mean that God created this world so that flesh would be a suitable medium for God's bodily presence.

At Christmastime we tend to make much of the fact that there was no room in the inn for Jesus. God came to visit, and we slammed the door in his face. "Use the stable out back," we said. "It's the best we've got left." It's a scandal.

In a real sense there was room in this world for Jesus. This material world was found suitable for the enfleshment of God's own Son. It's a scandal of the right kind, and maybe it tells us that the distance between God and humanity isn't as great as we sometimes fear. Perhaps, when the estrangement caused by sin is overcome, we'll find out just how close God and humans can be.

Light Works Best in the Dark

Dorothy Hoekema Graham '67   Matthew 5:16
Businesswoman; Cheshire, England

> *Let your light shine before others, that they may see your good deeds and praise your Father in heaven.* (Matt. 5:16, NIVI)

Have you ever tried to use a flashlight in broad daylight? It's not much use then, is it, except to illuminate a dark corner indoors? But if it's pitch-dark outdoors, the same flashlight can really give a lot of light. It seems that the darker the environment, the more light we get from a source. But the amount of light emitted by a source is actually the same no matter what the environment. Our eyes automatically adjust to different levels of lighting, but the flashlight does not. The flashlight, like any light, has the most effect in the dark.

Picture a room full of people. If only one person has a flashlight, that light will be seen and noticed by everyone in the room. If everyone has a flashlight, no single light will be as noticeable as a lone light would be. In a room full of people with flashlights there will be lights of different strengths — some will be very bright, others not as bright; some lights may seem to go for a long time without needing recharging; others may need frequent recharging. But all flashlights will need to be recharged or have new batteries at some point. They can't just keep shining all by themselves without a power source.

Jesus says that as Christians we shine with our deeds as well as with our words. What sort of deeds generate light? The fruit of the spirit (Gal. 5:22-23). But these can be difficult to put into practice. Shining the light of Jesus into dark places — doing a kindness for someone who would never do the same for us, forgiving someone who has treated us unfairly, or just being a friend to someone we would otherwise not have been friendly with — may not be easy or comfortable, but shouldn't we try to let our light shine especially where there seems to be the most darkness in our daily life? In the dark, a single light, even if it is not the brightest, can make a difference.

Listening

Psalm 147:1-9

Robert Koornneef '69
Pastor; Grand Rapids, Michigan

At various stages in my life certain passages from Scripture have stood out in bold print and have served as a focal point for me in my work. During the last ten years the third verse of Psalm 147 has emerged as a theme for my ministry with hurting people: "He heals the brokenhearted and binds up their wounds." As if to answer skeptics about this grand claim, the psalmist immediately underscores the fact that this promise is grounded in the works of God — his creation and his providential care (Ps. 147:4-9). But sometimes his providential care happens in surprising ways.

What has come home to me in a special way is the fact that God frequently uses ordinary persons to bring about his process of healing. Even more surprisingly, most of the time it is not so much the words we speak but our caring and loving presence with people in pain that makes the difference. It continues to amaze me that, after I do no more than just listen to them, people will say, "You have been such a help." One of the important things I learned as a chaplain with Hospice was to let hurting persons teach me what their pain is all about. It involves a conscious effort to be a listener — and so a learner — in each new situation and not to be some kind of expert.

While there are similar themes in the suffering of all people, I have come to see that everyone is a unique individual and that therefore reactions may not be stereotyped or assumed. One of the best ways to show our support for hurting persons is to ask open-ended questions that will encourage them to share their own particular stories.

With regret I remember times when one of our children would be crying because of a minor injury only to have their father declare, "Oh, it doesn't hurt!" It is so easy to be smart with someone else's pain and not to be an empathetic listener. As God's tools for healing the brokenhearted and binding up their wounds, we need to understand that this healing happens most readily when we are able to put aside our assumptions and expertise and simply listen carefully to the stories of each individual, including perhaps some whose paths we may cross this very day.

Slaughter of the Innocents

Stephen V. Monsma '58   Matthew 2:16
Professor; Malibu, California

> *When Herod realized that he had been outwitted by the Magi, he was furious,*
> *and he gave orders to kill all the boys in Bethlehem and its vicinity who were two*
> *years old and under. . . .* (Matt. 2:16)

Several years ago, while touring the Uffizi art museum in Florence, Italy, I suddenly came upon Daniele da Volterra's *Slaughter of the Innocents*. I stood in horror before the brutally realistic painting of burly Roman soldiers grabbing babies out of the arms of screaming mothers and running them through with their swords. This picture is a sharp contrast to the quiet, loving scenes that so many other artists have portrayed of Mary, Joseph, and the Baby in the Bethlehem stable.

"Why," I thought, "did the artist choose to depict this scene of horror?" I was repulsed by the picture, almost angry at the artist for painting it 450 years ago. But as I stood there reflecting on the scene before me, I started thinking that perhaps this picture captures the essence of Christ's coming into our world better than the sentimentalized, peaceful stable scenes, for if our world had indeed been a place of peace and quiet and of young mothers and fathers tenderly caring for their newborn babies, there would have been no need for Jesus Christ to come at all. If rulers such as Herod had been just and respectful of people's rights, if there were no death and violence in our world, God would not have needed to come in human form at all. The very reaction of a jealous, selfish, power-hungry politician — who vainly tried to defend his throne by violence — demonstrated the depth of our world's need for Christ.

It also struck me that this killing of the innocent children of Bethlehem presaged Jesus' life, a life lived in a world of pain, sickness, violence, death, faithless followers, and, ultimately, his own excruciating death at the hands of the same Roman government.

As I turned away from Volterra's painting, I could see that perhaps this painting preaches the good news of Jesus Christ in a more powerful, more accurate way than the more appealing, sweeter renderings of the holy family in the Bethlehem stable do, and I breathed a prayer of thankfulness for God's amazing grace that sent Jesus to our world, a broken world, that we might live forevermore.

'Fill Thou My Life'

Psalm 31:14-16

Leslie C. Vander Griend Ruiter '85
Attorney; Seattle, Washington

When I was an exuberant college student, it seemed to me that faith was about grandiose things — leading ministries, fighting injustices, incorporating theology into science or politics. The second stanza of the familiar hymn "Fill Thou My Life, O Lord, My God" shocks me now and shows me that faith can also be extremely personal, even homely: "Praise in the common words I speak, life's common looks and tones, in fellowship enjoyed at home with my beloved ones, enduring wrong, reproach, or loss with sweet and steadfast will, forgiving freely those who hate, returning good for ill."* Numerous times I had sung this hymn blandly, thinking that the text about "enduring wrong" surely meant enduring persecution (or at least disrespect) from the outside world for my Christian beliefs and lifestyle. But this 1863 hymn writer understood well that those closest to us can cause the most pain. He also understood that the cumulative effect of slightly unpleasant behavior among family members can cause hatred, by which God is not praised.

When in my thirties I was gravely hurt by the behavior of someone close to me, I wallowed in grief and thought my joy had vanished. Such pain was not supposed to come from inside the family circle. But the hymn both chided and comforted me: My own faith response had to include kindness in little words, looks, and actions at home and must also include enduring wrong, reproaches, and loss inside the home. God intends to be praised in common household kindness and by forgiveness of those closest to us when they inflict pain. As a music major, I took no class in how "each fret, each care [shall] be turned into a song." But God has been good in teaching me this lesson. Only he could have turned this bitter life experience into increased reliance on him and truer understanding of forgiveness. Only God could have healed this relationship after what had happened. God has brought back my joy, and my common words and my song shall praise him.

"So shall no part of day or night from sacredness be free."

"The Least of These"

Ronald Cok '80   Matthew 25:31-46
Laboratory head; Rochester, New York

> *For I was hungry and you gave me nothing to eat, I was thirsty and you gave me*
> *nothing to drink.* (Matt. 25:42)

When I was a child, I lived in Africa, where I collected local handicrafts — ebony and ivory carvings and artifacts made of leather and stone. In that culture there was no set price for goods; buyers and sellers negotiated, and usually the person with the greatest need for an item would be willing to pay the most for it.

One year there was a great famine in the north, and people traveled south seeking food. Taureg folk from the desert, dressed in flowing robes and headdresses, became a common sight where we lived. Late one dark, rainy night, a Taureg boy about my age came to our house. He wanted to sell me his dagger. It was beautiful — handmade, double-edged, and curved, with patterns carved on both sides of the blade. It had a black leather handle and scabbard with the traditional ball at its tip.

I offered the boy twenty shillings, and he agreed immediately. That was very strange. I had expected a counteroffer. So I offered ten shillings; he agreed again. When I offered five shillings, the boy nodded mutely. I went into the house to fetch my money, thinking, "What a great deal!" I paid the boy, and he turned and vanished into the dark night.

Only later did it occur to me that this boy desperately needed the money, perhaps for food. I might have given him some food if he had asked, but by then it was too late. I had lost my opportunity, and it would not come again. I still have that knife — and the memory of what I did and what I did not do to get it. For me this experience completely colors my understanding of Matthew 25:44-45: "'Lord, when did we see you hungry or thirsty or a stranger or needing clothes or sick or in prison, and did not help you?' He will reply, 'I tell you the truth, whatever you did not do for one of the least of these, you did not do for me.'"

Who are "the least of these"? Where do they live? Where do you see them? Are they those who matter least to you? Are they someone else's children? A boy needing food? A young man or woman who needs work, a mother who needs support, or a family in need of a home? If you or I meet them today, how will we respond? We may not have another chance.

The Last Word

Revelation 22:6-21;
Isaiah 1:18; John 7:37

Gordon Spykman† '49
Calvin professor emeritus;
Grand Rapids, Michigan

Behold, I am coming soon, bringing my reward, to repay every one according to what he has done. I am the Alpha and the Omega, the first and the last, the beginning and the end. (Rev. 22:12)

In the Bible the first Word is God's. The last Word, too. And all along the way God keeps sending forth His Word. All these words, says Christ to John, are "trustworthy and true." In the beginning God spoke his Word, "Let there be . . . ," and so it was. At the crossroads of history the Word became flesh in Jesus Christ, and dwelt among us. Now, as the curtain falls, it is still the Word of God which governs our lives. The world is unthinkable apart from God's Word.

The final Word, which echoes through this closing scene, is "Come!" In the beginning God said to man, "Come walk with me." Through the prophets and apostles God said, "Come, let us reason together." In Christ, God said it again, "Come unto me all ye who labor and are heavy laden." Now in the end all the players in this drama, like an antiphonal choir, join in this chant: "Come, Lord Jesus, come quickly!" "Let him who is thirsty come!"

The call to everlasting glory comes to us today as the call to obedient discipleship. What more could God say that He has not said? The next move is ours. Let us keep His Word and live it.

Notes and Acknowledgments

January 3   * Heidelberg Catechism, Question & Answer 1. Taken from the *Psalter Hymnal*, copyright 1987, CRC Publications, Grand Rapids MI 49560. Used by permission.

January 20   * Thornton Wilder, *Our Town* (New York: Coward McCann, 1938), p. 125.

** Thomas Merton, *Thoughts in Solitude* (New York: Farrar, Straus & Cudahy, 1958), p. 42.

January 24   * Martin Luther, "Last Sermon in Wittenberg," 1546.

February 10   * "O Love That Will Not Let Me Go," text by George Matheson.

February 17   * "Praise, My Soul, the King of Heaven," text by Henry F. Lyte, 1834, alt., in *Psalter Hymnal*, 4th ed. (Grand Rapids: CRC Publications, 1987), No. 475.

March 15   Reprinted from an insert in *The Banner*, February 15, 1999. Used with permission.

March 20   * "Jerusalem the Golden," text by Bernard of Cluny, 12th cent.; tr. John M. Neale, 1858, alt.

March 21   * Julian of Norwich, *Revelations of Divine Love*, Revelation 13, chapter 27.

March 27   * George Herbert, "The Agonie" (from *The Temple*), lines 17-18.

March 28   "Blues 92," copyright © 1999 by Calvin Seerveld. All rights reserved. Used with permission.

April 13   A previous version of this devotional was printed in the Sherman Street Christian Reformed Church *Lenten Devotional 2000*. Reprinted with permission of the author.

April 27   * "May the Mind of Christ, My Savior," text by Kate B. Wilkinson,

1925, in *Psalter Hymnal,* 4th ed. (Grand Rapids: CRC Publications, 1987), No. 291, stanzas 1, 5, 4.

May 23   * "If You But Trust in God to Guide You," text by Georg Neumark, 1641; tr. composite, in *Psalter Hymnal,* 4th ed. (Grand Rapids: CRC Publications, 1987), No. 446, st. 1.

June 8   * Annie Dillard, *Pilgrim at Tinker Creek.* (New York: Bantam Books, 1974), p. 82.

June 12   * "Now unto Jehovah, Ye Sons of the Mighty," in *Psalter Hymnal,* 3d ed. (Grand Rapids: CRC Publications, 1976), st. 3.

     ** "When Peace like a River," text by Horatio G. Spafford, 1873, in *Psalter Hymnal,* 4th ed. (Grand Rapids: CRC Publications, 1987), No. 489.

June 18   * "According to Thy Gracious Word," text by James Montgomery, 1825.

June 19   * Clarence Jordan, *The Cotton Patch Version of Luke and Acts: Jesus' Doings and the Happenings* (New York: Association Press, 1969).

     ** John Timmer, *The Kingdom Equation* (Grand Rapids: CRC Publications, 1990), p. 64.

June 27   * "If You But Trust in God to Guide You," text by Georg Neumark, 1641; tr. composite, in *Psalter Hymnal,* 4th ed. (Grand Rapids: CRC Publications, 1987), No. 446.

June 28   * Heidelberg Catechism Question & Answer 1. Taken from the *Psalter Hymnal,* copyright 1987, CRC Publications, Grand Rapids MI 49560. Used by permission.

July 2   * Heidelberg Catechism Question & Answer 27. Taken from the *Psalter Hymnal,* copyright 1987, CRC Publications, Grand Rapids MI 49560. Used by permission.

July 11   * Richard Mouw, *Uncommon Decency: Christian Civility in an Uncivil World* (Downers Grove, IL: InterVarsity Press, 1992), p. 58.

August 1   * Annie Dillard, "Keeping It Simple," *Architectural Digest,* June 1996, p. 36.

August 2   * John Calvin, *Institutes of the Christian Religion,* ed. John T. McNeill, tr. Ford Lewis Battles (Philadelphia: Westminster, 1960).

August 10   * "This Is My Father's World," text by Maltbie D. Babcock, 1901, in *Psalter Hymnal,* 3d ed. (Grand Rapids: CRC Publications, 1976), No. 374, st. 2.

August 22   * "God Moves in a Mysterious Way," text by William Cowper, 1774, in *Psalter Hymnal,* 4th ed. (Grand Rapids: CRC Publications, 1987), No. 434 st. 1.

September 5   * From "The Belgic Confession," translation copyright © 1985, CRC Publications, Grand Rapids, MI 49560.

September 28   * From Question and Answer 1 of the Westminster Shorter Catechism, 1674.

October 18   © 2000 by Richard Leach. All rights reserved. Used with permission.

October 23   * Dutch hymn translation used with permission of Irene Wiersma and William Spoelhof.

   ** Heidelberg Catechism Answer 26. Taken from the *Psalter Hymnal*, copyright 1987, CRC Publications, Grand Rapids MI 49560. Used by permission.

November 20   * From the CRC form for communion: "Celebration of the Lord's Supper," © 1964, CRC Publications. Taken from *Psalter Hymnal*, 1987, © CRC Publications, Grand Rapids MI 49560. 1-800-333-8300. Used by permission.

November 26   * Lionel Basney, "Dream of the School," in *Keeping Faith: Embracing the Tensions in Christian Higher Education*. Essays and Pieces on the Occasion of the Inauguration of Gaylen J. Byker as President of Calvin College. Ed. Ronald A. Wells. (Grand Rapids: Eerdmans, 1996).

December 3   * From the CRC "Form for Baptism of Infants," in *Psalter Hymnal*, 2d ed. (Grand Rapids: CRC Publications, 1934).

   ** "No Disappointment in Heaven," text by F. H. Lehman.

December 5   * Robert Southwell, "New Heaven, New War," lines 27-28.

   ** "Once in Royal David's City," text by Cecil F. Alexander, 1848, in *Psalter Hymnal*, 4th ed. (Grand Rapids: CRC Publications, 1987), No. 346, st. 5.

December 21   * From "O Little Town of Bethlehem," text by Phillips Brooks.

December 24   "Echoes of Mary's Song" is part of a forthcoming volume to be published by Wm. B. Eerdmans Publishing Co., Grand Rapids, MI. Used with permission.

December 29   * From "Fill Thou My Life, O Lord, My God," text by Horatius Bonar, 1863, in *Psalter Hymnal*, 4th ed. (Grand Rapids: CRC Publications, 1987), No. 547.

December 31   Reprinted from *TODAY*, May 31, 1978. Used with permission. Scripture quotations in this devotional are not from the NIV or NIVI.

Index of Authors

371